The Enigma
of Consciousness

A Spiritual Exploration of Humanity's
Relationship to Creation

The Enigma of Consciousness

A Spiritual Exploration of Humanity's Relationship to Creation

By D. Dean Graves

BOOKS

London, UK
Washington, DC, USA

CollectiveInk

First published by O-Books, 2024
O-Books is an imprint of Collective Ink Ltd.,
Unit 11, Shepperton House, 89 Shepperton Road, London, N1 3DF
office@collectiveinkbooks.com
www.collectiveinkbooks.com
www.o-books.com

For distributor details and how to order please visit the 'Ordering' section on our website.

Text copyright: D. Dean Graves 2023

ISBN: 978 1 80341 565 9
978 1 80341 578 9 (ebook)
Library of Congress Control Number: 2023937335

A CIP catalogue record for this book is available from the British Library.

Design: Lapiz Digital Services

UK: Printed and bound by CPI Group (UK) Ltd, Croydon, CR0 4YY
Printed in North America by CPI GPS partners

The author of this book does not dispense medical advice or prescribe the use of any technique as a form of treatment for physical, emotional, or medical problems without the advice of a physician, either directly or indirectly. The intent of the author is only to offer information of a general nature to help you in your quest for emotional and spiritual well-being. In the event you use any of the information in this book for yourself, which is your constitutional right, the author and the publisher assume no responsibility for your actions.

We operate a distinctive and ethical publishing philosophy in all areas of our business, from our global network of authors to production and worldwide distribution.

Table of Contents

Foreword

The first Age of Enlightenment was a cultural and intellectual movement that emerged in Europe during the 17th and 18th centuries. It was characterized by a focus on reason, empirical evidence, and the belief that individuals were capable of improving society through their efforts. One of the key characteristics of the Age of Enlightenment was the emphasis on rationality and scientific inquiry. Enlightenment thinkers sought to understand the natural world through observation and experimentation, and they believed that reason and evidence should guide all aspects of human life, including politics, religion, and morality.

The vestiges of the Age of Enlightenment prevail today but the hegemony resulting from this transformative age is indicative of a single elementary stepping stone in humanity's consciousness evolution. It is now time, or past time, for humanity to take the next step and move beyond the Age of Enlightenment's limitations. *The Enigma of Consciousness* provides essential information that can aid humanity with a fundamental understanding of itself, its purpose, and a guide to take the next step forward along the evolutionary path but it's incumbent upon the reader to assume the responsibility and enact the necessary changes in themselves to effect a significant change in the population.

Acknowledgments

The list of people that have contributed to my current condition of being and that have stimulated my awareness to the extent that I have been able to write this manuscript would be very long, and even then, I know I would forget to include too many teachers and guides. They have all been messengers to me of things that I needed to learn to become an adequate messenger of this information. Therefore, I will simply say thank you to all those who have shared my life's experiences. I am eternally grateful for your contributions.

Introduction

The objective of this manuscript is to provide the reader with truthful information that will aid their progression along the enlightenment path. In the Earth experience, much if not most of the information about the world and who we are is lost to distortion and access to truth is either completely lacking or severely contorted. Accurate, truthful information is essential to counteract the foibles of falsity and superstition but it is incumbent upon the individual reader to recognize the information as truth, surrender false beliefs and perceptions, and choose truth over distortion.

The mission of this manuscript doesn't include creating a club, religion, or organization of any sort. There is nothing to join or dogma to subscribe to but there is a significant onus placed upon readers to become aware and to be discerning about prevailing perspectives and how they may differ from the information offered herein. However, if the information offered in the manuscript doesn't resonate with you, meaning it doesn't feel like truth, then we ask that you simply dismiss it and leave it for others who do find it helpful. We have no desire to convince you of anything that doesn't ring true.

An individual's behavior is a direct reflection of his/her degree of enlightenment and the goal of the manuscript is to improve the behavior of everyone in the world by promoting their evolutionary consciousness advancement. This is an ambitious task but the longest journey begins with a single step, and as individual behavior changes, so changes the behavior of groups, and as groups change so changes the quality of life available to all.

The measure of a person's enlightenment is reflected in his/her happiness because the more enlightened, the less pain and/

or suffering created in daily life. Even so, happiness is a relative measure because the pursuit of enlightenment is the pursuit of infinity and offers an infinite number of possible paths to its attainment. The intended method to choose the path appropriate for you is to select the path that feels right. Every person is enlightened to the degree they have allowed themselves to be enlightened, which means that every individual controls the path and velocity of their enlightenment success.

Everything is consciousness and every person is imbued with the potential for enlightenment because they are designed with the potential to be aware; the tool necessary to further enlightenment. Awareness of the self is the universal key to enhancing enlightenment and empowers the individual to discern truth from distortion, which is important because Creation consists of a series of distortions made various by the experiencer's degree of enlightenment. It is only when we can surrender attachment to the authenticity of the distortions that we can experience greater truth and, thereby, further advance enlightenment. The Buddha instructed his audiences to question everything and we encourage you to do the same.

How to Read the Chapters

The chapters are presented as a course of study with each new chapter building upon the previous one. While it's not necessary to read all of them in order, it would be helpful, if for no other reason than there is a unique nomenclature used to describe aspects of the material that aren't generally available elsewhere. If you don't understand the vocabulary used, the material will have much less value.

The initial chapters are crammed with necessary overview information to better understand the information in later chapters. For example, in Chapter 1 we explain the purpose of creation, the beginning of creation, the first distortion of the

Creator that is the foundation for all creations, and many other concepts necessary to comprehend the forthcoming information. If you are familiar with the RA Material available through L/L Research, LLC, you will be ahead of the game because much of the material will be familiar, but there is more information offered here that will hopefully provide a deeper understanding and the ability to more practically apply it to your journey.

Chapters 2 and 3 continue to provide background information on the structure of creation describing densities, dimensions, soul streams, and, for the most part, the workings of the Creator Being levels of consciousness. Chapter 4 explains the beginning of physicality as we know it and Chapter 5 continues explaining the lower foundational and experiential densities that humans enjoy. Chapter 6 begins to explain the human experience on Earth and other planets that the population experienced before Earth. Chapters 8 through 11 discuss the Earthly population's historical experience, its primary purpose at the level of consciousness currently being experienced, the nature and purpose of stress, and much more.

Chapter 12 discusses meditation and mindfulness and the importance of each in the evolutionary process, especially among the Earthly population along with major developmental problems encountered on Earth including anger, addiction, and control dramas. Chapters 14 through 25 present information on the Archetypical Mind which is the blueprint for how humans process thoughts and why we perceive things as we do. Chapter 26 explains "Wanderers", a very special addition to the Earth experience of very special people that have volunteered to be a part of the experience to help it along.

Chapters 27 through 31 are a series called the "Human Condition" and more specifically explain why we are the way we are and why we continue to experience pain and suffering. These chapters also offer the prescription for how to advance ourselves through the plight of the current Earth experience and can be very helpful in transforming the lives of those individuals still enjoying the lowest experiential density. "Forgiveness" is the topic of Chapter 32 which is a furtherance of the healing begun in the previous chapter.

Enlightenment is important because it is the process of consciousness' evolution. The process requires the surrendering of attachments to the authenticity of distortions and seeing things as they really are which requires the recognition and acceptance of the truth. In truth is the realization of freedom from the artificial constraints imposed by false beliefs, superstition, and self-imposed suffering. We swim in a sea of truth but we seldom can recognize and accept the truth.

It is through the process of enlightenment that we learn of the Law of One. Briefly summarized, the Law of One explains that:

> all things are one, that there is no polarity, no right or wrong, no disharmony, but only identity. All is one, and that one is love/light, light/love, the infinite Creator.
> ~ RA, from *The RA Material*

Chapter 1

Creation

It's always best to begin at the beginning, so we will start by explaining the beginning of creation and the following chapters will expand upon this foundational knowledge. By itself, understanding creation is not a requirement for advancing individual enlightenment but the information can be a significant comfort when confronted with the prospects of surrendering perceptual distortions that have been the foundation of humanity's beliefs for many lifetimes. Information is light and the more truthful the information, the more confidence it provides the experiencer in their endeavor to surrender false or misunderstood information that keeps them confined within the lower dimensions of the evolutionary experience.

It's also helpful to know and understand because what we experience as humans on Earth is a microcosmic experience of the macro experience of Creation. In school, it was always frustrating to me when the subject matter being presented began from the micro and, over an extended time, eventually presented an overview. Teaching a subject in this way just seemed less productive for many reasons, but usually, it required rote memorization of seemingly useless information with no grasp of the practical implications until we were eventually able to piece together the big picture. It seemed the most ineffective way to provide an understanding and instill motivation to delve deeper into the subject matter.

Describing the big picture of creation first, and then explaining how it has been refined to create our current subset experience, helps us understand the significance of our contributions in relation to the whole. It provides a context for us to understand how trials and tribulations are purposeful and why they are necessary to fulfill creation's purpose. Everything begins with one source which we can identify as the Creator. This is the essence of the *Law of One* and at no point does creation become anything other than the One.

Some of you may wish to make the phrase God interchangeable with the Creator but the conventional perception of God and the actual Creator are very different concepts. God is a finite term created by religion(s) and constrains the perception of an infinite Creator because it requires a God and a separate creation (mankind). The more accurate identifier for the Creator should be the one infinite Creator but we haven't gotten to the explanation of how the Creator becomes infinite, so, for now, we will simply identify it as the Creator.

The nature of a God, any god, begins as a concept, and thereafter, can only be a concept but the Creator begins and ends as reality. To prepare for creation, the Creator projects itself as a concept, actually, two concepts, to facilitate an environment by which the purpose of creation can be fulfilled and the initial ambition for Creation satisfied. The Creator is the only thing that is "real" and not conceptual.

Before the beginning of creation, the Creator is a mystery and so we say that creation begins and ends in mystery. This may be unsatisfying to you but there are reasons that the Creator remains a mystery to consciousness which we will discuss in future chapters. What you can know more completely is *you* and, since all is one, learning about and becoming aware of yourself is to *know* the Creator. Knowing the Creator is the objective of all of creation and until you decide to undertake the task of exploring and becoming aware of yourself with aplomb and cease holding a "victim in need of a savior" perspective, the Creator will probably remain a mystery.

While we remain "in time" it is difficult for us to grasp that Creation has ended or that the conclusion was never in doubt.

2

Because there is only one source for the beginning and end of creation, the outcome of creation was always inevitably the same but the nature of the Creator is forever changed because of what happens in the middle. We, who are living lives, are fulfilling the purpose of creation, but without the possibility of altering the inevitable destination.

Because of where we are in the process, we perceive everything to have a beginning, middle, and end but the reality is that there is only one complete experience of creation without incremental sections such as a beginning, middle, or end. This is, in part, a limitation of where we are in the process because the understanding of simultaneity requires the capacity to perceive experience without partitions. It may be helpful to shift the perspective of creation from a linear journey or path with a beginning, middle, and end to an elastic ball with infinite simultaneous expansion and contraction capabilities.

Shedding the propensity to categorize every experience is an important part of the enlightenment process. We do this by becoming aware of thoughts and then taking control of them. For most people, becoming aware of thoughts requires that they first become aware of emotions and learn to explore the self through emotions. We use emotions to interpret every thought processed, so learning to become aware of emotions begins a process of reverse engineering awareness from emotions to the thoughts that we attract.

When we substitute the perception of creation from a linear process with a beginning, middle, and end to an infinitely expandable elastic ball we begin to see how the infinite nature of creation ensures constant stability with no possibility of deviation from absolute balance. We gain a reformed perspective of truth because it's put into the context of the infinite and shifts the perspective from a lower consciousness view to a higher one.

A perspective from outside of the elastic ball doesn't recognize polarity. It is only because of our limited perspective from within the elastic ball that we only see a portion of the experience, and therefore, polarity. Our limited perspective from within the creation process is the result of an intentional design that, when combined with other characteristics of our experience, encourages us to be more unique in our interpretations of experience.

The beginning of an understanding of the macro picture of the enlightenment process begins with the Creator's initial choices that began creation. Before creation, the Creator had a desire which prompted a decision predicated upon awareness. The desire was to *know itself*.

> **Creation's purpose is to provide a mechanism that allows the one infinite Creator to know itself by experiencing itself!**

The awareness that guides the structure of creation and satisfies the initial desire was that it must experience itself to know itself. That means it had to feel rather than just think. Direct experience is the foundation for the design of creation.

Even though Creation is a thought experiment, it's the most viable means possible to facilitate the Creator knowing itself by experiencing itself because, other than conceptually, the Creator cannot be distorted to be anything other than oneness. From this moment forward, as you read this manuscript and live your life, remember to put all experiences within the context of this simple but complete understanding of the purpose of creation. Most, if not all of the information we offer in the coming chapters, will be additional explanations of how this purpose is being fulfilled by the potentially infinite number of distortions that we experience as humans on Earth and as a small but integral part of creation. Knowing the purpose of creation is also the ultimate answer to the question "Why would that be so?" that we recommend you ask yourself whenever you feel resistance to the veracity of the information being offered.

Having identified the initial desire of the Creator ("to know itself") and determined the best means to satisfy this desire ("by experiencing itself"), the Creator began to implement the design. The Creator is everything. Imagine if you know you are everything and, therefore, cannot be directly distorted; how could you go about experiencing yourself?

In truth: the Creator is the only thing that there is. There was no physicality and no other beings of any sort. How could the Creator possibly experience itself? Think, for a moment, about how we currently can know ourselves. We interact with others and the environment, don't we? We learn to observe others conducting their lives and we either emulate them or reject their behavior but, regardless of what we accept or reject from the world around us, we rely upon interactions with that world to teach us about ourselves. We learn by analogy. In some way, every person, place, or thing we interact with brings us a messenger as part of the interaction and we choose to either accept or reject that message but, in doing so, we learn about ourselves.

If you are all that there is you can't interact with others because there are no others but, because you are the Creator, you can construct a scenario to accomplish your objective. If you are all that there is you can't just create another you that also is all that there is to interact with because there can't be more than one all that there is. If you were able to create a scenario that would allow you to candidly know yourself by experiencing yourself, you would also want to take the potential for experimenter bias out of the equation so the interactions would truly be an adulterated mirror reflecting an unbiased and truthful reflection of yourself. If it were anything less you'd just be creating a doll to play with.

The Creator created a thought experiment in which it was both inside the thought as a distorted conceptual projection of itself, and outside of the experiment as its undistorted self. To accomplish this, the distortion concept that was created was the *perception of separation* from its true self, otherwise known as *free will*. This accomplished the desire to create a conceptual being that could interact with the undistorted original Creator and also created an environment in which to further develop the thought experiment of creation.

But, before projecting itself as a distorted version of itself, the Creator needed to project two concepts. One that is foundational and a constant, and the other that serves as a variable to "color" the foundational concept. The foundational concept was infinity, accomplished by the Creator simply thinking the thought of infinity. The Creator conceptually projected itself as the environment of infinity, which became the nature of the Creator itself, and thereinafter, transformed the Creator into the one infinite Creator.

Having projected the concept of infinity, the one infinite Creator then thought a second thought, separate from the thought of infinity but paired with it. The second thought was *"intelligence"* which functions in conjunction with the initial thought of infinity to create an environment for creation called *"Intelligent Infinity"*. All of the creation we experience is constructed within the conceptual environment of Intelligent Infinity and functions within the limits of its characteristics.

Pairing intelligence with infinity creates the environment for a multitude of creations but the environment and all of the potential creations within it remain conceptual. The unstated implication is that there are other environments, different from, but equal to Intelligent Infinity, functioning parallel to Intelligent Infinity. Speculation suggests that other characteristics can be conceptualized and paired with infinity to create entirely different environments to serve as canvases for other creationary thought experiments. Even a human artist has multiple canvases on which to paint.

It's also interesting to note that the concept of infinity and the concept of intelligence do not merge into one concept but maintain separate characteristics to form the environment. Every thought, regardless of whether it is an original thought of the Creator or originated by a downstream fractal of the one infinite Creator, is contained within a geometric shape called a torus. The concept of infinity is completely within a single torus. Likewise, the concept of intelligence is completely within a different torus.

At the option of the torus creator, the torus (concept) can either maintain its stand-alone status and function in conjunction with other tori or it can surrender its independence and merge into a new torus or concept, providing a different effect from that experienced by maintaining its independence. Variances can be seen in behavior resulting from the same concepts when they are merged versus when they retain their independence and function cooperatively. A simple illustration of the potential of these conceptual interactions is seen in considering a whole and its parts.

A table is a whole thing but consists of the assembly of various parts to make it a table. A table is one torus but to be a table each part, the legs and tabletop, surrendered its torus. The torus of each part merged into the torus we perceive to be a table, thereby, creating the new table concept.

Earlier, we discussed the Creator's preparation for creation. The Creator projecting itself as an environment-creating concept has only prepared the field within which creation may be constructed. The Creator is now the one infinite Creator but still has inadequate means of fulfilling the purpose of creation by experiencing itself. Even though the Creator has projected two concepts working in union, the new concept of Intelligent Infinity is undistorted from the originating source.

Another important element must be added to begin creation. Remember, before the Creator projected itself as a concept, it determined the preferred way to know itself (the initial desire of creation) was to experience itself but it cannot interact with and thereby experience itself while both parts irrefutably know they're still the same entity. To experience itself, the conceptual projection of the Creator must be the subject to the actual Creator's object, which means it must be distorted so it can interact with its originating non-conceptual self while perceiving itself as separate. In other words, even though the undiminished mirror image part of the Creator remained the one infinite Creator, it must be able to perceive itself as autonomous.

The Creator must trick its conceptual self and by doing so create a vehicle that would allow the conceptual self to interact with the non-conceptual self as a peer. Remember that this is entirely conceptual and there is nothing physical. In our physical worldview, this would be somewhat similar to a science fiction story where a person is cloned. The original you would know that you were the original and retain all of the characteristics of you, even though you could physically see and interact with another person that looked like you. The cloned you would perceive the original you as a separate person and be able to act independently from the original you.

The distortion installed within the conceptual Intelligent Infinity environment is also created by the Creator projecting (thinking) the first distortion into the conceptual self, an analog projection of the original Creator. The first distortion that began creation was the concept of free will. We often think of free will as the ability to think or act independently of other people. The dictionary even defines free will as *"the power of acting without the constraint of necessity or fate; the ability to act at one's discretion"* but we have the option to act at our discretion only because we perceive ourselves as an autonomous being.

Free will is more accurately defined as *the perception of separation* which is necessary before we have the choice to act at our discretion. Discretionary action is the result of free will, not free will itself. *The projection of free will created the first analog projection of the Creator which is consciousness, thereby beginning creation.* This basic design for the thought experiment also established the template for the further development and expansion of creation.

The conceptual analog projection of the Creator, distorted by free will, retained all of the characteristics and creative capabilities of the undistorted Creator as well as preserving the desire to know itself by experiencing itself. The analog projection of the Creator, distorted by free will, is called *consciousness*. All of creation is consciousness which is simply a mirror image of the one infinite Creator that perceives itself as an autonomous being.

Free will is a distortion and consciousness endlessly potentiates diverse experiences because every deviation in the degree of free will distortion creates a different consciousness lens with which to view an experience. Free will functions as an intoxicant causing a greater perception of separation as free will is increased. The more free will that is added, the greater the perception of separation from the Creator and the more independent the resulting behavior. The less free will the lesser the perception of separation and the less independent the resulting behavior.

Consciousness is *"Creator-ness intoxicated with free will."* The same effect results when a person drinks more alcohol. The more a person drinks, the less aware they are of their senses, environment, and interactions with others. They are less able to think clearly or function responsibly because the whiskey is interfering with their inherent abilities by numbing their awareness.

Free will numbs units of consciousness to who they truly are by clouding the lens through which they view themselves, to act stupidly, and generally behave as drunkenly as if they were drunk on whiskey. To varying degrees, all consciousness is intoxicated by the distortion of free will. The process of enlightenment is the process of sobering from the intoxication of free will and becoming, once again, aware of who we truly are.

Consciousness

The conceptual analog projection of the one infinite Creator that is consciousness functions with a perceptual partition between the Creator and themselves, all within the concept of Intelligent Infinity. Intelligent Infinity pervades every part of consciousness but consciousness isn't pervasive to Intelligent Infinity. Intelligent Infinity exists quite nicely without consciousness but consciousness cannot exist outside of the Intelligent Infinity environment.

The experience of creation begins with the creation of consciousness, which creates a sub-environment of Intelligent Infinity that is populated with consciousness in a variety of degrees of free will intoxication. By consciousness populating all of consciousness, it also simultaneously creates a series of environments that corresponds to the declining ranges of consciousness made possible by the escalating free will intoxication. Intelligent Infinity is the all-encompassing enveloping environment of all creations but the analog projection of the Creator that is consciousness is its own environment within Intelligent Infinity. Several other environments are created in a similar fashion, which we will discuss when we explain those corresponding ranges of consciousness in future chapters.

The projection of free will into the analog projection of the Creator serves as the template for the further development of creation. As consciousness interacts as a separate being with the one infinite Creator, consciousness develops unique characteristics and behaviors previously unknown to the Creator. It began to create a unique pattern, and since the one infinite Creator is only interacting with a portion of itself, the Creator began to learn of itself by experiencing itself in ways that would not have been possible without having created consciousness.

Creating consciousness created the first subject/object relationship. The portion of the Creator that is undistorted is the object (the "Creator as the object") and, of course, knew that it was the Creator. Consciousness is the "Creator as the subject" and perceived itself as a separate entity from the "Creator as the object", believing itself to be able to enjoy experiences independently. Consciousness, at this level, is an undiminished distortion of the Creator with the same desire to learn of itself by experiencing itself and, therefore, proceeded to develop the expanded creation accordingly.

With the stated purpose of creation as the primary motivation, consciousness developed creation by incrementally investing increasing quantities of free will into itself as analog projections. This created multiple layers of consciousness, distinguished by their degree of free will intoxication, which had the effect of creating a series of subject/object relationships replicating the original subject/object relationship. The object always observes the subject and thereby learns of itself. The effect of creating multiple layers of consciousness was to create a scale with the consciousness at the top, the least distorted, knowing itself to be a part of the Creator and at the bottom of the scale having no idea the Creator existed, much less that it was a part of the Creator.

Our Earthly population's experience isn't on the bottom of the scale but we are on the low end of it. We rely upon subject/object interactions with other people, places, and things for experience and it's the experience that guides the inner dialogue within a person. We potentially vacillate between the subject/object role with every thought. Vacillating between the subject and object is the learning method which is the process of learning by comparison and contrast (AKA analogy).

Humans learn by comparison and contrast which is the analogy. By alternating the subject/object perspective from thought to thought we potentially experience two sides of the same coin and may learn what we like by experiencing what we don't like. Awareness is our tool to learn to take control of this process and begin to shun those thoughts and/or perspectives that displease us and pursue those that do please us. This is how we learn to use discretion and advance our pursuit of enlightenment.

The more aware we are the greater the opportunity to hold the object perspective and learn the lesson that is included in a thought. The less aware we are, lost within the illusion of creation, the less able we are to pay attention and recognize the lessons being brought to us. The choice of either the subject or object view of every thought is how we create our uniqueness, just as the original "Creator as the subject" began to create its pattern of consciousness. Awareness is the tool that allows us to surrender our perception of separation and assume the object's role over the subject.

The process of enlightenment requires us to be aware of our thoughts, surrender the propensity to experience the thought as the subject, and employ awareness to experience thought as the object. Increased enlightenment is the natural result of undertaking this thought-by-thought exercise. We surrender our perception of separation and learn who we truly are. Through the process of enlightenment, we gain nothing because we already are what we seek but we must surrender the distortions that keep us from knowing and experiencing greater truth.

Consciousness has experiences and interprets them in ways that were unique to the "Creator as the object". This allowed the "Creator as the object" to learn of itself in ways that wouldn't have been available had the subject/object relationship not been established. Because of the uniqueness of Consciousness' perceptions, it began to form a *"pattern"* more clearly identified as a "pattern of consciousness", and each new interpretation of experience often further enhanced the uniqueness of the pattern.

The Creator's mechanism to permit it to learn of itself by experiencing itself was working and so it decided to put the plan into full production mode. Full production consisted of numerically expanding creation into an infinite number of reiterations of the initial subject/object relationships which is the concept of "manyness". Until this point in the creation process, there was only the "Creator as the object" and the "Creator as the subject" (consciousness). The concept of "manyness" is simply the reiteration of the original subject/object relationship an infinite number of times which facilitated the simultaneous development of an infinite number of patterns of consciousness all following the same basic design to create an infinite number of creations.

The infinite number of subject/object relationships between the "Creator as the object" and consciousness are all within the single concept of Intelligent Infinity. It is also probable that other characteristics of the Creator have been paired with infinity to create other conceptual environments equivalent to Intelligent Infinity, each one being populated with an infinite number of creations led by a unique pattern of consciousness. We lack a descriptive word for what this entire system would be called other than the *Apeiron* of creation because it is potentially vast beyond our wildest imagination.

Chapter 2

Distortions • Inherent Characteristics • Law of Confusion

Consciousness is the "Creator as the subject" that interacts with the "Creator as the object" and feels its participation in those interactions as an autonomous being, establishing the initial subject/object relationship. The first subject/object relationship has been presumably replicated a numerically infinite number of times so that there are an infinite number of co-creators (subjects) to the Creator's object, all operating harmoniously independent from one another, and an infinite number of creations. The proliferation of co-creators prompted the co-creators to regulate themselves by adhering to a self-imposed "Law of Confusion".

The "Law of Confusion", also known as the "Law of Free will", is always subordinate to the "Law of One" and is an agreement among the Creator as the Subject patterns of consciousness to not interfere with each other's creative endeavors. Therefore, each Creator as the Subject can develop a creation experience without undue influence from other patterns of consciousness, which is important to provide the uniqueness and diversity desired to fulfill the foundational purpose of creation. The Law of Confusion is a real-life doctrine that shares similarities with the "prime directive" used to guide the explorations of the fictional *Star Trek* television series.

While the "Law of Confusion" is subordinate to the "Law of One" it is still a foundational condition for all experience within the particular creation that we share and we presume it to be equally as foundational in all other creations. However, the "Law of Confusion" can be violated whereas the "Law of One", by its very nature, cannot. The "Law of Confusion" is primarily violated by consciousness participating in the lower ranges of the experience every time they choose to inhibit another person's free will. Interactions between higher and lower consciousness beings, such as humans, will enjoy strict adherence to the law. The more elevated the consciousness the lower the potential for a violation of the Law of Free will.

Every pattern of consciousness participating in creation as higher consciousness knows that its perception is that of the distorted-by-free-will-Creator but also, enigmatically, perceives itself as separate, according to its degree of free will intoxication. Every pattern of a higher consciousness being knows every other pattern of consciousness, no matter the degree of free will intoxication, as another part of itself and, because of its awareness of itself as the Creator, works in absolute harmony with every other pattern of consciousness without rivalry, competition, or contest. The mutual agreement of all patterns of consciousness to honor the absolute nature of free will by honoring the Law of Confusion and allowing each other to explore the Creator without interference is also incorporated into and made a basic tenet of every aspect of creation.

At the Creator Being levels of consciousness, nothing is hidden. Everything is known or available to be known by every aspect or fractal of the Creator. If one pattern of consciousness has an idea, all the other patterns of consciousness immediately have access to it. Secrecy is an abomination in practice and impossible when you know that "all is one".

Also, there is absolutely no need for duplication, which means that there are no duplicated parallel universes or any other similar theoretical creation structures such as those woven into many Earthly theories of existence. There is a commonality of experience but no duplication and it is only our naive perceptions of creation that lead us to promote the possibility of a duplicate.

As we stated in previous episodes, creation is only possible because of the distortion that creates consciousness. Consciousness itself results from the distortion of the one infinite Creator, the conceptual analog projection of the Creator, by the free will concept which facilitates behavioral independence. In the series of compounding distortions within the creation that we experience the next foundational distortion is energy.

"Infinite Energy" is created by the "Creator as the subject", the least free will intoxicated consciousness, acting upon an inherent characteristic archetype of the Creator that we call love. When we say "acting upon" we mean projecting the thought of Infinite Energy into the archetypical characteristic of love because every action is a thought that distorts some aspect of the Creator's projection of itself as a concept. All that we experience is a distortion of the archetypical concept of love but love is not the compassionate bonding emotion that humans usually think of when they announce a love for another. Love is a condition of being, an inherent characteristic of the Creator that incorporates infinite capacities and allows "every" experience we have to be the opportunity to explore the self, no matter whether it appears to us to be a positive or negative experience. We shall spend the better part of a future chapter talking about love, but for now, understand that free will, as a distortion archetype of the Creator (not inherent), acted upon love to create "Infinite Energy", creating the next distortion within the creation that we experience.

Intelligent Infinity is the clay from which all creations are made, including the singular creation that we experience. Within the creation that we experience, the creation of Infinite Energy by the "Creator as the subject" established the foundation for all further development of this particular creation. You should understand that the labels "Consciousness" and "the Creator as the subject" are interchangeable because there is no difference between what these two phrases are identifying.

Consciousness begins as an undiminished fractal of "the Creator as the object" and when the distortion of "manyness" proliferated an infinite number of creations there was no benefit in duplicating experience in any other creation. To enhance its self-exploration, the basic purpose of creation, consciousness decided to explore itself by structuring a scheme of diminishing fractals of itself which is also the same basic design prolific in all other creations. This is accomplished by consciousness projecting increasing degrees of free will into itself creating a potentially infinite number of stratified fractal layers of consciousness. Since free will has the effect of being an intoxicant each diminishing fractal of Consciousness is more intoxicated on free will than the layer above.

Free will, the perception of separation from the Creator, meant that each new fractal would perceive itself a little more independent of the Creator and serve as a new subject to the preceding layer's object. The process of investing greater free will to create ranges of consciousness replicated the original subject/object relationship created when the "Creator as the object" created the "Creator as the subject". As this process continued the clarity of the subject/object roles of the more free will intoxicated consciousness became less apparent to the participating lower consciousness but remains blatantly obvious to the observing higher consciousness beings.

Every fractal of consciousness, created by increasing free will intoxication, led to new patterns of consciousness being created that became unique because it was able to interact with the other aspects of creation and interpret those experiences from its independent autonomous perspective. The initial "Creator as the subject" grouped fractalized layers into a system of eight ranges of consciousness with itself as the undiminished top layer or eighth range of consciousness. Within creation, the eighth range of consciousness is still functioning as an undiminished fractal of the "Creator as the object" but the other seven "lower" ranges are intoxicated to an increasing degree and functioning with an increasingly independent perspective of themselves with increasingly diminished capabilities. For example, the seventh range of intoxicated consciousness would hold a greater perception of its autonomy with diminished capabilities from the eighth undiminished layer; the sixth range would hold a greater perception of autonomy with diminished capabilities from the seventh layer, etc.

Each grouping constitutes a range of consciousness called a "density". For our purposes, the term may be simply expressed as a range of consciousness distinguished by the quantity of free will and diminished Creator capabilities. The 7th Density is a fractal of the 8th Density; the 6th Density is a fractal of the 7th Density, etc.

The description of the layers of consciousness being densities is equatable to the concept of molarity in chemistry. In chemistry, a solution provides a foundation for increased or decreased concentration of a substance within the solution, Similarly, the higher the concentration of consciousness, in relation to the concentration of free will, the higher the density. The lower the concentration of consciousness, in relation to free will intoxication, the lower the consciousness. Consciousness, within the solution of free will, becomes less dense and more perceptually spaced apart, and the consciousness level declines.

The entire system is still consciousness that is simply distorted to varying degrees by the concept of free will. Each diminished layer is still ultimately the "Creator as the object" and is still the one infinite Creator experiencing itself. At no point is an aspect of consciousness functioning independently other than in its perceptions of independence from the one infinite Creator.

All densities, other than the eighth, are further divided into incremental layers called dimensions. If a density were a mile, then a dimension would be an inch. As we have experiences and explore the self, the design intends that we will incrementally surrender our perception of separation dimension by dimension, thereby allowing ourselves to become more multidimensional and increase our consciousness by surrendering our free will intoxication. This is the process of evolution and the process of becoming enlightened.

Because everything begins as the "Creator as the object" and through the distortion of perceptions we become "the Creator as the subject", which includes you and me, we have nothing to gain along this process of evolution. However, as the Buddha taught, we have lots of stuff (distortions) to get rid of. Becoming enlightened is the process of surrendering our perceptions of separation from the one infinite Creator which allows us to incrementally relearn who we are from the perspective of the unique personality created as a result of our experiences. We have experiences in all dimensions and all densities of consciousness. Just as the first "Creator as the subject" became a pattern of consciousness unique to the "Creator as the object", we have become and are continuing to develop a unique pattern of consciousness that we are creating as a result of how we interpret experiences.

Some very interesting things happened at the 7th Density level of consciousness. Before the concept of "manyness" was extended to the 7th Density, one of the most interesting things emerging was that certain characteristics of the one infinite Creator became delineated. These characteristics are an inherent part of the Creator, but, before the 7th Density fractalization, were indistinguishable from the whole. Because these characteristics are inherent to the one infinite Creator, they are simply referred to as the "Inherent Characteristics".

Five Inherent Characteristics gave rise to the foundation for the balance of creation that we experience. These characteristics are awareness, love, wisdom, unity, and stillness. Repeating the subject/object relationship design, each of these five characteristics became a pattern of consciousness with their own identity within the 7th Density and perceived themselves as separate from each other as well as the other patterns of consciousness established as 7th and 8th Densities. Awareness had its own identity, became its pattern of consciousness, and, just like other patterns of consciousness, began to have perceptually autonomous experiences.

Love, wisdom, unity, and stillness began an equivalent enterprise of having experiences and developing their personalities too, but each of the patterns of consciousness of 7th Density was not devoid of the other Inherent Characteristics. For example, awareness was predominantly awareness but it was also love, wisdom, unity, and stillness. Love was predominantly love but it was also awareness, wisdom, unity, and stillness because, even though it perceived itself as a separate pattern of consciousness, it was still ultimately the one infinite Creator experiencing itself.

Each of the Inherent Characteristics has an identity and a name, which further enhanced their distinction from each other. Awareness is known as SA (spelled S–A), Love is known as RA (spelled R–A), Wisdom is known as LA (spelled L–A), Unity is known as YA (spelled Y–A), and stillness is known as KA (spelled K–A). Free will, the first distortion that began creation, also has its own identity and became known as Melchizedek. The five Inherent Characteristics and free will are archetypes of the Creator at a 7th Density level of consciousness.

In addition to the delineation of the Inherent Characteristics, it was necessary to replicate free will in each of the lower densities, therefore, 8th Density Melchizedek created 7th Density fractal Melchizedek, which perceives itself as a separate identity (pattern of consciousness) from the 8th Density Melchizedek. Therefore there is both an 8th Density Melchizedek and a 7th Density Melchizedek. They were able to simultaneously exist both as separate and in unity as one because of the increased free will intoxication and resulting distorted perception. 7th Density Melchizedek acts (thinks) independently from 8th Density Melchizedek because of this perception.

The source "Creator as the object" interacts with the identity known as 8th Density and knows that there isn't any separation between itself and 8th Density. It irrefutably is aware that "all is one" and that Melchizedek is a distortion of itself that perceived itself as separate. Likewise, when the 8th Density identity Melchizedek interacts with its creation of the 7th Density identity known as 7th Density Melchizedek it is aware that it is just a part of itself and when 7th Density Melchizedek interacts with the five Inherent Characteristics, RA, SA, LA, YA, and KA, it too is aware that it was only interacting with itself.

Archetypically speaking, Creation at the 7th Density level consists of 7th Density Melchizedek, SA, LA, RA, YA, and KA, which are all independent autonomous functioning patterns of consciousness. Unlike the five Inherent Characteristic patterns of Consciousness that aren't exclusive to the other four, Melchizedek is exclusive of each of the five Inherent Characteristics because it's a distortion. Retaining the same desire to know itself by experiencing itself, each of the five Inherent Characteristics began to further develop creation.

8th Density Melchizedek is a pattern of consciousness that is inseparable from the Creator as the Subject because it's the concept that creates the autonomous perspective and gives birth to the Creator as the Subject. The 7th Density Melchizedek is a pattern of consciousness that's interwoven with each of the five Inherent Characteristics that have been delineated but depending upon the dimension of the density remains identifiably independent. The 7th Density Inherent Characteristics are both their environment and pattern of consciousness and each Inherent Characteristic archetype maintains a single independent perspective (mind) spanning the entire range of dimensional perspectives (experiences) of the density, until they don't, having integrated into the unified mind of 8th Density. For example, in the 7th Density, RA is both an environment and an independent pattern of consciousness, as is each of the other four Inherent Characteristics, evolving towards the surrender of its independence and any perspective other than the unified mind/perspective of the Creator as the Subject.

While the Inherent Characteristic remains an independent pattern of consciousness, they function with a bias towards their predominant characteristic to a decreasing degree as they evolve towards unification and reintegration with the Creator as the Subject. The bias emerged as the characteristic delineation emerged, increased as the density dimensions were created, and resulted in the behavioral characteristic called a "racial mind", relative to the dimension of experience. The lower the density dimension, the greater the bias towards the racial mind. RA (love) has a racial mind predisposed toward the characteristics of love, SA has a racial mind of awareness, and the other Inherent Characteristics function similarly according to their own bias.

Each of the five Inherent Characteristics projected into their independent environment a potentially infinite quantity of consciousness (it's all conceptual anyway) that was also biased towards their Inherent Characteristics and functioning within the 7th Density range of consciousness. Within each racial mind bias, consciousness is further fractalized by the addition of more free will to create the range of consciousness that comprises the 6th Density. Within 6th Density, the concept of "manyness" is again applied which created an infinite number of 6th Density beings, each with its own identity biased towards a characteristic, but in harmony with all of the other 6th Density identities of their own sourced Inherent Characteristic and those of the other four archetypes.

The creation of the 6th Density facilitated significantly expanded possibilities in the diversification and implementation of the creation design. Consciousness' awareness of unity with the one infinite Creator below the 6th Density can be made variable in a way that is not possible with the relatively minimal (compared to lower densities) levels of free will intoxication found in the 7th and 8th Densities. 6th Density consisted of an infinite number of patterns of consciousness that initially obtained its uniqueness from interactions with itself and higher consciousness but the desire was to create a system that would also incorporate experience from interactions with lower levels of consciousness below 6th Density.

6th Density became a transitional density that separated the nature of the higher densities from those of the lower densities. Relatively speaking, 6th Density is designed to be a more experientially "hands-on" or day-to-day manager density of the lower consciousness densities while creating its environment and still retaining its capabilities as a Creator Being. While consciousness enjoying the 7th and 8th Densities is always aware of the most minute experiences of the lower five densities, it is the 6th Density that gets the call to create and manage consciousness' experiences in the lower five densities.

To accommodate the intention and the density design, 6th Density simultaneously created the lower five ranges of consciousness by adding several new distortions to the established practice of simply increasing free will intoxication. Instead of simply investing more consciousness and creating more intoxicated ranges of consciousness, relying upon the increased intoxication alone to provide a diversity of behavior, individual 6th Density patterns of consciousness invested into their environment a stream of consciousness that would vertically span the full range of free will intoxication from 1st through 5th Density. A single stream of consciousness is called a "soul stream" and allows consciousness in a soul stream to cumulatively amass experience from its evolutionary journey through the lower densities while experiencing uniqueness on an incremental dimensional level. In other words, the creation of soul streams allows the Creator to know itself even more intimately by experientially exploring itself most incrementally.

Within a single soul stream, the consciousness of the 5th Density is a fractal of the 6th Density, the 4th Density is a fractal of the 5th Density, etc. but all originate from an individual aspect of the source 6th Density entity. The originating 6th Density entity is called the "Higher Self" and establishes a mezzanine role of intermediate creator and coach to all levels of the soul stream while any part remains in the lower five densities. This design also allowed for the implementation of the process we know as evolution, AKA the enlightenment process.

Initially, some consciousness was invested as 5th Density, some at 4th Density, etc. but, when the switch was turned on and the machinery of creation was put into motion, the effectiveness of a soul stream became greatly magnified. Inherent to every aspect of consciousness was a programmed desire to return to its source. This meant that 1st Density desired to return to the source but to do so it had to evolve through 2nd Density, then 3rd Density, etc., and consciousness' pattern of consciousness uniquely matured as a result of its cumulative experiences in each density. This greatly enhanced the uniqueness of the patterns of consciousness evolving through the creation and greatly enhanced the infinite number of opportunities for the Creator to know itself by experiencing itself.

Initially, when the machinery was first "switched on", the experience was only possible in a limited fashion because inexperienced aspects of, for example, 5th Density aspects were interacting with other inexperienced 5th Density aspects but, as the process operated and consciousness evolved upward from lower density to higher density, the evolved consciousness brought with it the cumulative experience from the lower densities. Consciousness "graduates" from density to density by surrendering free will intoxication as it explores itself. In other words, as consciousness incrementally learns who it is, it increases its consciousness level. When consciousness surrenders free will intoxication it knows itself to be the Creator to a greater degree, hence it becomes more enlightened.

In densities one through five, consciousness is the same consciousness that populates 8th Density but, because of significant free will and other distortions, it doesn't appear to us to be the same at all. Below the 6th Density, two other distortions are coupled with increased free will intoxication to enhance the uniqueness of experiences. Below the 6th Density, the characteristic of intelligence and the nature of energy became altered and variable. There is significant additional information necessary to explain how and why these two distortions are used and why they are so effective in expanding uniqueness so we will defer to future episodes for these explanations.

The densities are grouped according to consciousness' abilities and subsequent service that it can provide to the creation experience. 6th, 7th, and 8th Densities are considered "Creator Being" densities because they are primarily responsible for creation's design, implementation, and operation. Densities one and two are considered foundational densities and densities three, four, and five are experiential densities. Each descending density is a fractal of the one above, and each provides an important step in the process of the Creator knowing itself by experiencing itself.

Each of the five Inherent Characteristics and Melchizedek is an archetype of the Creator in the 6th and 7th Densities but, to expand creation more significantly, more distortions of these archetypical Inherent Characteristics were created in the 6th Density. The five Inherent Characteristics of 6th Density were acted upon by 6th Density Melchizedek to create 26 additional 6th Density archetypical distortions which are not sustainable above 6th Density because they are not inherent to the Creator. In other words, they don't exist above the 6th Density. The infinite consciousness of the 6th Density becomes infinitely diverse because every lower consciousness environment (1st through 5th Densities) mixes and matches some or all of the 32 archetypes (5 Inherent Characteristics, free will, and 26 distortions) to facilitate unique experiences in the lower densities. The particular environment/experience we enjoy is comprised of 9 of these archetypes and includes the five Inherent Characteristics, Melchizedek (free will), and 3 of the 26 distortion archetypes.

At the level of consciousness that we all share, we don't know what we don't experience so it has not yet been possible for me to know what the other distortion archetypes are that we don't experience. One of the three distortions that we do experience is the distortion of separation, which has a name just like the Inherent Characteristics and serves as a multiplier of the foundational perception of separation created by Melchizedek. The archetype "separation" is called "TA" (spelled T–A) which functions as a 6th Density archetype, the same as the five Inherent Characteristics. "TA" has the same creative abilities as a 6th Density Inherent Characteristic archetype even though it is a distortion archetype.

Another distortion archetype included in our environmental design is "DA" (spelled D–A) which is the distortion of movement or motion. Consciousness participating in other parts of our creation experience that do not include DA as one of its archetypes can't experience motion as we do, or at all, because it is not part of the design of the conceptual experience. The distortion archetype of motion is "change" and allows the progression of time as we perceive it.

"Melchizedek" is also a 6th Density archetype in our environment and is part of every other creation experience as well because it is the distortion that begins creation. "Melchizedek" automatically gets invited to every party. "Melchizedek" doesn't create lower-density experiences but it is an integral part of every aspect of every experience regardless of the level of consciousness.

The final archetype of our Logos is a distortion of a distortion. In other words, it is a second-tier archetype, a 6th Density consciousness, an accelerator to enlightenment (particularly in 3rd Density), and has been instrumental in magnifying and enhancing opportunities for the Creator to know itself by experiencing itself. It is the distortion of unconsciousness and is particularly instrumental to the lower ranges of the 3rd Density but it loses its effectiveness about midway through the density. The characteristic of unconsciousness is the distortion archetype called "Lucifer" which means light bearer or light bringer.

"Lucifer" is a name you may be familiar with from religious texts and has consequently been given a negative image but it is through the characteristics of unconsciousness that we are motivated to awaken from darkness and begin to "see the light" of truth. "Lucifer" is an archetype of the Creator instead of a devil and serves to intensify the experience of what we don't like so that we will be motivated to begin to be aware of what we do like at an accelerated rate. Invariably, truth is what we like and what allows us to surrender our perception of separation, become increasingly enlightened, and align in unity with the Creator.

The distortion of "DA" (movement) comes into existence because of Melchizedek acting upon the Inherent Characteristic of "KA". The archetype "KA" is stillness and the thought is one of polarity, which is the concept of movement. Movement results in change, and without movement, we couldn't experience change. Our entire experience of creation is predicated upon change, which is often frightening when we don't have the truth available to us. As we become more enlightened by increasing our dimensionality, we slow down and eventually directly experience stillness without the distortion of movement. The one infinite Creator is absolute stability and absolute stillness.

The distortion of "TA" (separation) exacerbates the foundational perception of separation that free will provides so that we perceive ourselves as autonomous units of consciousness and, at our level of consciousness, cocooned within a physical body, separate from all other beings. The distortion of "TA" is created by the archetype "Melchizedek" acting upon the Inherent Characteristic of "YA" (unity) by the creation of the polar opposite perception. Evolution is the process of surrendering separation in favor of unity or oneness.

The enlightenment process begins in a state described as "primordial darkness" which doesn't mean that it begins locked in a dark closet but rather that consciousness begins the process as a clean slate with no light so that it is in total innocence. Remember that light is information. Consciousness has experiences and, as the experiences are uniquely interpreted with emotion from a variety of perspectives distinguished by degrees of autonomy, allows it to co-create creation by developing unique patterns of consciousness which are "selves". Consciousness, as we experience it, begins with a perspective of separation ("TA"), in a condition of constant movement ("DA"), and unconscious ("Lucifer") but, as we become awareness ("SA"), we surrender our preoccupation and attachment to the authenticity of the distortions and choose to experience more of the Inherent Characteristics (truth).

"Melchizedek" (free will) is always the standard, allowing us to freely choose how we interpret experiences and consequently choose what we do like in preference to what we don't like. By doing this, in our density, we are learning to become awareness and begin to see and accept the truth. Once we become awareness, we will have surrendered the effects of "Lucifer's" unconsciousness and we will learn of the infinite love that is always present in "Infinite Energy".

This is the process of enlightenment. We are all in the process, whether we are aware of it yet or not, and we will all eventually be enlightened when we finally surrender all distortions and reunite with the oneness of the Creator. This is the Law of One.

The only question is how long we will choose to remain under the influence of the distortions and continue in chaos by vacillating between truth and darkness. How long will you remain within the confines of darkness before you finally begin to realize who you are, liberate your awareness, and return to unity with all that is?

Be aware that all that we have discussed so far is still without any of the physical aspects of creation. There are no universes, galaxies, solar systems, or planets. Just as the Creator projected itself as the concept of Intelligent Infinity, everything that comprises creation is conceptual. Understanding the foundational concepts is essential to a better understanding of truth and learning who you are.

Chapter 3

Intelligence • Intelligent Energy • Light

Chapter 2 explained the overall structure of creation and how seven densities were created as increasingly distorted fractals of the 8th Density by increasing the amount of free will and decreasing the density of undistorted consciousness in each successive fractal. We explained that the foundation for all of the creation that we experience is built upon the manifestation of the distortion of Infinite Energy, a distortion of the archetype love. We also explained that in the 7th Density, five Inherent Characteristics of the Creator are delineated, each with a perception of relative autonomy, and from the 7th Density, the 6th Density fractals were created within their autonomous perception according to an Inherent Characteristic bias creating multiple racial minds. Upon its creation, 6th Density assumed responsibility for the creation's further expansion and guidance of densities one through five.

Densities six, seven, and eight are Creator Being densities with the honor and duty to create and manage the exploration of the Creator through the further development of creation while still having experiences and developing unique patterns of consciousness of their own. Densities three, four, and five are experiential densities and the 1st and 2nd Densities are foundational densities. The nature of experience is significantly different in each density but all experience, regardless of the level of consciousness, retains the foundational purpose of creation, which is to provide the one infinite Creator with the opportunity to know itself by experiencing itself.

The architecture of the lower densities of creation allows consciousness to be a perpetual system, investing itself into the lower five densities and then guiding itself to have experiences at each dimension through self-interaction, learning of itself by alternately serving as subject or object, and incrementally evolving back to unity with the "Creator as the object" as a unique pattern of consciousness. The system of creation is timeless and always adapting to changes resulting from free will's co-creation of the experiences while new consciousness is constantly reinvested into the lower densities as matured consciousness moves through the system. This is similar to a school system that starts each new school year with new students in kindergarten replacing the previous year's students that have graduated to first grade, the first-grade student that has graduated to second grade, and so on.

Intelligence

Intelligence is the concept that is emphasized and paired with infinity to create Intelligent Infinity, the parental environment of many creations, including the one we experience. Other concepts may also be paired with infinity to serve as environments for other creations equally as vast and equally as productive as the ones experienced within Intelligent Infinity. Within the creations of Intelligent Infinity, all consciousness has unfettered access to intelligence according to its ability to be aware. In other words, intelligence is not contained within a pattern of consciousness but is potentially equally available to all consciousness, regardless of the degree of free will intoxication, which includes the lower densities.

Within the Creator Being densities, intelligence is universally available and immutably experienced but its employment is reflective of the level of consciousness according to the consciousness' capacity to access it. 8th Density, because it is undiminished from the "Creator as the object", shares the same intelligence. 7th Density is a consciousness fractal of the 8th

Density and demonstrates diminished capacities from the 8th but has the same potential to access intelligence. As abilities become more diminished in the 6th Density fractal, consciousness demonstrates a more focused perspective, which includes more limited access to intelligence because of the nature of the density, but not because complete access isn't available.

As free will intoxication increases in the experiential and foundational densities, consciousness becomes less able to be aware and experience infinity. The restrained perspective of diminishing consciousness is demonstrated in a more directed or limited focus away from the infinite and towards the finite. A good comparative illustration of this is how our vision functions.

When we concentrate on an object and narrowly focus our vision we do so to the exclusion of periphery objects. Other objects surrounding the object of our focus are still available to be seen and we may be vaguely aware that they are in our periphery vision but their "brightness" fades. Similarly, the "brightness" of infinity fades as free will intoxication increases and we become less able to experience the whole because awareness and access to intelligence become diminished. As free will intoxication decreases, we regain the ability to experience more infinity with uniform clarity and awareness.

Consciousness' intelligence is in direct correlation to its degree of free will intoxication. The aspect of consciousness that employs intelligence as a function is called the "mind" which is a creation of spirit. In the 8th Density, the spirit and the mind are synonymous with consciousness but, as consciousness becomes increasingly fractalized with increasing degrees of free will intoxication, effects that permit the unique shaping of a pattern of consciousness promulgate the mind distortion into the forefront of experiences. Access to intelligence becomes moderated by the mind's willingness, or unwillingness, to surrender its perceived independence from spirit.

The mind is a distortion of the spirit and, in the foundational densities, 3rd Density, and the majority of 4th Density, it's virtually synonymous with the "ego". The mind of 8th Density is identified as a "cosmic mind" and has unrestricted access to the intelligence of the Creator because the 8th Density is the 1st "Creator as the Subject" and an undiminished fractal of the "Creator as the Object". 7th Density is a diminished fractal of 8th Density and consequently has a somewhat diminished access to intelligence from 8th Density but shares the cosmic mind to the extent it can do so. Unlike the 8th Density, the 7th Density is further subdivided into dimensions and experiences both vertical and horizontal "manyness" so the higher dimensions of the 7th Density have greater access to undiminished intelligence than the lower 7th Density dimensions. Because of this design, there emerges a unique range of intelligence within the 7th Density as it does within all densities below it.

Vertical manyness is the fractalization of a density into dimensions with each descending dimension experiencing a slight increase in free will intoxication. Horizontal manyness is the replication of consciousness that perceives its independence from other patterns of consciousness and allows it to develop uniqueness. The combination of vertical and horizontal manyness has several benefits to fulfill the original purpose of creation because each horizontally and vertically delineated unit of consciousness can create itself, through the interpretation of its subject/object interactions with other units of consciousness, as a unique pattern of consciousness.

6th Density is a fractal of the 7th Density and the broadest ranges of consciousness of any of the densities, twice the range of any other density. It too experiences both vertical and horizontal manyness but, as with the 7th Density, the lower dimensions of the 6th Density have less access to intelligence than the higher dimensions. 6th Density also participates in creation with a racially biased mind, according to the sponsoring Inherent Characteristic, but the potential access to intelligence remains unconstrained.

The mind of the 6th Density is called the "root mind" which, in the upper dimensions of the 6th Density, is only mildly diminished from the cosmic mind of the lower dimensions of the 7th Density but still potentially able to access undiminished intelligence. The root mind serves as the source of the minds experienced in the soul streams that span the foundational and experiential densities and therefore it is the "root" of their formation. The root mind is racial because it is biased or flavored with one of the archetypes of the Creator, either Inherent Characteristic or distortion. The bias of the 6th Density root mind serves as a foundation for a Higher Self and is carried forward into the lesser minds of the lower densities. However, regardless of the flavoring, all consciousness of equal dimension potentially has the same access to intelligence.

A mind is a distortion of spirit created by the distortion of free will and, therefore, it is a creation of spirit. In the experiential and foundational densities, intelligence becomes more difficult to explain because below 6th Density the mind becomes significantly more distorted and access to intelligence becomes a variable not directly tied to the level of consciousness. We will come back to the mind when discussing the lower densities, but for now, we would like to clarify some things about the environments of the Creator Being densities.

We previously explained that the Creator Being densities were both an environment and an independently perceiving consciousness which means that the 8th Density is the all-inclusive environment for its creation, the 7th Density is subordinate to the environment of 8th Density and essentially shares the same environment of infinity, but 6th Density is disbursed within the multiple Inherent Characteristic environments created in the 7th Density. Every soul stream invested by the 6th Density into the lower densities is of the bias of the sponsoring 6th Density archetype and usually functions within the same biased environment, but not always.

Additional experiential variety can be obtained by projecting soul streams into an environment different from the bias of the sponsoring Higher Self. Earth is an excellent example of this because it began as a LA experience but, after the Maldek fiasco, RA (love) assumed the leadership role and the experience is now predominately a RA experience, functioning within a LA (wisdom) environment. This is just one of the numerous conditions that make Earth a unique and potentially challenging experience.

There are three primary categories of environments that the creation we enjoy offers and consciousness simultaneously participates in each of these environments according to its perceptual abilities. Consciousness' ability to be aware of the environment while within them is determined by its degree of awareness which is characteristic of its consciousness level. The nature of these three working environments has historically been described as a dream, within a dream, within a dream. Consciousness may participate with awareness in one or all three of these environments simultaneously but it is unusual for consciousness in the lower densities to be able to participate with awareness in more than one or maybe two of these categories at a time.

The 7th and 8th Density environment, the third dream, is described simply as "infinity", and every consciousness fractal functions within it, much like the outside shell of a Russian nesting doll set. It is possible for consciousness at every level of creation to experience the infinity environment directly, but it's improbable below 5th Density consciousness. Beginning with the 6th Density, the environment Earth's science has labeled as "time/space", or more colloquially the "metaphysical world", is nested within infinity and is the second dream. The environments of infinity and time/space are naturally occurring but nothing is created extracurricular to the environment characteristic of the density.

Earth's science calls the first dream space/time which is the conceptual perception of an authentic physical world. As time/space is nested within infinity, space/time is nested within time/space but, where time/space is a refinement of a higher consciousness environment, space/time is an effect and creation of 1st Density, the lowest consciousness density. The nature of consciousness' evolution is to evolve from a lower consciousness to a higher consciousness so we progress out of the exclusive perception of the authenticity of the 1st Density physical environment of space/time and into the experience of the 6th Density environment of time/space, and eventually, the 8th Density environment of infinity. In time, the authenticity of space/time simply fades away as perceptions are incrementally modified by higher consciousness awareness and consciousness becomes "unattached" to the physical.

The experiential densities simultaneously experience time/space and space/time but the 5th Density's primary environment is time/space with only an occasional visit, at their discretion, to space/time. 4th Density is a transitional density because it begins the density with the primary experience of space/time but, as free will intoxication subsides within the density, consciousness begins to transition its primary awareness to time/space. 3rd Density, the consciousness level that the historical and prevailing population of Earth still enjoys, is primarily aware of only space/time but can occasionally experience time/space with measured awareness during such intentional exercises as meditation.

Consciousness in the foundational or experiential densities, when experiencing space/time, is always incarnate in a physical body to one degree or another depending upon the density. As the creator of space/time, 1st Density consciousness is always incarnate, experiencing space/time exclusively during its entire tenure in the density, but 2nd Density experiences space/time while incarnate in a physical body and time/space during the time between incarnations. 3rd Density experiences space/ time through a series of lifetimes during which it "lives" in the physical world and the metaphysical world when it isn't incarnate or when it intentionally chooses to surrender the authenticity of the physical.

When a 3rd Density person dies, he simply changes his perspective of his environment by surrendering the physical body and its ability to experience space/time. In the lower densities, consciousness never actually leaves time/space but visits space/time as an analog version of its time/space self. Regardless of the density of experience, the mind always remains in time/space and, when it processes thought in the foundational or experiential densities, the thought is processed in time/space with only the fruit of the thought brought into space/time.

The cosmic mind of 8th Density is indistinguishable from the spirit, so the spirit and cosmic mind function as the same thing, but in 7th Density, a pattern of consciousness becomes a mind/body/spirit even though the body of 7th Density is not in space/time. The 7th Density body is purely conceptual which is nothing like a physical body because there is nothing physical. Consciousness isn't born and doesn't die in the 7th Density because it never leaves the environment of infinity. It is eternal as long as creation lasts and, yes, creation does have an end.

Like the 7th Density, the 6th Density is also a mind/body/ spirit but the body is a "light body", something closer to being recognizable as physical. In 6th Density, there is no distinction between being incarnate and not being incarnate because the

6th Density environment is time/space. All that we experience in the foundational and experiential densities is either the environment of space/time or, if we exert the effort to become more enlightened, time/space but we experience them purely via thought. The more "attached" we are to the physical world's authenticity, the less likely we are to be able to experience the time/space environment.

6th Density creates all of the thoughts and experiences of the foundational and experiential densities. Consequently, at its discretion, a 6th Density being may inject itself into space/time in whatever form it may desire by incorporating its appearance as a physical form into a thought(s). RA and other 6th Density beings have "walked among the Earth's population" in physical form in fairly recent Earth history.

Consciousnesses, within the experiential and foundational densities, experience two minds which are identified as the "deep mind" and the "ego mind". The ego mind is frequently the dominant mind of 1st, 2nd, and 3rd Densities but the deep mind is always available and increasingly gains prominence as consciousness awakens and evolves, graduates to 4th Density, and eventually transitions to 5th Density where the design for an experience that creates the ego, the Archetypical Mind, loses sway entirely. From 5th Density, the deep mind continues to expand, transform, and eventually integrate back into the source root mind with the fruit of all experience gained through its evolution.

The ego mind is probably the only mind that 1st, 2nd, and lower 3rd Density consciousness will experience while it remains within the density's dimensions. As consciousness evolves through the upper dimensions of the 3rd Density, space/time doesn't disappear but its authenticity does diminish, as does the dominance of the ego mind. The ego mind remains part of the experiences of 4th Density but it has significantly less sway as consciousness increases its dimensionality.

The ego mind is an important contributor to experience while consciousness is attached to the authenticity of space/time, but it was never intended to dominate to the exclusion of the deep mind, as it often does. Because of the ego mind, the variability of intelligence below 6th Density becomes a significant factor and an important aspect of diversifying opportunities for the Creator to know itself. The mind is synonymous with the ego and the perception of separation, and is responsible for the process of analogy which is our ability to choose what we like over what we don't like.

The prominence of the ego mind as the primary mind is invariably indicative of a greater perception of separation and the emergence of the deep mind as a moderator of the ego mind is indicative of declining separation perception. The ego mind is the sole source of all pain and suffering or joy, particularly in the 3rd and early 4th Density but, in some cases because of a mind/body/spirit's choices, endures well into 4th and 5th Densities. Everything experienced is done so in thought and the only thing a mind does is process thought. How the mind, or minds, is employed determines the nature of consciousness experience.

Intelligent Energy

Another significant distortion that facilitates consciousness' participation in the foundational and experiential densities is the 6th Density creation of "Intelligent Energy". Intelligent Energy is a distortion of Infinite Energy and is found only in the foundational and experiential densities. The issuance and regulation of the flow of Intelligent Energy to a soul stream is also one of the most significant mechanisms used by a Higher

Self to guide consciousness through the lower densities while preserving its free will.

Intelligent Energy is the fuel that energizes lower-density consciousness and is sourced directly from a Higher Self to a soul stream according to its density. Regulation of the appropriate Intelligent Energy flow to consciousness at a density level is accomplished by a system resembling a series of valves and governors called the chakra system which we will address in a future chapter. The combination of increased free will intoxication, a regulated Intelligent Energy flow, and the creation of the ego mind for the foundational and experiential densities are the elements that make it possible for consciousness to successfully explore creation at its most reduced levels.

Every pattern of consciousness (AKA mind/body/spirit) experiencing a foundational or experiential density has the same amount of Intelligent Energy available as every other mind/body/spirit participating in the density. Intelligent Energy flows directly from the Higher Self via a direct and constant connection but the individual mind/body/spirit has the free will discretion to allocate the energy as it chooses. Free will is paramount in the recipient's discretion of how it will use the energy because its discretion is the choice of how it will experience creation.

Light

Light is another important non-archetypical distortion created by Melchizedek acting upon LA or wisdom, similarly to how it acted upon RA or love to create Infinite Energy. Light is information and instructs Infinite Energy to be a certain way but light itself is not energy.

Creation is implemented as a series of subject/object interactions between various aspects of consciousness, according to its inherent or distorted characteristics. Intelligent Infinity can be understood to be white light or truth that incorporates all light from which creation is experienced according to the focus of the observing pattern of consciousness. It is the one infinite Creator projected as a concept and experienced from a distorted perspective, which undoubtedly will incorporate only a small portion of the infinite whole.

The environment of the 8th Density is the undiminished light (truth) of the Creator but viewed through the lens of a unique pattern of consciousness that perceives itself as autonomous from the Creator. The environment of the 7th Density is also the Creator's light or truth, viewed through the lens of a fractal somewhat diminished from the 8th Density. From the top to the bottom of the 7th Density range of dimensions, the lens through which light is experienced continues to dim from the initial 7th Density brightness. Behavioral characteristics of 7th Density become more unique as dimensions decline within the density because free will intoxication increases, which means the perception of separation increases, and the light, which is the same as 8th Density light, is perceived less completely.

6th Density is a fractal of the 7th Density and it too is both its environment (light) and conscious identity. As the dimensions descend within the 6th Density, even greater diverse perspectives emerge that manifest in a panoply of light colors. 6th Density diversity comes from its interactions with other archetypes, both Inherent Characteristics and distortions and the accrued experiences of the soul stream densities below, which causes 6th Density to be the broadest range of consciousness of all of the densities.

The focus of light may vary depending on the density and the dimension within the density but the source of the light/ information is always the same. All light/truth/information is of or about the five Inherent Characteristics, and anything other than that is deemed a distraction or distortion. Information on any aspect of the physical world is deemed transient and inconsequential other than how it may pertain to consciousness' further understanding of awareness, love, wisdom, unity, or stillness. The only information that is preserved after a lower-density incarnation is that which has expanded the understanding of the Inherent Characteristics which means that all other information that may have provided academic accomplishments will simply go into the ground with the body because it has no value outside of space/time or beyond the physical incarnation.

While light and the variations of light colors are consistent throughout the densities, the intensity of the light is not, but only because of consciousness' inability to perceive it. The white light of the 3rd Density appears significantly less bright than the white light of the 4th Density. Graduation from one density to the next is measured by the graduating consciousness' ability to "appreciate" the intensity of the higher density's brilliance. The higher the density experienced by consciousness, the more aligned with the one infinite Creator and the more intense the light.

For example, upon the death of a 3rd Density mind/body/ spirit, it "walks the steps of light" until it cannot tolerate the light's brilliance because the "brilliance of the light of truth" becomes too much for them to bear. The light of truth comes into direct conflict with their perceptions or beliefs, and they resist surrendering their degree of perception of separation in favor of the distortions. Where they stop is the dimension and/ or density appropriate for their current level of learning, AKA consciousness level. Mind/body/spirits leaving an incarnation upon the Earth have been "walking the steps of light" to determine if they are adequately prepared to graduate to 4th Density (or higher) or will remain in 3rd Density for another tour through a density experience to provide them with an additional learning opportunity.

Intelligence is comprised of two elements, which are both conceptual. The first element is awareness and this is the most important because it is an Inherent Characteristic of the Creator. The second element is information (light). Awareness endures beyond consciousness and, consequently, before and after creation. Information has value only as part of Creation and is a tool of consciousness to interpret its experiences while it journeys from Creation's beginning to its evolutionary end.

Chapter 4

1st Density

In the previous chapter, we introduced the concepts of infinity, time/space, and space/time as experiential environments. Infinity is the all-encompassing environment of the 8th and the 7th Densities; time/space is the environment of the 6th Density, within the envelope of infinity; and space/time is the environment created by 1st Density within the envelope of time/space but shared to decreasing degrees by the 2nd through 5th Densities. Evolution through the lower five densities is a transformation process that starts with the perception of an authentic space/time in 1st Density and progresses with an incrementally declining perceptual authenticity until it concludes the 4th Density experience. The perception of physicality is an effect of 1st Density, the lowest and most basic range of consciousness with the most significant distortions.

Knowing how these environments are formed helps with the understanding of the nature of consciousness' experiences in each density. Infinity, the 8th Density environment, is indistinguishable from the consciousness of 8th Density because the nature of its consciousness is its environment. This is also true of time/space, the 6th Density environment, but because time/space emanates from a lower level of consciousness and vibration than the 8th Density, it is much easier for the experiential densities to reach. The ability to experience infinity or time/space is always available to all consciousness, regardless of the density, but the awareness constraints, characteristic of the foundational densities and the lower dimensions of the 3rd Density, make it very difficult to do so.

The space/time environment is the product of 1st Density and a reflection of how it has developed a unique pattern of consciousness, so space/time environments vary enormously. The uniqueness of a space/time environment is a demonstration of the infinite variety afforded by free will because all consciousness begins 1st Density in precisely the same condition as any other but, even within the limits of our solar system, there is significant variety in a planet's formation. Space/time serves as the basis for experiences of densities two through five and significantly contributes to how it evolves within the environment.

The design of 1st Density is that consciousness will begin without light, which is information, and its capacities of awareness are suppressed through a series of limiting mechanisms to allow it to begin at a near zero point, characterized as "primordial darkness". Through alternating roles of subject and object interactions with itself, it integrates into four unique patterns of consciousness that initially coalesce into an independent organism of an equivalent consciousness level and then continue to coalesce into a larger comprehensive organism called a planet, which is a larger unique pattern of consciousness that functions with a cohesive codependence. This begins evolution with the common intent of allowing the Creator to know itself by experiencing itself at a 1st Density level. Remember that creation is a thought experiment in process, made possible through a series of distortions of the Creator by the Creator.

1st Density begins with consciousness in the most intoxicated state possible and, through interactions with itself, learns to integrate into an organism that functions in relative unity with the other 1st Density consciousnesses sharing the experience. The coalescence of 1st Density is a demonstration of consciousness escalation within the density and portends the participating 1st Density consciousness' eminent graduation to 2nd Density. Space/time, AKA the physical world, is the manifestation of consciousness' evolution within the density and is an expression of relative unity.

Before 1st Density begins, the criteria for a universe's experiences are established by selecting archetypes from a pool of archetypes consisting of the five Inherent Characteristics RA, LA, KA, SA, and YA, Melchizedek (free will), and 26 archetypical distortions, all of which are of a 6th Density consciousness. From this pool of 32 archetypes, chosen participants are mixed and matched in varying combinations to populate universes and create opportunities for the Creator's exploration of itself. The particular universe that Earth participates in is composed of nine of these archetypes; the five Inherent Characteristics, Melchizedek (free will), and three distortion archetypes, TA (separation), DA (movement), and Lucifer (unconsciousness).

Every star is home to a 6th Density archetype and our universe began with a single nine-star system, one star for each of the archetypes that were chosen to comprise our universe. Each member of the original star system primarily interacted with the other eight to form a unique star system pattern of consciousness and prompting the entire star system to bond and function as a single organism. The initial nine-star system served as a seed to further populate the universe and, when the concept of manyness was applied to the initial seed system, it resulted in an infinite number of other seeded systems to populate the universe. Each of the replicated systems also developed a unique pattern of consciousness according to its subject/object interactions and functioning as a single organism.

In addition to the replication of the nine-star seed systems, the seed systems themselves sponsored other nine-star systems according to their uniqueness, with each replicated system refining the sponsoring systems' characteristics into its uniqueness which resulted in the galaxies. Each galaxy shares the foundational racial mind of the sponsoring nine-star seed system. The nine-star seed system is a single organism that grew into an even larger galaxy organism that is part of an even larger universe organism. The uniqueness of a universe is the result of the accumulated personalities of its galaxies and the uniqueness of the galaxies is a product of the personalities of the nine-star systems within it.

The 6th Density consciousness of the stars explores itself by investing itself in soul streams which mature into solar systems by populating the lower five densities so they may have experiences and develop uniqueness through analogy. Planets are comprised of the lower five densities and the accumulated uniqueness of the consciousness participating in the planets accrues to the originating 6th Density consciousness occupying a star. Consciousness participates in the five lower densities through personal experience by the processing of thought, allowing uniqueness to begin from a near-zero starting point and incrementally progress to unity, thought by thought. How this is facilitated will be the focus of the explanation of the lower densities.

Other than the archetypes Lucifer and Melchizedek, the 6th Density archetypes occupying individual stars within a galaxy project consciousness to populate the lower densities according to its racial mind or distortion, eventually resulting in the manifestation of a series of planets which we call a solar system. Consciousness can either be projected to populate only 1st Density to allow the evolution of consciousness to populate densities two through five, or it can be disbursed to all five lower densities simultaneously. The mechanism of how to scale consciousness to the appropriate density was briefly addressed in Chapter 1 and it will be explained in greater detail at the appropriate time in a future chapter.

A star that is home to one archetypical aspect is predominantly that aspect but is also inclusive of all of the other eight archetypes but to a less prominent degree. The bias towards one archetype while still incorporating all of the other archetypes to a lesser degree is the same design for all of the archetypes comprising our universe. Initially, a star is home to only one 6th Density entity and is one mind, but as evolution welcomes more evolved individual souls back to its 6th Density origin after its progression through the lower densities, it becomes a social memory complex. A social memory complex consists of many individuated souls or patterns of consciousness who have greatly surrendered their perception of separation and function as one mind and one organism but with multiple individual contributing parts, each adding the uniqueness of their patterns of consciousness to diversifying and expanding the whole organism.

Because galaxies grow from a seed, the nine-star systems at the center of a galaxy are usually the oldest and most evolved within the 6th Density range. The nine-star system we participate in is located near the outer edge of the Milky Way galaxy and, therefore, is relatively youthful and more innocent, relative to consciousness near the center. The size of the galaxy is often an indication of both the seniority and power of the originating consciousness. While a single galaxy may be grown from a single nine-star system's experiences it always is the result of the consciousness of many nine-star systems' functioning cooperatively and diversely but always harmoniously to create the whole galaxy.

Most stars are in a binary orbit with another star, but with an odd number of stars in a cluster, one star must be in a solo orbit. In our solar system, the Sun, home to the 6th Density archetype LA or wisdom, has been the exception to the binary rule, until fairly recently. Besides the Sun, the other eight stars that participate in our star system include Sirius B which is home to RA or love, Sirius A, home to TA or separation, Alpha

Centauri A, home to TA or separation, Alpha Centauri B, home to SA or awareness, Cepheus A, which is home to YA or unity, Cepheus B, Melchizedek or free will, Zeta Reticuli A, home to KA or stillness, and Zeta Reticuli B, which is home to Lucifer or unconsciousness. The aspect of RA that has called Sirius B home is in the process of graduating to 7th Density and the star is in the process of transitioning to a black hole which occurs when a 6th Density archetypical social memory complex graduates to 7th Density and begins to absorb all of the consciousness and energy it has invested into a particular nine-star system. A new star, to be the new home of the aspect of RA that will continue to participate in our star system, is forming in a binary orbit with the Sun, and Sirius A will assume a solitary orbit.

Physicality first appears sometime (indeterminant period because the formation isn't "in time" and is individually determined by the participating consciousness) after a star's 6th Density aspect invests consciousness to begin a soul stream and the consciousness of 1st Density adequately matures to coalesce into a planet. 1st Density is the most basic foundational density which begins at the lowest level of consciousness and starts the process of evolution. Consciousness is prepared for the density by converting unformatted consciousness (known to Earth's science community as dark matter or dark energy) by absorbing it into a star for formatting (causing the star to appear to be physical material), significantly increasing free will intoxication, and establishing a minimal flow of Intelligent Energy.

Consciousness experiencing densities one through seven participates in creation according to a coding scale consisting of 64 steps with two layers activated at a time. The highest activated numbers indicate higher consciousness and the least free will intoxication, and the lower numbers indicate the lowest consciousness and the greatest free will intoxication. 1st

Density ranges from only two strands of coding activated to eight strands.

A 1st Density experience initially distributes consciousness among the four coding levels: two, four, six, and eight, creating four platform levels of consciousness within the density but with the fractional layers between the platform layers being further subdivided into a multitude of dimensions. While initially the strands of coding are assigned by the Higher Self, the design is that all consciousness will incrementally evolve through all of the intervening dimensions and platform layers of the density by surrendering its free will intoxication, incrementally increasing its awareness, integrating more completely into the planetary organism, and evolving to higher consciousness.

Consciousness participating in the lowest range of consciousness with only two strands of coding activated will evolve through the intervening dimensions to attain the next platform layer of four strands within the density. The same activity prevails within the whole density until consciousness has achieved 10 strands of coding which moves it into the lowest range of 2nd Density. The evolution of consciousness is designed to be incremental, allowing consciousness to explore itself and, consequently, learn of itself at each dimension.

While most consciousness works incrementally within a density and is permitted to progress at its own pace, it is fairly common that consciousness may be scooped out of the 1st Density pool and the coding activated to a new setting on the coding scale by the "grace of the Higher Self", which allows consciousness to participate in a new higher level density without having completed its full evolutionary tenure at the lower levels. Dimensions and Densities may be skipped entirely and the recalibrated consciousness will promptly demonstrate behavior relatively similar to all other consciousness of similar coding activation.

Consciousness in the foundational densities experiences creation in bulk and evolves into the more narrowly focused experience of 3rd Density that we currently enjoy as a population and are all familiar with. We, who experience the human range of consciousness, perceive ourselves to be a single unit of consciousness, otherwise identified as an independent mind/body/spirit, but a single unit of consciousness for 1st Density consciousness is as an element.

Consciousness with only two strands of coding activated is deemed to be charged positively, is a male or the subject experience, and eventually manifests as the space/time element of fire. Consciousness is naturally attracted to other consciousness of equivalent coding activation and tends to coalesce accordingly. Behavior at any level is characteristic of a level of consciousness, even in higher densities, but consciousness' behavior with two strands of coding activated behaves according to the properties of the element of fire.

Negatively charged 1st Density consciousness is female or the object and eventually manifests as planetary matter in all of its various forms because of dimensional diversity. Matter begins with eight strands of coding activated which, as with fire, advances incrementally from dimension to dimension between eight and 10 strands of coding (10 is the beginning of 2nd Density). Consciousness within the 1st Density range evolves from the lower levels to the higher levels, transforming itself, including its behavior and appearance, in the process as it experiences the different forms in between fire and matter.

Matter and fire are the two most polarized elements and two more levels are less extreme in their polarization but still characteristically male/subject or female/object. Water is polarized as a plus sign over a negative sign and is weighted more towards the subject or male consciousness but still consists partly of the female polarity. Atmosphere results from consciousness charged with a negative sign over a positive sign which is weighted towards the object or female bias but also incorporates characteristics of the male polarity.

The polarity distortions of 1st Density are biases that begin experiences way before anything physical manifests and are expressions of degrees of perceptual separation from the Creator. Matter, the negatively charged female/object polarity, perceives itself closest to the Creator, relative to the other levels of 1st Density consciousness. Fire, the positively charged male/subject polarity, perceives itself farthest from the Creator. There is absolutely nothing sexual or reproductive about the identification of male or female intended other than the degree of perception of separation from the Creator. As will be explained in greater detail in future chapters, the male/subject and female/object roles of the higher foundational and experiential densities are also based upon the degree of perception of separation from the Creator, most notably in the 3rd Density.

Water, polarized as +/-, is skewed towards the male/subject polarization being less positive than fire but more positive than atmosphere. Atmosphere, polarized as -/+, is skewed towards the female/object polarization being less negative than matter but more negative than water. The elements of 1st Density experience creation as one torus and one mind. In other words, water is one torus and one mind, the atmosphere is one torus and one mind, fire is one torus and one mind, and matter is also one torus and one mind. The water in your drinking glass, although it appears to be isolated within the glass, is still part of the one torus and one mind of water.

Consciousness in 1st Density is assigned its polarity but from that starting point it creates a range of perceptual separation within the element based upon analogy or "what feels good". Each element coalesces into an organism of shared perceptual separation, demonstrating the behavior associated with the element, and the four parts then coalesce into a larger organism that integrates the four elements and appears or behaves as the physical environment that we perceive with our senses. The appearance of physical form is the naturally occurring behavioral characteristic of 1st Density consciousness as it has chosen its degree of perceptual separation. Each element may seem electrically charged but the electrical nature of the charge is actually how the level of consciousness, the element, is interpreting and filtering the Intelligent Energy provided by the source star.

Once 1st Density consciousness reaches a relative degree of maturity and begins to form the larger element organism, it develops the physical appearance of the gases that science has identified as the beginning of a planet but "the gases" are the small units of the elements that have not yet coalesced. Within all of the five lower densities, the design is for consciousness to shed its perception of separation and incrementally join together in ever-increasing unity. The appearance of the physical is an indication of the escalation of consciousness within 1st Density as it eventually unites to form the larger planetary organism.

When consciousness coalesces into the four organisms, they are demonstrating their pattern of consciousness. When the four elements come together to form a larger planetary organism, inclusive of the four parts, they are forming yet another larger, more complex pattern of consciousness. The elements continue to coalesce until they become a planet that will be unique and reflect the characteristics of their pattern. Planets are all different in appearance and composition because, while the nature of the experiences may be similar to all other 1st Density experiences, the four elements have employed free will to interpret them and, therefore, shape their uniqueness.

The space/time environment is the inevitable result of consciousness' coalescence into a planet because that is the behavioral characteristic of 1st Density, but the specific blending of the four elements will be unique because the free will of the participating consciousness determines its appearance as a planet. Coalescence is a behavior and all consciousness will demonstrate very similar behavior if it shares the same level of dimensionality or consciousness. The uniqueness isn't that it coalesced but in the resulting characteristics of the space/time environment.

Interactions between the elements of the lowest density are random, timeless, and encourage diversity in the co-creation of the space/time environment. The Creator Being densities were created from a top-down approach by intoxicating consciousness with additional free will which means that they retained significant intelligence and light, even though they are a reduced fractal of the density above. 1st Density was formed by starting in "primordial darkness" at the bottom of the consciousness scale which means it has little or no access to intelligence or information at its beginning. The four elements of 1st Density randomly interact, discovering intelligence and information as consciousness learns of itself and surrenders its perception of separation.

1st Density's experience is also the beginning of a soul stream and, in our universe, originates with the racial mind of one of seven of the nine archetypes. Melchizedek and Lucifer do not originate soul streams but they participate in every experience created by the other archetypes. It is possible, and not uncommon, for one 6th Density archetype to begin a soul stream and another to assume the Higher Self role while it is still in process. This is the case for a significant number of soul streams comprising the Earth experience.

Once consciousness enters 1st Density it can't experience time/space until it graduates into 2nd Density. 1st Density's point of perception is always incarnate and constantly interacting with the other elements within the space/time environment that it created through its incarnation. In the minds of 1st Density, the authenticity of the physical is irrefutable but very myopic because that is the nature of a 1st Density consciousness.

As consciousness is elevated within the density, consciousness rises to the top and is skimmed from the pool of consciousness just like cream that has floated to the top of the milk is skimmed from the bucket. The skimmed consciousness is then moved to 2nd Density to continue its evolutionary journey. The criterion for consciousness escalation in 1st Density is the same as it is in all the densities and requires the surrender of free will, resulting in its sobering from its free will intoxication.

Everything we experience through our five senses as space/time is 1st Density consciousness and is as "alive" and incarnate as we are. The nature of its service to the Creator may seem more elementary than in higher densities but it is integral to fulfilling the purpose of creation. The collective consciousnesses of atmosphere, water, Earth, and fire are still individual patterns of consciousness, intelligent, and able to telepathically communicate with other consciousness willing to exert the effort to do so. As a 3rd or 4th Density mind/body/spirit on Earth, we can telepathically chat with an elemental consciousness as we are willing to exert the effort to be adequately aware.

The consciousness that is virgin to the creation process is constantly being reinvested into 1st Density by resetting its coding to the lowest setting but it mingles and interacts with all consciousness that shares the planetary experience. Interactions of the consciousness levels within the density serve as the stimulus to raise the consciousness of the lower levels more quickly. Every interaction of every pattern of consciousness is a teach/learn and learn/teach opportunity, no matter the level of consciousness. Every aspect of consciousness serves as either a subject or an object in every encounter.

There are several examples of planets that are in the process of 1st Density maturity within our solar system that have not yet hosted a density experience other than their own. Jupiter, Mercury, Neptune, and Saturn are all examples of varying levels of 1st Density maturity that have not yet been ready or chosen to host a density experience beyond the 1st. Saturn and its moons frequently host higher consciousness visits but not as the host planet for a density experience other than its own 1st Density experience. Planets closest to the creating star are usually the most mature and therefore appear to be the densest and the most physically formed.

Once 1st Density has matured into a planet, the planet can and usually does cooperatively host more than one density experience at a time. For example, Mars currently is a 1st and 4th Density experience, and Venus is a 1st and 5th Density experience. Earth is simultaneously a 1st, 2nd, 3rd, and 4th Density planet and has previously served as a host planet for an earlier 3rd Density experience that was just completed, the one we perceive to have been a part of. Also, there is another planet called Tara in our solar system on the same orbit as Earth on the opposite side of the Sun that has simultaneously been host to a 1st, 2nd, 3rd, 4th, and 5th Density experience. For a planet to host an experiential density experience, significant additional changes must take place beyond the criterion of a 1st or 2nd Density experience.

In earlier chapters, we presented the irrefutable fact that "all is one" which is the statement of truth known as the "Law of One". Everything is the Creator experiencing itself. The distinction between the densities and the subdivision of dimensions is awareness. Free will, or the perception of separation, is a distortion that convolutes awareness by causing the portion of the Creator experiencing creation identified as consciousness to perceive itself as separate from the Creator with reduced access to intelligence, thereby narrowing its focus.

8th Density has the awareness of the Creator that it is one with the Creator except for the distortion that it perceives of itself as a separate identity. Each declining density holds less awareness of the fact that it is the Creator experiencing itself without distinction and, because of its increasing lack of awareness, it loses the creative and intelligence capabilities of the Creator accordingly. 1st Density consciousness is as much the Creator as 8th Density, but because of its extremely limited awareness, it perceives itself as completely separate and existing only as the environment of a physical element within the physical world of its creation. Its mind remains in time/space because it is still part of its Higher Self's mind but distorted to perceive that it is absolutely separate. The nature of its perception of separation results in the creation of a space/time environment and its inability to be aware, even of its simultaneous existence in time/space. It is the mind or minds of 1st Density that remains in time/space, as all minds do, that holds its perspectives and creates the environment of space/time.

Consciousness experiences the 1st through the 7th Densities as a mind/body/spirit. Because of the limited capacity of consciousness in 1st and/or 2nd Density, the spirit that is part of the foundational densities is the spirit of the Higher Self but the spirit shall remain inaccessible to a mind/body/spirit's mind until it progresses adequately within 3rd Density. The mind is the perception of separation as shaped by its experiences or, in other words, its ego. The body in 1st Density is the manifestation of the physical form appropriate for its coding activation.

The mind/ego processes thoughts and perceives the physical manifestation to be a representation of the information provided in thought.

1st Density consciousness isn't born and doesn't die. It is always incarnate, experiencing space/time, while it remains in a 1st Density range of consciousness and so there is no opportunity to experience anything other than its incarnate self as one of the elements. Because of its perceptual limitations, it only knows space/time, and all change or escalation of dimensionality must occur within the environment by its incarnate self.

It is permissible that 1st Density consciousness can awaken to its perceptual limitations, surrender its free will intoxication, and zip through to 8th Density consciousness by skipping all of the intervening levels of consciousness, but that is highly improbable and it's not the design. The design of evolution in all of the densities is to incrementally have experiences at every dimension and, through experience and analogy, create a unique personality, thereby allowing the Creator to infinitely experience itself and consequently know itself.

In rare cases, 1st Density consciousness can sometimes exceed the expectations of the design when it has the opportunity to experience higher consciousness through direct contact with higher consciousness beings. For example, there are locations on Earth where higher consciousness beings have dwelt for prolonged periods, and the interaction of the 1st Density consciousness with the higher consciousness being has elevated that portion of the 1st Density consciousness beyond its prescribed level. The appearance of the location(s) isn't altered, but some humans can recognize these locations because the "energy" of the location feels really good.

The portion of 1st Density consciousness that has benefited from interactions with a higher, positively polarized consciousness being results in more consciousness cream rising to the top of consciousness milk to be scooped out and deposited in a higher density. A similar condition occurs when 1st Density consciousness in a location has experienced interactions with lower negatively polarized consciousness for a prolonged time. The distinction between positive and negative polarization will be explained as part of our 3rd Density presentation.

In summary, consciousness can only experience what it is aware of. Because 1st Density's capacity for awareness is very limited it can only experience the physical world, which is space/time. The single mind of its organism continues to exist in time/space but it is completely unaware of anything other than its incarnate, physical world experience. Therefore, it experiences only space/time until it is scooped out of 1st Density and into 2nd Density and, even then, it experiences time/space only between incarnations.

Earth-based humans are experiencing a very great opportunity for consciousness escalation because the planet identified as "Gaia" has transitioned from 3rd Density to 4th Density and is providing the entire population with the accelerated opportunity to do the same.

Chapter 5

2nd Density

Chapter 4 explains the different environments of creation, the seeding of universes, galaxies, solar systems, and the 1st Density. 1st Density creates the environment of space/time, which is of particular importance to those of us that retain a lower experiential density consciousness level because it is the primary if not only environment that we are likely to be aware of during an incarnation, as is enhanced by 2nd Density. The process of consciousness' evolution prescribes that we begin in "primordial darkness" and progress through an infinite number of dimensions by incrementally escalating our awareness until we eventually return to where we began, in oneness with the Creator.

After evolving through the dimensions of 1st Density, consciousness may be moved to 2nd Density. Between 10 and 16 strands of coding are activated and, by that simple modification to the coding, consciousness enters 2nd Density, automatically experiencing an increased Intelligent Energy flow and an elevated degree of awareness. Even though the modifications necessary to accommodate consciousness' transition may seem simple, it affords consciousness a completely new creationary experience.

2nd Density is also a foundational density, but, while 1st Density functions as a "stand-alone" density, 2nd Density must be conducted in harmony with a mature 1st Density experience because 1st Density creates the playground necessary for 2nd Density to exist. Because 2nd Density is a parallel but dependent enterprise to 1st Density, it benefits from the nature of 1st Density's coalescence into a planet and how well the two densities assist each other's evolutionary progress. They must learn to function cooperatively and harmoniously together by constantly adapting, balancing, and accommodating each other's changes.

1st Density consists of pooled consciousness divided into four elements with each element being contained within a single torus and functioning as one mind for the entire element. Evolutionary advancement within an element is incrementally achieved according to the dimensions within the element but consciousness within each partition pool flows seamlessly upward and downward through the density's dimensions. 2nd Density consciousness is also pooled, but the pools are grouped according to the many dimensional layers of consciousness, illustrated by its manifestation into a multitude of plants and animals.

2nd Density consciousness begins with 10 strands of coding and concludes with 16 strands activated. Consciousness progresses incrementally through the dimensions of each platform level within the density by having experiences, learning the lessons that the current dimension has to offer, sobering from its free will intoxication by escalating its awareness, and undertaking the next level of experience. The various species of plants and animals are the physical manifestation, the analog projections, of a pooled level of consciousness.

Each time a plant or animal becomes manifest, consciousness is projected from the species pool to live an analog life as a space/time experience of the dimensional pool of consciousness. When the incarnate body dies, the resulting change in free will intoxication during its incarnation is assimilated into the dimensional pool and when sufficient nondescript consciousness within the pool has been elevated, the cream that has floated to the top is skimmed off and moved to the next dimensionally higher pool. 2nd Density does not establish an enduring individual soul beyond the temporary plant or animal incarnation but the entire density serves as a refined transition phase between the gross bulk pooled consciousness of 1st Density and a more focused and refined 3rd Density experience.

For example, when a tiger is born it is random that a baby tiger is conceived but when conceived it is infused with the nondescript dimensional consciousness of the tiger pool. The cycle of life of a single incarnation is that it begins in innocence, a baby, with a level of consciousness indicative of the species pool, and, from that relatively clean slate, it has experiences according to the behavioral characteristics available at the dimensional levels of the consciousness pool. The incarnate tiger interprets experiences during its incarnation and, when it dies and its condition of being is added back into the pool, it either increases or decreases the median level of the originating pool of consciousness. If the results of the incarnation effect an increase in consciousness within the pool, a portion of pooled consciousness escalated beyond the median range of the pool is skimmed off and moved to the next corresponding dimensional pool of consciousness.

Likewise, if the incarnation results in a lowering below the pooled median range, it may be skimmed from the bottom of the range of the pool and moved to a corresponding lower pool of consciousness. Consciousness in 2nd Density is nondescript because no individual unit of consciousness is metaphysically sustained and it is thusly very fluid, flowing from level to level either upward or downward. This is not a significant change in mobility from 1st Density consciousness behavior but the consciousness of 1st Density doesn't have significant room to move dimensionally upwards or downwards because consciousness is pooled in such bulk and it is so low, to begin with.

The same process describing the tiger occurs with every incarnation of every plant or animal. Like 1st Density, 2nd

Density is timeless and there is no limit to the number of times it may go through the incarnation process or a specified period for it to evolve through the dimension. Since there is no preservation of an individual mind/body/spirit, the pool of consciousness functions as a vat of consciousness perpetuating a cycle of incarnations that will continue as long as the form of the particular species produces desired evolutionary results. Each pool of consciousness has a single torus and a single mind but a separate torus and mind are established for the term of an analog projection.

Before the infusion of 2nd Density consciousness into a body in gestation, all analog projection bodies consist of the manifested space/time ingredients of 1st Density consciousness. When an incarnated 2nd Density body dies, plant or animal, the 2nd Density consciousness leaves the body and the ingredients resume the 1st Density experience. The need for 1st Density ingredients is another of the many reasons a 2nd Density experience can only be conducted after a 1st Density experience has reached a certain degree of consciousness maturity.

The 1st Density ingredients incorporated into a 2nd Density body never leave the 1st Density torus. For example, water participating in a 2nd Density body always remains part of the torus and mind of the 1st Density water element, and matter participating in a 2nd Density body always remains part of the 1st Density torus and mind of the 1st Density matter element, and so forth. However, providing the incarnate body ingredients does tend to elevate the 1st Density consciousness because of the close interactive contact with the higher 2nd Density consciousness.

Even though 1st Density consciousness is always incarnate, it does simultaneously exist in both time/space and space/time as does all consciousness in the foundational and lower experiential densities. Simultaneous with the creation of a soul stream, when consciousness begins a 1st Density experience, a nonphysical time/space enduring body is created consisting of seven bodies. The nonphysical time-space body acts as a valve, regulating the flow of Intelligent Energy from the Higher Self. When consciousness is scaled to 1st Density only the 1st Density time/space body is activated, allowing a minimal flow of Intelligent Energy according to its dimension level with the other six bodies remaining in potentiation. 2nd Density continues the time/space body, but with both the first and second bodies of the nonphysical enduring time/space body sequentially activated and the remaining five bodies continuing in potentiation.

Every 2nd Density mind/body manifest in space/time is an analog of the corresponding time/space mind/body/spirit pool of consciousness that remains the corpus of its being. The time/space mind/body/spirit is enduring and survives a multitude of incarnations. The lessons learned through repeated 2nd Density incarnations accrue to the time/space pooled consciousness, but since elevated consciousness is frequently skimmed from the top of the pool, the dimensional range of the pool of consciousness remains relatively unchanged. Newly formatted consciousness can be regularly added to the pool to replenish what has been skimmed and relocated.

Ideally, consciousness is readily available from lower pools of consciousness to serve as a reservoir to add to every pool of consciousness when consciousness from a single pool is advanced. Because consciousness within creation functions according to free will, some pools advance consciousness more quickly than others, and often there are shortages or excesses at any given dimensional level of consciousness within the system. The consciousness level determines behavior and so consciousness may be added or subtracted from the system from within the system or from outside the system by modifying it according to the Intelligent Energy valve we are calling a time/ space body, and its behavior will conform to the behavior of other consciousness that is already in the pool. The objective is for consciousness to explore itself at all dimensional levels and this is possible because all consciousness is the Creator exploring itself, according to the Law of One.

As consciousness progresses through 2nd Density it doesn't preserve awareness of experiences from the various incarnations but it does constantly reflect changes in free will intoxication. It is the change in free will intoxication that allows an increased or decreased Intelligent Energy flow and corresponding increased or decreased dimensionality. Consciousness in 2nd Density flows freely among the dimensions because it is nondescript and functions as pooled consciousness.

The 2nd Density analog bodies we recognize as a species are vessels with which to experience each other and the space/ time world around them. Different body types are regularly created, transformed, or removed from the 2nd Density system. The continued use of a particular species vessel is based upon how effective it has proven to be in encouraging a variety of experiences. When a species becomes extinct it is not because of the blind force of nature's random hand but because the conditions that once made it a viable vessel for experiences have changed and it is deemed to be no longer providing adequate opportunity for consciousness' exploration of itself.

The 2nd Density incarnate experience is dramatically different from the 1st Density in many ways. 1st Density bodies do not have senses with which to interact with their environment because it creates the environment but the 2nd Density analog projections heavily rely upon senses to flavor their experiences. The 2nd Density analog projections are dependent upon the space/time environment and their bodies sense/interact with the 1st Density physical environment around them while also interacting with other 2nd Density consciousness. 2nd Density experiences consist largely of feeding upon other species to nourish their bodies and/or to be food to nourish other 2nd Density bodies, and it's through these sensory input interactions that they can have experiences and learn.

The lower the dimensions within 2nd Density the more mindlessly motivated consciousness is to simply survive within the environment. 2nd Density consciousness evolving by surrendering its perception of separation demonstrates its progress by integrating into increasingly larger organisms and eventually into social organisms. The 2nd Density consciousness picks up where the 1st Density consciousness leaves off, and, while it remains within the lower dimensions of the new density, its capacity to evolve is limited, demonstrating behavior, not unlike the seemingly mindless back-and-forth flow of consciousness between the dimensions of 1st Density. Consciousness within the lower 2nd Density dimensions doesn't intentionally merge into larger organisms and perpetually remains within the lowest dimensions with a focus on the most basic survival.

Behavior within higher dimensions of 2nd Density begins to develop the foundations of behavior we associate with a 3rd Density experience such as affection for others, caring for others, or a communal coexistence because the changes in behavior are indicative of the transformation of lower consciousness into higher consciousness within the density. The differences between 1st Density and 2nd Density and the diversity of behavior between the dimensional ranges of 2nd Density are demonstrations of variety in the degree of awareness of itself in relation to other 2nd Density analog projections, places, or things. The more evolved the consciousness the greater the demonstration of unity behavior, which prevails in all densities, even in the lowest ones.

Throughout the evolutionary process, the key ingredient that distinguishes one consciousness level from another is its degree of awareness. Fire, the lowest consciousness manifestation, is indiscriminate and is virtually unaware. Gorillas, one of the highest body types of 2nd Density consciousness, are, relatively speaking, very aware and demonstrate their awareness in how they care for the young, fellow members of their troop, and how they interact with their surrounding environment.

Awareness is the Inherent Characteristic that pervades and distinguishes between all levels of consciousness, including the Creator Being densities. In the foundational and lower experiential densities, awareness is elementary and is primarily concerned with awareness within a space/time environment and survival. As consciousness evolves into the middle ranges of 4th Density and 5th Density it surrenders attachment to the authenticity of the space/time concept and concerns for survival almost entirely because it has sufficient access to awareness and information to do so. The 4th Density consciousness becomes focused on identifying and resolving its perceived distinctions between itself and the Creator. Surrendering the ego and perception of separation, resulting in a greater acceptance of unity, becomes the motivation for consciousness' interactions with itself and other consciousness, and awareness is the tool that allows it to do this.

Evolution is a process that begins by perceptually sending consciousness as far away from unity with the Creator as possible, then guiding it back to where it began, expanded by all of its experiences and uniqueness, and in complete unity with the Creator. The phases of evolution within the space/time environment appear as the physical process of merging the small and simple into the large and complex. Units of 1st Density consciousness are very small and simple, even though we perceive their unification into planets to be large and complex.

The 1st Density's reality is composed of only four parts that make up the organism we call a planet, and consciousness participates as very small increments of one of the four elements. Humans, in their efforts to scientifically "know" the world around them, have interpreted these four small parts to be molecules, atoms, quarks, etc. but these are only biases of interpretation of how the four elements might appear and interact. In other words, because we have expectations of what the micro world is like, we have shaped the four elements into being the panoply of chemistry and physics particles that we expect them to be, which is the basis of the sciences.

Observing 2nd Density consciousness allows us to realize the joining together or the reunification of consciousness when we consider the diversity of bodies that populate the Earth as plants and animals, but much more unity is occurring beyond the physical bodies. The complexity of the bodies is one indication of greater unity, but the incarnate bodies begin to create socially cooperative units called families, flocks, troops, herds, colonies, etc. Bodies unite with other bodies for survival, the perpetuation of the species, companionship, and sometimes, in the higher dimensions of 2nd Density, even to potentiate loving behavior. The various species of incarnate consciousness that form social units are expanding the consolidation of consciousness beyond the physical.

All consciousness projected into the environment of space/time is an analog of time/space consciousness, functioning as if it is on stage in a theatrical production, and behaving according to the constructs of the character being portrayed. Regardless of the particular character or play, consciousness is always the conceptualized Creator distorted to perceive itself as separate from itself. The unmanifest time/space body in all of the foundational and experiential densities is the Intelligent Energy valve that regulates consciousness' relative participation in creation. If the valve is sufficiently open to only allow Intelligent Energy to flow through the unmanifest body to activate between two and eight strands of consciousness, then only the 1st Density body will be activated and consciousness will portray the character necessary to experience 1st Density.

If the 2nd time/space body is activated, then the valve is set to allow sufficient Intelligent Energy to activate between 10 and 16 strands of coding and consciousness will be able to participate in creation at a 2nd Density level. The unmanifest time/space energy body is the regulating mechanism and the unmanifest time/space ego mind becomes the repository for accumulated incarnate experiences. In the foundational densities, dimensional activation is often heavily dependent upon "grace" from the Higher Self to energize additional Intelligent Energy flow because consciousness is inadequately aware to do otherwise.

The manifested 1st Density body, one of the four elements, is the product/creation of the unmanifest 1st Density mind/ego because that is how it is capable of perceiving itself. Its self-perceptions transform from one manifested element to the next because the nature and capacity to process thoughts change. Its ability to perceive itself transforms as it matures. Fire becomes water, water becomes atmosphere, and the atmosphere becomes matter because consciousness can perceive itself differently with each advancing dimensional gain.

In all of the densities, the spirit always knows itself to be the Creator but, until the mind/ego surrenders its free will intoxication and sufficiently increases its energy flow, the spirit remains obscure or unrecognizable to the mind until the later dimensions of 3rd Density, and even then, only with an elementary recognition. The mind/ego primarily determines the nature of consciousness' experience of creation because of its inability and/or unwillingness to surrender its independent perception of itself. All intelligence is the intelligence of the Creator and the intoxicating effects of free will limit consciousness' access to intelligence and awareness which inhibits its ability to access spirit. Consciousness experiencing 1st and 2nd Densities perceives the mind/ego to be the sole "experiencer" of 1st and 2nd Densities.

When driving a vehicle with a manual transmission, the driver must engage a clutch to disengage the gears so that shifting from one gear to the next is possible without damaging the gears. Once the clutch is engaged and the gears have been shifted, the clutch is carefully released so that the new gear may be fully engaged to transfer the power from the engine to the wheels. The process of releasing the clutch encounters a friction point when the gears transform from not being engaged, to being engaged. If the clutch is released with the driver's awareness of this point, the gears can be engaged with minimal wear and tear on the gears and maximum comfort to the vehicle's passengers.

Each new dimension or density is a higher gear than the one below and as consciousness shifts from one dimension to another, or from one density to another, the degree of awareness of the driver and its ability to distinguish the friction point allows the transmission of change to be less bumpy and a more comfortable ride. When the driver lacks awareness, the shifting of gears from lower to higher may still be relatively accomplished but it is more difficult. Shifting from dominance of the ego mind to the spirit is improbable in the foundational densities but awareness is always available and the key to making the journey smooth or bumpy, no matter the consciousness level.

As presented in earlier chapters, creation is a thought experiment. In the foundational and experiential densities, the mind only processes thought but it doesn't create thought. The 6th Density Higher Self(s) create all thoughts for the foundational and experiential densities and all their perceptions come through thoughts. Experience is the mind's processing of thought, including its perceptions of the nature of the self and the environment. The degree to which consciousness can be aware varies from dimension to dimension and from density to density because of consciousness' variable ability to process thought according to its varying degree of free will intoxication.

Regardless of the thought, every thought holds the potential for the full awareness of the Creator, but the ability to employ awareness is governed by the degree of free will intoxication of the ego mind. A first-grade student has the potential to read and understand the complexities of a Shakespearian play, but because of limited access to awareness, experience, etc., he/she is highly unlikely to be able to do so. Likewise, foundational density consciousness has the potential to realize its unity as the Creator by the processing of a single thought, but, because of the governing of its awareness, it is highly improbable.

1st Density thought results in the perceptions that manifest in one of the four elements creating space/time, but this doesn't mean that a real physical world is created and exists independent of perception. It does mean that 1st Density authentically perceives itself as a body, manifest as one of the four elements, operating in unison, to create the environment of space/time. That is the limit of its perception of self as presented in thought.

2nd Density participates in Creation in cooperation with a 1st Density experience and it assumes the authenticity of the space/time environment because of its awareness limitations. A species pool of consciousness has a torus and ego mind and perceives itself independently from the space/time environment, which is a significant perceptual refinement over the bulk 1st Density element perception of itself. Each analog projection into a solitary species member is also a torus that creates an ego mind, identifies itself as a separate self, and processes thought independently from the species pool of consciousness.

Due to consciousness' limited awareness in 2nd Density, it can only perceive itself as the image of the self that is included in thought so, when tiger consciousness is projected into an infant tiger body, it is only able to perceive itself as an infant tiger. When a tiger matures the image included in a thought matures as well so the tiger perceives itself as getting bigger and stronger. As the tiger matures, it has random experiences and reacts to those experiences according to what it likes. It creates an emotional body that guides its reactions to all new experiences.

If, for example, a tiger has an experience in which he/she sees a potential food source, such as a man, and the experience results in a painful failure for the tiger, any future encounter with a man will likely be reacted to with fear or some degree of displeasure. The tiger will probably become predisposed to avoid similar future encounters, based on its previous unpleasant experience. The initial encounter becomes a bias that guides its interpretations of future potential encounters based on the emotions that it experienced.

In the initial experience, the man was only a catalyst for the tiger's emotional interpretation of the experience. It is the emotional interpretation of the experience (thought) that is of importance to the learning of the tiger in the incarnation. The initial experience was a combination of several ingredients that contributed to the tiger's interpretation, including the sensory input of the space/time environment, the emotional disposition of the tiger at the time, and ultimately the catalyst. When a sufficient number of similar feeling ingredients are again recognized by the tiger, they will likely recall similar fear feelings and cause the tiger to avoid the new experience.

If the tiger had the capacity for sufficient awareness it could become aware of the contributions of the different ingredients to its bias, assess each one for its validity as a contributor to a potential repeat of the initial experience, and either dismiss them or entertain them as accurate. The awareness would need to be of the thought(s) itself because all of the ingredients are only included in thoughts. The ability to become aware of thought is way beyond the limited parameters expected of 2nd Density, but it is possible, given that 2nd Density is still the same unified consciousness shared by all of creation.

The tiger's inability to be aware of thought and assess the ingredients of an experience perpetuates its inability to see itself as anything but a tiger. The perception of itself as a tiger is included in its thoughts and, since it is incapable of observing thought, it must live the life of a tiger. This limitation of awareness pervades 1st, 2nd, and 3rd Densities and creates an attachment to the authenticity of space/time, AKA the physical world.

The mind/ego is a distortion of spirit and the body is a creation of the mind resulting from its limited awareness of the self as the processer of thought. The body appears and functions according to the dictates of the mind but the mind can only process thought and if it's only able to extract certain content or it can only discern certain characteristics of the content, that is how the body will appear and function. Anything and everything that consciousness experiences in the foundational or experiential densities come through thought, created by the Creator Being densities and interpreted or co-created by the processing consciousness. Every thought, regardless of the content, will be interpreted according to the degree of awareness of the experiencer.

The conclusion from this is that the physical, which the foundational and lower experiential densities perceive to be authentic, is a distortion of the mind. Space/time is a distortion made authentic by the 1st Density mind which creates the environment for both the foundational and the lower experiential densities until awareness increases sufficiently in the 4th Density, to recognize it as distortion. Consciousness, experiencing any dimensions or densities, is only limited by its awareness. One of the universal effects of raising consciousness through the upper dimensions of the 4th Density is the progressive awareness that space/time is a distortion, an illusion, existing only in the mind.

Consciousness experiencing the 1st and 2nd Densities is nondescript because what is learned through its interactions isn't retained within the consciousness experiencing the density, but the fruit of the learning isn't pointless or lost. Consciousness is consciousness or, in other words, "all is one" and what is experienced and learned in the foundational densities is directly absorbed and retained by the sponsoring 6th Density consciousness. That, which is experienced and learned by any portion of consciousness, regardless of how it may perceive itself to be isolated or segregated from the whole, is experienced and learned by all and contributes to the purpose of creation equally. This is the "Law of One".

Since creation is a series of subject and object interactions, this behavior is replicated and reiterated to create what we perceive to be creation. The object always perceives itself as closer to the Creator and the subject always perceives itself as farther away, more independent, from the Creator. This is the reason for sexual genders; the female is always the object and the male is always the subject.

Beginning in 2nd Density the interactions of subject and object become significantly more complex than in 1st Density. 2nd Density introduces into the incarnate portions of its experience the concept of biology and experiences a specific design that allows for the more unique creation of a personality, even though it is not preserved beyond a single incarnation. The sexes, rather than the somewhat vague characterizations of 1st Density's interactions, become not only prominent but essential to consciousness' learning and advancement.

The biological design of species reproduction is that an offspring is born into innocence with corresponding physical limitations, which is a reiteration of the 1st Density beginning in primordial darkness. The newborn is innocent and has a relatively "clean slate" on which to write but, through interactions with other aspects of consciousness, it learns about itself and its surroundings and eventually becomes an experienced adult. Through the experiences of its life, it forms a unique personality (identity) resulting from its free will interpretations of experiences according to what it likes.

The essence of experience, according to free will, is for all consciousness to choose from a variety of experiences according to what it likes (AKA what feels good). As stated before, this is known as the "Law of Confusion" or the "Law of Free Will" and is applicable in all densities. Any intent to compel conformity to a standard by any other criteria, other than allowing every autonomous perceiving consciousness unit, is a violation of the Law of Confusion, no matter the level of consciousness.

2nd Density relies upon a more expository role for subject and object interactions than 1st Density. For example, 2nd Density heavily relies upon the sexes to provide learning opportunities. The male is always the subject and perceives itself as more autonomous from the Creator, and the female is always the object and perceives itself as less autonomous from the Creator. Required interactions between the sexes for mutual survival and reproduction significantly intensify and expand the learning opportunities for both subject and object.

The roles of males and females vary somewhat as consciousness moves through the dimensions of 2nd Density. In some species, the male provides the less dominating caretaking of the young role often associated with the female, and in others, the female provides the more dominant provider/ protector role usually associated with the male. Just as RA is not exclusively RA but only dominantly RA while still being inclusive of the other four Inherent Characteristics, a male is not exclusively male and a female is not exclusively female. Each sex incorporates characteristics of the other, thus providing subject/object interactions with other members of its species while simultaneously providing subject/object interactions within itself.

Consciousness reaching the higher dimensions of 2nd Density demonstrates a more consistently defined role for males and females. Males usually possess a greater ego than females and are frequently physically dominant because of greater physical strength or cunning. Females are characterized by sex and biological reproduction with usually a lesser ego than males. This is the foundation of the continuation of male and female interactions in 3rd Density but more is occurring than a biological interaction.

When consciousness interacts with other consciousness in the foundational and lower experiential densities, an invisible, but competitive, exchange of energy, Intelligent Energy, is occurring. When a male exerts physical strength to dominate other males, females, or the environment, it is competing for energy, potentially available to be extracted from the less competitive of the species or other animals. When a female is sexually available or "feeling/looking pretty or sexy", it is also competing for potentially available Intelligent Energy through interaction with males or other females. When it "wins" the competition, it feels better, and when it loses the battle it feels less good. Competition for energy, characteristic of higher 2nd Density and especially the lower dimensions of 3rd Density, either enhances or diminishes the ego and guides the interpretation of experience.

2nd Density greatly expands and intensifies consciousness' experience of creation over 1st Density but it too is a foundational density. Even though it is significantly more complex than 1st Density, it is not nearly as intense or complex as 3rd Density. Its diversity is illustrated by the wide range of plant and animal species which adds to the panoply of opportunities for consciousness experience.

Chapter 6

3rd Density

2nd Density is dramatically different from 1st Density, and 3rd Density is equally as dramatic, if not more so, in how it differs from 2nd Density. As consciousness moves from density to density its ability to co-create the density characteristics increases because the nature of the next higher density capitalizes upon and enhances what was begun in the previous one. Creation in the foundational and especially in the experiential densities is a school in which the Creator learns of itself and each density sets forth certain lessons that must be absorbed in the lower density to be able to do the work of the next. Similarly, when you were in third grade it was necessary to learn its lessons before you could advance because the third grade lessons were the foundation for the work of the fourth grade.

The foundational densities are timeless and experiences within them are random but 3rd Density is neither timeless nor random. An experience of 3rd Density has a very definitive beginning and ending which is approximately 75,000 years and, as RA explains, is "as regular as a clock." The actual number of years varies to accommodate the planet hosting the 3rd Density experience's orbit around the sponsoring star and the solar system's orbital journey through a galaxy.

The 75,000-year master cycle, or 3rd Density experience, is further divided into three equal segments of approximately 25,000 years. A 3rd Density experience is further sequenced by dividing the approximate 25,000 years into five smaller segments of approximately 5,000 years each. For example, the 3rd Density master cycle that Earth has just completed lasted for 78,000 years, divided into three segments of 26,000 years with each of those segments consisting of 5,200 years. The 3rd Density master cycle of Earth concluded in February 2016 and Earth has now become the host for a new shared 3rd and 4th Density planet.

When a 3rd Density experience concludes it is not automatic that the planet will become a 4th Density planet. Just as the beginning of the foundational density experience begins with a decision by the primary sponsoring archetype, a 3rd, 4th, or 5th Density experience is begun with a similar decision based upon need. If another 4th Density experience is not needed but another 3rd Density experience is, then it is probable that the same planet may host a new 3rd Density experience and begin another +/-75,000-year cycle. For example, the planet formerly known as Zenoa (now Venus) was host to a series of 3rd Density experiences for billions of years until approximately 775,000 years ago.

The Milky Way galaxy currently hosts approximately 67 million planets ranging from 1st to 5th Density and approximately 26% of them are 3rd Density experiences at various stages of progress. The Andromeda galaxy currently contains approximately 85 million planets hosting foundational and experiential density experiences and roughly 32% of them are 3rd Density experiences. Other than the newly begun 3rd Density experience on Earth, the solar system that we currently experience has only one other 3rd Density experience that is also just now beginning a new 3rd Density term on the planet Tara which is being hosted simultaneously with a 1st, 2nd, 4th, and 5th Density experience.

The 3rd Density experience is the lowest consciousness level of the experiential densities. Consciousness in 1st Density is nondescript because it doesn't have an identity other than the bulk identity of one of the four elements and, other than what is reflected in the pooled consciousness by a transiently increased awareness, it doesn't preserve learning from its incarnate experiences. Consciousness in 2nd Density is also nondescript because learning from its incarnate experiences is not preserved by the 2nd Density consciousness, but it does have significantly more refined experiences than 1st Density through its multitude of incarnations as various plants and animals.

Beginning with 3rd Density, for the first time in its evolutionary journey, consciousness is segregated into individual units of consciousness functioning as mind/body/spirits that can become "aware" and assume personal responsibility to increase their perception of separation or pursue greater unity with the Creator through its experiences. A defined time/space (metaphysical) mind/body/spirit repeatedly incarnates into multiple lifetimes and the learning, or lack thereof, is cumulatively preserved in its corpus and used as the foundation for its next lifetime, allowing for an accumulation of learning experience beyond the brief experience of a single incarnation. In this way, a unique consciousness pattern can be formed that transcends a single incarnation.

3rd Density is also the only density from which consciousness must "graduate". Just like a high school that requires its students to accrue a specific number of credits in a variety of subject areas to graduate, 3rd Density has a curriculum and all students must obtain the prescribed number of credits in various areas of study to graduate to 4th Density. Every incarnation is designed to provide a mind/body/spirit with experiences that will allow it to learn the subject matter, check off the curriculum requirements, and move closer towards graduation. Every mind/body/spirit retains free will and has the choice of doing the prescribed work, or not, and so the individual retains control of how quickly, or how slowly, they will graduate.

The curriculum has nothing to do with math, science, or language. The curriculum is comprised of experiences that will provide every student with the opportunity to learn about awareness, love, wisdom, unity, and stillness, the Inherent Characteristics. The only thing that is retained from lifetime to lifetime is what is learned about the Inherent Characteristics, which means, no matter how many MD or PhD diplomas are acquired during an incarnation, all that education goes into the ground at the end of the lifetime and the only thing that is preserved is what is spiritually enduring.

Consciousness is the Creator experiencing itself as a conceptual self. All learning about the physical space/time world is a distortion of truth and it is the intensity of the attachment to the distortions that significantly obscures and slows consciousness escalation. Learning about the physical world can be very valuable if it is used as a mechanism to increase the population's consciousness escalation, but in the Earth experience, the fruit of most science, technology, mathematics, etc. has been to enhance the stature or wealth of the individual, which are elements of an identity created for the prevailing lifetime and are only ego mind values. This is the nature of free will but the antithesis of the spiritual design and an unaware, unconscious objective devised by Earth's population.

3rd Density begins with 18 strands of coding activated and ends with 24. Consciousness may be elevated from 1st or 2nd Density to begin a 3rd Density experience, or it may begin its introduction into the evolutionary process by beginning in 3rd Density without any prior experience of the foundational densities. However, 3rd Density must be conducted on a planet that has achieved relative maturity in both of the foundational experiences. If a planet is hosting a 3rd Density experience, it was already hosting a 1st and 2nd Density experience.

On a planet experiencing a 1st and/or 2nd Density experience, the planet itself doesn't have an equivalent consciousness host other than the 1st and 2nd Density consciousness creating the foundations for experiences. Beginning with the 3rd Density, the planet itself has an equivalent consciousness that serves as a host for the population and will be experiencing the 3rd Density on an equivalent evolutionary journey. For example, Earth has been a 1st and 2nd Density planet with the consciousness of a relative density populating both of these foundational densities while concurrently having a planetary consciousness that served as a host 3rd Density consciousness of the 3rd Density population. Earth's host 3rd Density planetary consciousness has commonly been called "Gaia" and has been on an evolutionary journey independent of the population but in harmony with the 1st and 2nd Density consciousness.

If you will recall from previous chapters, the spirit of 1st and 2nd Density is the spirit of the sponsoring archetype, however, because consciousness is now at a suitably higher consciousness level than the foundational densities, each mind/body/spirit believes it is an individualized spirit with an independent perspective of self from the sponsoring archetype. Perception is important to understand because stress-provoking distortion perceptions are primarily a product or limitation proffered by the ego mind. The ego mind of the 3rd Density perceives that it has an individualized spirit, but, regardless of the perception, it is still the spirit of the Higher Self.

While the mind/body/spirit remains within the experiential densities, including 4th and 5th Densities, the perception of separation (free will as enhanced by TA) moderates the mind/body/spirit's ability to surrender itself to the spirit and realizes its unity. The spirit of 1st and 2nd Density is inaccessible because of the perceptual and intellectual limitations of consciousness, but it is still the spirit of the Higher Self. 3rd Density begins where the foundational densities leave off and it begins with the same limited ability to access spirit.

As awareness escalates through the dimensions of 3rd Density, consciousness may become aware of spirit, but, because it is still constrained by the ego mind, it probably still perceives that its spirit is separate from that of the Higher Self. It is usually not until the upper dimensions of the 4th Density that a mind/body/spirit can sufficiently surrender its free will intoxication to truly recognize itself as sharing the same spirit as the Higher Self. Recognizing and surrendering free will is always a feeling enterprise and not an intellectual one, regardless of the consciousness level.

When a mind/body/spirit reaches the upper dimensions of 4th Density, it will have spanned numerous dimensions to gain sufficient awareness to come to this realization and spend the remainder of its tenure in the density focused on the seasoning and acceptance of the newly revised perception. 5th Density picks up where 4th Density concludes and consciousness continues the process of surrendering free will intoxication and integrating itself into unity. Evidence of progress is first available in the 3rd Density when the mind/body/spirit achieves sufficient dimensionality to periodically surrender its preoccupation with the ego mind and allow the deep mind to emerge.

The "deep mind" is the same as the "root mind" of the 6th Density Higher Self, but it functions as if it were separate because of a greater free will intoxication. To come to the realization and acceptance that the 3rd Density mind/body/spirit shares the same spirit and mind as the Higher Self, it must adequately surrender its perception of its identity's authenticity, held sacrosanct by the ego mind. It is only the surrender of the identity's authenticity by exploring the self and experiencing the self that permits a mind/body/spirit to do this. As long as a mind/body/spirit remains myopically focused outside of the perceived self, and solely reliant upon the ego mind for thinking, it will continue to experience intense stress and suffering and be unable to move into the higher dimensions of the density.

Transition into 3rd Density activates the 3rd unmanifest time/ space body of the seven bodies that serve as the energy valve to regulate the flow of Intelligent Energy from the Higher Self. The 3rd Density unmanifest metaphysical body, the individual enduring corpus, always remains in the metaphysical world, and, similar to 2nd Density, 3rd Density beings experience the physical world through a series of mind/body/spirit incarnations that are analog projections of the unmanifest mind/ body/spirit (the corpus). Every analog projection into space/ time is an incarnation and the fruit of learning of each Earthly visit accrues to the unmanifest metaphysical mind/body/spirit upon death. This is a significant refinement of the 2nd Density experience that shares the experience of analog incarnations but only accrues consciousness changes to a nondescript pool of consciousness.

The 3rd Density unmanifest time/space mind/body/spirits usually simultaneously experience multiple lifetimes at once. When 3rd Density consciousness is low within the density range, usually at the beginning of its 3rd Density experience with only 18 strands of coding activated, it has sufficient Intelligent Energy to experience only about three simultaneous lifetimes. (The Earthly population, as a rule, currently only has enough energy to simultaneously experience one or two incarnations because of its developmentally delayed evolutionary progress.) As its consciousness elevates within the density range, usually near the end of its 3rd Density experience with 24 strands of coding activated, it can simultaneously experience as many as eight or nine lifetimes. The average Earth-experiencing human has lived over 3,900 lifetimes and some above 8,000.

Mental health professionals have identified a condition previously called "multiple personality disorder" when a patient would slip into different roles, usually without control, and demonstrate different personalities, gender identities, and voice characteristics with each role. Schizophrenia is another diagnosis with similar but somewhat different behaviors that results from the same condition. We can discuss the specifics of how this could be in future chapters, but, for now, when a person experiences emotional trauma in one lifetime it can be an unwelcome opportunity for the characteristics of other simultaneous lifetimes to seep into the traumatized one. It's nothing to be afraid of, but it usually will take work to effect healing of the condition, learn how to again take control of the seepage, and regain control of the mind.

A single 3rd Density incarnation is intended to microcosmically reiterate the entire evolutionary process from the beginning through 3rd Density and potentially beyond. Consciousness beginning the 3rd Density experience with its first incarnation begins with a completely clean slate in "primordial darkness", but with a 3rd Density consciousness capability. As a metaphysical mind/body/spirit experiences multiple incarnations, its consciousness level (with distortions acquired incrementally from previous incarnations) serves as a starting point for a new life as biases or prejudices to be healed by its awareness and surrendered or enhanced if they're polarizing negatively. Many biases and prejudices carried over from previous incarnations cause emotional pain and/or suffering in the new life, but potentially catalyze increased awareness and eventually promote healing of the distortions of its self-perception.

Since a 3rd Density experience can only begin on a planet that already has a mature 1st and 2nd Density experience in progress, a body type for incarnation is selected from the available 2nd Density bodies and adapted to accommodate the 3rd Density consciousness. For example, the ape body was selected as the most suitable for the 3rd Density Earth experience but any physical body with suitable design flexibility can be used. On a

3rd Density Sirius B planet, trees were chosen as the body type and proved to be a very productive 3rd Density experience.

Usually, on a planet without a 3rd Density history, there's a transition period when a 2nd Density body is adapted to accommodate the 3rd Density consciousness requirements. Preparing the body vessel in Earth's experience required about one and one-half generations for the transition to be completed. When an ape baby was randomly conceived, it was infused with a 3rd Density consciousness, and the transformation of the ape body into a more suitable 3rd Density body was begun. Because life on Earth is carbon-based, science assumes that carbon is necessary for biological evolution, but any substance can be used that is available because it is the infusion of the appropriate consciousness level into an organism that makes it viable.

The transition from 3rd Density bodies to 4th Density bodies is usually a less difficult process, but a 3rd Density body is more "chemical" and a 4th Density body is more "electric". Earth's current preparation for 4th Density cohabitation is requiring a modification of the chemical body we have become accustomed to because many children born since the year 2000 are 4th Density. The children are being born into "transitional" bodies which are still somewhat chemical but also more electric, and, as they mature and seed the next generations, they will be even more electric until the body is completely transformed to a 4th Density standard. It's anticipated, at some undisclosed future time, that the 4th Density and 3rd Density populations will be segregated into two simultaneous but non-interacting experiences and each density experience will enhance its destiny qualities as necessary.

After multiple incarnations into space/time, the metaphysical mind/body/spirit will have begun to form a unique personality (AKA consciousness pattern) based upon the interpretations of experiences of its analog mind/body/spirit's experiences in the physical world. In the same way that the Creator's archetypes began to find their uniqueness in 7th Density and more dramatically in 6th Density, 3rd Density consciousness begins to find its uniqueness which is preserved as the basis for future incarnations. Free will, the distortion inherent in all aspects of creation, allows consciousness to explore creation freely, within the defined parameters for the specific solar system experience, without interference.

A new baby born in 3rd Density is a mature metaphysical mind/body/spirit with a consciousness pattern of some degree of maturity. It begins life anew but with a preconditioning comprised of biases, consciousness level, and predilections that will guide its choices, likes, and dislikes until it can increase its awareness and take control of its thoughts. Conception is random, but the selection of the body's occupant isn't. The body's occupant will have been carefully chosen because the potential life experiences will provide the body's occupant with probable experiences that will assist the spiritual growth and development of the occupant's unmanifest mind/body/spirit.

A 3rd Density lifetime has a very specific design. The manifest mind/body/spirit is purposely born into innocence, just as 2nd Density consciousness begins an incarnation, with the intention that, because of its ego mind-created biases and prejudices, it will mostly experience what it doesn't like until it either becomes aware or hits a "bottom" when it cannot continue interpreting experiences as it has been because it's just too painful. He/she then has the opportunity to awaken and begin to surrender old behaviors and attitudes developed by the unaware ego mind perspective so it can begin to incrementally create what it likes.

Invariably, the period of a lifetime when the mind/body/spirit experiences what it doesn't like is the time while it's maintaining a false identity (collection of beliefs) and attempting to turn its own "wheel of fate". It intensely believes itself to be the false identity it has created from its experiences. All experience is emotionally neutral but the emotional intensity of an experience results from interpretation by the individual mind/body/spirit's application of an emotion. Every stress-provoking experience is self-imposed by the ego mind and not because any experience has brought the stress or is more emotionally intense than another.

Awakening or "bottom hitting" may take many lifetimes before the mind/body/spirit finds success, but it is also possible that it may occur during the first incarnation. It is only the ego's limitations and a lack of awareness that prevent them from awakening. As we have previously explained, the ego is synonymous with the ego mind and the results from the perception of separation, so the pain and/or suffering of life continues and intensifies until the mind/body/spirit begins to awaken and, of its own volition, begins to move forward along the evolution path by surrendering the ego, resolve its ignorance, and increase their awareness.

The purpose of this manuscript is to provide humanity with information that may serve to aid those individuals who are ready to awaken, surrender the ego, and evolve. Truthful information is helpful to the process, especially when an environment, such as Earth, has been so significantly contaminated with superstitions and falsehoods for many generations. Regardless of the availability of truthful information, it's still incumbent upon the individual to awaken, recognize the truth, heal the distortions of self-perception, and surrender the false identity because graduation from the 3rd Density is an individual process. There are no group graduations from 3rd Density.

Several things must occur in 3rd Density to graduate to 4th Density and these occurrences are sequential because it is a transformative process, and it's the design for consciousness' experiences. Whatever preamble to beginning consciousness' escalation may be fruitful for the individual mind/body/spirit, the first step is always an awakening. Awakening may begin with nothing more than the feeling of dissatisfaction or unrest with life's prevailing conditions. Grousing isn't helpful because it avoids transforming the self, which requires effort (work) that must include surrendering false perceptions and undertaking the necessary steps to explore the self. It is only through self-exploration that the opportunity to become adequately aware can be found.

Once the individual mind/body/spirit becomes aware of their awakening, it is necessary to invert attention from outside of the self to inside and begin to discover who the experiencer is. This is a process because it will require the incremental surrender of the ego mind to become familiar with the truly authentic self. This phase of the process may take several lifetimes or can be accomplished in a few years of a single lifetime, depending upon how earnestly the individual mind/body/spirit is committed to the process. Usually, pain and/or suffering is the initial motivator and the mind/body/spirit is "running away from the stick" as the motivation for beginning the work.

"Running away from the stick" remains the primary motivator until some success in surrendering the ego mind and attachment to the physical is achieved. There will be a time in every experiencer's life when a transformation from flirting with awareness into actually seriously working towards being awareness occurs. As the experiencer's self-confidence increases because of incremental success and they become aware that they are happier, they invariably become more diligent in the work. It is at this point that the individual mind/body/spirit "gets a bite of the apple" and the motivation transforms from "running away from the stick" to "chasing the apple" because the apple tastes good and more is very desirable.

Tasting the apple and then wanting more is a significantly more productive motivation because it has no upward limits and the willingness of the individual mind/body/spirit to quickly move forward is intensified. The process of surrender, the willingness of the individual to surrender the false identity created by the experiencer to induce others to give them love, requires consent. The underlying fear of getting more of the stick lessens and the individual mind/body/spirit develops more awareness of itself, ready to surrender more ego mind (identity) and explore itself with aplomb and enthusiasm. They cease to see the world as an evil swamp full of demons, snakes, and enemies that have been competing for success in life.

An immutable condition of 3rd Density is that it's necessary to become aware before becoming awareness. Being awareness is a condition of being, indicative of a person's success in achieving higher consciousness within the density and where true learning of the Inherent Characteristics begins. 3rd Density is the density of awareness and, to graduate from 3rd Density and do the work of 4th Density, it is essential to accomplish this condition.

Once consciousness in 3rd Density becomes awareness it can learn of love and experience love through the lens of awareness. All consciousness is programmed to explore and learn of the five Inherent Characteristics, as it is able, and the period in 3rd Density, when it experiences what it doesn't like, is the period before awakening to its life's mission. During everyone's pre-awakening time, they are irrefutably attached to the authenticity of the physical, mistakenly seek love from the physical world outside of themselves, and erroneously attempt to trick the world into loving them by promoting a false self-image (the identity). Therein is the stress, pain, and suffering created by the ego mind.

To spur awakening, a mind/body/spirit will either voluntarily awaken or will more often than not "hit a bottom", which motivates them to realize that the world cannot give them love and they must look elsewhere for the love they are programmed to need. If the outside world cannot give them love, the only other place to look is inside themselves and it's only there that they find love in infinite quantity. When consciousness looks inside, surrenders its attachment to the physical world's authenticity, and truly begins to earnestly explore itself do they realize that they are the source of love they sought. It is with this realization that, for the first time since it began its timeless journey through the foundational densities and its tenure to date in 3rd Density, it truly experiences love.

This is an essential requirement for graduation to 4th Density. The 3rd Density mind/body/spirit must begin to know itself and experience itself as the source of love because it has sufficiently surrendered its ego (identity) to allow itself to be a radiant conduit for the Creator's love. Once this plateau has been achieved, it serves as a foundation for even further accelerated evolutionary advancement.

So far, we have been describing some of the things that must occur in 3rd Density before consciousness may graduate to 4th Density. These requirements can be imposed upon participating consciousness and not before because, in 3rd Density, they're capable of becoming aware and assuming responsibility for their advancement, and the results are immutable for everyone once they do. However, there is one aspect of 3rd Density that can be singled out as the single most important feature that precedes all further consciousness escalation. That requirement is called "the choice".

Because consciousness can be aware and eventually becomes awareness in the 3rd Density, it becomes a significant co-creator of its experiences. Consciousness experiences creation with the mind by processing thoughts, so all experience comes to consciousness in thought. The individual mind/body/spirit determines how experience is interpreted on a thought-by-thought basis. Every time a thought is processed, consciousness, in the form of a manifest space/time experiencing mind/body/ spirit, decides how that thought is going to be interpreted.

When a thought includes interaction with another aspect of consciousness (person, place, or thing), the mind/body/spirit(s) exchange energy, Intelligent Energy. While consciousness remains within the lower dimensions of the 3rd Density, it functions chaotically and battles for energy with every interaction, which is a continuation of the survival behavior of the 2nd Density. When the battle is won, the mind/body/ spirit feels good (or at least better) but when it is lost it doesn't feel good. While the mind/body/spirit remains unconscious, the battle often motivates people to become more proficient as energy soldiers.

Constantly battling in this way creates an automatically reactive learned behavior because winning a battle provides immediate gratification. Winning incremental energy battles provides short-lived benefits but they must again immediately battle to get more energy. When an argument is deemed won, a new item is purchased on a shopping spree, you drive a fast car, or another person is "bested" in any way, there is a brief period of immediate gratification. It inflates the ego (identity) but deludes the experiencer into thinking that they need to win more pyrrhic battles or collect more transient toys.

The mind/body/spirit is making an unconscious choice (read: unaware choice) of whether to radiate or absorb energy. If the choice is to consistently absorb energy, it creates a habit that perpetuates a behavior to satisfy the need for constant immediate gratification, regardless of the consequences for other people. This is behavior indicative of immature consciousness dwelling in the lower dimensions of the density and is described as Service-to-self behavior. Service-to-self behavior is a choice that reinforces separation from the Creator, enhances the ego mind (identity), and, if continued, will potentially set the course of the person's progression through the balance of 3rd Density, 4th Density, and potentially even 5th Density.

Service-to-self behavior reinforces the false identity the experiencer has created and requires them to dominate and subjugate others to satisfy their perpetual need to restock the good feeling energy provided by winning the energy battles. While they remain incarnate, this ideology evolves into conditions labeled as narcissism, psychopathy, or sociopathy. These are distorted conditions of the experiencer that seldom mature within a single lifetime but require the shaping of a service-to-self metaphysical consciousness pattern over multiple incarnations. Their awareness becomes myopically, but intensely focused outside of themselves and does determine the course of their further journey through creation for many years.

The alternative is to choose to radiate energy with every thought and cease to participate with other mind/body/spirits in the competition for energy, which is known as the service-to-others path. Radiating energy results in the surrender of the ego mind, reunification with the Creator, and the experience of enduring joy and eventually bliss. This is the ultimate choice so important in the 3rd Density experience and what makes 3rd Density such an intense density. The service-to-others path is deemed the direct path through the creation and the service-to-self path is deemed to be the indirect path because, once the service-to-self path does awaken, potentially many billions of years down the road, they must return to where they dropped out of school and follow the direct path to achieve advancement in their evolutionary journey.

Both the service-to-self path and the service-to-others path may graduate to 4th Density but the criterion is completely different. Along the service-to-others path, the mind/body/spirit must choose to radiate energy in 51% of its thoughts. Along the service-to-self path, the mind/body/spirit must choose to absorb energy in 95% of its thoughts. The reason for the difference is that the service-to-self individual is choosing to not align themselves with his Higher Self, in the personification of the Creator, and, therefore, terminate their direct source of Intelligent Energy. They must learn to substitute the vital flow of Intelligent Energy from other sources than the Higher Self, which they do in 3rd Density by dominating and subjugating others.

If you will recall from previous chapters, all energy ("Infinite Energy") is a distortion by the Melchizedek (free will) archetype acting upon RA which is the Creator's love archetype. Intelligent Energy is a distortion of Infinite Energy, the energy used to power creation in the foundational and experiential densities, but, it's all still "love" energy. Radiating Intelligent Energy is radiating love energy and absorbing it is absorbing love energy. Radiating love energy is the process of unification with the Creator and absorbing love energy is the process of separating oneself from the Creator.

Intelligent Energy is a creation of the 6th Density. A 6th Density Higher Self is the persona of the Creator to the lower foundational and experiential densities and the only source of love energy to the lower densities, but, when a mind/body/spirit chooses to not align themselves with the Creator they're choosing to not align themselves with the Higher Self, thereby cutting themselves off from the constant flow of the very fuel necessary to sustain their survival. If a mind/body/spirit choosing the service-to-self path must be able to obtain the necessary Intelligent Energy from sources other than the Higher Self, where can it go to find it?

The only other possible source of Intelligent Energy is to "steal" it from other mind/body/spirits who are receiving the constant flow of energy directly from the Higher Self by deceiving them into giving it away. It isn't possible to break into a mind/body/spirit's private vault in the stealth of night and walk away with it. A targeted mind/body/spirit must agree to give their energy to the service-to-self person, but no aware mind/body/spirit would willingly give their Intelligent Energy to anyone in such a way. It would limit or deprive them of their evolution.

Service-to-self must rely upon deception to convince the targeted mind/body/spirit(s) to willingly give their energy to them, and domination and subjugation have proven to be the most effective tools for their deception. The most susceptible targets for domination and subjugation are those mind/body/spirits experiencing the struggles of the lower dimensions of 3rd Density because they are still spiritually naive, already in relative chaos, but they have a sufficient flow of Intelligent Energy to make the endeavor worthwhile. Neither 1st nor 2nd Density has sufficient Intelligent Energy flow or enough presence of mind to wittingly surrender their energy and, once consciousness has risen to 4th Density, it has too much awareness to participate in the deception. Just like Goldilocks, the lower dimensions of 3rd Density are "just right" to be susceptible to deception with enough Intelligent Energy flow to make it a potentially fruitful venture.

Once a mind/body/spirit graduates to 4th Density along the service-to-self path, they must sustain themselves entirely from the theft of Intelligent Energy from others, which means they are constantly in competition with other service-to-self denizens for the energy. Every vulnerable 3rd or 4th Density mind/body/spirit in Creation is a potential target and a potential enemy because they have something that the service-to-self mind/body/spirit desperately needs to survive. Every 4th Density service-to-self mind/body/spirit is constantly looking for a moment of weakness in others so they can use deception to steal more Intelligent Energy.

Intelligent Energy isn't something that can be stored until needed. From the Higher Self, it arrives as a constant flow and so, especially when periodically pilfered from others, it must be constantly replenished. The entire existence of a service-to-self mind/body/spirit is hunting and battling for more Intelligent Energy but, even more so, they must constantly defend against others attempting to confiscate what they have acquired. Imagine if you were a soldier in a 24/7, never-ending perpetual battle, but also have to be on guard that your fellow soldiers might shoot you in the back.

Graduating along the service-to-others path means that you have more completely surrendered the ego mind which results in an increased flow of Intelligent Energy directly from the Higher Self, increased awareness, and increased alignment with the Creator. Graduating along the service-to-self path means that you have enhanced the ego mind, resulting in a termination of the flow of Intelligent Energy from the Higher Self, decreased consciousness, and increased perception of separation from the Creator. The choice to follow the service-to-self path is known as polarizing negatively and the choice to follow the service-to-others path is known as polarizing positively. This is the most important choice of 3rd Density because it determines the course of future evolution.

Because of free will prominence, there are three possible paths through evolution. The first path is the most direct and is the experience of the positive polarization of a mind/body/spirit. The second path is the most indirect path which is the negative polarization of a mind/body/spirit. Along the negative path, a mind/body/spirit drops out of school and struggles to turn its wheel of fate, for potentially billions of years, until it finally must give up, and ironically return to the grade where it dropped out of school, only to follow the positive path to reunification with the Creator. The third path is when a negatively polarized mind/body/spirit becomes energetically bankrupt by failing to sustain itself with the theft of Intelligent Energy and is removed from Creation, returning immediately to the Creator.

Chapter 7

4th Density Transitioning from the Distortions • Healing 3rd Density

4th Density begins where 3rd Density leaves off. As previously stated, the 3rd Density is the only density from which consciousness must graduate to progress to the 4th Density. Each density has its criterion for consciousness' ability to participate but a "graduation" is not required.

If you will recall from the discussion on 3rd Density, one of, if not "the" most important experiences of consciousness in 3rd Density, is the choice. The choice is an individual choice by every mind/body/spirit participating in 3rd Density to choose to either radiate or absorb love energy. If an individual chooses to preponderantly absorb love energy they are deemed to have polarized negatively and are choosing to separate themselves from others and the Creator. If an individual chooses to preponderantly radiate love energy they are choosing to polarize positively and to align themselves more closely with the Creator.

The choice is made with every thought processed and graduation requires that the individual polarizing negatively absorb love energy in 95% of their thoughts because it is choosing to sever its reliance upon the sustaining Intelligent Energy flow provided by the Higher Self and must demonstrate that it can sustain itself through the theft of Intelligent Energy from weaker, more vulnerable mind/body/spirits. Those individual mind/body/spirits choosing to polarize positively are choosing to enhance their unity with the Creator, surrender their perception of separation (AKA free will), and experience an increased flow of Intelligent Energy, and so radiating love energy with every thought requires only a 51% success rate. In 3rd Density, there is much chaos as individuals vacillate back and forth for multiple lifetimes until they eventually become dedicated to a chosen path based upon demonstrated behavior. The confusion created by the vacillation greatly intensifies the experiences of 3rd Density and creates great pain and suffering among populations.

This has been Earth's population experience but other 3rd Density experiences are often much more harmonious with significantly less pain and suffering. Even within the 3rd Density chaos of becoming aware and eventually becoming awareness, most individual mind/body/spirits participating in creation on other planets have much less difficulty in reaching a choice of polarization. Earth's experience can only be characterized as extreme but still very productive in the Creator's desire to learn of itself by exploring itself.

In all 3rd Density experiences, the choice of polarization is arrived at by comparison and contrast, how all consciousness is designed to learn because of free will. However, once a choice has been made and the graduation criterion achieved, the mixing of polarizations in a single environment ceases. Those graduating along the negative path, the service-to-self individual mind/body/spirits, are normally transferred to an environment where they will interact primarily with only others who have also chosen the negative path. Those graduating along the positive path, the service-to-others individual mind/body/spirits, are normally transferred to an environment where they will interact primarily with others who have chosen the positive path.

Beginning in the 4th Density along the positive path, individual mind/body/spirits no longer learn by the elementary behavior of comparison and contrast of external stimuli. Greater awareness allows learning by comparison and contrast of internal feelings and awareness of greater or fewer degrees of alignment with the Creator. For those having chosen the negative path, the same stimuli prevailing in the 3rd Density provide significantly more learning by comparison and contrast of a different nature and hold significant opportunities for pain and suffering predicated upon the fear that took them down the negative path in the first place. Free will prevails and the Creator doesn't nod to one path or the other because both paths are providing the Creator with the opportunity it seeks, which is to know itself by experiencing itself.

4th Density begins with the energizing of 26 strands of coding and ends with 32 strands of coding energized. Those of us still alive on Earth are witness to the advent of a unique situation where a new 3rd Density experience is beginning as a parallel experience to a new 4th Density positive experience because it has been determined that the 3rd Density population requires extra assistance for a while. Even though we are in transition from an old 3rd Density experience to a new density mixed population, those 3rd Density adults who are alive are still able to choose to polarize until they die. These are the last 3rd Density mind/body/spirit individuals that will experience an exclusively 3rd Density on Earth for many years.

Most children who were born after 2001, and many born before, are 4th Density mind/body/spirits who have graduated along the positive path from Earth or another 3rd Density planet. Gaia became a 4th Density consciousness many years ago and has been progressing along a 4th Density evolution path since their graduation. Those not graduating will begin reincarnating as participants in a new +/-75,000 3rd Density experience in hopes that, with the influences of the parallel 4th Density experience, they will be able to surrender sufficient ego (free will intoxication) to polarize one way or the other.

4th Density can be characterized as consciousness' opportunity to heal from the "slings and arrows" of 3rd Density.

It begins much as we see in the faces and hearts of children alive today. There is still significant chaos that they carry from their own experiences in 3rd Density, and great chaos provided from the residual environment of the recently concluded 3rd Density planet, but they have a significantly higher consciousness with which to do the work of self-healing.

In 3rd Density, in addition to choosing the path of our polarization, we are tasked with becoming aware, and further, becoming awareness. It is from the perspective of awareness that we began to learn the lessons of love. In 4th Density, we pick up where we left off and eventually become love as we became awareness in 3rd Density. It is from the perspective of love that we will begin to learn the lessons of wisdom, the criteria for 5th Density.

Since the 3rd Density graduates are primarily going to be staying on Earth and are already polarized positively, I'm going to reserve an explanation of the experiences of the 4th Density negative path for a future chapter, other than by an occasional reference because the positive path deserves the spotlight here. The healing required in 4th Density is the healing of the attachment to the distortions of perception promulgated during 3rd Density. Most prominent among these is the attachment to the authenticity of the 1st Density space/time environment, which includes the physical body.

The 3rd Density body is a very chemical body but the body being experienced by the newly arrived 4th Density children is a blend of both chemical and electrical which is called a transitional body. Those mind/body/spirits continuing to experience 4th Density will continue to transition the body to a more electrical body until they eventually achieve sufficient consciousness to surrender the need for a physical body at all. They will continue to experience 4th Density for some time but without the requirement of a physical body.

Creation and the process of evolution is the enterprise of surrendering free will, consolidating consciousness, and returning to unity with the Creator. In 1st Density, consciousness is disbursed but tasked with the amalgamation of itself into the four elements that eventually form a planet and an environment of space/time. In 2nd Density, an amalgamation of consciousness continues as consciousness merges to form the variety of plant and animal species that works in conjunction with 1st Density consciousness. In 3rd Density, consciousness is isolated into individual units of mind/body/spirits that create individual units of consciousness but continue to amalgamate into social organisms with common perceptions and beliefs.

In 4th Density, the process of returning to unity continues where 3rd Density leaves off but with a significantly more dramatic effect. 4th Density begins with consciousness as individual units but progresses to consolidate consciousness into significantly less isolation. A single soul stream in 3rd Density consists of 394 individual units, each one perceiving itself to be an autonomous mind/body/spirit. When consciousness has sufficiently evolved, these 394 units will merge into 96 units, again, each one being an autonomous mind/body/spirit. Eventually, after all 96 units consent to surrender their attachment to an autonomous perspective and the distortions of space/time, the 96 units will form a social memory complex and function as one autonomous perceiving unit of consciousness.

Initially consolidating consciousness into 96 units, four into one, requires a significant surrender of the perception of separation (free will). Consciousness accomplishes this by sobering from its free will intoxication and becoming more aware of its unity in the Creator. The formation of a social memory complex, near the end of its 4th Density experience, is a continuation of the same process of sobering from free will intoxication. When 4th Density consciousness can consolidate into a social memory complex, it is a signal that it is ready to experience 5th Density.

Even though 4th Density consciousness is successfully merging and integrating, first the four into one and eventually 96 into one as a social memory complex, there remains a significant residual of the individual personalities created during 3rd Density. Consolidating consciousness is the process of surrender by each unit of consciousness and the motivation is increased good feeling obtained from the unity of consciousness. It just feels better to be part of the unity of consciousness than it does to remain an isolated unit of consciousness so we continue to learn by comparison and contrast but with significantly more beneficial results than choosing between chocolate or vanilla ice cream.

Throughout the entire evolutionary process, free will is sacrosanct and the degree of surrender of the individual identity is entirely up to the individual. All density experiences are only a plan or blueprint for consciousness to follow and if they follow it will achieve similar results to other consciousness having similar experiences but, since all consciousness is the Creator experiencing itself, all consciousness can exceed the plan limits and return to unity with the Creator at a much more accelerated rate. A single 4th Density experience does have a designed beginning and end but, where the 3rd Density is approximately 75,000 years and divided into three equal sub-cycles, the 4th Density has 30 million years in a single cycle and is not divided into sub-cycles. The average life expectancy of a 4th Density denizen is 90,000 years but the average tenure of consciousness in 4th Density is only 35,000 years which means it is common for 4th Density consciousness to progress more quickly through the density than the time allocated.

For most readers, it's difficult to imagine most of what 4th Density will offer them but the increased consciousness inherent in the 4th Density experience will transform the attachment to the authenticity of space/time. 4th Density mind/body/spirits will be able to move back and forth at will from a space/time to a time/space awareness, eventually experiencing only a time/space environment as they near the end of the density and surrender the anchor of a physical body. Pain and suffering will be nonexistent with only a slight discomfort upon death which would not even prompt a doctor visit in 3rd Density.

Bellicosity will quickly decline and disappear within the planetary population but it will become an issue with 4th Density service-to-self planets until they realize the futility of such behavior. This realization usually doesn't occur until the populace has been within the 4th Density experience for some time. Mars is currently a 4th Density service-to-self planet and their interference with the 3rd Density of Earth has been closely monitored, while still occurring, but many of those monitoring systems will be relaxed as Earth moves more significantly into the new density-sharing condition. Most of those graduating along the negative path from Earth will be relocated and probably added to the Mars population upon death.

Verbal communication will cease to be necessary as the 4th Density population begins to diminish reliance upon the rational/logical mind and learns to rely more heavily upon the deep mind which uses telepathic communication employed by most of creation. As telepathic communication increases, language barriers disappear because telepathic communication is the transference of unadulterated thought rather than the symbols of thought characterized by a language. Direct telepathic communication with the consciousness of all densities will become available to everyone, depending upon the willingness of the 4th Density mind/body/spirit to engage in communication with higher consciousness.

While 4th Density retains attachment to a physical body, ingestion of food substances will still be required but eating will become a distraction from the work that 4th Density consciousness deems important. Long leisure dining will become a rarity because it distracts from the time that could be spent doing the work of healing 3rd Density and advancing consciousness. This is one of the greatest glitches of 4th Density service-to-others because they lack the sufficient perspective to become unattached from the outcome, but it is part of the learning of the foundations of wisdom necessary to transition to 5th Density.

The population density will decline because a 4th Density service-to-others planet is significantly less densely populated than a 3rd Density planet. Incarnations as males and females will continue into 4th Density, and mating will still be an essential practice but, as consciousness escalates, the motivation for mate selection will transform. In 3rd Density, mating is designed to provide each other with lessons that each needs to learn based upon deficiencies in their curriculum but, after the initial stages of 4th Density, mating becomes a process of recognizing spiritual compatibility. This is the beginning of surrendering free will intoxication to merge into the four units of consciousness.

Once the population surrenders attachment to the authenticity of space/time and the body, it will no longer be necessary to begin an incarnation as children, so children will not be part of the population makeup and procreation will not be a motivator. Once the reliance upon the rational/logical mind sufficiently diminishes and we predominantly function with the deep mind, using telepathic communication rather than verbal communication, then mating will be accomplished with complete and utter candor and with the shared compatibility of the mutual desire to be of the greatest service. The interactions of subject and object will continue but with significant awareness of the interaction's purpose to explore the self, heal the self from free will intoxication, and propel each other to greater unity with the Creator.

In 3rd Density, we begin life as an innocent infant because each life is a microcosmic journey of the entire evolutionary journey. Even though the infant seems new, it is a fully matured 3rd Density mind/body/spirit experiencing a lifetime, predicated upon all the learning it has acquired from previous lifetimes. Once getting past the transitional stages of early 4th Density when we regain communication and awareness of time/space, we have access to all of the experiences of the soul journey and are working to heal the attachment to distortions that made many of the unpleasant experiences possible. It becomes no longer advantageous to remain in ignorance of who we really are.

What we seek is intimacy. Intimacy is an aspect of love that provides us with the feeling of unity, safety, security, unconditional acceptance, and comfort. While we remain unaware we seek intimacy with another mind/body/spirit which gives rise to the many love stories and novels about finding true love. In reality, intimacy must first be found with the self, and having found intimacy with the self and learning to see other selves as the self, we may then begin to find intimacy with another mind/body/spirit. We are never asked to love another self but to learn to love the one and only self we may know, and from that foundation, begin to see all other selves as the extensions of the self and automatically love them because we already love and are intimate with ourselves.

None of the Inherent Characteristics are exclusive of the other four. As we are learning from the perspective of awareness, we are learning of love, stillness, unity, awareness, and wisdom by actually becoming awareness. Awareness is the dinner plate, and love, awareness, stillness, unity, and wisdom are the foods served on the plate. Where awareness is the dinner plate in 3rd Density, love becomes the plate in 4th Density and the same five foods are served on the love plate, but they all are presented uniquely and differ from the lessons of 3rd Density because we are better able to appreciate and experience them to a greater depth of understanding.

In 4th Density, relearning the lessons of the Inherent Characteristic from the vantage point of love is what is being learned by both service-to-others and service-to-self. Love is the principal of all creation, and Infinite Energy, of which Intelligent Energy is a further distortion, is a product of love (RA). Love encompasses both the positive energy perspective, which is the focus of the service-to-others, and the negative energy perspective, which is the focus of the service-to-self. Whether positive or negative, it is all part of the relearning of the lessons of the Inherent Characteristics from the vantage point of love and all part of the balance of the one infinite Creator.

Whether the mind/body/spirit is graduating service-to-self or service-to-others, 4th Density is distinctly not like 3rd Density. There is a defined period for a 4th Density experience but there is not a harvest per se. Graduation from 4th Density must be as a group effort and is accomplished when the group is ready. "When the group is ready" means that the group has formed a social memory complex and achieved sufficient bonding to do 5th Density work.

Bonding for the service-to-self path means distinctly different things than bonding along the service-to-others path. Bonding within the service-to-self path means that a pecking order has been established and a sufficient number of mind/body/spirits have been beaten into submission so that they pledge allegiance to the most forceful leadership. This establishes a hierarchy that transcends 4th Density into 5th Density because both densities require the theft of Intelligent Energy to survive. All of the 4th Density service-to-self beings become minions to do the bidding of 5th Density negative beings.

Bonding for the service-to-others path is predicated upon the continued elevation of consciousness. As consciousness continues to rise, the individual self, who has already become aware and learned to be love, begins to see the other self(s) as the self and begins to extend the self-love to the other self as well as itself. The group that is formed is formed with the other members of the soul stream that graduated to 4th Density together. The goal of the 4th Density is to form a "social memory complex" with the other members of the soul stream.

At no time are we ever expected to love another mind/body/spirit either in 3rd Density or 4th Density. We are expected to reduce the perception of autonomy (free will intoxication) sufficiently to be able to see other selves to be the same as our self, which is what inevitably occurs when we become love. Loving another is not possible. Loving ourselves and seeing all other self(s) as the same as our self is not only possible but it is the design of how we will reintegrate ourselves into the one infinite Creator.

Soon after graduation to 4th Density our individual mind/body/spirit tori will join with three other mind/body/spirit tori (a total of four 3rd Density mind/body/spirit beings) and form a new 4th Density mind/body/spirit tori that will incorporate the four mind/body/spirit tori. This forms one 4th Density entity that merges our individual 3rd Density mind/body/spirit's tori and permits the expansion of our mind/body/spirit into greater unity with the one infinite Creator. Once this is accomplished, by the continued elevation of our consciousness and relearning the lessons from the perspective of love, we continue to consolidate our beingness.

Our new 4th Density being/torus, which incorporates the four mind/body/spirit tori of 3rd Density, works to form the social memory complex that will signal our readiness to graduate to 5th Density. Our new 4th Density torus will integrate with 95 other new 4th Density tori to form the social memory complex by forming a new torus to encapsulate all 96 4th Density beings.

We maintain the newly formed consolidated 4th Density mind/body/spirit and integrate the tori into the social memory complex so that we function both individually and collectively. In the course of our 4th Density evolution, we will have expanded our perception of self sufficiently to perceive all 96 4th Density beings, which are composed of a total of 384 3rd Density mind/body/spirit tori, to be one being/unit, sharing the perception of self and self-love.

Because of their greater awareness and higher consciousness, 4th Density beings recognize a greater number of dimensions (AKA levels of consciousness) within their density. On the deep sea diver's depth dial the settings begin at 26 and range upward to 32. Experiences are still paramount in 4th Density but the mind/body/spirits of this level of consciousness are refining and cleaning the limiting conditions left over from 3rd Density. Many of the experiences in the early phases of the density are often focused on healing the residual emotional baggage carried over from the 3rd Density with the density goal of becoming love.

Once an experience occurs in the 3rd Density, along with its interpretation, it is preserved in perpetuity. The clearing or healing of the emotional baggage in the 4th Density is from 3rd Density but with the 4th Density lens. When we form our expanded 4th Density self we are co-sharing the experiences of all three of our counterparts as well as our own experiences and cumulatively healing each other.

When we form a social memory complex we are doing similar things with all 95 of our counterparts in anticipation of incorporating those "other selves" into our self as a social memory complex. Every 3rd Density experience of the four parts into one consolidation will be experienced by all four participating parts. Every 3rd Density experience of the 96 into one consolidation will be experienced by all 96 parts. Everybody experiences everyone else's experiences from the unique perspective (personality) that they bring to the group.

To reiterate; the purpose of creation is so that the one infinite Creator may know itself by experiencing itself. Every 3rd Density mind/body/spirit begins the process of experience with a single solitary interpretation of a prepared experience. The results of that experience are preserved and re-experienced from the unique personality of all of the other mind/body/spirits providing a vast panoply of the diversity of interpretation for the Creator's reservoir of opportunities to know itself. Experiences are not haphazard or accidental. Every experience that we have in 3rd Density is designed to explore a specific part of the one infinite Creator.

Incarnate portions of a 4th Density people do have a visible body that, on Earth, will probably look very much like the 3rd Density body, but the body is primarily electric as opposed to the chemical body of 3rd Density. 4th Density beings can and do interact with 3rd Density but service-to-others choose to do so infrequently and only in exceptional cases. The reason for this rarity is that they respect the sanctity and value of the 3rd Density experience and they know that interaction between 3rd and 4th Densities may bring into question the veracity of the conditions created for the 3rd Density environment. Again, this is called the "Law of Confusion" or the "Law of Free Will" and prevails in all of the higher densities above the 3rd.

4th Density service-to-self has no such compunction or reservations about interfering with the 3rd Density experience. Those who do have direct experience are called "crusaders" because their primary purpose is to steal energy from the more innocent 3rd Density beings and to recruit (tempt) followers to the service-to-self path. They are instrumental in implementing the commands of 5th Density service-to-self which are always self-serving in their need for more energy. The objective of all service-to-self contact is the subjugation and domination of the 3rd Density population by 4th Density crusaders, including the 3rd Density mind/body/spirits seeking graduation as a service-to-self candidate because harvesting the 3rd Density Intelligent Energy is the only way the service-to-self can maintain their required supply.

The fully converted 4th Density body is designed to last 90,000 years. The body of a 4th Density service-to-other entity is often retired before its potential duration because the average tenure in 4th Density service-to-others is only +/-35,000 years, even though 30 million years constitutes a 4th Density cycle of experience. A service-to-self body may be adjusted to transition to 5th Density but this seldom happens because the average tenure of life in 4th Density for a service-to-self entity well exceeds a single body's life expectancy, potentially lasting billions of years.

There is no physical illness in the 4th Density, no pain or suffering, as we know it, and each being may potentially freely communicate with all of the creation telepathically. The only pain is a slight discomfort upon the death of the body that would not even be enough for treatment in 3rd Density. The conditions of pain and suffering, as we experience them in the 3rd Density, are transcended when graduation to the 4th Density occurs. From 3rd Density, graduation to 4th Density does require the surrender (death) of the 3rd Density body so the myth of ascension from 3rd Density to 4th Density is just that, a myth or, in some rare cases, a ploy of deception by service-to-self crusaders.

In future chapters, we will discuss the different types of beings that share a 3rd Density experience. When we say that ascension is a myth we mean it is a myth for a 3rd Density being because the purpose of 3rd Density is not to escape. Some beings are incarnate to serve as examples or guides for how we can live our lives and how we may grasp the controls and guide our own life up and beyond 3rd Density but they don't ascend. Jesus and the Buddha are two examples of these beings and they didn't ascend because it would have given the wrong message to the populace. In most cases, the appearance of ascending beings is those of service-to-self polarity playing upon the ego of the unsophisticated 3rd Density population to gain domination through worshipful supplication.

Having been vaulted past the chasm of dimensions that separates 3rd Density and 4th Density, 4th Density gains access to two major increases in abilities which become necessary to do 4th Density work. The first of these is the ability to move between time/space and space/time while incarnate in a 4th Density body. The second is a significant change in the interaction with time. 4th Density beings work with time but no longer are "in" time, and may move both backward and forward along a timeline (explained in Chapter 6).

For roughly the first half of the 4th Density experience, the service-to-others participants contend with war but not among themselves. Wars exist between service-to-self and service-to-other planets but once the service-to-self reaches a certain wisdom point then wars become passé and they no longer feel the need for bellicosity. Conflict continues but the arena becomes thought battles and the pursuit of more energy takes on a more empyrean nature.

As we raise our consciousness we participate less and less with the physical and more and more with the ethereal. The higher consciousness levels of the service-to-others path travel all of creation without ever leaving their lounge chair but the service-to-self must continue to promote some degree of physical travel because they remain attached to the authenticity of the physical and detached from the Higher Self. Everything is conceptual and as we can participate in that understanding more completely we have fewer of the confinements and restrictions that we now experience so completely in 3rd Density.

4th Density does not need children because, once projected into a fully transformed physical body, we will not have the forgetting or a veil. We do not begin a lifetime in ignorance with the plan of overcoming ignorance and awakening. We are learning the lessons of the Inherent Characteristics from the vantage point of awareness, which is an entirely different pursuit than overcoming the chaos of the 3rd Density and taught in a completely different atmosphere by completely different methods.

We will incarnate in both female and male genders but partnering or mating will be a result of literally seeing the energy of another person and knowing they will be a match with our energy. Since we are learning to see all other selves as extensions of ourselves, all other beings become partners in our journey. All beings become our "soul mates" and all are worthy of our love because they are simply extensions of the self.

Chapter 8

Emotions • Chakras • Polaris

If an experience was purely an intellectual exercise of the mind there would be very little, if any, variety of experiential interpretation from one person to the next. All experiences would be matter-of-fact with virtually no uniqueness and it would be improbable that a variety of personalities or patterns of consciousness could develop with any significant diversity, able to explore creation as the Creator intended. To successfully fulfill the purpose of creation it was necessary to create a mechanism that would distort the pure intelligence functions of the mind and make it possible for consciousness to "feel" experience interpretation and, thereby, determine what it likes and dislikes.

In previous chapters, we discussed the different minds that serve the densities as free will intoxication is increased and we will rely upon your recollection of those discussions in what we present here. The first mind began with the first distortion which was free will, and made creation possible by creating the first "Creator as the subject". The first mind is the "cosmic mind", which possesses the equivalency of the Creator's knowingness and awareness but perceives itself as separate from the Creator because of the free will distortion.

The cosmic mind is synonymous with the 8th Density spirit. The only difference between the "Creator as the object" and the "Creator as the subject" is perception. Perception is a product of awareness and limited or distorted awareness results in limited or distorted perception, which means that the first mind holds a limited or distorted perception because of limited or distorted awareness. The aspect of the 8th Density consciousness, which is the first separate identity from the Creator as the object and proffers a distorted perspective, is the mind, the cosmic mind.

The 7th Density shares the cosmic mind and the 8th Density spirit but it is a fractal of the 8th Density because it is more intoxicated with free will than the 8th Density and perceives the spirit through the lens of its more distorted mind. The 7th Density cosmic mind is the result of an even more limited or distorted awareness and, consequently, holds a more distorted perspective. As the 7th Density is incrementally subdivided into dimensions, awareness diminishes accordingly, becomes more distorted, and causes perspectives to become increasingly limited or distorted.

The continuation of consciousness fractals into the 6th Density further dilutes awareness and the resulting escalating limitation or distortion of perspectives continues also. The spirit of 6th Density is still the undistorted spirit of 8th Density but its ability to be aware of this diminishes with every declining dimension because its awareness is incrementally decreasing, resulting in its perspectives becoming more distorted in favor of its perception that it is a separate identity. Its free will intoxication limits its mind's ability to be aware and perceive that its spirit is synonymous with the undiminished spirit of 8th Density. The diminished awareness also promulgates its free will distorted mind into greater prominence in its experience of creation.

The emergence of increasing perceptions of autonomy illustrates that a mind, any mind, is a perception of independence from other aspects of consciousness. The 8th Density that begins creation and is consciousness perceives itself as autonomous from the one infinite Creator and, therefore, creates the cosmic mind. The 7th Density begins with an autonomous perception from the 8th Density and the one infinite Creator but quickly becomes numerous minds segregated horizontally by the racial nature of their Inherent Characteristics, and further vertically distinguished according to their descending dimensions.

The 8th Density functions as a single organism because there are no mind subdivisions but the 7th Density is both a single organism (the cosmic mind) and comprised of multiple organisms. A mind's borders are defined by wherever the experiencing unit of consciousness perceives its autonomy begins and ends. As consciousness evolves from the lowest densities to its place of origin, minds will transform from the most isolated self-perception to, eventually, total unity. At every transformative step along the way, the prevailing mind (the autonomous perceiving self) is transforming the nature of the experiencing organism, exploring itself "as creation" by experiencing itself, therefore, fulfilling the purpose of creation.

Perception has two elements to it: an intellectual understanding or "knowing" and a nonintellectual "feeling" (qualia). The 6th and 7th Density consciousness "knows" intellectually that it is the same spirit as the 8th Density and is actually "one" with the undistorted Creator but it doesn't completely "feel" that it is. The surrender of free will intoxication begins with an intellectual "knowing" that "all is one" but the hard part, and the most important part, is the "feeling" that consciousness is one with the Creator.

In a previous chapter, we explained that the greater the free will intoxication the more myopic awareness becomes and the less able to experience completeness. We used the comparative experience of vision and explained that at the level of consciousness we all experience, the more we focus attention on an object the less aware we become of periphery objects. When free will intoxication increases in the 7th and 6th Densities, awareness decreases as the focus becomes incrementally more myopic and directed towards a more limited perspective.

In every density and at every dimension, the mind is the distortion of spirit that perceives itself as a separate identity, according to its degree of free will intoxication. Creating an infinite layering of minds by shaving consciousness into ever smaller slices of spirit provided the Creator with the opportunity to enjoy the ability to experience itself from numerically infinite perspectives along a one-dimensional path, a vertical exploration of creation, but, by its nature, it doesn't permit a diverse perception and/or exploration. While one dimension on the consciousness scale may differ in its perspective from any other, because of the uniqueness of its capacity for awareness, all consciousness sharing that dimension will essentially behave the same. Consciousness, sharing a particular dimension only because it was assigned that particular dimension, has little means of making analogies and, therefore, no means of establishing personal likes or dislikes, a unique personality, or diversifying its experiences because it has no emotions with which to experience itself.

To allow consciousness to explore itself horizontally and diagonally, it was necessary to create a conceptual mechanism that would allow it to go beyond simply interpreting experiences according to its vertical dimensional free will fractal. The scheme employed was for consciousness to vibrate, which means that all consciousness below the 8th Density was caused to vibrate at different speeds according to its consciousness level. The uppermost dimensions of the 7th Density vibrate the fastest and the lowest dimensions of the 1st Density vibrate the slowest. Everything in between is scaled according to its dimension and density.

In a previous chapter, we explained that Infinite Energy was created by free will, which is synonymous with 8th Density consciousness, acting or thinking upon the Inherent Characteristic of love. The 8th Density thought created the concept of Infinite Energy which resulted in the vibration of consciousness in all densities below the eighth. Infinite Energy "is" synonymous with vibrating consciousness.

Light is information, a distortion of wisdom, the Inherent Characteristic of LA, and an archetype of the Creator. 8th Density shines as an infinitely bright white light because it is the "Creator as the subject" and shares the same status as the source of information within creation as does the Creator because it is the undistorted fractal of the "Creator as the object" that is distinguishable only by its free will distortion. Densities seven through the first are fractals of the density above with each density having its unique perception of a white light fractal called its inner light or Polaris. Each density light fractal is dimmer than the one above, not because it is dimmer, but, because of its more limited awareness, it observes the white light through a thicker and more distorted lens. When the Polaris shines into the layers of vibrating consciousness called densities and its dimensions, colors become illuminated.

Each density reflected a color indicating its degree of distortion on the vibration scale according to the speed of its vibration with the 7th Density, the fastest vibration, radiating a violet color, 6th Density an indigo color, 5th Density a light blue color, 4th Density a green hue, 3rd Density a yellow hue, 2nd Density an orange color, and 1st Density, the slowest vibration, the color red. These are the colors in the order of the colors of a rainbow. A rainbow is the result of white light shining into a prism, water vapor serving as a crystal, and creating the panoply of colors which is the same effect as the Polaris of each density shining into the vibrating consciousness stratified into dimensions. Within the densities, the vibration levels were further subdivided into the layers identified as dimensions, and the rainbow colors are reiterated.

The specific colors and their order of appearance are the results of an arbitrary choice by 8th Density. Since we are deep within the evolutionary process, science would say that the colors appear, and appear in the order that they do, because it is a natural law but they could be in any other order or not appear at all just as easily if that had been part of the original choice. Since it was an original choice, the appearance and order of the colors are pervasive in all the densities throughout the creation that we experience but the colors, appearing as a result of the corresponding speed of the vibration or movement, are distortions of perception.

The prism effect is reiterated within the 7th Density. 7th Density perceives white light or undiffused light to be a little less intense than the white light of 8th Density, and it shines into the vibrating consciousness of its dimensions duplicating the rainbow effect within the density. The 6th Density's perception of the Polaris, which is a little less intense than the light of the 7th Density, is also stratified into the rainbow colors as it is diffused through the vibrating consciousness that comprises its dimensions. The process continues throughout the experiential and foundational densities exactly the way it does in the 6th and 7th Densities with the Polaris of each succeeding density perceived less brightly than the density above. When we "graduate" from the 3rd Density we will "walk the steps" of light until the intensity of the light becomes too bright, and it is there that we will stop to continue our experiential learning of the curriculum of evolution.

The coding system of a single density divides the dimensions into four platform levels, but in between each platform level is a range of dimensions. A density is divided into seven segments, also represented by one of the seven colors of the rainbow, four platform levels, and three spaces in between. When the white light is stratified into layers within a density, truth is being stratified into incremental layers according to consciousness' awareness ability and, in the context of evolution, where consciousness is progressing upwards through the densities in its return to closer unity with the Creator, attainment of truth is gained in increments that correspond to the layers of light. Remember that consciousness surrenders distortions to move out of darkness and into light as it evolves and moves up the consciousness scale, dimension by dimension.

As with a rainbow, the greatest color intensity is in the middle of the color banding but each color transitions into the next adjacent color as the vibrating speeds transition to the next vibration range, so the perimeter of the color banding seems less bright than the middle. The brightness of the color is indicative of where consciousness is in its transition from lower dimensions to higher dimensions within the density. For example, 1st Density consciousness with two strands of coding activated is the lowest vibrating range and is red. The range of dimensions between two strands and four strands of coding is orange; four strands of coding is yellow; the dimensions between four and six strands are green; the sixth strand is light blue; the dimensions between six and eight are indigo; and the eight strand is violet.

The vibration color ranges are reiterated in each density so, in 2nd Density, consciousness with 10 strands of coding activated is red, the range of dimensions between 10 and 12 is orange, 12 strands of coding activated is yellow, and so forth. Energy appears as a vibration or wave pattern because consciousness itself vibrates and illuminates the colors of the vibration frequency. Energy vibrating in the red range is referred to as "red-ray energy", orange vibrating energy is referred to as "orange-ray energy", yellow vibrating energy is identified as "yellow-ray energy", etc.

Each color range of vibrating energy offers different properties, and consciousness vibrating according to the different vibration ranges demonstrates different behavior. Red- and orange-ray energy, 1st, and 2nd Density colors are always foundational and usually grounding properties but they aren't associated with a specific Inherent Characteristic or archetype. The nature of the behavior of both 1st and 2nd Densities is that they provide the basic experience of moving from complete dispersion to relative unity as 1st Density consciousness consolidates into a planet and 2nd Density moves from isolated single cell units of consciousness to relatively unified social groups, randomly learning of the Inherent Characteristics without preference, relative to their capacity to be aware.

The 3rd Density is "yellow-ray energy" and is characterized as an awakening or "awareness", and corresponds to the sequentially 1st Inherent Characteristic, SA. 4th Density is "green-ray energy", characterized as "love", the 2nd hierarchical Inherent Characteristic, RA, and 5th Density is "blue-ray energy", characterized as "wisdom", the 3rd Inherent Characteristic, LA. 6th Density is above the experiential densities and the lowest range of the Creator Being densities identified as "indigo-ray energy", the range of the 4th Inherent Characteristic "unity", where YA has prominence and where all polarities are resolved. 7th Density is "violet-ray energy" and the Inherent Characteristic of "stillness", KA, where all the experiences of the lower densities are collected, integrated, and any remaining distortions of perception are surrendered. The Inherent Characteristics are hierarchical because of the necessity of reclaiming the characteristics of the archetype to facilitate the greatest comprehension of the next hierarchical level and not an indication of the value of one over the other.

The vibration characteristics of different energy colors are experienced as emotions that are used to interpret or "feel" experience beyond the process of thinking thoughts. According to the design of the Earthly Archetypical Mind, no thought can be processed until an emotion is applied to the thought. A thought is an incremental experience, in and of itself, but we usually attract a series of similar thoughts or follow a momentum trajectory of thoughts into the experience because of our limited ability to isolate a single thought. Limited awareness restricts the ability to isolate individual thoughts in the lower densities, hence, the task for the 3rd Density consciousness is to become aware and then actually become awareness.

The application of an emotion is a functional part of the Archetypical Mind and the system that allows or requires us to apply an emotion is an essential function of the mind's design called the "chakra system". When we apply emotion to thought we are exploring the self as a unique personification of the Higher Self but, in the foundational densities, 3rd Density, and the lower dimensions of 4th Density, emotions are usually applied according to the limited capabilities of the ego mind. The greater the chaos directing the interpretation of thought the more intense the experience of emotions experienced by a mind/body/spirit.

In 1st Density, each of the four elements has an independent set of chakras but, because 1st Density consciousness only experiences space/time, the element only has one set of space/time chakras. 2nd Density experiences both time/space and space/time, which means every pool of consciousness has a time/space set of chakras, and every analog projection into space/time as a plant or animal has a space/time set of chakras that are functionally independent of the species pool but integrated and incorporated into the pool of consciousness upon death. 3rd Density also experiences both time/space and space/time, and every time/space mind/body/spirit has a chakra system as does every independent perceiving analog projection into space/time. Similar to the 2nd Density, the analog projections in the 3rd Density living timelines are functionally independent, but the results of their experiences are absorbed and incorporated into the corpus time/space mind/body/spirit upon death.

4th Density is a different experience from 3rd Density but the density begins with the same procedural experience of incarnating into analog mind/body/spirits as do 3rd Density people. 4th Density is a transitional density that is intended to allow for the healing of 3rd Density experiences and distortions. To progress through 4th Density, consciousness must surrender its attachment to the physical and cease to incarnate into space/ time, but until that occurs, it will continue to have the same or a very similar experience as 3rd Density consciousness, in so far as incarnating into analog mind/body/spirits. A 4th Density mind/body/spirit will begin the density with a chakra system for the time/space mind/body/spirit and a functionally separate chakra system for every analog projection into space/time but, as it surrenders its attachment to the physical and ceases to incarnate into space/time, it will only retain its time/space chakra system.

5th Density begins where 4th Density ends and, for 4th Density consciousness to graduate to 5th Density, it must form a social memory complex. The 4th Density social memory complex, in comparison to a 6th Density social memory complex, is significantly smaller and not nearly as unified. A 4th Density social memory complex still is an amalgamation of individual mind/body/spirits that each retains its chakra system, as does, for the most part, a 5th Density social memory complex. However, a 5th Density social memory complex, as consciousness progresses through the dimensions of the density, is larger and becomes increasingly unified. The independent functioning of the 5th Density mind/body/spirits, and their chakra systems, eventually begin to merge and consolidate into the 6th Density social memory complexes where they eventually merge into "one" as consciousness becomes unity.

We have already explained and emphasized in previous chapters that "all is one" and all perceptions of individuality, including 8th Density's independence, is a distortion of perception, a thought experiment. The explanations of the design of creation in the experiential and foundational densities in particular presume that the reader understands that "all is one" and the information we are providing is intended to aid the reader in surrendering distortions and perceptions that hinder evolution through the dimensions. The limitations of language require us to speak in terms that indicate distinct separation and independence of beings so that it may have some familiarity but, in reality, there is no separation at any level, other than in its perception. This is the "Law of One".

That having been said, the chakras are part of the energy system that helps compartmentalize and maintain a mind/body/spirit in creation. The energy system in the foundational and experiential densities begins with the "inner light" or "Polaris" of the 6th Density Higher Self. The honor/duty of serving as a Higher Self is generally reserved for consciousness organisms that have progressed within the density to the upper half of the density dimensions. 6th Density is the density of "unity" and progressing to the upper half of the dimensions indicates that they are beyond dimensions such as movement (DA) or separation (TA), and only a very tiny part, if any, of the perception of autonomy remains other than as a social memory complex.

The Polaris of the Higher Self is conceptually compartmentalized to form a soul stream which is further compartmentalized to conceptually form the individual mind/body/spirits participating in creation as part of the soul stream and populating the foundational and experiential densities. Every mind/body/spirit participating in the lower densities conceptually has its own Polaris or inner light but it practically is only a compartmentalization of the Higher Self's Polaris which, in turn, is ultimately the 8th Density Polaris. In 1st Density, this means that the four elements separately perceive and function as if they have an independent inner light. In 2nd Density, each species pool perceives that it has its own Polaris, and each of the species pools is further compartmentalized so every plant or animal analog projection into space/time perceives that it has an independent inner light.

In 3rd Density, every metaphysical mind/body/spirit perceives that it has an inner light, but it still is only the conceptually compartmentalized allocation of the Higher Self's Polaris as seen from a significantly more distorted lens. The same perceptions pervade the 4th and 5th Density beings while always remaining the Polaris of the Higher Self. All consciousness in any density perceives itself to have an independent Polaris, but it is still the one originating Polaris of 8th Density viewed from the fractal perspective of a more free will intoxicated consciousness with a reduced awareness capacity (AKA the distorted lens).

The chakras, of both the time/space mind/body/spirit or the multitude of analog projections into space/time, are illustrating the ranges of vibrating consciousness made detectable by the shining of the light, similar to blowing smoke into an otherwise invisible flow of air. The 7 vibrating ranges of consciousness within a unit of consciousness are density-appropriate reiterations of the 7 Densities below the 8th Density, and especially in the foundational and experiential densities, they serve as the course curriculum for what is to be learned to progress through evolution. Chakras are a framework for emotion, a maze constructed from Intelligent Energy, but they do not apply emotion to an experience. Only consciousness can "feel" by the application of emotions, but it does so according to the pattern of distortions sequentially presented to it as the chakras.

To put the process of evolution into motion using the chakras, it is necessary to channel energy, Intelligent Energy, through them. The chakras are an integral adjunct to the processing of thought through the Archetypical Mind, and I must apologize for repeatedly referring to the Archetypical Mind without having discussed it yet, but everything is integrated and we are attempting to explain things as completely as possible, and in an orderly fashion to allow the reader's most comprehensive understanding. There is a specific step in the processing of thought according to the Archetypical Mind called the "Experience of the Mind" when the mind requires emotion to be "felt" before it continues its process. It is an integral part of the thought process because it is "the" point when individuality is heightened and uniqueness is stimulated.

Intelligent Energy flows directly from the Higher Self to the time/space body or bodies, in sequential order. In the 1st Density, only the 1st time/space body is energized, which "is" the 1st time/space chakra, allowing between two and eight strands of coding to be activated. In 2nd Density, both the 1st and 2nd time/space bodies are energized, activating between 10 and 16 strands of coding, which also "is" the 2nd time/space chakra. The flow of Intelligent Energy increases in the 3rd Density which activates the 3rd time/space body, the 3rd time/space chakra, and opens the strands of coding sequentially from 18 and 24. In the foundational densities, the flow of Intelligent Energy is regulated by the "grace" of the Higher Self, which simply means that the Higher Self widens or narrows the flow valve at its discretion. As previously explained, consciousness is nondescript in these densities because experiences encountered and lessons learned are not specifically preserved to advance its progress through evolution.

In 3rd Density, the progression through the density requires the individual mind/body spirit to become sufficiently aware to be able to choose which path, positive or negative, to follow and, in so doing, open or close the energy valve necessary for its continued evolution. To graduate from the 3rd Density to the 4th Density along the positive path, it is necessary to energize the 4th time/space chakra while still within the range of 3rd

Density consciousness. Activating the 4th chakra is not a result of the grace of the Higher Self, but it only is activated or opened because the individual mind/body/spirit has become sufficiently aware, undertaken the necessary work to sufficiently heal the distortions, and learned the course curriculum sufficiently to progress further. In other words, consciousness potentially attains sufficient awareness to be able to "take control" of its progression through evolution and assume responsibility for its return to the Creator by sobering from its free will intoxication.

Because 3rd Density consciousness potentially becomes awareness, it isn't restricted to advancing only to 4th Density. With sufficient work, it may skip a grade, or in very rare circumstances, skip two grades. Upward advancement through the densities becomes less structured and more flexible.

In the 1st Density, Intelligent Energy flows only into the 1st time/space body and through it, flowing then through all six remaining chakras in sequential order. Changes to its mind and body, its pattern of consciousness, resulting from the emotions used to interpret the thoughts processed, then create the modified 1st Density consciousness that attracts the next thought. Once it completes its initial lap through the chakras, it will have finished its full cycle at the 1st Density level.

In 2nd Density, Intelligent Energy flows from the 1st time/space body/chakra and then to the space/time chakras of each analog projection, returning to cycle through the 2nd time/space body/chakra, and then back to the same space/time chakras of the analog projection to complete another lap before its full chakra process journey is complete. In 3rd Density, Intelligent Energy adds a lap through the 3rd time/space body/chakra, and then back through the space/time chakras before it completes its trip. After Intelligent Energy flows through all three of the time/space bodies/chakras and three laps through the space/time chakras, emotion is applied to interpret the thought and the thought continues its processing journey through the Archetypical Mind design.

Within the Archetypical Mind, the thought is paused at the "Experience of the Mind" module until Intelligent Energy completes its trip or trips through the time/space chakras. Intelligent Energy doesn't feel emotion but only energizes consciousness vibration according to the pattern of consciousness formed by previous thought processes. Only consciousness can create or feel the emotion, but Intelligent Energy "energizes" the emotion according to the mind/body/ spirit's pattern of consciousness.

Regardless of the density, consciousness projected into an analog space/time mind/body/spirit has a chakra system that begins an incarnation with all seven chakras activated. Intelligent Energy is portioned from the time/space mind/body/spirit to the analog incarnations according to the number of coding levels energized. 3rd Density begins with only 16 strands of coding activated, which results in a lessened capacity to project simultaneous incarnations than later in its density evolution when it has 24 strands activated and it will have reached the upper dimensions of the density. When it begins the density experience, it doesn't have sufficient Intelligent Energy flow yet to power more incarnations successfully.

When the mind/body/spirit opens the 4th time/space chakra, it adds another lap through the 4th time/space body/chakra and then repeats the journey through the entire space/time chakra set again. When the 5th time/space body is energized, it again will add yet another lap through the time/space chakras but 5th Density consciousness no longer incarnates into space/time. The consciousness in the upper dimensions of the 4th Density and all of the 5th Density will have released its attachment to the physical perceptions of space/time and, therefore, no longer projects itself into analog mind/body/spirits. 4th Density signals its readiness for 5th Density by surrendering its false identity completely, surrendering the authenticity of the 1st Density physical environment, and forming a social memory complex. The 5th Density functions completely as a social memory complex. But, even in these densities, it is unlikely to fully surrender all of its autonomous perspective of its metaphysical consciousness pattern, so the individual time/space mind/body/ spirits that comprise the social memory complexes of upper 4th and 5th Densities usually maintain an individual chakra system while participating in a social memory complex.

The 4th Density is a transformation density that allows consciousness to heal from its manufactured distortions of the 3rd Density. Consciousness' progression through the 4th Density dimensions will allow it to merge and integrate itself into a larger organism or, in other words, significantly surrender its perceptual autonomy and participate in an elementary social memory complex. When it does this but remains within the lower dimensions, it will incarnate into a single analog space/ time projection which is an undiluted reflection of time/space itself. The children who have been born since the year 2008 are mostly beginning the 4th Density journey and are more of their whole being, which means they have the awareness and energy capacity to significantly transform the Earth experience as they mature into adults.

Once again, we must qualify our explanation of the process by saying that this is the path and process for those individual mind/body/spirits choosing to polarize service-to-others, or, in other words, the positive path. Those choosing to further distance themselves from the Higher Self, as a personification of the Creator, do not seek to elevate their consciousness and do not increase their flow of Intelligent Energy from the Higher Self. Upon graduation from 3rd Density, they choose to sever their attachment to the Higher Self by severing the flow of Intelligent

Energy completely, which means they must find a substitute source for it because they still are required to sustain their participation in creation through an Intelligent Energy flow. As we previously discussed, the only other source is through the practice of dominating and subjugating unaware 3rd Density mind/body/spirits to trick them into giving up some portion of their Intelligent Energy allocation.

The stolen energy follows the same path into and through the service-to-self chakras as if it was coming from the Higher Self, but one significant difference in its flow within the system is that it bypasses the 4th time/space body/chakra entirely. The characteristic of the 4th time/space body/chakra and the 4th space/time chakra is love, and those choosing the negative path consider love to be folly. In place of love, they choose the "feel good" experience of a short-term energy burst obtained from the immediate gratification of their desires, obtained by dominating and subjugating others. We shall discuss the service-to-self path and characteristics in greater detail in future chapters but, for now, know that the functioning of the chakras is different along the negative path.

To briefly review: the "white light" within creation originates with the "Creator as the object" and the white light of 8th Density is a metaphorical replication of this light. The Polaris of 7th Density is the same 8th Density light but seen with the distorted eyes of a consciousness fractal of 8th Density. The same 8th Density is seen by all sequentially descending densities but each density views it from its increasingly fractal perspective, meaning that it sees it less clearly.

Within the foundational and experiential densities consciousness is compartmentalized, corresponding to its degree of free will intoxication and experiencing the 8th Density Polaris to be a significantly dimmer illumination because of its limited perspective and perceiving it to be its own. Consciousness vibrates and the vibration causes the light to stratify into colors corresponding to the velocity of the vibration. Intelligent Energy is directed into the vibrating consciousness from the lowest to the highest which allows consciousness to "feel" and use those feelings to interpret thought.

The chakras directly correspond to the densities and the densities directly correspond to the Inherent Characteristics. In the foundational densities, consciousness' awareness is very low and experiences are random with no specific characteristics being assigned but all Inherent Characteristics are potentially equally available to be experienced and explored to the extent that consciousness may be aware. Similarly, the chakras in these densities do not characteristically have specific emotions or feelings that they facilitate.

When consciousness advances to 3rd Density, randomness becomes orderly and the chakras take on specific characteristics associated with the Inherent Characteristics. The 1st chakra remains nondescript but is often associated with a variety of emotions emerging as a result of basic concern for non-survival. Like the 1st chakra, the 2nd chakra is associated with low and slow vibrating emotions which humans have labeled with such names as shame or guilt without necessarily a predominant corresponding positive emotion.

The 3rd chakra corresponds with the 3rd Density and the Inherent Characteristic of "awareness". The 3rd Density is tasked with becoming awareness in preparation for graduating to the 4th Density, but awareness requires a significant surrender of free will intoxication. Using the metaphorical example we previously presented, it is necessary to leave first base to get to second base which prompts fear in many people. Fear is the primary negative emotion associated with the 3rd chakra, but unlike the 1st and 2nd chakra, it has the corresponding positive behavioral characteristic called courage.

The 4th chakra corresponds to the 4th Density and the Inherent Characteristic of "love". In the 3rd Density, after consciousness has become awareness, it is tasked with learning the lessons of love from the vantage point of awareness. Love, like awareness, is not just a positive emotion or vibration but spans a full spectrum of both positive and negative vibrations that can feel very good and very bad. Even when we are experiencing "what we don't like" we are learning the lessons of love, just the negative side of the equation.

The 5th chakra corresponds to the 5th Density and the Inherent Characteristic of "wisdom". We can demonstrate the behavioral characteristics of wisdom in the 3rd Density, but it is primarily the focus of the 4th Density after consciousness has become love, similar to how it became awareness in the 3rd Density. The 3rd and early 4th Density dimensions associate emotions and conditions such as truth, trust, responsibility, and self-expression with the 5th chakra and offer an equally broad variety of vibrations and interpretations of these feelings as love does.

The 6th chakra corresponds to the 6th Density and the Inherent Characteristic of "unity". The sequence of vibrating energy through the chakras begins with the lowest chakras not having a readily identifiable corresponding positive emotion to the low vibrating negative feeling and concludes with the 6th chakra offering no readily identifiable corresponding negative emotion to its high positive vibration. The most easily understood feeling emanating from the 6th chakra is calm, peace, or completion.

The 7th chakra corresponds to the 7th Density and the Inherent Characteristic of "stillness". The 7th chakra doesn't have an associating emotion, either positive or negative, but reflects an average of all of the lower six chakras' balance. This is, relatively speaking, a reflection of 7th Density too, as consciousness has progressed through the foundational and experiential densities, through 6th Density, and is now preparing for reintegration in 8th Density with a return of all of the cumulative experiences and uniqueness of its journey through creation.

Chapter 9

The Self • The Ego • Emotions

Evolution is the process of self-discovery. The self is a concept that continuously changes as we evolve from the lowest levels of consciousness to the highest, but from the Creator's perspective, the concept of self never changes. It is always the absolute Creator exploring itself from an infinite variety of vantage points.

However, for consciousness, the concept of self isn't viewed from the press box. It's viewed and experienced from its limited perspective of being on the field, in the game, and on the scrimmage line. Because of its limited perspective, consciousness frequently has great difficulty remembering its original objective.

By design, the concept of self begins with the most disbursed and chaotic perspective possible with minimal competency with the tools necessary to make an accurate observation of whom or what the self is, but consciousness always has the appropriate tools and resources necessary to accomplish the immediate evolutionary task in the environment being experienced. Even within the lowest levels of consciousness, it is incumbent upon consciousness to employ awareness to discover the available tools and implement them to accomplish its specific mission. Evolution requires consciousness to be proactive from the beginning because "at no point" is consciousness ever a hopeless victim in need of saving.

Within 1st Density, the concept of self dramatically evolves as it progresses through the density's dimensions. Each disbursed unit of consciousness has an identity that it perceives as the "self". Consciousness is inherently attracted to other consciousness of equivalent awareness and so 1st Density consciousness with two strands of coding activated is attracted to other consciousness of equivalent coding activation. A shared perspective and shared behavior create a sense of familiarity which provides a degree of comfort, even at this low position on the consciousness scale. But, the attraction to similar consciousness is not the only pull on consciousness because awareness dictates that, as soon as it begins to find a modicum of comfort at its current level, it will increasingly be attracted to higher consciousness and, consequently, it will soon begin to model higher consciousness behavior.

All consciousness is programmed to return to its source and the condition of its source is absolute total stability. Compared to 1st Density consciousness with two strands of consciousness activated, consciousness with four strands of consciousness activated is more stable, and so, two strands of activated consciousness seek to activate four strands. Even though consciousness with two strands activated finds comfort in the familiarity of bonding with other two-strand consciousness, it is simultaneously motivated to seek greater stability and, therefore, it is inclined to change its behavior by mimicking consciousness with four strands activated. Its free will choice always guides its actions to either stay the same or change, depending solely upon what "feels" right.

Mimicking the behavior of higher consciousness eventually results in increased awareness as lower consciousness ends their mimicking when they become higher consciousness. Awareness is both the discovery tool and the healing tool that transforms consciousness at all levels and inevitably transforms its self-perspective. By design, consciousness is programmed to seek greater stability and uses real-time interactions with higher consciousness models to learn how to behave according to the characteristics of greater stability. This is the practical and experiential implementation of subject/object relationships resulting from consciousness interactions.

Experiencing the relative comfort of familiarity by bonding with other consciousness of equivalent awareness but simultaneously being programmed to seek greater stability may seem paradoxical. Often, it creates an internal conflict that governs lower consciousness' willingness to change its perspective of self. The internal conflict is fostered by a lack of awareness which appears as confusion between stasis and stability, creating emotional pain and/or suffering. Stasis is "staying the same" and it is desirable to lower consciousness because it's familiar, even though it may not be comfortable, and shuns change. Seeking greater stability requires acceptance of change which is the defining difference between stasis and stability.

Until consciousness reaches the upper dimensions of the 3rd Density or higher, the paradox of stasis and stability stimulates "fear" which is the antithesis of and distortion of love. Consciousness becomes familiar with the prevailing emotional characteristics of the self and, through its experiences, it becomes comfortable with the limits and capabilities of its prevailing limited perspective. To protect their current condition and, thereby, not have to change themselves, they try to exert relative control of the world around them, hoping to remain as they are while still garnering more of what they like. Relative control often manifests as some type of force, either active or passive, which usually includes deception and/or untruthfulness with the self and others. Mimicking others to become higher consciousness requires them to surrender their prevailing perspective of the self and its related behavior characteristics, which results in them eventually stopping attempts to control or limit change by managing the world around them.

To surrender the perceptions of self and experience self-honesty, every mind/body/spirit, especially in the foundational densities, 3rd Density, and lower dimensions of 4th Density, must allow themselves to become vulnerable. Consciousness becomes vulnerable by increasing its honest awareness of the self which results in the eventual dissolving of false perceptions, cessation of clinging to stasis, and becoming open to change, thereby allowing it to experience greater stability. With every thought processed, consciousness at all levels is provided the opportunity to surrender a little bit of its false identity in favor of greater stability. It is allowed to surrender its prevailing perspective of self, intoxicated with free will, and predisposed to preserve its identity as a separate self, in favor of greater unity with the Creator.

This is the "choice" of 3rd Density but it is a process pervasive to all consciousness experiencing evolution. The 3rd Density is just the first level of the consciousness journey through evolution that includes the intention for consciousness to have sufficient energy, awareness, and tools to effect lasting results. Every time consciousness in the foundational or experiential densities processes a thought, it is provided the opportunity to choose fear and preserve the prevailing image of self, which is stasis; or, surrender the prevailing image of self, choose greater stability by surrendering more free will intoxication, and evolve to higher consciousness, which is stability. This is the process of a mind/body/spirit either radiating love energy by aligning more completely with the Higher Self and surrendering its perception of a separate self or absorbing love energy and separating itself by preserving its separate identity.

Choosing stasis by serving the self is a fear-based approach and choosing stability is a love-based approach that serves others. The perspective of a separate identity, reinforced by self-deception, fear, and absorbing love energy creates a perpetual cycle of chaos sustained by repeating futile efforts to manage the world through force. The entire process of evolution and the purpose of creation is to explore the self through experiences. Every thought/experience processed requires consciousness to interpret it with emotion and it is through those emotions that consciousness creates its uniqueness.

The story of the baseball player who is on first base but wants/ needs to go to second base is a metaphorical paradox for staying the same or changing. First base is familiar and there is relative stability if there is no change, but, beginning in 3rd Density, he/she becomes sufficiently aware to know they can't rely on a lack of change because everything is in motion which, by its nature, is change. Moving upwards along the consciousness scale requires surrendering the familiarity of the current level of consciousness to move up to the next level, an action that can only be undertaken by the experiencing mind/body/spirit. Current and future happiness is contingent upon changing a perspective of self predicated upon choosing fear and the relative feeling of comfort provided by the familiarity that comes with the prevailing level of consciousness, or becoming vulnerable, choosing love, and surrendering the familiar in favor of the unknown based upon faith.

Surrendering the stasis perspective of the current level of consciousness to move to a higher level of consciousness and greater stability requires the transformation of the perspective of self, and the model for the new self is always available by observing and mimicking higher consciousness. Repeatedly, from the beginning experiences of consciousness in 1st Density through the last levels of consciousness in 7th Density, consciousness is required to transform its perspective of self a countless number of times but there is always a model provided to emulate. At each incremental step along the way, faith is required to surrender stasis at the current level to experience greater stability at the next. Consciousness inches its way along from the known to the unknown at each dimension, predicated upon faith in itself and its newly revealed awareness, but not faith in some unseen mysterious character.

The awareness developed by the incremental process allows the mind/body/spirit to learn to have faith in itself, and by that faith, it learns its power. This is important because power is significantly different than force. Force is a distortion of power created individually or cumulatively by mind/body/spirit(s) directing it outward from the self to manipulate the world around it so that it doesn't have to change. Physics tells us that the issuance of force inevitably creates an equal and opposite force, and this is an important learning experience as consciousness attempts to exert force to manage the world around itself to compel the world to meet its expectations. Using force to attempt to compel the world to meet our expectations, rather than being "in the moment" and experiencing "what is", is the source of all stress.

When consciousness has sufficiently elevated its awareness, usually midway through the 4th Density, if not before, it realizes that force is futile and forever after surrenders force to power because power is the Creator. This is an immutable experience for all consciousness when it allows itself to sufficiently surrender fear and have trust in power as it's found within the self. Learning its power through unity is an important part of the process of exploring and learning about the self and, ultimately, the Creator.

All consciousness in the foundation and experiential densities experiences creation as a mind/body/spirit. The spirit is the spirit of the Higher Self which, in turn, is the spirit of 8th Density, and which, in turn, is the one infinite Creator. The spirit will remain inaccessible until the mind surrenders sufficient amounts of its self-created false identity to allow the spirit to emerge. When it does emerge, it will probably seem like an independent identity from the spirit of the Higher Self, even though it's a part of itself because it perceives the spirit through the distorted lens of lower consciousness. It recognizes the spirit for the first time through its mind, which is an event that usually occurs near the end of its 3rd Density experience as it prepares to graduate to 4th Density.

The mind is a creation of spirit which inevitably creates the distorted lens through which it observes the spirit called the false identity that is the natural product of free will intoxication. The mind "is" the spirit that perceives itself as separate from the Creator and allows the mind/body/spirit to co-create its experience by employing analogy to create its unique pattern of consciousness. Its metaphysical pattern of consciousness is a distortion of the mind, made possible by the free will distortion of the mind's separate identity (AKA the "ego"). Through its analog projections, the metaphysical consciousness pattern is uniquely shaped by the distorted perception(s) of self, conflagrated by how it has emotionally interpreted thoughts. It is the mind's processing of a thought that takes the thought/experience through the chakra system. The chakra system applies emotion, which is the interpretation of the thought used to alter its pattern of consciousness and prepares it for the next thought.

Remember, creation is a point-in-time experience. A single thought is fully processed and the fruit of that process modifies the mind/body/spirit. The mind/body/spirit that has just been modified attracts a new thought and perpetuates a cycle that modifies the mind/body/spirit over and over again. With awareness, the mind/body/spirit continues to learn with each process and eventually decreases its vacillation along the consciousness scale, establishing a pattern of a more consistent forward progression while retaining its uniqueness.

The body is a creation of the mind and the nature of the body is the result of the thoughts being processed, but it also provides feedback from the environment to the mind to aid in the mind's interpretation of the experience. When the time/space mind/body/spirit experiencing the foundational densities, 3rd Density, or the lower dimensions of the 4th Density projects an analog of itself into space/time, every thought processed will include the body image of the lifeline as modified by its experiences. The body image is constantly altered as the mind/body/spirit adjusts its pattern of consciousness and reflects those changes in its body image. The body is a reflection of the nature of the mind/body/spirit's pattern of consciousness.

In the 1st Density, consciousness evolves from the chaos of unformed dispersion floating within the concept of voluminous space to relatively stable unity as a cohesive planet by bonding with other consciousness. At every dimension along the way, consciousness is required to change its perspective of self and its perceived identity to create a new, more unified higher consciousness identity. 1st Density consciousness becomes codependent upon other consciousness so it may experience the relative stability available at this level, which requires it to surrender its autonomy perceiving self-identity numerous times in the process.

The spirit of 1st Density is the spirit of the Higher Self which is inaccessible to the mind of 1st Density because of the lower consciousness' high degree of free will intoxication. The minds of 1st Density are the minds of the elements which result from free will intoxication and the perceptual compartmentalization of the spirit. The manifested bodies are the physical elements that we see, feel, hear, smell, and touch which contribute to the mind's interpretation of thoughts for all consciousness sharing the experience and still perceiving the authenticity of the physical world. How the minds of the four elements work and bond together will be determined by their willingness to harmonize, and the resulting appearance and functioning of the planet reflect its degree of harmony. Earth, without the interference of the 3rd Density population, is a very harmonious 1st Density experience.

In 2nd Density, the evolution of consciousness picks up where 1st Density ends and diversifies itself by forming a multitude of time/space species pools that project themselves into the environment of space/time as "living" organisms, initially disbursed as isolated units of consciousness that we recognize as single cell plants and animals. Every species pool has its mind and every analog projection into space/time has its mind that functions independently from the species pool. Similar to the experiences of 1st Density, consciousness' evolution progresses within the density and is evidenced by the merging of single independent cells into small organisms and eventually into larger more complex organisms. The perception of self becomes more complex too because each species pool creates a perspective of self and every analog projection into space/time also creates its own, independent perspective of self.

1st Density creates the environment of space/time with significant diversity throughout the planet and 2nd Density capitalizes upon the planetary diversity by varying the uniqueness of the bodies of the plants and animals. More than any other foundation or experiential density, 2nd Density varies the body portion of the mind/body/spirits as the basis of its exploration of the self, but this is necessary because of the limitations of the level of consciousness and its mind's limited capacity to become aware. Varying the nature of consciousness' experiences by varying the diversity of 2nd Density body types is relatively cumbersome when contrasted with the more nimble experience of varying the mind in 3rd Density, but it accommodates the limitations of 2nd Density consciousness.

3rd Density begins where 2nd Density ends, with consciousness assuming the form of an enduring time/space mind/body/spirit that cumulatively preserves the nature of its experiences from multiple incarnate analog projections and allows the perspective of the self to mutate and change over multiple incarnations. Thoughts processed by the mind become the primary instruments of change for consciousness' experience because the 3rd Density mind has a greater awareness and, therefore, the capacity to process thought. Consciousness begins 3rd Density as a "clean canvas" with its exploration of the self guided by the design constraints of the relevant Archetypical Mind. From its starting point, analog projections into the space/time environment are tasked with becoming a unique identity or ego (ego mind) from which to experience its limited perspective of creation; constantly mutating and adjusting its perception of self as its awareness grows until it can significantly surrender its attachments to distortions in favor of truth.

At each stage of the evolutionary process, consciousness relies upon feelings, or emotions, shaped by the chakra system, as the mechanism to interpret experience. It is because of the chakra system that consciousness can employ the process of analogy to determine what it likes or doesn't like and thereby creates the uniqueness of its pattern. Since 3rd Density is the first level of consciousness that cumulatively preserves the fruit of its experience, the chakra system assumes a significantly more important role, not only in individual experiences but as a reflection of the cumulative progress of consciousness through the densities' dimensions.

Consciousness experiencing 3rd Density as a mind/body/spirit has the first three time/space bodies activated, which means that Intelligent Energy is provided in adequate quantity to power these three bodies. A single metaphysical mind/body/spirit simultaneously projects itself into multiple space/time analog projections by allocating portions of its Intelligent Energy to each analog projection, usually in equal quantity. Each analog projection follows a timeline, which it selects according to its prevailing metaphysical pattern of consciousness from within a set of timelines, and experiences the events of that timeline by assigning an emotional value to every thought.

Timeline thoughts are sequentially encountered one at a time by the incarnate mind/body/spirit because it is the next designed experience on the timeline and the prevailing thought is held in the "Experience of the Mind" phase of the Archetypical Mind until an emotion is applied to it. The emotion can only be applied by the mind/body/spirit processing the thought and its results because of the prevailing nature of the distortions comprising its pattern. No experience or thought holds or brings any emotion with it, which means every experience or thought is emotionally neutral. The flow of Intelligent Energy energizes the chakra system and negative emotions are felt because the energy flow encounters resistance, thereby promulgating an "I don't like it" emotion associated with which chakra (assessment point) within the system the resistance is felt.

Where Intelligent Energy encounters resistance within the chakra system is where there is an attachment to a distortion that needs "healing" or surrender. Every thought processed through the mind includes a message or a portion of a message that provides the experiencing mind/body/spirit with the opportunity to learn the lessons of the Inherent Characteristics and reduce its free will intoxication by healing emotional baggage and/or surrendering a faulty belief included in its false identity. It is incumbent upon the experiencing mind/body/spirit to become aware of what the message is, as it relates to its current pattern of consciousness, and, by "letting go", surrender its attachment to the distortion.

The degree of resistance can be small or large enough to block the continued flow of energy through the remaining chakras. If it is small, and not addressed, it may continue to serve as an impediment to the free-flowing Intelligent Energy until it eventually becomes large. When it becomes large enough, it can alter the behavior of the mind/body/spirit by significantly lowering awareness until it seems that it is regressing along the scale. A 3rd Density mind/body/spirit with a large degree of chakra system obstruction may potentially remain a 3rd Density consciousness but behave as if it is a 2nd Density consciousness.

For example: during World War II, some members of the Nazi SS that were guards and/or executioners in the concentration camps were reported to experience sexual excitement and even orgasmic ecstasy over the torture and execution of the captives. The guards remained 3rd Density or "yellow-ray" consciousness but they behaved as if they were severely distorted or 2nd Density "orange-ray" consciousness. Consciousness behaving as an orange-ray is a characteristic of individuals or groups relying upon bellicosity to manage the world which is the cornerstone for mind/body/spirits that are in the process of polarizing or have polarized negatively. Large portions of the Earth's current population still function with these conditions: remaining 3rd Density consciousness but behaving as an orange-ray or 2nd Density consciousness.

The application of emotion is how consciousness interprets creation, so the application of emotion is reflective of its current pattern of consciousness. Its pattern, which is synonymous with its ego, is a distortion of its mind and the product of how it has interpreted its experiences heretofore. If a mind/body/spirit retains a relatively low consciousness and continues to dwell within the lower dimensions but is still yellow-ray, it will probably be relying upon fear or heartache, in one or more of their myriad forms, as the primary emotion to interpret most or all thoughts. After an emotion is applied to the current thought, the thought continues on its journey through the structure of the Archetypical Mind and the processing mind/body/spirit has the further choice to continue to sustain its limited perspective by absorbing love energy or transform its prevailing pattern by radiating love energy.

If the mind/body/spirit is aware, it will choose to change its pattern of consciousness, if only incrementally, by overriding its prevailing pattern and radiating its love energy. If it isn't yet aware, it will probably allow the constraints of its prevailing pattern and limited perspective to sustain its behavior of absorbing its love energy. When it is choosing to radiate its love energy, it is deciding to surrender its free will intoxication and evolve slightly closer in alignment with the oneness of the Creator. When it chooses to absorb its love energy, it is choosing to maintain or even enhance its free will intoxication and reject its alignment with the oneness of the Creator.

As awareness continues to grow within the mind/body/spirit, it enhances the ability to override its propensity to "react" to the emotion and to "take control" of its thoughts. By doing this, it is learning of its "power" and, when it becomes awareness, its perspective of self dramatically transforms and takes control of the velocity with which it can heal the self and align more completely with the Creator. The nature of consciousness' experience becomes increasingly immutable because the process becomes more focused on surrendering false perceptions and aligning more completely, but uniqueness is always maintained because each mind/body/spirit approaches the process from its unique perspective of the self.

The objective for the density is to learn awareness, and from that vantage point, learn the lessons of love. Consciousness has experiences, feels the self-determined appropriate emotion, becomes aware that the experience is a message of something that needs to be healed, and "surrenders" or changes the condition within its pattern that needs healing. Awareness is both the discovery tool and the healing tool of what needs to be healed.

Once the conditions have become healed and the mind/body/spirit is cleared of accumulated distortions, the mind/body/spirit will continue to have experiences and continue to apply emotions but, instead of "reacting" unconsciously and applying the emotional distortions representative of a lower consciousness pattern, it can respond to the experience with a more appropriate emotion and "put it down" once the experience is completed. Experience will continue to bring messages to the experiencing mind/body/spirit, but, with awareness, it may use the experiences to further advance its evolution by surrendering more of its free will intoxication, thereby raising its consciousness. The perspective of self continues to transform with every thought, but instead of either regressing along the consciousness scale or continuing to vacillate between one step forward and one step back, a consistent forward momentum can be maintained and significant progress can be made.

As previously stated, when consciousness begins its 3rd Density experience it begins with a clean slate, but the clean slate is programmed to perceive itself in "primordial darkness" as an individual separate identity, having "no" information or light, in constant motion, which is synonymous with chaos, and unconscious or unaware. From this platform, it begins to process thoughts or experiences. As a result of its interpretation of its experiences, soon into the experience of 3rd Density, it forms a pattern of consciousness or ego that serves as the basis for new experiences but repeatedly transforms with the processing of every single new thought. The procedure becomes a routine cycle of a) attracting a thought; b) processing a thought; and c) transforming the pattern of consciousness according to the fruit of the thought, and then, beginning the cycle again.

The average adult person alive today, as part of the Earth's population, has experienced over 3,900 lifetimes as part of their 3rd Density tenure with some exceeding 8,000 lifetimes. The perspective of self has incrementally transformed after the processing of every thought during every lifetime and continues today. The perspective of self is constantly changing but it does reach a stage when the process itself dramatically slows down as consciousness is elevated.

When a mind/body/spirit sufficiently surrenders its free will intoxication to become awareness, it activates the fourth time/space body while still incarnate as a 3rd Density mind/body/spirit. Until this occurs, the mind/body/spirit continues to perceive itself as an independent identity, cocooned within a body. Evolution is a process, so a mind/body/spirit evolves slowly to allow it to digest or "season" its experiences as it progresses through all of the phases from the lowest to the highest. Within 3rd Density, the more intoxicated with free will the more isolated and independent a mind/body/spirit perceives itself to be.

While a mind/body/spirit remains within the lower dimensions of the density it perceives other mind/body/spirits as rivals and feels that it is in "competition" with all others for what it needs. What every mind/body/spirit is preprogrammed to need is love, but it isn't preconditioned to feel what love should feel like, so it pursues an undefined conceptual goal, having to imagine what love feels like. We described in an earlier chapter that, while consciousness remains within the lower dimensions of 3rd Density, it competes with other mind/body/spirits for energy and every experience requires an energy exchange. When one mind/body/spirit wins the competition for energy it feels better, but, when it loses an exchange, it feels worse.

Because consciousness is unaware during the competition phase of its evolution, it mistakes the "feel good" feeling resulting from winning an energy completion as love. It experiences "immediate gratification" from the "feel good" feeling and, while consciousness remains unaware, it is motivated to hone its skills to be able to be more successful more often in winning the competition for energy. This behavior creates the basis for a philosophical distortion that can become ubiquitous to the entire 3rd Density experience. The distortion is described as the "Concept of Empire", which simply is the belief that "I can be enhanced by diminishing you".

The "Concept of Empire" has been an integral part of the population of Earth way before the 3rd Density experience on Earth began, creating sometimes dramatic conflicts between the two resulting polarities. The Concept of Empire philosophy originates in fear, the opposite of love, and uses fear as a tool to deepen its effectiveness. Because it is founded upon the distortion of love and requires repeated success in the competition for energy, it is enhanced by lowering consciousness and the practice of reinforcing the ego and a perception of an independent identity. This philosophy has created a divergent path to the evolutionary process design, even though it is ultimately doomed to failure because "all is one", and there is only one possible conclusion for evolution.

The Concept of Empire is the foundational behavior and philosophy that established the contrasting option for the "choice" of 3rd Density, where a mind/body/spirit either pursues its separation from the Creator by dominating and subjugating others to "steal" their energy or chooses to align with the Creator and reject the deception of those polarizing service-to-self. In the phase of the Earthly experience we currently enjoy, the "choice" is intentionally being induced with significant intensity, but without prejudice or judgment, for all mind/body/spirits alive on the planet today. The 3rd Density experience on Earth has ended and those beings that are still incarnate, that have not qualified for graduation, still have the opportunity to do so but choosing to polarize service-to-self or service-to-others is imperative. It has been determined that Earth, for some period, will be a mixed 3rd Density, beginning a new +/-76,000 cycle, and 4th Density service-to-others planet after the conclusion of the previous 3rd Density experience and those who are graduating service-to-self will be relocated elsewhere to continue their evolution.

As a mind/body/spirit approaches the activation of the fourth time/space body, which is synonymous with the activation of the fourth time/space chakra, 3rd Density experiences become less competitive because its perception of self is transforming more consistently to align with the path of higher consciousness. The attachment to the authenticity of the physical world eventually begins to loosen its grip, and what previously was a clear-cut perception of an independent mind/body/spirit begins to transform as it begins to see other mind/body/spirits as extensions of itself, rather than "others" to compete against. It is at this point, in the evolution of the perception of self, that the mind/body/spirit has sufficiently progressed along the consciousness scale and has sufficiently learned the lessons of love to do 4th Density work and becomes ready for graduation as a positively polarized mind/body/spirit.

When a 3rd Density mind/body/spirit adequately surrenders enough free will intoxication to open the fourth time/space chakra, it experiences love more frequently and consistently. Love is an Inherent Characteristic and archetype of the Creator, and reaching the fourth chakra opening milestone allows consciousness to feel the feelings that accompany that degree of awareness. Love is an awareness available to all consciousness, but, to feel love, it is necessary for consciousness to "get out of the way" by becoming aware of the self as a unified part of the Higher Self and the Creator and to surrender its ego enough to reduce its perceptions of separation. Consciousness feels love because it feels its "Creator-ness" and begins to "be" the love that it has sought through all of its evolutionary development.

Within the 3rd Density experience, becoming aware allows a mind/body/spirit to establish a greater degree of order in its experiences which, in turn, allows it to have a clearer lens through which to observe the self and its experiences. When it becomes awareness, it will have incrementally cleaned the lens that it uses to observe the self and its experiences. What becomes clearer is feeling. We learn by analogy and when we can distinguish the feeling of a short-term burst of Intelligent Energy, gained from the immediate gratification of winning the competition for energy over another mind/body/spirit, from the constant connection to love available by simply surrendering free will intoxication, love wins.

Until we become awareness and open the fourth time/space chakra we seek love from outside of ourselves by "tricking" the world into loving us but experience after experience teaches us that the world cannot love us. We are creating and experiencing what we don't like. If we are lucky, which means "if we pay attention", we become aware and simply awaken to this fact and intelligently look for alternative places, other than the outside world, to look for love. If we are not lucky, meaning that we are stubborn and continue to beat our heads against the wall trying to force it to finally give what we want and need, we will "hit a bottom" when we absolutely, positively cannot continue living the way we have been living.

Either way, if the outside world cannot love us, the only other place to look for love is inside the self. It is only when we begin to be honest and aware of ourselves that we begin to finally find what we want and need. By looking inside and learning to be honest with ourselves, we can begin to discover and heal the distortions that have caused us so much difficulty.

By looking inside, forgiving ourselves for being human, and giving ourselves permission to identify and experience the love that we inevitably "are", we begin the find what we have sought all along.

Every person reading this manuscript is the Creator experiencing itself. Every person has within them everything that they want and need. The final phase of 3rd Density evolution is the process of surrendering the distortions of perception that cloud consciousness' lens through which it observes the self, so it may allow the self to feel the love that it already is. There is nothing to gain; there is only "stuff" to get rid of.

Chapter 10

Service-to-Self

In previous chapters, we have highlighted specific tasks for consciousness to undertake in the experiential densities to evolve. 3rd Density was described as the most intense density of all of the densities for a variety of reasons and the lessons of the density are extremely important because how consciousness makes its choices from the lessons offered determines its course through the remainder of its tenure in the experiential densities. In the 3rd Density, consciousness is tasked with three significant duties which are 1) awakening; 2) becoming awareness, and 3) choosing whether it will either work to align more closely with the Creator or separate from it. Those choosing to separate from the Creator will not awaken or become awareness.

The universal characteristics of consciousness in 3rd Density are that it begins the density with the time/space perception of the self as an autonomous mind/body/spirit and projects itself into space/time as multiple analog mind/body/spirits, some simultaneously. Every analog projection also perceives itself as an autonomous identity, cocooned within a physical body, and independent from all other consciousness sharing the experience. Under these conditions, the time/space mind/body/spirit is provided the opportunity to begin the density experience as an experiential virgin, able to cumulatively preserve the fruit of its experience interpretations to uniquely "create" a consciousness pattern. All consciousness beginning its tenure in the 3rd Density begins the experience on an equal footing, with the same degree of coding activation, the same quantity of Intelligent Energy flow, and the same awareness tools in potentiation.

When a 3rd Density experience begins, participating consciousness incarnates into space/time bodies and interacts with other incarnate space/time bodies by sharing experiences. Experiences are synonymous with thoughts and the space/time mind/body/spirit processes thoughts with 3rd Density capacities. Some analog projections incarnate as males, that are predisposed to be the subject in the lifetime, and some will incarnate as females, that are predisposed to be the object, but from the beginning of the 3rd Density experience and because each mind/body/spirit incarnates into multiple analog projections simultaneously, the time/space mind/body/spirit is both male and female at the same time. Each interaction with other 3rd Density incarnate mind/body/spirits, the co-experiencing 2nd Density consciousness, and the 1st Density created environment allows them to learn about themselves through analogy.

The objective is to eventually become awareness, and through the awareness lens, learn about love, but when consciousness begins from scratch, in chaos, ignorance, and unconscious, *it must also discover what love is.* Before consciousness discovers what love feels like, it determines that some experiences feel better than others, and, through analogy, it learns to create behavior that feels better. Behavior results from thoughts and the selection of new thoughts is, for the most part, based on its interpretation of previous experiences. The nature of its behavior is a product of its degree of awareness, and, consequently, it behaves according to its level of consciousness, or how far it has inched up the dimensional scale.

Analogy dictates that we learn by trial and error, and, when awareness is low and consciousness retains the limited perspective characteristic of the beginning conditions of the density, consciousness will often consistently choose experiences that don't feel good in search of ones that do feel good. There is no limit to how many experiences a person can have that don't feel good before it awakens, the first definitive phase of its evolutionary progression. To limit a bias from the initiating Higher Self and preserve free will in the experience, the process begins without any prior programming of what love should feel like.

Mind/body/spirits serve as the subject or the object to each other in every experience, and inherent in every subject/object interaction is an exchange of energy, Intelligent Energy. While a person dwells within the lower dimensions of the density, getting more Intelligent Energy from an exchange feels better than losing Intelligent Energy, and, as explained in Chapter 9, winning an energy battle creates a temporary feeling that feels good. If you would like to review a more specific explanation of this process then we encourage you to review the information in the earlier chapter explaining the confusion between stasis and stability that creates the philosophy and behavior of the "Concept of Empire".

The "Concept of Empire" is the foundation for the polarity of the experiential densities. The polarity is the conflict between those mind/body/spirits that have not become aware, rely upon winning the energy battle to experience immediate gratification (which is often mistaken as love), and, consequently, polarize negatively, and those who do become awareness, experience the enduring feelings of love, and polarize positively. Those polarizing negatively are identified as service-to-self and those polarizing positively are identified as service-to-others. These are only characteristics of different vantage points of consciousness but are still inherently part of the "oneness" of the Creator.

We have heretofore described the evolution through the foundational and experiential densities as beginning in a state of dispersion and ending in an increased state of unity or harmony. Because a mind/body/spirit cumulatively preserves its learning beginning in 3rd Density, its evolution through the experiential densities is one long process that begins with a perspective of being completely autonomous and culminates in the unity of 6th Density, but it does this in phases identified as the 3rd, 4th, and 5th Densities with each density being a different phase and subdivided into countless dimensions. The choice between polarizing negatively, the service-to-self path, and polarizing positively, the service-to-others path, is the single most important task of 3rd Density because it will determine the nature of consciousness' experiences in both 4th and 5th Densities. Making the "choice" in 3rd Density is required for "graduation" from 3rd Density because, not only does it select the nature of mind/body/spirit experiences in the higher densities, it determines where and in what environment those experiences will be presented.

Earth, for the 3rd Density experience just completed and the new one just begun, is a "second chance" planet. The population has been consolidated from 16 different 3rd Density experiences that have already participated in, but not graduated from at least one previous 3rd Density experience. Of the 16, three were major contributors and 13 were minor contributors. Because the mind/body/spirits preserved their patterns of consciousness, formed during previous 3rd Density experiences, they brought with them significant distortions from which to begin their reinvigorated endeavors to graduate from the density.

As an example of the source of the emotional baggage, one of the major population contributors began their 3rd Density experience on the planet Zenoa, which we now call Venus, approximately 850,000 years ago, and has experienced five previous 3rd Density experiences. The first 3rd Density experience on Zenoa completed the entire +/-75,000-year cycle and graduated some portion but not all of the population. The non-graduating population began a second 3rd Density experience on Zenoa, but midway through the second segment of the new experience, the conflict between the polarizing segments of the population destroyed the atmosphere, requiring the entire 3rd Density to be terminated. Until this event, Zenoa had successfully hosted successive 3rd Density experiences for over two billion years.

The 3rd Density population of Zenoa, which we will identify hereafter as the Zenoa–Earth population, was relocated to the planet Maldek to start another +/-75,000-year 3rd Density experience from the beginning. Maldek was a planet in orbit around the Sun between Mars and Jupiter. Again, midway through the middle segment of the master cycle, conflicts between the polarizing factions of the population resulted in the destruction of the planet and the end of the Maldek 3rd Density experience. The remnants of Maldek are seen as the "asteroid belt" between Mars and Jupiter.

After the destruction of Maldek, the population needed significant healing because the mind/body/spirits were in a "knot of fear" and unable to function. Part of the healing process for many people included incarnating on Earth as a "big foot" creature where they remained a 3rd Density consciousness but experienced a quasi 2nd Density incarnation. For some, the healing process continues, but not necessarily as a big foot incarnation. It will still be necessary for the individual people to eventually graduate from the density by meeting the same criterion as all other acolytes.

The Zenoa–Earth population started another 3rd Density experience, the fourth attempt to complete a 3rd Density experience and graduate on Mars. Unfortunately, history was repeated and during the middle one-third segment of the master cycle, the conflict between the polarizing service-to-self and service-to-others factions of the population again resulted in the destruction of the atmosphere and the experience had to be terminated. From Mars, the Zenoa–Earth population was transferred to Earth, the ape body was adapted to accommodate a 3rd Density body type, other populations were consolidated, and the Earth experience began a little over 75,000+ years ago.

For the Zenoa–Earth population, the newly started Earth experience is the sixth attempt to graduate, having only completed two of the five previous attempts. The recently finished Earth experience was not without some extreme difficulties. At the beginning of the 3rd Density experience, the face of the planet looked very different than it does today because there used to be a continental land mass between North America and Europe that was destroyed as a result of the bellicosity between rival service-to-self and service-to-others factions. The continent was the most densely populated area of the planet and was named Atlantis, and, as a result of the final conflict with nuclear and other "crystal weapons", sunk beneath the waves in approximately 8441 BC, leaving only a few survivors from either side to rejuvenate the 3rd Density experience. We don't know if the other 15 contributing populations brought as many distortions with them, but the Zenoa–Earth population's history alone was a significant contributor to the difficulties of the Earthly experience.

As a mind/body/spirit polarizes more significantly towards the service-to-self path, it becomes necessary for it to become increasingly adept at extracting Intelligent Energy from other people. It is not possible for them to actually "steal" the energy directly because the energy donors must agree to surrender their energy. To convince them to give up their energy, it's necessary to use deceit because, invariably, if the donors were aware of what was happening, they wouldn't willingly participate in the energy harvest.

In earlier chapters, we explained that 3rd Density metaphysical consciousness patterns simultaneously incarnate into multiple analog projections in space/time with the flow of Intelligent Energy from the Higher Self usually allocated equally to the projections. As a consciousness pattern veers to the negative path, they begin to concentrate the energy into a single analog projection. Concentrating the energy allows the projection of martial additional strength to dominate and subjugate weaker people. The philosophical Concept of Empire, "that I can be enhanced by diminishing others", becomes the service-to-self rationale for this behavior.

Domination and subjugation are the primary tools negatively polarized people use to extract energy from others who are undecided in their polarization, unaware, and still in relative chaos. Domination and subjugation work best if the targeted people feel inferior or a victim of some other 3rd party oppressor. The deception continues by convincing the targeted people that they need to be saved by the stronger, more capable subjugator.

Fear becomes weaponized by suppressing awareness, limiting light (or information), and enslaving those mind/body/spirits that they consider weaker than themselves, either physically and/or psychologically. Those polarizing service-to-self are themselves fear-based but have sufficient familiarity with the characteristics of fear to be able to use it to enslave others with weaker energy resources (AKA less awareness). A common effect of consolidating energy into a single 3rd Density incarnation is relatively greater intelligence.

Intelligent Energy is what energizes the space/time chakras, fuels awareness, and allows consciousness to activate the time/space bodies (time/space chakras). Beginning in 3rd Density, consciousness has sufficient awareness to assume the responsibility of furthering its journey through evolution; consequently, it isn't limited to energizing only the 3rd time/space body. In fact, for those people who are polarizing positively, graduating from the 3rd Density experience requires them to liberate enough energy to open the fourth metaphysical chakra. When a 3rd Density person polarizing negatively gains adequate proficiency, they will intentionally skip opening the 4th chakra entirely because they fear surrendering their ego (AKA false identity), and consider love to be folly, but instead, will use their energy absconding proficiency to energize the fifth metaphysical chakra, bypassing the fourth.

Intelligent Infinity is the conceptual environment (see Chapter 2) within which creation is begun with the projection of the conceptual distortion, free will. Intelligent Infinity is the canvas on which creation is painted and it is always present, even though consciousness in the lower densities is usually unaware of it. When an evolving person opens the 4th metaphysical chakra, they may become aware of the presence of Intelligent Infinity. At this level of consciousness, Intelligent Infinity functions within the person as "increased energy" and is experienced as increased fuel to further escalate awareness.

This process is sometimes described as Intelligent Infinity entering the top of the chakra system and proceeding downward through the chakras until it meets the upward flow of Intelligent Energy, but Intelligent Infinity is omnipresent and doesn't flow. Access to it becomes available for incorporation into consciousness' experience of creation as the evolving acolyte can become aware of it. This is true for people polarizing positively or negatively, but since the negative path doesn't open the 4th chakra, those choosing the negative path access Intelligent Infinity at the 5th chakra, which requires significant effort.

People polarizing negatively "weaponize" Intelligent Infinity to enhance their ego identity and further hone their skills of dominating and subjugating other consciousness. People polarizing positively are actively dissolving the ego (false identity) and enhancing awareness. The positively polarizing person's identity, formed during their tenure in 3rd Density, begins to dissipate and the person's authentic self begins to integrate into "all that there is". Their perception of self as a separate identity becomes vulnerable to greater truth because they can "feel" increasing unity.

People polarizing negatively intentionally bypass the 4th metaphysical chakra and work to deceptively abscond with enough energy to power the 5th metaphysical chakra, leaving the 4th metaphysical chakra in potentiation. When they're successful in garnering enough energy to open the 5th metaphysical chakra, they too can access Intelligent Infinity and begin to incorporate it into their experience by also enhancing their awareness but in a limited and distorted manner. For consciousness along the service-to-others path, the addition of Intelligent Infinity provides them with the ability to surrender their distortions more quickly and completely so that they may evolve more efficaciously, but it has other effects along the service-to-self path. By continuing to point their awareness outside of themselves, thereby, enhancing their false identity, and "weaponizing" Intelligent Infinity, the service-to-self path enlists the additional resources to intensify the use of force through domination and subjugation to confiscate even more Intelligent Energy.

Negatively polarized people can advance to both the 4th and, eventually, 5th Density strength because they are excellent deceivers and become increasingly ruthless, dominating and subjugating other weaker or less mature people to extract more energy. They prey upon other consciousness, especially in the lower dimensions of 3rd Density, to maintain a source of Intelligent Energy to remain in evolution. If they fail to do so, their participation will disappear and dissolve into unformatted consciousness, which is still the one infinite Creator. While consciousness remains within the experiential densities, access to Intelligent Infinity doesn't substitute Intelligent

Energy but it does enhance it. Every aspect of creation is the Creator learning of itself by experiencing itself and there is no judgment or condemnation for the choices made by fractalized consciousness, but there is often headshaking disbelief.

The act of connecting to Intelligent Infinity is available to all consciousness within creation, including the consciousness exploring the foundational densities, but the 1st and 2nd Density consciousness doesn't have the awareness to recognize and incorporate it into its experiences. When consciousness has progressed to the upper dimensions of 3rd Density through their initiative, they will have achieved sufficient awareness to be able to identify and incorporate Intelligent Infinity into its experiences on a very elementary basis. For consciousness choosing the positive path, awareness incrementally removes the blinders from its eyes as they begin to incorporate more of the periphery into its primary focus. The stricture of its identity begins to loosen and with each step forward it can identify more with the unity of all consciousness.

Awareness for those along the negative path also is enhanced as it garners more strength through the addition of increasing quantities of borrowed Intelligent Energy, but it has the opposite effect of consciousness polarizing positively. Because the development of negatively polarized consciousness is distorted, awareness is unbalanced and increased Intelligent Energy flow increases the perception of identity and the resulting ego. Adding the ability to connect to Infinite Energy increases awareness for consciousness along the negative path too, but only as may be experienced within the limiting parameters of its false perception of self and ego. If the wheel on your car is wobbly, accelerating only increases its wobble.

Consciousness following the service-to-others path is surrendering its perception of separation, integrating, and merging into unity with the Creator, so it is incrementally becoming one with the Creator again. Consciousness choosing service-to-self intensifies its perception of separation, increases its attachment to distortions, and preserves and enhances the ego identity initially created in the 3rd Density. Service-to-self mind/body/spirits are in perpetual competition with every other aspect of consciousness because they are rivals for Intelligent Energy to sustain their very existence, even with other aspects of negatively polarized consciousness. Increased Intelligent Energy makes them stronger and more forceful, but the stronger they become, the more isolated they become.

Negatively polarized consciousness is concentrated within the Orion star system but it has outposts run by regional managers throughout the universe. Once a mind/body/spirit graduates from 3rd Density along the service-to-self path, it is probable that they will remain on that path for billions of years, themselves being dominated and subjugated by stronger service-to-self mind/body/spirits until they can win enough energy battles to elevate their position in the service-to-self community. The social structure of service-to-self consciousness is much like a pyramid marketing scheme. There are lots of minions in the 3rd and 4th Densities that do the work of harvesting energy but few 5th Density mind/body/spirits that oppress the minions and perpetuate their enslavement.

6th Density is the density of unity but a service-to-self mind/body/spirit can master the confiscation of energy process so proficiently that it reaches the lower dimensions of 6th Density strength (not consciousness level), but only for an instant. It isn't possible to be in unity and separate at the same time, so mind/body/spirits following the negative path are destined to "hit a wall" where they cannot go any further. At this point, if not before, to advance and return to the Creator, they must surrender all of the strength and identity they have built up over the billions of years within the service-to-self ranks, return to the density where they dropped out of school (3rd Density), and begin again by following the service-to-others path through the densities. There is no other way to advance out of the experiential densities than to follow the service-to-others path.

Even though Gaia has graduated to a 4th Density experience and Earth has become a dual experiential density hosting both a 3rd and positive 4th Density planet, large portions of the population still currently incarnate are struggling to advance and graduate from 3rd Density. Service-to-self factions are hard at work to harvest as much energy as possible from those remaining people before the source evaporates. The 3rd Density populations on Earth, Zenoa, Maldek, and Mars endured overt efforts from service-to-self factions to hinder their progress so the energy-sapping could be sustained. These 3rd Density experiences have been very fruitful for the service-to-self pirates and seriously convoluted the population's experiences but also provided the Creator with significant opportunities to experience itself in unpredictable ways.

Probably more than any other condition, the degree of interference in the population's experiences for thousands of years has caused the Earth experience to be one of the most intense and difficult 3rd Density experiences ever. Even though the Zenoa–Earth population and other consciousness contributors have been under intense assault for a long, long time, it has also always had a significant number of dedicated coaches and cheerleaders, and the transition from 3rd to 4th Density has been the entire universe's super bowl to watch. Service-to-self does not honor the Law of Confusion so they have no compunctions about violating other consciousness' free will but service-to-others do. Not only do the Creator Beings honor the free will of lower consciousness polarizing positively, they equally honor the free will of consciousness polarizing negatively.

The degree of interference that the Earth's population currently experiences is comparatively subtle when compared to earlier times because 5th Density service-to-self is now relying upon the suppression mechanisms and distorted cultural ideologies established and historically programmed into the population. Earth's fairly recent history reflects that service-to-self has been much more interactive and in direct contact with the population to instill fear and distract the population from successfully evolving. Once service-to-self has established a reliable source of energy, they strive to preserve and sustain the source by making it self-perpetuating from generation to generation. Essentially, the extraction of energy from large portions of the Earth's population is on autopilot, self-perpetuating their spiritual enslavement through self-imposed ignorance, reliance upon superstitions, and the unconscious reinforcement of false beliefs and outright lies.

When service-to-self reaches 5th Density strength, in some ways, it's very wise and it uses that wisdom, in conjunction with its vantage point of being outside of time and its other abilities, to play upon distortions and exacerbate fear and perceptions of victimhood. To some degree, they need people to implement the energy harvest from within the 3rd Density experience and be the "agents" of their deceit. Establishing a class of unconscious 3rd Density agents also creates a steady supply of souls polarizing negatively to replenish the generations of new 4th Density minions to continue to serve the 5th Density upper echelon. In the Zenoa–Earth experience, it has been relatively easy to recruit service-to-self agents by promoting beliefs of superiority based on skin color, wealth, religion, physical size, debt, war, education, etc.

In Earth's "not-too-distant" past, service-to-self has been more physically present and interactive with the population. For example, the Lines of Nazca, Easter Island heads, and

Stonehenge were all created by 4th Density service-to-self beings and have no purpose other than to stimulate fear within the populations at the time. In the present day, almost all of the UFOs sighted in the skies or "close encounters of the 3rd kind" are 4th Density service-to-self intrusions attempting to stimulate fear.

Because service-to-self lowers its consciousness level while gaining strength by pirating Intelligent Energy from a 3rd Density population, it retains a significantly greater attachment to the space/time illusion than positively polarized consciousness. For example, 4th Density service-to-self has significant technological capabilities and must rely upon physical vehicles for transportation, but 4th Density service-to-others are more inclined to connect to universal consciousness which alleviates much of the need for technology. 5th Density beings, service-to-self or service-to-others, can create "portals" to traverse the universe, and 4th Density service-to-self minions often use portals created by their superiors to travel the universe and employ their deceptions. Earth currently experiences several service-to-self portals terminating in Russia, the Middle East, Venezuela, and other less prominent locations where the population is under stress from autocratic leadership.

Service-to-others are less inclined to physically travel because, as their awareness rises, they're able to participate in the experiences of geographically distant places telepathically. 5th Density of either polarization can physically appear in whatever form they desire and are not limited to a single physical body shape or style. During consciousness' tenure in the early dimensions of the 4th Density, people aren't able to manipulate their physical appearance yet.

Creation is a thought experiment experienced in thought, but thought, in the foundational and experiential densities, is created by 6th Density consciousness. 5th Density is not able to create thought, but they can see and manipulate timelines comprised of a string of thoughts which allows them to bend a thought from one timeline to another. A set of timelines being experienced by a 3rd Density mind/body/spirit offers a full range of possibilities which includes everything from the most positive to the most negative. Negatively polarized 4th Density only marginally have the capabilities of manipulating thought directly when they advance to the upper dimensions. All that is necessary to disrupt a 3rd Density mind/body/spirit's stream of thought is to temporarily bend a more negative fear-based thought stream into the current timeline being followed and the aberrant thoughts will likely be accepted as if they were their own.

An extremely small minority of people may have a 5th Density service-to-self mind/body/spirit bending negative thoughts into their path, but the 4th Density service-to-self are much more active in trying to do so because they are the minions responsible for harvesting energy. Most of us don't need help coming up with negative leaning thoughts because the current condition of our pattern of consciousness attracts the next thought, and, if we retain a significant quantity of emotional baggage in need of healing, that alone will be a more than sufficient magnet to attract a plethora of negative thoughts that contribute to surrendering energy. The remedy is the same for negative thoughts guided into our path as it is for one of our self-attracted negative thoughts, which is to become aware of it and simply dismiss it.

We mentioned earlier that service-to-self is centralized in the Orion star system but has outposts throughout the universe. The service-to-self portion of creation is structured with a very distinct pecking order based on who is controlling more energy. The top echelon is the most proficient at absconding with energy, and at manipulating and oppressing other service-to-self subordinates to stave off challenges to their energy sources or their domain. As it is/was on 3rd Density Earth, those who control the wealth and power don't want things to change and so they promote stasis and keep things the same.

To make force and intimidation successful, it is beneficial to cause the environment experienced to be one of constant chaos. The higher echelon service-to-self mind/body/spirits keep their minions off balance and in a constant state of chaos, because, if they were ever able to find a point of stability, they might be able to institute a coup and depose the existing rulers from their thrones. This is true, not only for the dimensionally higher realms of the service-to-self world, but it is also true of how they attempt to program and disrupt a single 3rd Density experience, such as Earth. If conditions become too reliable in the 4th Density service-to-self ranks or their 3rd Density targets, instability is artificially instigated to stimulate chaos and ensure that the minions are kept off balance.

When a mind/body/spirit graduates from 3rd Density along the service-to-self path, they automatically are thrust into a 4th Density planet population for further incarnations as a 4th Density negatively polarized mind/body/spirit. They immediately become a minion to a 5th Density ruling mind/body/spirit and must compete for a position in the 4th Density pecking order. Newly minted 4th Density service-to-self mind/body/spirits immediately begin to compete against other 4th Density service-to-self mind/body/spirits, most of which have been playing the game for millions, if not billions of years, so they are experientially disadvantaged. One individual that we know who graduated to the service-to-self path from the Earth experience was a strong and ruthless bad actor named Genghis Khan, who is now an inglorious shipping clerk in 4th Density.

The population completing Earth's most recent 3rd Density experience produced a mixed graduation with some polarizing and graduating along the service-to-self path, and others graduating along the service-to-others path. Most of the population remains in 3rd Density and will repeat the new 3rd Density cycle on Earth, some for the sixth time, to learn the density's lessons. Those graduating service-to-self will probably integrate into an existing 4th Density service-to-self experience occupying Mars. Venus, formerly Zenoa, is home to a solitary 5th Density regional manager for the "Orion Group".

While it may feel appropriate to consider those polarizing negatively as a "bad" thing, it is important to remember that "all is one" and all consciousness is just another part of you. The service-to-self path is just another path to unity with the Creator, albeit an exceedingly long and troubled one. The answer to how to respond to the demands, efforts of intimidation, or attempted domination by those polarizing service-to-self is to simply reject their overtures and continue along your chosen positive path. The rejection may require some significant application of resistance on your part, and that is okay, but only if it is in response to their force and you can feel love for them despite their attempts to hinder you.

If their overtures trigger an emotion other than love within you, it is a message to you, and about you, of something that needs to be healed with awareness. Missing the opportunity to become aware of what it is within you that needs healing and then not committing to the task of healing the condition lessens the value of the experience for both of you. While consciousness remains in the 3rd Density and the lower dimensions of the 4th Density, every experience provides the experiencing mind/body/spirit with an opportunity to learn of the self more completely. Learning comes from awareness and awareness fuels the escalation of consciousness and its evolution.

Chapter 11

Stress • Healing • Love

A primary characteristic of the 3rd Density experience is stress. If a mind/body/spirit experiences stress, it is an indication that there is a need for additional healing through awareness escalation. It is a message and a motivator to become aware of what it is (belief) within us that we need to become aware of and heal, AKA surrender or process an emotion because stress doesn't feel good. Stress is solely the result of an awareness deficiency and is an excellent measure of a person's perception of separation or "free will intoxication".

When a person experiences stress, they are interpreting thoughts primarily from a perception of a unit of consciousness in isolation and with a strong identity separate from all others. Most probably, they are sincerely attached to the authenticity of the physical world, with a myopic perspective of the self, and little or no awareness of their concurrent metaphysical world participation. In other words, their belief in an authentic perception of self-autonomy compels them to experience only problems and they struggle to identify and resolve those problems from within the environment of the problem's source. The greater the stress level, the more pain and/or suffering experienced, but consciousness potentially learns the most and escalates awareness the most when it is the most uncomfortable.

Stress/suffering is one of the most significant mechanisms available to motivate the evolution of consciousness from the lower dimensions of the experiential densities to the higher. Since 3rd Density is the density of awareness, when consciousness first has the potential to become aware, stress can be the most beneficial motivator to propel consciousness through the dimensions. Consciousness can know it is uncomfortable, assume responsibility to awaken, and undertake the necessary steps to resolve its discomfort through awareness.

Numerous 3rd Density experiences enjoy significantly less stress than the 3rd Density population of Earth, and some don't incarnate into space/time analog projections of themselves at all. In those 3rd Density experiences, the evolutionary progression of consciousness participating in those endeavors proved to be lethargic by comparison. Stress is not a mandatory experience of 3rd Density, but it is a common characteristic, created in varying degrees by the consciousness participating in the experience. Stress can be debilitating, but, when putting it into the timeless perspective of creation, it is one of the greatest tools available to aid evolution. It is most effective while consciousness remains in the lower dimensions of 3rd Density because its inevitable eventual result is increased awareness, gained from experiences.

If you asked most people what stress is they will probably respond with a description of some condition that results from stress ranging from a physical malady or illness to mental confusion or illness. Certainly, these conditions are a result of stress, but they are not "stress" itself. Stress manifests the same in all people, depending upon their degree of awareness and the pattern of consciousness they have created, but how we resolve stress, in other words, transform the experience of what we don't like into experiences of what we do like, varies according to the experiencer's degree of awareness.

Simply defined:

Stress is the difference between our expectations and how things really are.

As presented in earlier chapters, consciousness experiencing 3rd Density does so as a time/space mind/body/spirit that perceives itself to have an individual identity, perceptually isolated from the multitude of other mind/body/spirits of similar understanding and perception of self. The time/space mind/body/spirit simultaneously projects itself into space/time as analog projections. Each analog projection experiences space/time according to the characteristics of a timeline in either a male or female body with certain physical and mental attributes. While the consciousness level of the time/space mind/body/spirit remains low, the specific timeline is chosen by the Higher Self, but, as its consciousness level and awareness rise within the density, the selection of the timeline is increasingly chosen by the mind/body/spirit's perspective of need and preferences of the experiences necessary to provide a stimulus for the aspects of the Inherent Characteristics that need to be learned.

A lifetime is a set of timelines that are all variations upon the central character. The set of timelines consists of a range of experiences that will allow anything from the most positively polarizing experience to the most negatively polarizing experience and almost everything in-between. Where within the range of timelines the analog projection begins its incarnation is determined by the prevailing pattern of consciousness of the time/space mind/body/spirit. If the time/space mind/body/spirit's pattern of consciousness has already achieved a level of awareness that is skewed towards a positive polarization, then it will enter the timeline towards the positive side of the range. If it has shaped its existing pattern to follow a negative path, then it will enter the range of timelines towards the negative side of the range.

Polarizing positively or negatively is an incremental process that usually takes numerous lifetimes to achieve with each new lifetime providing the metaphysical mind/body/spirit the opportunity to build upon what has gone before. The choice of following a negative path or a positive path is not influenced by the Higher Self or others because the purpose of creation is to provide consciousness with the opportunity to experience creation according to its free will choices, thereby allowing the Creator to explore itself by experiencing itself without precondition or bias. Any mind/body/spirit analog projection can experience the same timeline character along a positive path or a negative path, but the pattern of consciousness that begins the timeline will likely perpetuate momentum along one path or the other.

Until a time/space mind/body/spirit has acquired sufficient experience and achieved a relative degree of awareness it will probably vacillate between a positive path and a negative path. This means that, while incarnate, a space/time mind/body/spirit will spend a lot of time jumping back and forth from the positive side of the timelines to the negative side. This behavior is chaos but it allows the mind/body/spirit to utilize analogy to determine what it prefers. It is the trial and error method of learning about the self and further shaping its unique pattern of consciousness.

There is a purpose in creating an incarnation process that progresses incrementally as 3rd Density humans experience it. Humans are born into innocence during which time the infant is closely tied to its unmanifest self (that portion of itself that is not incarnate). During its time as an infant, its mind is the mind of the unmanifest self, its physical abilities, etc., are extremely limited, and only its 1st time/space chakra is processing Intelligent Energy through its space/time chakras. The space/time chakras are all fully open (all seven) and available, but the energy source and depth of experience are restricted because it is only making one lap through the space/time chakras which makes the nature of its experience very simple.

When an infant becomes a toddler, the 2nd time/space chakra opens. It is obvious when this has happened because the "terrible twos" begin and everything is "mine, mine, mine". The mind/body/spirit is learning its power in relationship to others on a one-to-one basis. They are testing others and using the trial and error method to find their position in relationships with other people, places, and things.

When consciousness is in the infantile stage, stress is experienced but results primarily, but not exclusively, from physical discomfort. In the toddler stage, when the 2nd time/space chakra has opened and Intelligent Energy is making two laps through the space/time chakra system, the nature of its experiences becomes much more complex and it experiences equal portions of physical and emotional stress. Of course, the stimulus for its stress expands during the 10 years or so of its experiences with only the first two time/space chakras open, but the nature of its learning is essentially consistent. It is during this time that the emotional foundations, both brought forward from its unmanifest pattern of consciousness and as amended by its interpretations of its current timeline experiences, are formed which will serve as the basis of what it is to learn and heal during its lifetime.

While in 3rd Density, the mind/body/spirit will continue to function with only the first two time/space chakras open until it experiences puberty. The beginning of puberty is the opening of the 3rd time/space chakra, and the focus expands from the limits of learning its place on a one-on-one basis to learning its position in the world. The mind/body/spirit will continue to function with only the first three time/space chakras open until it undertakes the task of becoming aware and intentionally opening the fourth time/space chakra which signals its readiness to graduate from the 3rd Density. Evolving into the next phase, which opens the 4th time/space chakra, may take a lifetime or many lifetimes, and, while the mind/body/spirit remains a 3rd Density consciousness, must be undertaken by the aware and conscious interpretations of thoughts being processed because it doesn't automatically open.

Once the mind/body/spirit has met the criterion for graduation from 3rd Density to 4th Density and completed its last incarnation as a 3rd Density consciousness, it will begin to incarnate into a service-to-others 4th Density experience, different than the 3rd Density experience it just left, with a consciousness level somewhere within the lower dimensions of the density. The process of sequentially opening the time/space chakras will be very similar to that experienced in the 3rd Density, but the infant is born with the first two time/space chakras open. Also, an added step will automatically open the fourth time/space chakra, since the opening of the 4th chakra was achieved during the earlier incarnation as a 3rd Density mind/body/spirit. The time frame for when the 4th time/space chakra will open for those Earth children born since +/-2000 is difficult to specify because of the variables in the characteristics of Earth's transition to the 4th Density experience. The majority of the Earth's population is still finishing its most recent 3rd Density experience while the 4th Density inhabitants are being born. The lower 3rd Density population continues to weigh down the planetary consciousness' escalation.

When the Earthly 3rd Density experience began, the average life expectancy of an incarnate mind/body/spirit was approximately 900 years. By the end of the first 25,000-year sub-cycle, it had dropped to approximately 700 years. After the destruction of Atlantis in approximately 8441 BC, the average life expectancy was only about 35 years. The cause of the decline in life expectancy was that the cumulative consciousness level of the population dropped precipitously over the term of the 3rd Density experience, and, even now, has only recently escalated to approximately 75 years.

Gaia, the 4th Density consciousness of the planet, is fully experiencing 4th Density and has progressed approximately halfway through the density's dimensions, but the residuals of the low-dimension 3rd Density population continue to work on their 3rd Density advancement. This adds to the difficulty in predicting when the new 4th Density residents, the children born since the year 2000 (and some others before then), will fully experience the 4th time/space chakra, but this will probably occur while in their early twenties. Until then, they will behave and appear to function much like the 3rd Density generations before them.

When Earth's 4th Density heirs do open the higher chakra, they will begin to demonstrate significant behavioral changes, equally as dramatic as when the 2nd and 3rd chakras open, because the changes will include a significant predisposition towards consideration for others, compassion, and caring. In addition to the 4th time/space chakra opening, they will have ceased incarnating into multiple simultaneous analog projections, which means they will have an increased energy flow and all of their Intelligent Energy will be available to power the single incarnation. The chaotic lower consciousness 3rd Density Earth experiencers should also be transforming because the mind/body/spirits polarizing negatively are being removed from the consciousness pool. These relocations will hopefully purify and stabilize the population so that Earth will be only a more stable 3rd Density enterprise and a 4th Density service-to-others experience.

Until a 3rd Density mind/body/spirit becomes aware, it will probably be living one timeline while distracted by aspects of several other timelines. In other words, it will be having the experiences and processing the thoughts of the predominate timeline but dreaming of other timelines running parallel to the one it is on. Both the timeline that it is on and the ones providing the daydreams are stories, and, because it is unaware, it often gets lost in the story(s). While it remains unaware and lost in the story, it can have little if any awareness of the self that may be living the story but separate from the story.

The story(s) is the play, but an actor is portraying a character within the play. When the actor forgets that he is only a character in the play, he primarily lives with the expectations prompted by the story, unaware of the truth, and so, he experiences stress. Stress results from trying to compel the play to provide the actor with what he needs but the play and all the characters in the play are just that, characters in a play, and cannot provide the actor with what he needs. What the actor ultimately needs is what consciousness is programmed to explore, which is love.

A timeline is chosen from within a set of timelines because the prevailing condition of the pattern of consciousness resonates with that timeline, and the experiences on that timeline will be most valuable to learn what is needed at that time. When we are unaware of "what is", in other words, the lessons of the timeline we are currently on, we miss the lessons most important to us at that very moment. When we are focused on our expectations of how things should be, we are trying to manage the world around us to meet our expectations. We remain unaware of what we can become aware of and the thing that we can control (change) to fulfill the most basic need that all consciousness shares.

When we are living according to our expectations we are attempting to "turn our wheel of fate". We are trying to manage the world around us to induce the "world" to give us what we need, which, at the level of consciousness currently being experienced in the Earth population, is love. While we remain unaware and lost in the authenticity of the character in the play, and even the play itself, we create stress because neither the character nor the play is real, but we remain attached to the illusion in the hopes that it will somehow magically provide us with the love that we need.

Instead of discovering the truth by exploring and discovering it within and through the self, we attempt to "trick" the world into loving us by conforming to how we perceive the world wants us to be. We fail to use the analogy process to truthfully assess what it is that we like, and settle for what we believe the world wants us to be, based on the false belief that "if we do conform", the world will love us. While we remain unconscious, we mistake the burst of energy, Intelligent Energy that we receive from winning energy battles, as love and settle for the photograph instead of the experience.

Ultimately, stress results from our expectation that the world can and should love us, but the truth of the matter is that the world cannot love us, and, until we reach this awareness, we will continue to experience stress in varying degrees of intensity. Reaching the awareness that the world cannot love us can come to us in one of two ways. Either we awaken, become aware, and honestly surrender our expectations that the world should love us, or we hit a bottom when we absolutely cannot keep doing the unsuccessful things we have been doing. We are compelled to surrender our expectations of being saved by some elusive "thing" in the world.

Finding love is a very skillfully designed process. We begin evolution pre-programmed to explore love, but we aren't provided with any guidance on what love feels like. The onus of discovering where love is and what love feels like is entirely upon the individual consciousness experiencing the 3rd or 4th Density, the individual mind/body/spirit. Until we surrender the perception of separation (AKA free will) sufficiently to open the 4th time/space chakra, we won't truly know what love feels like and won't be able to experience love.

Every unit of consciousness, every mind/body/spirit experiencing creation, is the Creator experiencing itself. The love that we seek is within every person but it is only accessible through the self instead of outside the self. Every person is the source of the love that they seek and a conduit for it. When we allow the ego to dissolve by surrendering it, we begin to feel the love that is already within us. We begin to realize that we are a conduit for love, realizing that we already have everything that we seek.

There is absolutely nothing that we need from the world, other than support for our physical body because there is nothing else the world can give us, it's an illusion. We have everything that we need within us, and, as we raise our consciousness level and align more completely with the Creator, the perspective that the world should and could love us transforms, we surrender stress, and we surrender our false identity expectations in favor of becoming aware of "what is". For the first time, in the long journey through the foundational and lower half of the experiential densities, we begin to know what love feels like and we know it feels good, so we want more of the good feeling. We become aware that our perception of separation is the only hindrance to our feeling love more completely, and so, we are motivated to evolve from the lower consciousness perspectives of separation to the higher consciousness perspectives of unity.

Love is something that we give or radiate because it's who we are, not something that we get. When we surrender our perception of separation and allow ourselves to be truly honest with ourselves, we expand our awareness. Expanded awareness allows us to feel more like a part of the Creator. When we become vulnerable, we surrender our false identity and become honest with ourselves, able to identify previously hidden obstacles to evolutionary advancement. We begin to correctly identify fear as the ultimate culprit that keeps us locked away from trusting ourselves.

Fear is a distortion of love, and, when we become aware of the fear that we have stored within us, it dissipates because awareness is both the discovery tool and the healing tool that allows us to feel love. Once we deal with the deep-down fear and become aware that we can trust ourselves, we begin to experience what we really and truly seek, beyond just loving ourselves. We begin to develop an intimacy with ourselves, and intimacy is really what we desire. We are the Creator, and, when we allow intimacy with ourselves, we are allowing intimacy with the Creator, the ultimate stability and unity.

There is a saying, "It's easy to be enlightened in the guru's cave but difficult when in the village." Enlightenment is a process, the process of surrendering perspectives of separation and transforming the perspective of the self to being in unity with the source. In the phase of evolution that we share, we still must participate in village life but we must also learn to regulate the degree of participation so that we can allow ourselves regular visits to the guru's cave. By doing this, we allow ourselves the opportunity to experience analogy and the potential to observe the variations in the awareness of the self between the two environments.

Life is an incremental process of learning about the self by becoming aware of the chaff, discarding it, and retaining that which is valuable. When we visit the guru's cave, we can become aware of both the chaff and the valuable, and, because of awareness, it's easier to discard the chaff in favor of the valuable. If we never visit the guru's cave, we will probably know only the chaff. When we allow our mind to predominately live in the guru's cave, only visiting the village when necessary, the village becomes the analogous antithesis of the guru's cave and our measure of how we are progressing with self-discovery.

The village visits become an opportunity to season or curate that which we have experienced in the cave and become even more aware of our true being.

It is possible to become aware while we participate only in village life, but it is improbable. To begin to heal from unconsciousness and transform the perception of the self through self-awareness, daily retreats to the guru's cave must be incorporated into a daily routine. When learning anything new and desiring to achieve a relative competency, it is important to diligently practice the new thing until proficiency is achieved. It is by becoming aware that we transform the self and surrender attachments to false expectations that cause us to experience stress.

To solve any problem, it is first necessary to become aware that there is a problem, and then begin to diagnose the problem itself. It is fairly easy to identify stress as a problem because of the unpleasant accompanying feeling or emotions, which often lead to eventual illnesses. When we fail to acknowledge and resolve stress at the time of experience (AKA the message about what needs to be healed within us), the unpleasant feeling usually escalates into a physical illness. The unpleasant feeling or emotion is simply a flashing neon sign pointing to something in our pattern of consciousness that needs to be dealt with.

We have reiterated numerous times throughout this writing that we learn by analogy. When we encounter experiences that repeatedly trigger the same unpleasant feeling or emotion and we repeatedly ignore the unpleasantness and continue to repeat similar behavior or interpret the experience with the same emotion, we are habitually choosing what we don't like over what we do like. We are tasked with exploring ourselves, but if we continue to unconsciously experience stress because we are repeatedly choosing what we don't like, we are failing to be honest with ourselves. Everyone is preprogrammed to need love. To motivate consciousness to explore itself in search of the love that it already is, it experiences the unpleasantness of stress.

Consciousness intentionally begins a 3rd Density experience without an inkling of what love feels like, but, by interacting with other consciousness and utilizing the process of analogy, it establishes an ever-changing pattern to its consciousness and begins to get an idea of what love feels like. The pain and suffering of stress, being unaware of what we like, and repeatedly choosing what we don't like motivates consciousness to become aware. The only question is, "How much pain and suffering will it take before consciousness begins to awaken and become aware?"

There is both a "you" that is living the timeline or story and a "you" that is independent of the story. Becoming aware is becoming aware of the "you" that is independent of the story and distinguishing between the two. The "you" that is enmeshed in the story experiences all stress and lives in the village. The "you" that is independent of the story already lives in the guru's cave.

Acknowledging the existence of the "you" that is independent of the story is "awakening" and the simple act of identifying its existence allows the work of healing to begin, but it is just the beginning. The act of acknowledging the "you" that is independent of the story allows your perspective of life to change, but you must still work diligently to surrender the attachment to the "you" that lives in the story. All problems exist in the story, so, the "you" that lives in the story knows only problems and attempts to manage the world around them to lessen or control the problems. The "you" that is independent of the story has no problems.

The "you" that lives in the story only has access to the "ego mind", but the "you" that is independent of the story has access to the "deep mind", the mind that is a diluted part of the cosmic mind and synonymous with the collective consciousness. When a mind/body/spirit acknowledges the "you" that is outside of the story and exerts the effort to more clearly distinguish the "you" within the story from the "you" that is outside the story, truth becomes apparent. The chaff becomes easily distinguishable from what is valuable and the chaff begins to fall away. The two "yous" still coexist but the perspectives of the "you" outside the story become much more desirable.

We coexist in both the metaphysical world and the physical world. The "you" inside the story lives only in the physical world and knows only its problems, but the "you" that lives outside the story lives in the metaphysical world, where there are no problems. Resolving stress is the process of becoming aware and getting to know the "you" that lives in the metaphysical world. It is the process of surrendering the attachment to the story and, in the process, surrendering the perception of separation, thereby elevating dimensionality.

It is the process of self-transformation from lower consciousness into the beginnings of a higher consciousness perspective based upon faith because no proof is available in the 3rd Density other than how it feels. The process continues, solely motivated by the increased awareness of the experiencing consciousness because it feels better, and the "you" outside the story is promulgated into the forefront of perception. As fears of surrender are overcome, intimacy with yourself, based upon trust, develops and the mind/body/spirit moves from being aware to being awareness.

The only thing that changes is perspective. The perspective of self as a victim of the story transforms to the perspective of Creator-ness, fully in control of how it interprets experiences. This change of perspective, as a result of self-awareness, is very humbling because it is ego dissolving. Those people polarizing along the negative path do not share this experience because they do not become aware and don't surrender their ego.

The immutable measure of how you are doing is how happy you are. The more you become aware and eventually become awareness, the happier you get, regardless of what is happening in the story. Stress dramatically reduces and eventually disappears, because with increased intimacy with the "you" that is outside the story, the greater love you feel.

In previous chapters, we stated that the Inherent Characteristics are hierarchical. We learn the lessons of awareness and enter the school of love. We learn the lessons of love and advance to the school of wisdom. We learn the lessons of wisdom and advance to the school of unity, and eventually to stillness.

Awareness, love, wisdom, unity, and stillness are just labels that we use to distinguish between the degrees of awareness of our Creator-ness. Awareness begins our identification with the Creator and love is just a higher degree of awareness of our Creator-ness. Beyond love, wisdom is just a higher degree of awareness of our Creator-ness and so on through stillness. It's a hierarchical scale of how much we are aware of Creator-ness.

Reducing or eliminating stress begins the process of feeling Creator-ness, and stress, pain, and suffering are the motivator to induce us to move from the bewilderment of chaos toward relative stability. We begin by understanding what stress is and beginning to surrender our attachment to the authenticity of the "self" that lives in the village. We begin to know the true self by making friends with the self that lives in the guru's cave.

Chapter 12

Meditation & Mindfulness

In the previous chapter, we discussed stress and how it manifests from a lack of awareness. We also explained the necessity of a daily visit to the guru's cave to permit familiarity with the "you" that lives outside of the "village" so you can employ analogy to distinguish what you like from what you don't like. To be able to do this, it is necessary to leave the village, at least mentally, to have a basis of comparison of the two "yous" that are participating in the current lifetime. This is how perspective is gained to allow a mind/body/spirit to efficaciously heal itself and advance its dimensionality during an incarnation.

The most effective tool available to accomplish these goals is meditation. While meditation may currently be fashionable in new-age circles and has received endorsement by some media outlets, it isn't widely accepted by the populace, probably because people find it difficult or lack an understanding of its benefits. A common misunderstanding is that a meditator can stop his or her thoughts and, thereby, escape stress.

This may be true of mind/body/spirits that have advanced to the upper dimensions of 4th Density or even 5th Density but the population of Earth is comprised of a predominantly 3rd Density population with an emerging 4th Density one. As a rule, 3rd Density and the lower dimensions of 4th Density consciousness don't have sufficient awareness to move out of time and, consequently, can't stop thoughts. As explained in previous chapters, time is experienced because of the constant flow of thoughts presented in a programmed sequence, so it is highly improbable that stopping thoughts will be possible until long after everyone's current incarnation is over.

In earlier times, parents would send their teenage children to live with a spiritual guru so that he or she could tutor them in spiritual matters. The teenagers would be an apprentice of sorts for some time until they had achieved competency in basic concepts at which time the guru would dispatch them into the forest, desert, or mountains, whatever was locally appropriate, with the instructions to remain there until they could stop their thoughts in meditation. After months or sometimes years, the students would return to the guru and confess either their success or failure.

If they professed success, he would send them back into the woods to meditate more diligently, knowing that they were lying. If they confessed their failure, he would tell them, "Now you are ready to learn." The guru wasn't being cruel but deemed it necessary for the student to come to this realization as a result of their awareness. The realization of their limited capabilities was a significant indication of an escalation in self-awareness and a significant surrender of the ego because the student must be honest with themselves to do so. From a stress perspective, they became aware of their expectations, surrendered them, and became aware of "what is".

The practice of meditation has very simple objectives because all meditation does is increase concentration and awareness. Many people believe they are good at concentration because they focus on projects at work, academic studies, or other activities requiring focus, but the concentration that meditation builds is not focused on things outside of the self. It is focused solely inside the self, where the guru's cave begins and the village leaves off.

Many people may also say that they are very aware of people and things around them or may even have keen intuitive insights into people or situations. The awareness that meditation increases is not the awareness of people, places, or things but awareness of the self. All of meditation's benefits are of and for the development of the self and not to enhance an identity, social position, or intellectual interactions in the world around them.

The purpose of creation is so that the one infinite Creator may learn of itself by experiencing itself. By redirecting concentration and awareness to inside the self, the two aspects of the self begin to rectify themselves as inseparable perspectives of the same self, working to fulfill creation's purpose. Exploring the self as completely as possible is everyone's purpose in life and the reason for participating in evolution. All other duties, purposes, or activities, the "story", simply provide the opportunity to fulfill the purpose of creation.

The objective of meditation is to improve concentration and awareness which then can be used to discover the self, explore the self, and make adjustments to the perceptions of the self to surrender free will intoxication and align more completely with the Creator. Progression towards this end advances incrementally but the velocity of progress depends entirely upon how diligently and honestly the individual mind/body/ spirit invests itself in the process. If meditation is practiced once a week or occasionally, then progress will be slow, but if meditation becomes a daily practice or multiple times a day, advancement will be much more profound.

The lifetime tenure of a meditation practice can be divided into two phases that are not mutually exclusive. Phase one is focused on healing the self of distortions collected during the period of life(s) when we are unconscious, which cumulatively incorporates all lifetimes to date, including the current one. Phase two begins when a relative degree of success has been achieved with phase one, and directly focuses on dissolving perceptions of separation. Practically speaking, the two phases overlap but there is a point when phase one is all but complete and phase two becomes the primary focus.

The incarnate self is an analog projection of the unmanifest self with the sole purpose of exploring itself through its experiences, interpreting those experiences from the vantage point of its unique pattern of consciousness, and then surrendering identity to allow for greater unity with the Creator. While we remain unconscious, we use a large portion of the Intelligent Energy flow to sustain the portage of the emotional baggage that we have created. Emotional baggage is the result of previous lessons that were not completed and keeps a mind/body/spirit stuck in a perpetual loop of experience until the processing of those experiences is completed. The emotional baggage distorts our perceptions and supports the pattern of consciousness that perceives itself as separate from the Creator.

Meditation allows us to turn off the perpetual input from our senses which allows us to re-task the expenditure of the energy required to run our senses to awareness. You become able to more clearly identify the temporary "you" within the story as distinguishable from the enduring "you" that is outside of the story. This activity allows us to gain perspective, by the process of analogy, of who we are. The thoughts continue to flow but, with additional energy and awareness, we can become observers of the thoughts as if we were standing on a riverbank observing the water flow in front of us. We have the opportunity to go into the guru's cave, away from the village.

While in the guru's cave, without the constant barrage of our senses and other experiential stimuli, our awareness becomes heightened. We can more fully become aware of the self outside of the story and begin to identify characteristics of the pattern of consciousness and emotional baggage that have been guiding the interpretation of experiences. This is important because it is through the awareness and surrendering of the emotional baggage that we accomplish the healing necessary to successfully fulfill phase one of the meditation process. The emotional baggage shapes the pattern of consciousness, which is a distortion of the self, and, when distortions are surrendered, it is possible to align more completely with the Creator.

The process of healing is an incremental one that only we can accomplish because we are the only ones that know our experiences and the only ones that can see or feel what is going on inside. It is intentional that we have these limitations because we are tasked with exploring the self from the unique vantage point that we have created. Many people may have similar experiences but no one has interpreted those experiences with the same emotion or intensity of emotion. Each of us is the Creator tasked with exploring the self from our unique perspective.

Meditation allows us to utilize analogy to advance dimensionality and transition from the chaos of the 3rd Density to the greater stability of the 4th Density. When we enter into meditation, we are visiting time/space. In time/space, there are no problems, so, we can experience a vacation from the chaos and problems of the space/time village. When we go on holiday, we return to our daily routine of experiences with a new, more relaxed perspective and the same is true of our return to the village from a regular visit to the guru's cave.

There are several good commercially available writings on how to. It is helpful to find a good meditation instructor that can guide your practice but the most important aspect of learning to meditate is just do it, and do it often. Also, finding a group or class to meditate with is helpful because it creates a shared energy that can amplify the meditation experience. Once you have attained a relative competency with getting into the meditation state of mind, meaning that you have at least identified the "you" outside of the story and can return to that perspective consistently, then it is important to begin to direct your practice to self-healing.

Ultimately, the objective is to become aware of thought (not stopping thought) but, initially, it's very difficult to identify individual thoughts or even identify a stream of thoughts, however, it is fairly easy to identify emotions. Emotions are part of every thought, and emotion comprises emotional baggage. In an analog projection, consciousness experiencing space/time, emotional baggage serves as an obstruction to the flow of Intelligent Energy through the space/time chakra system and emotions are stored geographically according to the chakras. The accumulated obstruction feels like a body sensation but the nature of the specific sensation will vary. Often, it feels like energy movement or tightness in a localized area but it may be more generalized and simply feel like resistance.

Most of the emotional baggage collected from 3rd Density experiences will have to do with either heartache or fear because love is what we are tasked with learning and fear is a distortion of love. Fear is like french fries at McDonald's. No matter what sandwich you get, it's likely that you are going to get fries with it.

Likewise, no matter what emotion is experienced, it is likely fear will accompany it, so there is usually lots of fear-based emotional baggage to discover and release. Fear is a 3rd chakra emotion and so we mostly store fear in the 3rd chakra, located in the solar plexus below the 4th chakra. While meditating, if you feel a body sensation in your solar plexus, it is probably some form of fear. Most emotional labels have a multitude of synonyms, and when we identify labels like fear or heartache, we intend to include all of the synonyms.

Love is the emotion associated with the 4th space/time chakra which is located at the heart and, while meditating or mindful, if you become aware of a body sensation in this part of the body, you are probably identifying the emotional baggage accumulated as heartache. Fear and heartache will dominate the focus of the healing process for most people on

Earth because of the design of our 3rd Density experience. If you have experienced physical maladies in the solar plexus or area of the heart, it is probably a manifestation resulting from the inability of Intelligent Energy to flow freely through that part of the energy system. The body is a manifestation of the mind and the mind applies emotions to thoughts as prejudiced by consciousness' prevailing pattern.

Guilt is an exacerbation of fear, stored in the upper portion of the 2nd chakra, and shame is an exacerbation of guilt, stored in the lower portion of the 2nd chakra. Females are usually able to identify obstructions in the 2nd chakra more easily than males because they are often able to identify physical sensations in their lower body as a result of their menstrual cycle. Nevertheless, males must work diligently to bring awareness to these areas of the body and effect healing.

Another area of the core body that stores significant emotional baggage is the throat, where the 5th chakra resides. It's difficult to specify a specific emotion other than the condition of frustration here but it is a prominent area of difficulty for most people. Such characteristics as responsibility, truth, trust, and self-expression are associated with the 5th chakra, and emotional baggage stored here can affect voice or physical organs located in this area of the body including the body's nervous system because the chakra incorporates the nerves in the spinal column.

A more primal version of fear will be stored in the 1st chakra, located at the perineum or felt along the pelvic bone. 1st chakra body sensations are usually difficult to identify for both males and females but emotional baggage stored here will manifest into systemic illnesses that affect the entire body such as autoimmune or skin diseases. Primal fear is associated with a fear of non-survival and is a fairly simplistic fear when compared to the more general fear of the 3rd chakra.

Awareness, as developed and focused in meditation, is both a discovery tool for what needs to be healed and the healing tool because when we discover the problem we are shining light into darkness. Emotional baggage results from the storage of the incomplete processing of emotions used to interpret experiences during our lives, and until the processing is completed, we haven't learned the lessons of those experiences. Emotional baggage may be accumulated from lifetime to lifetime through the consciousness pattern of the metaphysical self, so there may be a significant amount of baggage to release. The motivation to do the work is not only spiritual growth but physical healing in the current lifetime.

On discovery, healing might be immediate and complete, but minimally, a significant improvement can be realized. It is a process and requires a commitment by the meditation practitioner to effect changes. It may be a "one-and-done" experience or it may require repeated visits to experience the desired results. Results vary due to a variety of conditions including the size of the emotional baggage mass, the degree of the practitioner's awareness, or the intensity of the practitioner's resistance to letting the emotional baggage go.

Beginning to heal is not a complicated process. Sit down to meditate, surrender the mind to the calm of meditation, and become aware of where within the body you feel sensations. Some sensations may be in the extremities but most are going to be in the core of the body. There are numerous secondary chakras distributed throughout the body but they are all tied to the core chakras and working on the core chakras will most likely clear any obstructions in the secondary ones.

When beginning the work, use actual life experiences as a pointer to stimulate the emotional baggage that needs attention. Simply ask the body's energy system to bring to mind what experience needs immediate attention. An experience will come to mind and you can then use that experience to feel the emotion. Allow yourself to feel the emotion as deeply as you can and focus awareness on it. It will have a beginning when the experience is recalled and as the emotion begins to be triggered; a middle, until the emotion reaches its zenith; and an end, when the emotion ceases.

If the focus on emotion is lost during meditation, simply bring the feeling back into awareness and pick up where you left off. While focused on the sensation, it may move within the body. If it does, keep the focus on the sensation and follow it. Emotions are layered and, for example, may start with heartache, move to fear, and then move back to heartache for the next layer.

Even though we perceive an experience to hold emotion, emotional baggage is not tied to a specific experience but, rather, it's stored in a nonspecific bulk. Initially, experiences can be used to trigger stored emotions but relying upon experience will soon become ineffective because the experiential triggers become cleared. More of the nondescript emotional baggage will remain which will be apparent because the practitioner escalated concentration and awareness. While doing the work of healing in meditation, concentration and awareness will have been strengthened and these enhanced tools should be adequate to discover and clear the remaining emotional baggage without relying upon experiences.

After experiences have disappeared, continue the healing work by focusing awareness on the geographic area of the chakras within the body. By this time, familiarity with what emotional baggage feels like should be apparent, and awareness and concentration can be used to focus on the feeling and continue healing without a corresponding experiential trigger. The day's work is complete when there is a feeling of lightness, usually fatigue, and no other experience immediately comes to mind. The next day (or later in the day after some rest), return to the same routine and wait for either another experience or sensation to come into awareness.

With diligent, honest, and dedicated work, all emotional baggage can be healed which leaves the practitioner in a liberated condition, ready for new experiences that are not prejudiced by a predisposition towards the old emotional baggage. While emotional baggage is prevalent, experiences are interpreted with reactions, but after clearing, they can be responded to with a more appropriate emotion. A mind/body/spirit will continue to process thoughts but, with full access to its energy and awareness now available, experiences can be fully processed at the time of their occurrence, and emotions can be "laid to rest" without accumulating new emotional baggage.

Phase two of the meditation process can and often does overlap with phase one. Once the emotional baggage is substantially healed, it's time to begin working diligently on awareness of the unmanifest self, which will include connecting to the Higher Self. The pathway will have been significantly cleared of obstructions, and with the new awareness, the mind/body/spirit can focus on surrendering free will intoxication, which further heightens awareness and increases dimensionality.

It's the plan for all 3rd Density mind/body/spirits to go through the same process. It's how consciousness evolves and transcends the chaos of lower-density consciousness. It requires work, hard work, and transforms consciousness from a victim perspective in need of salvation to one in unity with the Creator. Consciousness learns of its power as the Creator by assuming responsibility for its advancement through the dimensions of the density. The reward for the hard work is an escape from chaos and confusion, happiness, love, honest intimacy, and, eventually, graduation to the next higher density where there is no pain or suffering.

Phase one of the process can take a single lifetime or numerous ones, depending on how seriously and diligently the mind/body/spirit undertakes the process. The results are immutable and inevitable for all consciousness experiencing 3rd Density. Those mind/body/spirits not ready for graduation from the Earth experience, indicative of not undertaking the process, have been transferred to the new 3rd Density experience recently begun on Earth, to begin another +/-75,000-year experience in the hopes that, in the new 3rd Density experience, they will awaken from unconsciousness sufficiently to undertake the process and graduate. There is no condemnation for not undertaking the process or graduating because "all is one" and creation is a thought experiment in which all of the consciousness' experience is the Creator experiencing itself.

Mindfulness is an expansion of what is learned in meditation, a way of living that permits a mind/body/spirit to take the awareness gained during meditation with them throughout the day. In other words, maintaining the perspectives gained in the guru's cave while returning to the village. Holding awareness inside of the body, instead of letting it wander unwarily on the outside, allows the mind/body/spirit to unattach from the intensity of the village experiences and the problems. Once the emotional baggage is significantly cleared, awareness allows the mind/body/spirit to be "in the moment" and experience life without, or at least with significantly reduced, chaos.

Imagine straddling the yellow line of a two-lane country road with one foot on either side of the line. One side of the road is the village and the other is the guru's cave. When the body weight is shifted to the foot on the village side more stress is experienced, more awareness is focused on problems, and less awareness is available to maintain the guru's cave perspective. When the body weight is shifted to the foot on the other side, the guru's cave side, less stress is experienced, fewer problems are encountered, and more awareness is focused on how the village is aiding spiritual growth.

Feeling the weight of the body shift from one foot to the other is very similar to feeling awareness shift from being the subject of problems to being the observer, the object in the experience. Learning to shift conscious awareness to the object perspective allows less attachment to the experiences and less subjectivity to the emotions. Emotions are essential to interpret every thought processed, but becoming aware of the emotions used to react to experiences allows the choice of selecting another emotion or using the same emotion with less intensity. This is learning of power from a higher consciousness perspective, lessening unconsciousness, surrendering free will intoxication, and learning who you are while incrementally unattaching from the authenticity of the physical.

Experiences in the village will make demands upon the mind/body/spirit's awareness to varying degrees. The mind/body/spirit that has become awareness can allocate awareness according to fluctuating demands of the village experiences, but, when the demand is over and the experience completed, retract its awareness and energy back inside the self to regain its guru's cave perspective, ready for the next experience. The mind/body/spirit will continue to have experiences but without exhaustion of its awareness.

Chapter 13

Control Dramas • Anger • Substance Abuse

Consciousness begins its evolutionary journey in the condition of primordial darkness or, in other words, from "scratch", without any preconditioning or programming other than a desire to return to its source. Inherent in the desire to return to the source is the need for love, which means, as we seek love, we are exploring the full range of love including its positive "feel good" and negative "doesn't feel good" aspects. As consciousness progresses beyond the phase of evolution that humanity currently shares, the exploration of love will yield to wisdom, wisdom will yield to unity, and, eventually, unity will yield to stillness. Once consciousness becomes stillness, its journey will be almost complete but it will continue its journey by surrendering the last vestiges of consciousness' distortions.

At every step along the way, the discovery and exploratory tool is awareness, and that means it's a path of discovering "what already is" but from a unique vantage point. Consciousness begins evolution in "primordial darkness" and everything must be discovered, but, because awareness is the discovery tool, what is brought into awareness is made prominent according to the discovering consciousness' likes and/or dislikes. Because of the nature of analogy, consciousness has absolute free will to choose "what it likes" or "doesn't like", and, from an infinite number of possibilities, is allowed to pursue choices based purely upon what it prefers. "What" is discovered is immutable, but consciousness is encouraged to create uniqueness in an identity through its independent interpretation of experiences, and, from the unique vantage point of its identity, it views the immutable self (AKA the Creator) differently.

In the foundational and lower experiential densities, consciousness constructs the uniqueness of its identity which perceives its discoveries as truth, but, because its perceptions are prejudiced by its identity, they are often contrary to the immutable truth. Near the end of the 3rd Density in the higher dimensions of the density, because of an escalated awareness, the building of a separate identity ceases and reverses the process because consciousness becomes able to recognize truth through a less prejudicial eye, transforming the identity-building process into an active endeavor of surrendering its identity so that it may experience greater immutable truth and unity with the Creator. Evolution reaches the peak of its separation perspective and now begins to surrender identity to feel greater love, stability, and unity. Resistance to unity incrementally subsides and eventually ceases.

The unique pattern of consciousness or ego that 3rd Density consciousness creates is predicated upon distortions of perception, the potentiated formation of which is intentional. An ego is shaped by how a mind/body/spirit has interpreted experiences, primarily during analog projections of itself into space/time, and consequently, consciousness is encouraged to "go off the beaten path" and explore itself through distortions without restriction. Because the design encourages self-exploration through distortions, it potentiates a high probability of consciousness accumulating significant emotional baggage that supports its ego identity and perpetuates its attachment to the distortions. Distortions and the resulting emotional baggage are variances from the truth which compel an ego to be inconsistent with the truth.

If for no other reason, we know emotional baggage is a distortion because it doesn't feel good, demands the diversion of significant energy to carry it, and requires a depletion of the mind/body/spirit's resources to sustain it. When emotional baggage is poked by experience, a mind/body/spirit is reminded of the baggage's presence and learns to avoid the poking catalyst so that it doesn't feel the stimulation of the emotional baggage. It creatively avoids becoming aware of the presence of emotional baggage by trying to make the catalyst, the experience poking the emotional baggage, go away.

To do this successfully, a person must attempt to manage other people and/or conditions around them to meet the identities' expectations, which is the essence of stress. Stress invariably results from the effort to preserve the authenticity of identity. The physical illnesses and mental/emotional manifestations of stress result from efforts to defend the identity from authenticity challenges. An identity is a victim's perspective and all efforts to protect an identity are purely defensive.

Becoming aware of ego distortions allows consciousness to heal the emotional baggage and move beyond its need to defend an identity, thereby allowing the surrender of its victim perspective in favor of truth. In a lifetime, we are provided with the opportunity to be "big": when the ego is allowed to be prominent, and "small": when the ego is significantly challenged, but the objective is to learn to be big and small at the same time. When we can be both big and small at the same time is when we will begin to see the immutable truth of who we are because the ego begins to dissolve.

Consciousness' perception of separation is experienced as an "identity", and the life of an identity can be graphed through the entire evolutionary process from 1st Density through 7th Density as

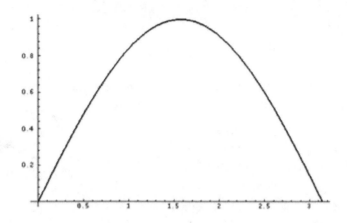

the upper half of a sine wave. It begins as a point in "primordial darkness", where the perception of separation is at its most intense, consciousness is unformed and in complete dispersion before an identity has been created. As it begins to interact with itself, it begins to form a 1st Density identity and the graphed wave begins to rise. In 2nd Density, the wave illustrating the identity's prominence rises even higher because awareness and intelligence increase, but so does the attachment to the authenticity of the distortions. In 3rd Density, the perception of separation, attachment to the authenticity of the distortions, and eminence of its identity reach their peak for most consciousness polarizing positively, but, towards the end of the density, as consciousness awakens to truth, it begins to decline.

4th Density is a transformation period and a healing opportunity for consciousness as identity begins to rapidly decline in favor of truth and the graph line descends towards greater unity. 5th, 6th, and 7th Densities pick up where the prior densities leave off, tasked with surrendering even more free will intoxication in favor of greater unity (the identity is completely surrendered at the end of the 4th Density). The entire path of creation is the path of evolution that begins with the perception of total dispersion, creates a perceptually irrefutable ego identity, and concludes with the complete surrender of all identity, all distortions, and total truth (AKA unity) with the Creator. The only difference between consciousness at the beginning and end of evolution is its perception of separation which potentiates the creation of an identity. Consciousness' creation of an identity has great value because it allows the Creator to explore itself by experiencing itself and affords learning for the Creator, both as the identity escalates and as it declines through the evolutionary journey.

Consciousness is very creative when it comes to defending identity, and creates a variety of mechanisms to avoid feeling emotional baggage being poked. The more creative it becomes, the more strenuously emotional baggage is poked because the avoidance mechanisms are predicated upon force and force creates an opposite force of equal measure. While consciousness remains within the lower dimensions of 3rd Density, still competing for Intelligent Energy through perpetual pyrrhic energy battles, one of the predominant behavioral characteristics is to use control dramas as the basis for interactions with other people to increase its opportunity to win energy battles and temporarily feel better. It also learns to create and use anger to manipulate experiential catalysts and avoid having its emotional baggage poked, but possibly the most devastating and significant avoidance behavior is the abuse of substances (drugs, alcohol, etc.). All three of these conditions are learned behavior, indicative of a lower consciousness, with the primary purpose of defending identity and avoiding becoming aware of "what" within the self requires healing.

Unconscious employment of control dramas, anger, and substance abuse are all addictive because they temporarily are effective in allowing a person to avoid feeling the unpleasantness of the emotional baggage and transforming from unconsciousness to being aware. They are uniquely addictive and are not mutually exclusive because employing one does not preclude the simultaneous use of the other two. A person can be under the influence of a substance while angry and simultaneously employing the control dramas. The control dramas are behaviorally addictive because they are temporarily effective and common to most people within the Earth experience; anger is emotionally addictive because it too is often temporarily effective; and substance use is both physically and emotionally addictive for the same reasons.

Consciousness within the lower dimensions of 3rd Density will go to great lengths, even death, to avoid identifying and feeling the emotional baggage. The emotional baggage can be perceived to be of tremendous size and intensity because it isn't always accumulated from only the current incarnation. Remember, an incarnate mind/body/spirit is an analog projection of its time/space self, and emotional baggage is usually accumulated over a multitude of incarnations and stored in the time/space mind/body/spirit as the pattern of consciousness. A single analog projection can and often does, access the entirety of the time/space emotional baggage in addition to the emotional baggage directly stored from its current space/time incarnation.

Control Dramas

The four control dramas are learned from interactions with other people and the selection of which control drama to use varies according to the personality preferences of the individual consciousness. Their purpose is to effect the extraction of Intelligent Energy from other individuals in daily battles for energy, thereby providing the participating people with a temporary feeling of identity strength and/or suppression of the emotional baggage. While the individual space/time analog projection will probably use one control drama method more than the other three, all four may be used alternately to obtain the desired results.

As consciousness becomes more aware and rises through the dimensions of the density, the use of the control drama methods subsides and eventually ceases. Employing the control dramas facilitates the extraction of Intelligent Energy from other people, and, for those people polarizing positively, the theft of Intelligent Energy reaches a point when it is no longer desirable or necessary to feel better. Those people polarizing negatively will not only continue to use them to extract Intelligent Energy from others, but they will also hone their skills to enhance the control drama techniques to exact even greater quantities of energy. The use of control dramas doesn't heal the emotional baggage, but it does help to remain unconscious and become numb to its presence.

Control dramas are behaviors and become personality traits because they serve as the foundation for a person's interactions with others. The control dramas, in no particular order, as represented by animal characteristics, are:

1. The "Tiger"
2. The "Opossum"
3. The "Spider"
4. The "Excited Puppy"

Each one of the dramas can be equally effective in extracting Intelligent Energy from other people, and, when alternated in the course of an experience, often create a push-pull effect to keep the target of the drama off balance or in temporary chaos.

The "Tiger" is a control drama popular with males because it is often most effective when employed by a person who has created a strong or dominating identity, but females may use it as a primary technique too. The behavior is characterized by aggression, and when coupled with other identity-reinforcing characteristics, such as physical strength, physical attractiveness, sensuality, intellectual superiority, or financial wealth, becomes a common technique to dominate and/or subjugate others. When it doesn't work or ceases to be successful in extracting Intelligent Energy in a particular experience, it will be exchanged for another drama, often the "Opossum" technique.

The "Opossum" technique is the opposite of the "Tiger", and is characterized by a "poor me" or "nobody-loves-me" attitude, feigning weakness, and may create a push-pull effect that can catch the targeted person off guard, much like suddenly lessening the tension on a tug-of-war rope. The same confusion can result from a person employing the "Opossum" technique first and then suddenly substituting the "Tiger", again catching the target person off guard after the target allowed their defenses to become relaxed. Unless the target mind/body/spirit is very aware, they may find themselves being dragged along in the mud of the exchange with no means to gain traction and regain their competitive posture.

A mind/body/spirit employing the "Spider" technique is very patient, plays "hard to get", and allows the target person to attempt to employ its favorite technique until it wanders into the Spider's web. The Spider technique is characterized by aloofness and is often used by people to appear above all the fray and chaos by mysteriously possessing some mystical knowledge or information. When the targeted person finally weakens and offers himself to the Spider to garner the mysterious insight, the Spider pounces and extracts the energy that was the object of its behavior all along.

The fourth control drama technique is the "Excited Puppy" which is often characterized by an invasion of the target's personal space and/or a constant barrage of questions. The invasion of personal space catches the target off guard or triggers confusion, and the constant questioning often prompts a surrender response from the target of "here's my energy, just go away." The "Excited Puppy" is the opposite of the "Spider" technique but it is often used in tandem, much like the "Tiger" and "Opossum" techniques are used. The techniques don't need to be paired as we have presented them but they often are because they work effectively together to create chaos in the target's disposition. Commonly, a skillful energy pirate will alternate between all four techniques until a suitable confiscation of energy is obtained.

In one form or the other and with varying degrees, the control dramas are consistently used until a person has achieved some degree of awakening. The more proficient the practitioner the more subtle the energy theft overtures may appear and the more successful the enterprise. When a person successfully uses these techniques, they are benefiting from an immediate "feel good" gratification by an Intelligent Energy boost in place of their need for love, but substituting the immediate gratification avoids the required introspection and awakening.

Because consciousness temporarily "feels better", it seldom is motivated to seek beyond immediate gratification, much like being satiated after a meal and not realizing that the cupboard is bare with nothing to eat for the next meal. The "control dramas" require the application of some degree of force to be successful, and as long it is successful it is probable that the practitioner is going to repeat the behavior until the control dramas prove inadequate or fail. The proliferation of control drama behavior adds to the predisposition toward a chaotic environment for all consciousness participating in the immediate environment. The behavior is common among lower dimension 3rd Density consciousness, continues for all consciousness polarizing negatively in 4th and 5th Densities, but ceases for consciousness polarizing positively near the end of its 3rd Density tenure.

The typical design of a lifetime for those choosing to polarize positively is that they will unconsciously battle for energy until they are unable to continue because they are failures in their energy-battling ways and become sufficiently aware, motivated by the pain and/or suffering that results from failure, to be able to decide that they cannot continue doing the same thing. They hit rock bottom because of their energy bankruptcy and are forced to change by ceasing to try to control the world around them to meet their expectations. It isn't required that mind/body/spirits enter an energy bankruptcy condition but humans have proven very resistant to change without an extreme experience as motivation. The alternative to the control drama energy pirating behavior requires consciousness to look inside the self, heal the emotional baggage, surrender its identity, and discover they are the source of what they seek.

The design of a negatively polarizing mind/body/spirit's lifetime is such that they will continue to find success in their energy-pirating enterprises so they are not motivated to become aware. The consistent success in energy confiscation reinforces their false identity and they practice enhancing the techniques, mastering immediate gratification from Intelligent Energy gains, but never knowing love. Exploring the self and surrendering identity versus reinforcing identity is the service-to-others or service-to-self choice of 3rd Density. The control dramas are simply a technique or created behavior to avoid becoming aware and doing the required work of sobering from free will intoxication.

Anger

Anger is another technique to avoid becoming aware of the accumulated emotional baggage and doing the work to heal the baggage so that a sobering from free will intoxication can occur. Anger is an emotion but it's a secondary emotion, a defensive emotion, created by the ego mind, unlike the primary emotions such as fear or heartache that arise from distortions within the chakra system. The primary emotions facilitate perceptual distortions within a person's pattern of consciousness and result in emotional baggage. The primary emotions offer potential lessons to allow a person to explore the self, and, consequently, allow the Creator, as personified in a person, to explore itself by experiencing itself.

Anger doesn't explore anything but allows a person to temporarily avoid feeling the emotional baggage stored within, and, much like the "control dramas", allows a person to avoid becoming aware and surrendering their free will intoxication. Experiences (AKA thoughts) allow a person to interact with other people, places, and things as either the subject or object to experience themselves, learn about themselves, and become more aware of who they are. Experiences are messages to the experience participants about themselves that are designed to aid them in becoming aware of the ego identity distortions, surrender them through awareness, and, thereby, become more attuned and in alignment with the Creator. Anger is a secondary defensive emotion used to make the experience that is triggering the emotional baggage "go away" so they don't have to feel the emotional baggage or identity beliefs that no longer serve them.

Whenever a person gets angry they are missing the opportunity to look inside and identify the underlying emotional baggage or false ego-creating beliefs being triggered by the experience. Within the emotional baggage is the lesson about the self that will allow the individual to heal the distortion, surrender more of their free will intoxication, and advance its dimensionality. Anger suppresses awareness and reinforces unconsciousness; therefore, it keeps us from evolving.

When consciousness becomes aware of what anger is and what it's doing, it can be used as a pointer to aid the development of awareness. Because it is easily recognized, when a person learns to recognize that anger is arising, stop, and look underneath the anger, it is fairly easy to identify the underlying primary emotion that is the real culprit in need of attention. Once the underlying emotion is identified, a person can use awareness to discover the depth of the primary emotion and allow it to dissipate. This is the healing process described in the earlier chapter discussing "Meditation & Mindfulness".

Substance Abuse

The last method we will discuss, used by mind/body/spirits to avoid doing the required work of healing identity distortions and evolving, is lumped into the category of substance abuse which generally includes all drugs, alcohol, and/or smoking. Substance abuse is more complicated than the previous methods because it adds the element of a physical distortion and/or addiction. A physical addiction makes the behavior more complicated because it distorts the mental faculties necessary to become aware, but it's employed for the same purpose as the "control dramas" and "anger".

Why does anyone smoke, drink alcohol, use drugs, overeat, over-sex, gamble compulsively, etc.? Without exception, the honest answer is to attempt to "feel better". So, what doesn't feel good? Without exception, the honest answer is emotional baggage.

The body is a product of the mind and the mind instructs the body "how to be" with every thought. Once the mind has instructed the body to include a need for a substance, the body will thereafter include, in its per thought report to the mind, the condition of the need for the substance until the mind provides a corrective instruction to the body that it no longer needs the substance. Just like when a computer is programmed to perform a certain task until it is instructed otherwise, the body will continue to tell the mind, with the processing of every thought, that it needs the substance.

This is true for other illnesses too. Once the mind has instructed the body to include the condition of an illness, the body will manifest the illness and continue to report the manifestation to the mind with every thought. Cancer is a prime example of this behavior. The body may be genetically predisposed towards developing cancer but the predisposition may never be enacted because the mind never needs to use the experience of cancer to guide the person's evolutionary development.

The potential for illness is often incorporated into a timeline as a catalyst for the awakening of the person during its incarnation or to keep it on the evolutionary path chosen before incarnation. If needed, it can be activated at the discretion of the mind or spirit to catalyze the person to redirect their timeline trajectory and realign with their pre-incarnate goals or mission. Franklin Delano Roosevelt (FDR), the 32nd president of the United States, was an excellent example of this.

FDR had a mission to alter the course of service-to-self domination built into his timeline, but the fulfillment of the mission required a very delicate balance because of the environment and temptations of politics that could distract him from the pre-incarnate mission. As a safeguard, polio was potentiated in the timeline, to be used as a catalyst to limit his ability to go "off script" from the pre-incarnate mission. As anticipated, he began to succumb to the temptations and his unmanifest self triggered the catalyst which successfully brought his incarnate self back to the original mission, but, had he not been so distracted, the illness wouldn't have been necessary.

Substance abuse hinders the brain's ability to be a clear channel, a filter, for thought and it is necessary to clean the substance from the body before any substantive awareness can develop. Lots of people experiencing substance abuse "get clean" over and over again but repeatedly relapse because seldom is there an adequate support system to guide them in their awareness development and emotional baggage healing. Emotional baggage is the underlying motivator for substance usage, and until a mind/body/spirit undertakes the task of healing the underlying baggage and developing awareness, the propensity to use the substances will probably remain.

All healing, physical, emotional, or mental, is achieved with awareness. Awareness is both the discovery tool and the healing tool, but it isn't an awareness of the world outside of the self that heals. We all are tasked with exploring the self and healing the self is only an elementary phase of self-exploration.

Chapter 14

Introduction to the Archetypical Mind

Included in the Appendix is a chart that will be helpful to your understanding of the information.[1]

Creation is a mechanism the one infinite Creator uses to explore itself by experiencing itself. It includes a series of environments that begins with Intelligent Infinity and becomes diversified with the creation of free will, the first distortion. Each new sequential environment is a conceptual refinement of the one above so that they appear as if a series of nesting dolls, one contained within the other that concludes with the environmental setting that you (the reader) are currently experiencing with your eyes, ears, and other senses. However, an environment, no matter how close or distanced from the original environment, is purely conceptual and has little or nothing to do with anything physical other than our distorted perception of its authenticity.

Time, a conceptual component of creation, is designed to be a theatrical script, primarily for 3rd Density, providing a series of scenarios or experiments that permit the exploration of the Creator by potentiating consciousness' ability to learn of itself, the Inherent Characteristics, by experiencing itself. All scenarios/experiences are replicated in a variety of condition-appropriate environments to allow diversity in the experience and to explore the depth and breadth of the lessons to be learned. Regardless of the environment or the experience, the constant objective is for the "Creator as the subject" to explore the five Inherent Characteristics.

The environments and experiences implement the theatrical production and staging of creation. The most significant aspect of creation is the "Creator as the subject", otherwise known as consciousness: the actor that is thrust onto the stage and costumed as the character to be portrayed. The "Creator as the subject" (a mind/body/spirit, AKA a person) is carefully prepared to make it possible to deliver a stellar performance, just as the environment and the script are meticulously prepared.

It may seem that creation has mysteriously and randomly developed and it is certainly true that there is a significant element of free will and randomness in the exploration, but "all is one" and the exploration of the self is infinitely experienced through the diversity of individual units of consciousness conducting their autonomously perceived exploration. A single unit of consciousness employs free will to explore itself from a finite unique perspective, but, when all of the units of consciousness are finished exploring an environment through a multitude of experiences, and from its unique identity lens, the experience will have been infinitely explored. Our task, as a finite unit of consciousness, is to explore ourselves, and through our autonomous perceiving exploration, we contribute a small part to the Creator's infinite exploration of itself.

Because the physical body costume is the only portion of the character portrayal that we can tangibly identify, we tend to believe it is the only preparation necessary for our mind/body/spirit's entry onto the stage. The body costume that we slip into at our birth is a significant contributor to the nature of our incarnate experience, but it is transient and only a contributing factor for a single lifetime. The single most significant element in shaping the consciousness pattern's experiences is the Archetypical Mind.

The Archetypical Mind is a process design or blueprint for processing thought that mixes and matches the archetypes comprising a universe. In our particular experience, nine archetypes are used to construct the Archetypical Mind because the design of the universe is founded upon these same nine aspects of the Creator. The nine archetypes are uniquely mixed and matched to form a series of modules that shape how a consciousness pattern and all of its analog projections will process thought.

If you imagine a person without the formatting of an Archetypical Mind being like electricity without a wire, you may begin to get an understanding of why an Archetypical Mind is necessary. Electricity, without a wire, cannot be easily channeled to perform work. Similarly, a mind/body/spirit, that has been distorted to function with a significantly reduced consciousness level (i.e. within the lower five densities) and without an Archetypical Mind, would be unfocused and unable to effectively do work. The nature of all work within creation is always to explore an assigned territory of the Creator through the concept of self. As we evolve through the densities the only real change to the mind/body/spirit is the perception of self.

As an individualized portion of the "Creator as the subject", each person, each mind/body/spirit, is a "self". The self is the assigned portion of the Creator that we are to explore and investigate. Regardless of the density of consciousness, the self is the only element of our experience that we may "know" and the only element that we may change. As consciousness evolves through creation, the concept of the self transforms from the chaotic misperception of individuality in 3rd Density to the ultimate perception of unity that characterizes knowing that "all is one".

We learn of the self through experiences and therefore the self is the Creator learning of itself by experiencing itself. As we learn of the self through experiences we are incrementally relearning about the Inherent Characteristics of the Creator. Just as every environment is a refinement of the one above, the fruit of every thought is added to our beingness and we become a refinement of our previous self. Because we are imbued with free will, we have the opportunity to choose whether we will use the thought to bring us closer to unity or gravitate further away.

Catalyst(s), delivered with every experience/thought, is our lesson for the moment, and while we remain lost in the throes of lower consciousness, we perceive it to be brought to us randomly as part of a physical "real" world that exists independently of us. We bring each other messages that provide us with the opportunity to explore the self and, therefore, explore the Inherent Characteristics of the Creator. The more aware we are of this process and the messages (the thoughts) themselves, the more productive we may be in our evolution participation.

You may ask, "So what, if thoughts or experiences are random and/or un-channeled? The exploration of the Creator would happen through randomness whether the mind/body/spirit is channeled or not." This may be true but the Creator, and subsequently the "Creator as the subject", is intelligent in addition to being infinite. Rather than relying upon "1,000 monkeys with 1,000 typewriters to eventually write a complete Shakespearean play", the Creator's intelligence prescribes meticulous planning, preparation, and design to direct consciousness to be efficacious explorers.

The environment is carefully designed and planned. The script (AKA time or timelines) is carefully and intricately written to specifically provide a variety of experiences and still allow for free will improvisation or interpretation. Awareness, the electricity within the wire, is contained within a conduit to allow it to improvise but also be directed to exactly where it needs to go to explore. The experiencer is guided by the programming limits of the exploration so that it stays within the margins of its assigned territory. The self, as perceived according to the degree of awareness of the experiencer, is its assigned territory.

The Archetypical Mind functions very similarly to a spacesuit because, when an astronaut puts it on, they are unable to experience anything that doesn't pass through the spacesuit. The spacesuit determines how he/she will experience an environment. Likewise, when we put on the Archetypical Mind, the Archetypical Mind determines how we will experience an environment and process thought, but neither the spacesuit nor the Archetypical Mind experiences anything. Consciousness is the only agent of change in all of creation and the Archetypical Mind serves as a channel to guide consciousness as it journeys through creation.

There are a multitude of Archetypical Mind designs within a universe, with each design incorporating only the archetypes selected to comprise the universe experience. All of the archetypes will be used but none can be added that are not part of the universe design. In our particular experience, all nine archetypes are used to design the Archetypical Mind which means that we have incorporated all five Inherent Characteristics, free will, and three archetypical distortions.

If a universe is designed to incorporate all 32 archetypes, then the Archetypical Minds designed within that universe will be comprised of the 32 archetypes. If a universe design incorporates only the five Inherent Characteristics, then all Archetypical Minds will be designed with only the five archetypes. The mixing and matching of the archetypes are intended to provide a standard that can be used to explore the Creator as completely as possible with the characteristics arising from the particular archetypical configuration. There are significant other factors that greatly vary experiences, even with the same archetypical selections, because of the variability of free will choices by the participating consciousness that allows the explorations to become infinite.

We often retain the same Archetypical Mind throughout our tenure within the foundational and experiential densities. The same design serves 1st Density through 5th Density, but, because of the characteristics of consciousness as dictated by the density, how it serves a mind/body/spirit in each density is different. 3rd Density and the early experiences of 4th Density are the only densities where mind/body/spirits are totally within time but the Archetypical Mind remains a spacesuit during the periods when consciousness is only in time/space. Consciousness doesn't function without an Archetypical Mind while it remains within the foundational and experiential densities.

The Archetypical Mind guides how thoughts are processed, and, since consciousness continues to wear the Archetypical Mind when it isn't incarnate, it will continue to process thoughts in time/space and throughout the remaining experiential densities, including 4th and 5th Densities, but it will have less sway as awareness rises. Consciousness continues to have experiences after it shucks the "mortal coil" that it occupies in space/time, albeit with less intensity because it will continue to process thoughts as the consciousness pattern. The primary difference between the thoughts experienced while "alive" and when "dead" is a change in perspective, which is significantly altered by the change in the environment, conditions, and the nature of its catalyst.

In time/space, consciousness doesn't have the veil or the forgetting. It isn't processing thought through a space/time analog self, but directly through the enduring consciousness pattern. Experience is still experiencing and learning but the experiences are much less intense than processing similar thoughts in space/time, and, consequently, much less productive in provoking exploration of the self.

The Ego Mind

The ego mind is a product of the Archetypical Mind while an analog projection's awareness is low. It is indicative of the 3rd

Density, the lower dimensions of the 4th Density, and of those people who have graduated to higher densities choosing to polarize service-to-self. The ego mind creates and sustains the perspective of an authentic physical world, and, consequently, sustains both low consciousness and the propensity to repeat the cycle of stress and suffering.

Consciousness swims within an ocean of truth but its inability to be aware of it is because of unconsciousness. Even towards the higher dimensions of 3rd Density, as it evolves and works to liberate itself from the constraints of the ego mind and the distortions that create it, it can more readily experience truth. A greater awareness in the 3rd Density exposes the deep mind, which is always underlying the ego mind and provides the ability to process thought through the lens of awareness. The design of the Archetypical Mind promotes the creation of the ego mind, anticipates and facilitates its function, and guides a person's transformation away from it to rely upon the deep mind as it grows through the experiential densities.

When graduating to the 4th Density as a service-to-others mind/body/spirit, consciousness will have somewhat transformed its reliance on the ego mind into the deep mind. If graduating to the 4th Density with only the minimum dimensional calibration necessary for graduation, consciousness will still have more work to do in the 4th Density to complete the transformation of the ego mind. When a mind/body/spirit is eventually successful in completely surrendering the ego mind, the additional dimensional accesses that permit it to move from a space/time perspective to a time/space perspective become available.

Upon graduation to 5th Density consciousness gains the added dimensional ability to create the appearance of an incarnate body to whatever form it may choose at the time. A 5th

Density consciousness won't usually project an analog of itself into space/time unless it does so on a limited basis to interact with a lower-density being. It will retain the time/space body but the space/time body will be discretionary and changeable as may be deemed appropriate for the prevailing experience. Consciousness will continue to process thoughts with the deep mind as guided, but significantly less constrained, by the Archetypical Mind, availing consciousness of a significantly greater awareness of truth.

Those polarizing service-to-self have a much more convoluted experience. Service-to-self does not transform the ego mind, however; they do gain significant access to dimensional abilities because of an increased flow of Intelligent Energy, resulting from a more focused ability to steal it from weaker people. Service-to-self's access to increased dimensional abilities is never complete or balanced because its access has been gained through reliance upon distortions and a resulting unstable force, without the balance afforded by following the course curriculum of evolution.

Geographically, an Archetypical Mind serves a solar system. Every planetary experience within a solar system will be based upon the same mind design which anticipates all of the foundational and experiential densities. If a mind/body/spirit shares or graduated from an Archetypical Mind of the solar system it is considered an "inner plane" being. If a mind/body/spirit does not share an Archetypical Mind it is considered an "outer plane" being. Sharing an Archetypical Mind does hold a certain heritage quality but the nomenclature of inner or outer planes applies only to mind/body/spirits still within the experiential densities. Once consciousness has attained 6th Density awareness, it may be an alumnus of a particular Archetypical Mind but it is no longer subject to any of its constraints.

It is common to be an exchange student to another solar system during a soul's journey through a density and experience one or more lives as a graduation candidate within the system. The visiting exchange student must surrender their home Archetypical Mind and don the one currently in use by the solar system being visited. Visiting another 3rd Density experience as an exchange student and wearing the Archetypical Mind of the visited planet can potentially be a difficult adaptation but the experience can significantly accelerate the liberation of a mind/body/spirit's awareness.

It is possible and common for a mind/body/spirit to permanently transfer from an experience in one solar system to another experience in a completely different solar system. More often than not, the two solar systems in the exchange will be sponsored by the same Higher Self or, at least, by the same archetype. However, there are exceptions as demonstrated by the many Zenoa/Earth survivors of the Maldek destruction that began evolution with a "LA" Higher Self and exchanged their affiliation for a "RA" Higher Self. Also, lots of other consciousness left the solar system entirely and transferred to other planets in other solar systems.

The population of Earth is a good example of mind/body/spirits swapping Archetypical Minds. Because Earth is a second chance planet, an amalgamation of 16 different 3rd Density groups were assembled here under the prevailing Archetypical Mind with only a fraction having originated 3rd Density with the same mind. Even though this behavior is possible, there are potentially additional complications for a mind/body/spirit in changing Archetypical Minds after a significant resume of experience has been accumulated under one. These complications are believed to have contributed to some of the difficulties that Earth's population has experienced over the 75,000+ tenure of the recent 3rd Density experience.

The Archetypical Mind Design

Earth's Archetypical Mind consists of nine archetypes configured into 21 modules. Free will is one of the nine archetypes and participates as the foundation for all of the modules but isn't specifically included in any of the mind's module designs. Free will is the first distortion of Intelligent Infinity that makes creation possible but the free will of the Archetypical Mind is a 6th Density fractal version of the 8th Density creating archetype.

The Modules of the Archetypical Mind

Earth's Archetypical Mind's 21 modules are divided into three groups of seven with seven serving the mind, seven serving the body, and seven serving the spirit. These three aspects of the self, the mind/body/spirit, are segregated into three columns with each of the seven modules pairing two archetypes and stacked sequentially within each column. The modules also serve as a flow chart of how a thought enters the mind and how it is processed:

Mind	Body	Spirit
Great Way of the Mind	Great Way of the Body	Great Way of the Spirit
Transformation of the Mind	Transformation of the Body	Transformation of the Spirit
Significator of the Mind	Significator of the Body	Significator of the Spirit
Experience of the Mind	Experience of the Body	Experience of the Spirit
Catalyst of the Mind	Catalyst of the Body	Catalyst of the Spirit
Potentiator of the Mind	Potentiator of the Body	Potentiator of the Spirit
Matrix of the Mind	Matrix of the Body	Matrix of the Spirit

← ← ← ← ← ← ← ← ← ← ← Freewill → → → → → → → → → → → → →

A thought process begins at the bottom of each column, with the three modules comprising the matrix category including the Matrix of the Mind, the Matrix of the Body, and the Matrix of the Spirit. The second sequential category is the potentiator category which includes the Potentiator of the Mind, the Potentiator of the Body, and the Potentiator of the Spirit. The matrix and potentiator categories are paired as a subsystem within the Archetypical Mind. Their function is to receive the fruit of the previous thought that has been brought into space/time from time/space and modify the mind/body/spirit accordingly, in preparation for the processing of the next thought.

The modification of a mind/body/spirit in preparation for a thought process reoccurs after the completion of every thought, making every thought a "point-in-time" experience. Once a thought produces fruit, the fruit of that completed thought is delivered to the Matrix and Potentiator to modify the mind/body/spirit before the next thought is attracted. The modification of the mind/body/spirit is the result of the fruit of the previous thought having been brought into space/time and modifying the magnetic nature of the person before attracting the next thought. All thought is processed in time/space and only the fruit of the thought is brought into space/time.

The third module of each column is the "catalyst" category and includes the Catalyst of the Mind, the Catalyst of the Body, and the Catalyst of the Spirit. The fourth module of each column is the experience category which includes the Experience of the Mind, the Experience of the Body, and the Experience of the Spirit. The fifth module in each column is the significator category and, as you may guess, includes the Significator of the Mind, the Significator of the Body, and the Significator of the Spirit.

These three categories: the catalyst, experience, and the significator are also grouped as a subsystem within the Archetypical Mind to guide the mind/body/spirit in the processing of thought. Processing a single thought through these three categories constitutes a single experience, the fruit of which will be forwarded to the matrix and potentiator categories to modify the mind/body/spirit while it remains within the foundational densities and lower dimensions of the 3rd Density. The Archetypical Mind does not "experience", but serves as a process template for the mind/body/spirit that is doing the experiencing.

The sixth category is the "Transformation" category and consists of the "Transformation of the Mind", "Transformation of the Body", and "Transformation of the Spirit". The "Transformation" category potentially participates in the processing of every thought beginning with consciousness' introduction into evolution but its contributions will usually not be recognized by the participating consciousness until the 4th Density. It doesn't significantly contribute to the fruit of a thought process until the consciousness can recognize it.

The seventh category is the "Great Way" category and consists of the "Great Way of the Mind", the "Great Way of the Body", and the "Great Way of the Spirit". The "Great Way" category doesn't participate in the processing of an individual thought but establishes the environment for the entire mind. The "Great Way of the Spirit" is the omega and the "Matrix of the Spirit" is the alpha of the entire process with all of the other modules falling in between these two parameters of experience. Twenty-one modules comprise the Archetypical Mind. Each module makes a unique contribution to the process of a thought and is integral to the mind's functioning. Productively contemplating the workings of the Archetypical Mind requires consideration of the contributions of each module individually, as part of the category in which it participates (matrix, potentiator, etc.), and as a contributor to the Archetypical Mind as a whole.

The mind/body/spirit exists independently of an Archetypical Mind but, when consciousness begins the evolutionary journey and puts on the spacesuit, it repeatedly modifies itself according to the results of its self-exploration. The modification begins from the condition of a clean canvas and follows its evolutionary development according to the design of the mind. By "design" we mean the mind/body/spirit is formatted according to the perspectives created by the conditions (distortions) and algorithms of the Archetypical Mind. An example of distortion is the belief that there is a physical world within a volume of space and we are inserted into it at birth which gives rise to a predisposition to be attached to the physical.

A unique interpretation of the experiences presented to the mind/body/spirit is the brush that paints upon the blank canvas creating a unique personality in all of creation. Painting upon the canvas is not so much what touches us, as it is how we touch the experiences we encounter. All experience is emotionally neutral, and consequently, the value of experience is a result of the application of emotions by the unique personality of the experiencing mind/body/spirit.

Through the design of the Archetypical Mind, the reader may also see the incremental nature of experience. All consciousness begins the evolutionary process in the same condition, as a completely blank canvas. As it is incrementally presented with catalyst within variable but carefully designed environments, it slowly deviates from the sameness and interprets experiences from a unique vantage point. Over a multitude of lifetimes, the uniqueness of a developed personality becomes increasingly diverse so even if a mind/body/spirit were to duplicate a catalyst within an environment at a later point in evolution, it would afford a significantly different experience.

The design of time and the environments of our experiences are intended to complement the incremental nature of the Archetypical Mind's functioning. The beginning of a 3rd Density experience appears to be full of incomprehensible "gross" experiences which have a significantly overwhelming effect, relatively speaking, upon the mind/body/spirit. As the personality develops and the person's awareness grows, gross content transforms into more subtle and incremental content because of increased awareness.

This is true of the overall journey through evolution as well as reiterated in a single lifetime. The gross experiences of youth, full of motion and chaos, potentially give way to the more subtle experiences of adulthood, assuming awareness grows within the individual. Of course, the individual is the magnet that attracts the experiences so the more unaware it becomes in adulthood, the more fruitful the experiences become as a person ages. A mind/body/spirit can direct the nature of its experiences by how it can increase awareness and balance the self.

The design always anticipates flexibility. If consciousness chooses to remain unaware and chronically repeat the foibles so characteristic of remaining in ignorance, it is provided with that opportunity for as long as it needs to motivate awakening. If they choose to shift gears and proceed more quickly along the path than was anticipated, that too is possible. The whole plan, regardless of how slowly or how quickly consciousness progresses through the plan, is to explore the depth and breadth of the self through awareness.

Chapter 15

Overview of the Workings of the Archetypical Mind

In Chapter 14, we introduced the concept of the Archetypical Mind as the process template for thought and began to explain the general parameters for how thought is processed by the mind, according to the Archetypical Mind that Earth experiences. This chapter continues where the previous chapter leaves off by explaining a general overview of how it works.

The purpose of a personality is so the Creator may learn of itself by experiencing itself, "uniquely". The experiential densities (3rd, 4th, and 5th) provide us with the opportunity to relearn of and about the Creator by exploration and discovery of the self. In 3rd Density, we are tasked with learning about the Inherent Characteristics through the lens of SA (awareness), and the Archetypical Mind is strategically designed to facilitate this. When we learn of the Inherent Characteristics through the lens of awareness, it means that we must become awareness through the opening of the 4th and 5th chakras (and potentially the 6th chakra) and then simply continue to have experiences but with the enhanced ability to recognize greater truth in each experience.

After we adequately learn of the lessons of 3rd Density and graduate to 4th Density we will relearn the Inherent Characteristics through the eyes of RA (love). To accomplish this we must become love, just as we are to become awareness in the 3rd Density. Relearning the Inherent Characteristics by becoming love is not the task of 3rd Density because it requires the foundations afforded by becoming awareness and acquiring the level of consciousness that corresponds to 4th Density.

The ability to experience the one infinite Creator is available in every thought but the design dictates that we proceed through the process incrementally so that we may explore the depth and breadth of every dimension that we evolve through. It is the completeness of every experience uniquely interpreted that is the goal, not the speed with which we may progress through evolution. No matter where in the evolution of consciousness we may currently reside, the experience is perfect. It may not be joy-filled or comfortable but, it is exactly what we require now because we have chosen it as a result of a careful reflection of our current needs.

Once we graduate to 5th Density we will learn to become wisdom and, through the lens of wisdom (LA), we will continue to relearn the Inherent Characteristics. Evolution can be understood to be a course of study in which we are simply progressing from one course topic to the next in the sequence necessary to enhance our greatest learning opportunities. In the process, we are systematically overcoming the conditions of 3rd Density that initially set us on the evolutionary track naked and afraid, and ultimately concludes with our reunification with the Creator.

The 5th Density is the last density served by the Archetypical Mind and the strategic placement of LA (wisdom) into the individual archetype modules reflects this. Towards the later stages of our evolution through the 5th Density, we begin to prepare for reintroduction into the 6th Density, the density of unity. The archetypes YA (unity) and KA (stillness), the focus of 6th and 7th Densities respectively, are included as a sub-current in all of the modules and mixed into various modules of the Archetypical Mind but we lack the consciousness to become unity or stillness until we graduate out of the experiential densities.

Each module of the Archetypical Mind has an archetype as an initial "object", or "logos", and as an initial "subject", or "sub-Logos". The archetypical characteristics of the initial object/Logos establish the characteristic of the module when we begin our journey and will continue to do so as long as we remain in lower consciousness. This is the period of our evolution where we are primarily learning what we don't like and functioning with only the lower three time/space chakras open.

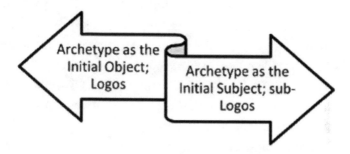

As we continue to have experiences, having developed a resume of things we don't like, we begin to activate awareness and either integrate the initial object/Logos archetypical characteristics with the archetypical characteristics of the subject/sub-Logos or exchange roles so that the initial archetypical characteristics of the object/Logos become the subject/sub-Logos, and the initial archetypical characteristics of the subject/sub-Logos become the object/Logos. The internal workings of the module indicate that the position of the object and subject remain unchanged but our capacity to prioritize the contributions of each does change as we increase awareness and select the behavior characteristics more aligned with our escalating consciousness. We regulate the contributions of the Archetypical Mind based on the recognition and balance of our personal power.

Where the initial object/Logos is a distortion (TA, DA, or Lucifer) the module offers an archetypical characteristic called a condition. The conditions create basic elements of the distortion of our 3rd Density experience and as we raise our consciousness these conditions become naturally surrendered to truth. The conditions created and surrendered to truth include such things as the ego and "I" perspective but also include other distortions such as time, movement, and authenticity of physicality. One condition is not necessarily limited to an individual module but may be created by the combined contributions of two or more modules.

Two modules begin as conditions while we are naive in our journey but we transform their contributions to become algorithms as we overcome unconsciousness. The other two serve as the starting point and ending point for the entire evolutionary journey through the experiential densities. One of these is the alpha and is populated with a distortion in both the object and subject position and the other is the omega and both subject and object are populated with the same Inherent Characteristic archetype, requiring the two modules to be harmonized and integrated into unity before we can complete the experiential journey. All of the other 19 modules are in between the alpha and omega modules and provide the mystery for the journey between the two.

Most of the modules are algorithmic and are constructed solely of Inherent Characteristic archetypes in both the object/Logos and subject/sub-Logos positions. Each of the 15 algorithmic modules provides a unique and specific function to the mind depending upon the position of the module within the flow of a thought process. The algorithmic modules do not exchange the priority of the initial object/Logos and the initial subject/sub-Logos but integrate them as we learn to raise our consciousness and balance the workings of the two archetypes.

Fifteen modules are algorithms because each one contributes only a portion of the solution to the equation we are calling the Archetypical Mind and functions as a single gear within a machine. When we can synchronize the functioning of the algorithmic modules and integrate the alpha and omega modules we will have achieved the criteria for graduation from the experiential densities (not just 3rd Density) and move into 6th Density unity. One might say that the entire Archetypical Mind's purpose is to create an enhanced illusion of separation from the Creator while providing a road map and breadcrumbs to lead us back to where we began.

As we relearn the Inherent Characteristics from the perspective of awareness in 3rd Density, the perspective of love in 4th Density, and the perspective of wisdom in 5th Density, we are overcoming the conditions and the Archetypical Mind. Conditions are just a result of the spacesuit effect and as we raise our consciousness through the processing of thoughts (AKA having experiences) they just dissolve. We naturally substitute distortions and illusions with the truth.

Archetypical Minds that serve other Logos (solar systems) within our universe will share a similar mixing and matching of the same nine archetypes that comprise our Archetypical Mind. The closer the apparent physical proximity to our solar system the more likely the design of the Archetypical Mind is very similar to ours. The further away the solar system seems to be geographically the greater the likelihood that the Archetypical Mind design will have significant deviations from ours.

Mind/Body/Spirit

Integral to the design and function of the Archetypical Mind is the construction of the mind/body/spirit. The ordering of the mind/body/spirit is a reflection of the function of the individual aspects as it relates to the Archetypical Mind. The function of a mind, any mind, is to process thought, and prioritizing the mind first before the body and spirit indicates that the mind is the primary processing unit when we begin, but also suggests the spirit's potential substitution of priority as we evolve through the densities.

The mind is created by the free will intoxication of spirit and, therefore, is the "Creator as the subject" and the spirit is the "Creator as the object". The purpose of creation is for the Creator to learn of itself by experiencing itself and so the mind ("Creator as the subject") is given prominence in leading the interpretation of experience until the mind/body/spirit sufficiently evolves to know that all is one and voluntarily surrenders its overabundance of free will to again become only the spirit. The body has no intelligence but contributes to the choices of the mind by reporting on the illusions of the perceived physical world and reflecting the condition of the mind/spirit balance.

The column of mind modules assumes the lead by directing a thought step by step through the categories. Until the mind/body/spirit activates the spirit portion of itself by opening the 4th time/space heart chakra, the mind functions as a tyrannical demagogue dictating the disposition of every thought processed based upon fears and biases. Its only contributing cohort is the body that is reporting the physical sensory data input to the mind with every thought processed and then reflecting the mind's decisions in its appearance and health. Once processed through the three experience categories of the Archetypical Mind, the fruit of that process is forwarded to the mind modules of the matrix and potentiator categories so they may use it to modify the mind/body/spirit before attracting the next thought to be processed.

The mind module of the catalyst category begins the processing of a new thought by accepting the new thought attracted by the modified resonance of the mind/body/spirit and begins the processing. The mind module of the catalyst category contributes its assessment of the thought and passes it along, with the input from the catalyst category, to the mind module of the experience category. The experience category contributes its input and passes the thought, with the cumulative input from both the catalyst and experience categories, along to the significator category, etc. When a thought is processed it is received into the category through the mind module, processed through the other activated category modules, and from the category's mind module passed along in sequence to the next category.

While a thought is being entertained by a category, the mind sends the content of the thought first to the body and, after the spirit portion has been activated, to the spirit with the instruction to report the module's input to the mind. Whether the spirit portion of the mind/body/spirit has been activated or not, the mind remains the decision maker of how the thought will be processed while we remain within the experiential densities. The mind reviews the input provided by body and spirit and rules on how the thought will be interpreted for the category before it passes the thought on to the next category above. The processing of thought through the mind/body/spirit is not a democracy of the three elements because the mind is the undisputed dictator until it voluntarily relinquishes authority to the spirit.

With every thought processed, the mind may choose to weigh the input from the body only, as is the case while we remain in lower consciousness, or receive and incorporate the input from the spirit along with the body, as is the case when the spirit has been activated. The more dictatorial the mind remains in processing a thought with only input from the body, the more stress and suffering the mind/body/spirit will experience. The more the mind surrenders control to the spirit, the greater happiness and greater ability to recognize truth are available to the mind/body/spirit.

This is important to understand because as long as we retain a significant ego (perception of separation) the mind resides under the influence of unconsciousness and will ignore the input from the spirit. That means that the mind is basing its interpretation of all thought with only the input from the body, which offers no added intelligence, and the mind's limited intelligence is predicated upon the distortions (conditions) of the Archetypical Mind. In other words, the mind, because of its limitations, insists upon interpreting life from the perspective of the ego, which is ignorance.

During this phase of evolutionary experiences, we are living life with only the 1st, 2nd, and maybe the 3rd chakras open while we experience what we don't like. We are exercising our free will by "turning our own wheel of fate" and encountering stiff opposition to finding what we like from all directions. At best, we have become aware but not yet able to become awareness and, therefore, have yet to begin to lift ourselves out of the chaos of 3rd Density, as imposed by the conditions of the Archetypical Mind.

Until we open the 4th time/space chakra, we are only able to experience a minimal consciousness level. We are functioning without access to the spirit portion of our being. We remain in pain and suffering, firmly lashed to the "Wheel of Samsara" and fully experiencing the "slings and arrows of outrageous fortune".

We remain mesmerized by the authenticity of the physical and the perspective that we are victims of life. We can only see ourselves as separate from the Creator and that we live in a physical world of dichotomy. The "conditions", created by the distortions that comprise many of the initial modules of the Archetypical Mind, are our reality and we are unable to see much, if any, of the truth in which we swim.

How the Archetypical Mind Works

By itself, the Archetypical Mind does not work. The Archetypical Mind is a process template that funnels a thought through its maze. A thought includes an environment and a catalyst processed and experienced as a holographic film (program) being played through a mind/body/spirit complex's projector which we interpret as life. The experience of time is the experience of thought being processed through the Archetypical Mind while we are incarnate in space/time. Thoughts continue to be processed through the Archetypical Mind while we are in time/space but, by comparison, it is like the bulb on the projector is switched to dim.

The environments that are a part of thought, whether in space/time or time/space, are a series of refinements with each subsequent environment being refined from a more general environment that precedes it. The thought of creation is the one relatively complete thought of 8th Density. The thoughts of 7th Density are less complete because they are more specific and more narrowly defined than the one thought of 8th Density.

6th Density thoughts are a refinement of 7th Density thoughts and are less complete than 7th Density because, according to the level of prevailing consciousness, they allow for a further modification of the ability of the experiencing mind/body/spirit to recognize the degree of truth available. The 7th Density recognizes less truth in a single thought than the 8th Density, and the 6th Density recognizes less truth in a single thought than the 7th Density. This is the process of refinement that allows the dissection of the mind/body/spirit ("Creator as the subject") through observation of the various behaviors that emerge according to its ability to perceive truth.

6th Density produces thoughts for the experiential densities and 6th Density is a fractal of 7th Density. All experiential density thoughts are refinements of 6th Density thoughts that are created or refined specifically for the experiential densities. The refinement of thoughts for the experiential densities anticipates a broad range of consciousness capacity to recognize the truth within thought because it incorporates three significantly different densities.

Thoughts are not further refined within the experiential densities, which means that thoughts are not refined into 5th, 4th, and 3rd Density thoughts. We will essentially process the same thoughts in the 5th Density that we do in the 3rd Density. The distinction between 3rd Density thoughts and 5th Density thoughts is the ability of the processing mind/body/spirit to recognize and extract the truth from the thought based solely upon the consciousness level of the individual(s).

Mind Fractals

All of the mind(s) of creation are a series of step downs from the mind of the Creator, which is identified as the "All Mind". The All Mind is inherent to the Creator's beingness and is indistinguishable from the wholeness of the Creator. The All Mind is a concept, an environment within which creation may be constructed and it is synonymous with Intelligent Infinity without distinction.

The spirit portion of our mind/body/spirit is the same spirit that is the one infinite Creator and it ultimately cannot be diluted or lessened in any way, but it can and is significantly obscured from awareness. It is the Polaris light of our beingness and it is our Creator-ness. The spirit creates the mind and the mind is governed by the degree of intoxication of free will to allow us to obscure our perception of spirit and allow us to participate in the different levels of consciousness we call densities.

The mind is our distorted perception of self. As the intoxication of free will increases, expanding the preeminence of the mind, we perceive ourselves to be further removed from the wholeness of the Creator. As we surrender our free will we simultaneously surrender the mind and incrementally increase the awareness of the self as the Creator again. We return to where we began, seeing it again as if for the first time.

From the wholeness of the Creator's undistorted being, the concept of mind within creation is both created and refined by application of the increased intoxication of free will, first to the cosmic mind of 8th Density, and subsequently to the 7th Density cosmic mind. The 8th-density cosmic mind is also an environment that serves as the concept for the development and construction of creation. It is only distinguishable from the "all mind" because it perceives itself as possessing free will and, therefore, being separate from the "all mind" of the Creator.

The 7th Density cosmic mind is a refinement of the 8th Density cosmic mind which means it perceives itself from the perspective of an increased intoxication of free will. It also becomes a mind/ body/spirit at this level and, in addition to the delineations of the Inherent Characteristics, it enters into the system of coding designed to fractalize the layers of consciousness we know as the densities, all made possible because of the intoxication of free will. The cosmic mind(s) of 7th Density also serve as environments for the further development, diversification, and construction of creation.

In 6th Density, the mind is stepped down again to become the "root mind", which again is accomplished by the increased intoxication of free will. The root mind of 6th Density is also an environment and it is constructed as a mind/body/spirit participating in the evolutionary coding system that governs fractalized consciousness. When 7th Density consciousness is defined as a fractal, as a result of the increased free will intoxication, it becomes a co-creator of the evolutionary process, as does 6th Density consciousness.

The root mind differs significantly from the cosmic mind(s) of 7th Density in several respects. The root mind of the 6th Density is constructed by increased intoxication of free will over the 7th Density but it also is more intensely directly feeling and experiencing the experiences of creation. It is at the 6th

Density level that distortions as archetypes are introduced to expand and diversify the development tools of creation beyond the Inherent Characteristics.

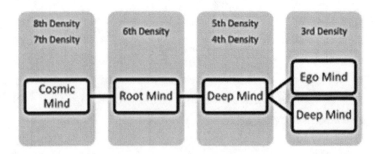

The deep mind of the experiential densities is a significant deviation from the root mind of the 6th Density. The deep mind is not an environment but becomes the primary experiencing aspect of a mind/body/spirit within the foundational and experiential density environments. The consciousness of the Creator Being(s) holds the perspective of free will, but within the experiential densities (deep mind), significant additional free will is added to the extent that it constructs an ego.

Even more free will is added to further intoxicate consciousness in the foundational and experiential densities but, in addition, consciousness is modified from a 6th Density level to reduce its working ability. A reduction in working ability is accomplished by restricting the flow of Intelligent Energy through the mind/body/spirit's energy system which functions similarly to installing a governor on the fuel injection system of your car. The full potential of your car's engine remains intact, but because it cannot get enough fuel to burn it can only access a limited portion of its potential power. The restricted flow of energy significantly compounds the intoxicating effects of free will by limiting the mind/body/spirit's working capacity by depriving it of the Intelligent Energy (fuel) that it needs to realize its potential power.

Within the experiential densities, the 5th Density experiences the greatest flow of Intelligent Energy (fuel) and functions with the greatest capacity to experience the most complete truth in the thoughts that it processes. The 4th Density experiences an increased flow of Intelligent Energy over the 3rd Density but less than the 5th Density. 3rd Density is the most deprived of the Intelligent Energy flow within the experiential densities which allows for the creation of the ego mind and the extreme perception of separation from the Creator that begins the 3rd Density journey. Regardless of the chaos that may ensue from the domination of the ego mind at the early stages of 3rd Density, the deep mind is always prevalent, running like an underground river underneath the turbulence of the ego mind.

All mind/body/spirits enjoying an experiential density experience the same potential flow of Intelligent Energy as every other mind/body/spirit sharing the density. In the 3rd Density, the flow of Intelligent Energy through the space/time chakra system becomes baffled because of the collection of emotional baggage. Healing, in the 3rd Density, is the process of clearing the emotional baggage through awareness to facilitate the free flow of Intelligent Energy through the time/space and space/time chakra system enough to allow the further opening of the time/space chakras. It is simply the process of surrendering the chaos and distortions of the ego mind to allow the mind/body/spirit to function at its full capacity, which signals its readiness to do the 4th Density work.

The ego is the result of enhancing free will to the point of establishing the ego mind as the governing aspect of the mind/body/spirit in 3rd Density and the service-to-self factions in all experiential densities. In the 3rd Density, the ego (AKA ego mind) is dominant while the mind/body/spirit remains within the ignorance of "unconsciousness" and the throes of the resulting chaos. For those polarizing service-to-others, evolution through the experiential densities is the process of surrendering the ego mind to incrementally allow the experience of the deep mind.

Chapter 16

The Ego Mind • Transcending Minds • The Thought Cycle

Beginning with the cosmic mind of 7th Density the environmental refinements of each fractal and diversification assume a "racial mind" quality. For example, RA (love) is an Inherent Characteristic of the Creator and it's distinguishable from the other four Inherent Characteristics. The distinguishable qualities of love become manifest in experiences as behavioral characteristics and, relatively speaking, assume racial qualities that define the nature of a mind by fractalization of the original template. In the Creator Being densities, the behavioral characteristics are only perceptible because of the awareness of higher consciousness but, as consciousness is increasingly intoxicated with free will, the distinguishable characteristics become ever more apparent.

The same is true of each of the other four Inherent Characteristics, and the racial qualities of each become further refined with each new diversification or dilution. Paradoxically, even in the lower densities, the delineation of an Inherent Characteristic does not isolate or completely segregate that characteristic from the other four aspects. In other words, LA (wisdom) is still love, stillness, unity, and awareness, but the dominance of consciousness is that of LA which is what provides the racial aspect and the diversity of experience interpretation.

The dominance of the mind as the prominent aspect of the mind/body/spirit makes the racial mind qualities possible and the concept of segregating consciousness into a mind/body/spirit begins in the 7th Density and is further fractalized into the 6th Density with the creation of the "root mind". 6th Density's root mind is created within the flavoring of a racial mind of the 7th Density Inherent Characteristic. In addition to the additional 26 distortions that are created in the 6th Density and become archetypes at this level, experience below the 6th Density becomes even more diverse because intelligence itself becomes a variable.

In the mind/body/spirits of the 6th and 7th Creator Being Densities, intelligence is indistinguishable from the corpus of the mind, which means that all 6th and 7th Density consciousness shares the same access to intelligence capabilities. When the root mind is fractalized into the deep mind, consciousness emerges with the ability to segregate intelligence from the corpus of the mind and make it a variable. Varying intelligence within mind/body/spirits makes every experience infinitely more diverse in addition to the already infinite diversity afforded by changes in consciousness level, the environment, and a variety of catalysts.

Free will intoxication fractalizes consciousness and creates the mind along a vertical scale with each new fractal behaving in a manner less in line with the source but essentially the same as every other aspect of consciousness fractalized to that degree of intoxication. The chakra system, the time/space body, is incorporated into the design of consciousness' experiences which allows consciousness with the same placement along a vertical scale to interpret experiences according to analogy or what it prefers, which allows consciousness to explore itself along both a horizontal and diagonal scale. When access to intelligence is made a variable in the experiential and foundational densities, consciousness can explore itself along an unstructured fourth measurement which is difficult for us to illustrate other than as an untethered cloud overlaying the first three scales.

The vertical scale is the exploration of the self according to awareness, the horizontal scale is the exploration according to love, the diagonal scale is the exploration according to wisdom, and the unstructured fourth measurement is an expansion beyond the confines of a scale and is the exploration according to unity. There is still a fifth measurement that is even more difficult to conceive of that is the exploration according to stillness. The combination of distortions of consciousness allows the Creator to know itself by experiencing itself completely and deeply because it is the infinitely incremental exploration of infinity, according to the Inherent Characteristics.

In 3rd Density, after opening the heart chakra and activating the spirit portion of the mind/body/spirit, consciousness begins to be able to intuitively directly experience the Creator. The person becomes awareness and can learn of the Inherent Characteristics through the lens of awareness. Until consciousness sufficiently surrenders free will to allow itself to have a direct intuitive experience, it is primarily repeating the cycle of collecting more of what it doesn't like. A person is relying upon limited and variable access to intelligence to make it more successful in a minute-by-minute immediately gratifying but pyrrhic battle for increased energy to feel better.

The Archetypical Mind is designed for the foundational and experiential densities because it directs and motivates consciousness to explore the Inherent Characteristics based on what it prefers but restricts it from wandering too far off the desired path of evolution. There is a dramatic difference in the purpose, function, and abilities of each foundational or experiential density but the Archetypical Mind is designed to serve each of these densities without change. That is, the design of the Archetypical Mind doesn't change but the experiencing consciousness changes and, consequently, how the Archetypical

Mind serves the journey through evolution in each density level is significantly different.

The Ego Mind

The Archetypical Mind and the deep mind serve all five foundational and experiential densities but 3rd Density contends with the most intense conditions created by the mind that obscures a person's authentic self-perception. The deep mind, the authentic mind of the experiential densities, is obscured within the foundational densities too but the awareness and intelligence of consciousness within these lowest densities make it almost irrelevant. Within the 3rd Density, the Archetypical Mind creates the ego mind, which serves as a veneer over the deep mind and occludes the deep mind from detection until we begin to intentionally explore the self below the surface of daily "village life". The veneer of a mind called the ego mind is steeped in the illusions of the distortions and conditions intentionally devised by the Archetypical Mind which deceptively endears a 3rd Density graduation candidate to its fantasies of the authenticity of the distortions and conditions.

Especially in the elementary dimensions of 3rd Density, the fantasies or conditions are significant and severe, and a belief in their authenticity often becomes intensified as the mind/body/spirit begins to have experiences through processed thoughts. An attachment to the authenticity of the beginning conditions, by design, is how all consciousness begins its 3rd Density journey. The conditions include ignorance, innocence, primordial darkness, constant movement or change, and a few others that are secondary to these basic distortions but the effect is that the unit of consciousness beginning the journey is wiped clean of any experiential biases that could contaminate the uniqueness of its 3rd Density experience.

The conditions of innocence and primordial darkness are intensified by causing the mind/body/spirit to be mentally and, consequently, physically in constant motion. While consciousness remains within the lower dimensions of the density, movement ensures perceptual chaos and is a foundational condition of 3rd Density consciousness in the universe of our shared experience. It's also a basic mechanism that motivates an organism to explore itself through interactions with other consciousness and its environment.

Innocence and movement are cornerstones of the ego mind and significantly contribute to the creation of consciousness' unique pattern. Movement is change and it is necessary to experience constant change to employ an analogy, the mechanism consciousness uses to choose "what it likes" over "what it doesn't like". The Creator is "stability" and the more intensely consciousness perceives itself to be separated from the Creator, the greater its feeling of chaos. Chaos doesn't feel good, and so, consciousness experiencing perceived chaos is motivated to seek the stability of higher consciousness as it incrementally evolves closer to the Creator (AKA returning to source).

The 1st, 3rd, and 5th Densities and 1st, 3rd, and 5th chakras are considered primary levels. 1st Density begins in complete dispersion and concludes with relative unity as consciousness coalesces into a planet. 3rd Density begins as a dispersion with consciousness experiencing an independent identity in isolation and concludes with it becoming awareness and partially surrendering the independent identity perspective. 5th Density begins with the initial perspective of a social memory complex comprised of a multitude of individual mind/body/spirits and concludes with the social memory complexes bonding into unity and graduating to the unity of 6th Density.

Consciousness, in the experience of 3rd Density, begins with the mind portion of the mind/body/spirit within the

Archetypical Mind being programmed to perceive itself as independent of every other mind/body/spirit, the Creator, and also holding an "I" perspective. The ego is predicated upon this perception, that a person is separate and autonomous in the creation and must figure out how to survive and prosper. The ego mind develops from the resulting mindset created by high levels of intoxication of free will that causes a mind/body/spirit operating with a reduced flow of Intelligent Energy to believe that it is completely separate from the Creator, innocent, and dealing with constant change. The ego mind allows the creation of fear, which is a distortion and the antithesis of love, and allows consciousness to explore "what it doesn't like" so that it may discern "what it does like".

The ego mind is the initially dominant mind that interprets thoughts, while consciousness remains within the lower dimensions of the density, but also guides a person from innocence to awakening by directing it to experience repeated stress and suffering. A mind/body/spirit experiences primarily what it doesn't like while it remains under its umbrella. The nature of its experience is the result of an aggregate of conditions that cumulatively serve as a negative motivation for it to evolve in the form of stress and suffering. It is the stick that drives it forward, motivating it to escape the pain until it tastes the carrot and shifts its motivation from avoiding the negative to seeking more of the positive.

While consciousness remains within the confines of the ego mind and perceives itself as separate from the Creator, it will perceive itself as a victim. There are three stages of victimhood and consciousness will cycle through the three stages which begin with the common view of the world as hostile, making it necessary for it to constantly battle for survival. Victimhood progresses from playing on the battleground as a loser to playing on the battleground as a winner when it improves its playing skills and becomes an aggressor. The third stage of victimhood, the stage before it begins to surrender the ego mind into the deep mind, is the rescuer when its perceptions are focused on the need to rescue others from the battlefield, transforming the center of its focus from the self to others.

The battle raging among consciousness, because of the limited perceptions of the ego mind or minds, is a product of the limitations and confines of the lower three time/space chakras and the distortions created by the Archetypical Mind. The process of surrendering the ego mind to the deep mind coincides with the beginning of the heart chakra opening and radiation of love in thought processes, instead of vacillating between radiating and absorbing the energy. The ego mind, the interpreter and promulgator of stress and suffering, will be surrendered soon after graduation to 4th Density if consciousness is polarizing service to others. If it is choosing to polarize service-to-self, the calamities created by the ego mind become enhanced and the ego mind is not surrendered until it cycles through the service-to-self evolutionary process to find itself returning to the evolutionary point of departure where it dropped out of school.

Mind/body/spirits can flirt with the connection to the deep mind in 3rd Density, as it awakens and intentionally works to raise its consciousness, but being out of the ego mind and fully within the territory of the deep mind usually doesn't occur until after some tenure in 4th Density. A mind/body/spirit can intuitively connect to the deep mind when it retreats to the "guru's cave" while in meditation. It is between the thoughts attracted and processed with the ego mind that it sinks into the awareness of the deep mind and begins to have direct intuitive experiences of the Creator.

Through the deep mind, consciousness spiritually advances and accrues knowledge of the Inherent Characteristics, incorporates that knowledge into its "beingness", and carries it forward from lifetime to lifetime. Clinging to the ego mind perpetuates its stay within the Wheel of Samsara, but surrendering it sets it free from the cycle of stress and suffering. Developing awareness by becoming aware surpasses the confines of the ego mind when it awakens the spirit portion of its mind/body/spirit and activates the 4th time/space heart chakra.

Transcending Minds

The Archetypical Mind facilitates the conditions of the ego mind from the beginning of consciousness' introduction into the evolutionary process. It is the mind that completely perceives itself as separate from the Creator and contributes to the creation of the "I" perspective. We have described the service-to-self path as holding a different philosophy than service-to-others but the philosophy is founded upon the Archetypical Mind's creation of the ego mind and the resulting fear of surrendering the ego to a unity perspective that spawns its creation. The service-to-self path is founded upon the ignorance of the fallacy of the identities' authenticity and fear of their loss of identity.

As consciousness graduates to the 4th Density service-to-others' experience, attachment to the ego mind decreases and the deep mind or spirit emerges more prominently as the dominant portion of the mind/body/spirit. Even in 3rd Density, as consciousness progresses in polarization towards service-to-others and alignment with the Higher Self, it begins to lessen the domination of the ego mind and begins to experience the connection to the deep mind. Development of inward awareness is the tool that allows a mind/body/spirit to surrender the ego mind's white-knuckled grip, and begin to open the 4th heart chakra and awaken the spirit.

The ego mind keeps consciousness attached to the authenticity of the physical and tied to the lower dimensions of the density. Only when it begins to surrender the ego mind is it able to experience the qualities of the Inherent Characteristics of the Creator through the lens of awareness and allow them to become a more radiant part of the self. A rising tide lifts all boats and this occurs simultaneously with the opening of the heart chakra, which only occurs for those polarizing to the service-to-others path.

Even in 3rd Density, the deep mind, which is the same as the cosmic mind stepped down to the capabilities of consciousness within the experiential densities, serves as background music to the ego mind. It is always there, waiting for a mind/body/spirit to recognize it, pay attention, and allow its melodic harmonies to pervade its awarenesses. Obtaining an understanding of the workings of the Archetypical Mind aids a mind/body/spirit in the process of transforming the ego mind and becoming aware that the deep mind is the subtle backdrop to its entire experience of 3rd Density.

Unlike the ego mind, consciousness never transcends the deep mind. The deep mind expands from the limitations of 4th Density awareness into 5th Density awareness. From the 5th Density, it grows and expands into the root mind of the 6th Density and eventually into the cosmic mind of the 7th and 8th Densities.

Truth is infinite and an unchanging constant, never varying from its completeness, however, consciousness' capacity to be aware of truth varies with its degree of sobering from its free will intoxication and its surrendering of its attachment to the distortions. The mind is the discovery tool that allows the Creator to observe and experience itself, thereby learning of itself. It is through the mind that consciousness rediscovers truth and knows itself as the truth in which it swims.

The Thought Cycle

The Archetypical Mind is the design for how a thought is processed and the processing of thought is how experience is accomplished through a subject/object interaction. Upon completion of the processing of the thought and before the attraction of the next thought, a mind/body/spirit becomes a "point-in-time" fractal of the Creator. It is modified from the previous pattern of consciousness by adding the fruit of the newly completed thought to create a new pattern of consciousness, albeit a possibly minutely perceptible modification. The exploration of infinity is accomplished infinitely through incremental steps.

The Archetypical Mind that Earth experiences creates seven conditions at the beginning of the evolutionary journey. Consciousness processes thoughts throughout its tenure in the lower five densities but, beginning midway through the 3rd Density, it will begin to work and overcome these seven conditions which will allow it to potentially experience greater truth in every succeeding thought. The seven conditions created by the Archetypical Mind create the illusions or conditions that make the experiential densities possible and define the evolutionary process for consciousness experiencing our solar system.

We have already disclosed the creation of the ego mind and referenced the "I" perspective as two of the conditions created. The other five conditions created include the perceptions of space as a volume, perception, and authenticity of physicality, motion, bodily health or illness, and ego-defining biases and prejudices. The lower the consciousness the more adamantly the 3rd Density mind/body/spirit adheres to the "authenticity" of a physical world experience and supports the perception that its existence is irrefutable.

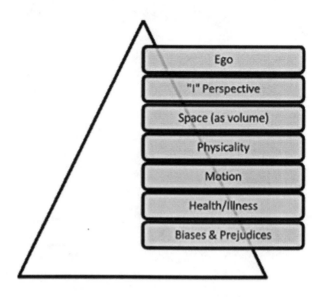

The seven conditions are either reinforced or reduced with the process of every thought. While consciousness remains within the foundational or experiential densities, the processing of thought consists of a mind/body/spirit:

1. beginning as a "pattern of consciousness",
2. attracting a thought,
3. processing a thought,
4. modifying the pattern of consciousness by the incorporation of the fruit of the process results, and
5. the attraction of another thought to repeat the cycle based upon the condition of the newly modified pattern of consciousness.

For every thought that we attract the process is repeated until it completes a full cycle through the Archetypical Mind. While we remain within the foundational or experiential densities there is never a point when a thought is not somewhere in the process. This means that we experience the Archetypical Mind structure in both space/time (while we are incarnate) and time/space (while we are "in-between" lives).

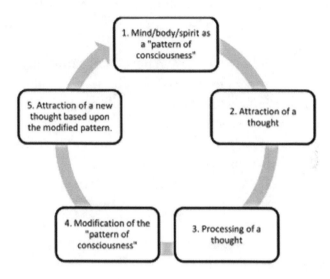

The process is infinitely repeated and can be illustrated as either an ascending or descending spiral. Ideally, the modification will incrementally create an ascending spiral and bring the mind/body/spirit more in alignment with the Higher Self by a reduction of the belief in the irrefutability of the conditions. In this case, the processing of the next thought will reveal greater truth than the one before. However, this is not a requirement and seldom works so ideally until we awaken, open the 4th chakra, and begin to surrender the authenticity of the conditions or distortions.

The spiral in the Earth experience has frequently become more of a repeating flat circle because of the chaotic battle between service-to-self and service-to-others factions. This has created a condition of spiritual entropy. The cycle can become a descending spiral, moving the object further away from alignment with the Higher Self which results in increased fear and polarization towards service-to-self. The direction through evolution is chosen by the individual mind/body/spirit but the direction is seldom consistent until it makes the aware choice of whether it will polarize positively or negatively.

The Body in the Archetypical Mind

As part of the design of the Archetypical Mind, a mind/body/ spirit chooses the healthy functioning of the body with every thought processed. The incarnate body is part of the timeline chosen to experience the incarnation, but the health and/or physical condition of the incarnate body is a manifestation of the choices made. For most people, the body paraded around during an incarnation becomes a monitor for the choice of balance between the ego mind and the spiritual deep mind.

The walking around body of space/time, the analog projection of our time/space self, is only a costume donned to play the timeline role being experienced. The time/space self also has an enduring body which, in the experiential densities, consists of the yellow-, green-, or blue-ray body that will remain throughout the evolutionary journey and reflect the pattern of consciousness created through experiences. The costume bodies, the analog projection into space/time, will die at the appropriate time and disappear with the termination of the character role being portrayed.

The Archetypical Mind in Space/time and Time/space

While consciousness remains within the experiential densities there is no period that it isn't within the guiding influence of the Archetypical Mind. For most mind/body/spirits incarnate in 3rd Density, the only perception employed is from within the timelines and subject to the conditions of the Archetypical Mind, unless extra effort is exerted to more fully awaken from the dream, which is possible. As consciousness ascends through the densities, the Archetypical Mind holds less sway on the processing of thoughts or, in other words, consciousness begins to peer through the dense fog of the ego mind.

The ancient spiritual teachers describe consciousness' participation in creation to be a dream within a dream, within a dream. The innermost dream, the most familiar, is space/time when the analog projection is repeatedly incarnating within a timeline and its perspective is the most restrictive phase of the 3rd Density experience. Dream #2 is consciousness' experience of time/space when it remains within the Archetypical Mind but its awareness isn't limited to an incarnate identity or the timelines. Dream #1 is the experience of creation from the vantage point of infinity which is the matrix of creation and the environment of 8th Density.

Every time consciousness becomes more aware, it increases its level of consciousness in increments, which is synonymous with becoming more aligned with the Higher Self. Each increase in consciousness level is an experience and inclusion of more dimensions into the awareness field. Eventually, these small increases in awareness add up to the major mystical abilities that transcend the conditions of the Archetypical Mind such as confounding the "natural laws".

Chapter 17

Introduction to the Matrix Modules of the Archetypical Mind

The matrix category of the Archetypical Mind establishes conditions that contribute to the formatting of the mind's patterns of consciousness and significantly contribute to how it will perceive experiences while it remains within its auspices. All Archetypical Minds are unique and do not necessarily have the same matrix category or any of the other categories included in the design that Earth's population experiences, but this discussion is primarily about the design that serves Earth and its solar system. The matrix category establishes the beginning parameters for the experience. It shapes the mind's early perceptions and how a thought is processed, thereby establishing the foundational nature of how a participating mind/body/spirit may experience the environments and catalysts presented to it in thoughts.

Consciousness forms a definitive pattern as a result of its unique interpretation of experiences, but it's a pattern formed within common perceptual boundaries imposed upon all consciousness within the same Archetypical Mind. The Archetypical Mind serves the foundational and experiential densities and consciousness, evolving through the 1st and 2nd Densities, and concludes the density with a unique but common pattern shared by all consciousness within the experience. Consciousness evolving from the 1st Density experience of Earth to the 2nd Density will begin the 2nd Density with a common pattern of consciousness.

3rd Density is the first density that establishes an "I" perspective and preserves its cumulative learning from lifetime to lifetime but consciousness begins the density with commonality to its consciousness pattern from its 2nd Density experience. Soon after consciousness enters the 3rd Density, the mind/body/ spirit's patterns begin to become unique and distinguishable from all others, primarily because of an "I" perspective. The matrix category creates conditions that are universally shared by all consciousness within the Archetypical Mind that significantly contribute to the creation of the "I" perspective. The conditions are distortions of perception that persist until the individual mind/body/spirits become sufficiently aware to surrender the authenticity of its perceptions and, thereby, overcome the conditions by recognizing truth through the distortions.

After donning the spacesuit called the Archetypical Mind, the matrix category initially formats the mind/body/spirit according to its conditions and continuously modifies the consciousness pattern according to the results of processed thoughts. The nature of creation is change but it's experienced in increments as if it were a still photograph. Change occurs as consciousness' perceptions change but the experience of a changed perception only happens when the fruit of a thought process is incorporated into its consciousness pattern. The matrix category remains unchanged throughout consciousness' journey through the foundational and experiential densities, but the recognition and acceptance of the conditions and/or distortions vary as the mind/body/spirit's degree of awareness changes.

The more consciousness can sober from free will intoxication, the more it surrenders the "I" perspective and the less authentic the conditions of the Archetypical Mind. As always, awareness is the discovery tool and the healing tool to advance consciousness through the evolutionary journey. The more aware consciousness becomes, the less authentic the perception of self as an independent identity and the less authentic the conditions created by the Archetypical Mind.

Within the lower dimensions of 3rd Density, consciousness' ability to stretch beyond the confines of the conditions of the Archetypical Mind is severely limited because of its lack of awareness. It is highly improbable that consciousness will be able to discern anything other than the absolute authenticity of the distortions as reality. However, after multiple lifetimes and countless individual experiences, the stricture of the conditions potentially lessens as the individual's awareness increases, resulting in changes in perception. The Archetypical Mind remains the same but the escalation in consciousness experienced by a single mind/body/spirit as a result of its consensual increases in awareness lessens the tenacity of its grip on the distortions.

Graduation to 4th Density continues the process of transforming the limiting perceptions created by the matrix category and other modules of the Archetypical Mind. Regardless of the experiential density being experienced, consciousness consistently reassesses the Archetypical Mind conditions, allowing it to potentially grasp greater truth in every thought. The primary difference between the beginning of 3rd Density and 4th Density is that 3rd Density begins in a significantly higher degree of chaos and must first create or discover a foundation for stability before it can proceed to experience truth. 4th Density is a transformative and healing opportunity for consciousness after the chaos of 3rd Density and has the advantage of picking up where 3rd Density left off, adding additional stability to the foundation of awareness and truth already discovered.

Stability increases and chaos decreases with each dimension gained which permits additional access to the truth with each incremental step. Graduation to 5th Density continues and accelerates the process from where 4th Density leaves off and allows the greater surrender of the same conditions and a continued transformation of consciousness to allow an even greater experience of truth. 5th Density remains within the auspices of the Archetypical Mind but, as consciousness advances through the density, the mind and its conditions have a decreasing sway.

Consciousness experiences 5th Density as a social memory complex but, to a declining degree, individual mind/body/spirits still retain identities and process thoughts and the matrix still functions to modify the individual consciousness patterns with the fruit of its thoughts. The perceptions of self are dramatically transformed from the self-centered "I" perspectives of the lower ranges of 3rd Density, and the degree of deviation of thought interpretation from one mind/body/spirit to the next is increasingly minimal. The fruit of every thought still modifies an individual mind/body/spirit participating in the social memory complex to allow increasing integration into a unified organism but also modifies the entirety of the social memory complex. The lower the dimensional experience within the density, the more the individual mind/body/spirits participating in the social memory complex alter their patterns of consciousness; but the higher the dimensional experience, the more the changes affect the unity of the social memory complex's pattern.

Flow of Thoughts

The matrix and potentiator categories work in tandem as a sub-process within the Archetypical Mind. They are not participating in processing thought but they do receive the fruit of the thought process and use that fruit to modify the mind/body/spirit's consciousness pattern. Together, the matrix and potentiator categories prepare the mind/body/spirit to attract and process the next thought.

As earlier stated, the Archetypical Mind serves all consciousness within the foundational and experiential densities but access to the full mind is gained incrementally. While consciousness remains in the foundational densities or the lower dimensions of the 3rd Density, it employs the mind, the body, and the spirit columns of the matrix and potentiator categories but only the mind and body columns of the catalyst, experience, and significator categories. Only when consciousness surrenders its free will intoxication sufficiently to open the metaphysical 4th heart chakra does it begin to add access to the spirit column of the catalyst, experience, and significator categories. When graduating to 4th Density, a mind/body/spirit adds access to the transformation category in all columns.

No matter the level of consciousness, all thoughts are processed in time/space, and only after the fruit of the thought modifies the consciousness pattern does the experience become part of the space/time experience. The only way a thought or experience becomes part of space/time is as a result of the modification of consciousness' pattern. Thought becomes part of space/time because the 3rd Density mind/body/spirit perceives itself within the limits of the Archetypical Mind's conditions. When a thought is processed by a 3rd Density mind/body/spirit, the fruit of the thought modifies both the immediate mind/body/spirit's consciousness pattern and, similar to a social memory complex, the collective pattern of the planetary population.

When consciousness graduates from 3rd Density and advances to the appropriate dimensional level within 4th Density where it is no longer within time, the processing of thought continues but the character of thought changes significantly because of changes within the experiencing consciousness. The ego mind surrenders itself to the workings of the deep mind, which dissipates its confidence in the authenticity of the Archetypical Mind's conditions. The 4th Density mind/body/

spirit's perceptions eventually become liberated from most of the restrictions of the conditions and the mind/body/spirit becomes able to move between the environments of space/time and time/space at will. When this occurs, those polarizing service-to-others are restricted from interacting with lower consciousness until they have adequately learned how to shield themselves from detection.

Every Archetypical Mind module continues to play a significant role in the processing of thought but the contributions of some modules become more evident after consciousness has escalated to the level that it can be aware of the modules' effects. The fruit of the thought is received by the Matrix of the Mind and then forwarded to the Matrix of the Body and the Matrix of the Spirit for input. The Matrix of the Body and Matrix of the Spirit respond with their input, and the input is either accepted or rejected by the Matrix of the Mind. The Matrix of the Spirit is the alpha of the entire mind's design and creates the foundational condition for all consciousness within the foundational or experiential densities, and its contributions to every thought process continue while consciousness remains in the lower five densities, but it progressively has less sway until it eventually becomes harmonized with the mind's omega module.

Until the 4th heart chakra and the spirit portion of the mind/body/spirit become activated, the pattern of consciousness is modified only by the fruit of the previous thought according to the conditions created by the Matrix and Potentiator categories. In the modules of the Archetypical Mind above the Matrix and Potentiator categories and concurrent with the 4th heart chakra activation, the mind begins, for the first time, to recognize input from the spirit. This adds significant intelligence to the mind's interpretations and begins to lessen the authenticity of the Archetypical Mind's conditions which lessens their influence on the entire thought process. But, until the spirit is awakened, consciousness will continue to process thoughts according to the distortions created by the Matrix and Potentiator category.

The resulting foibles can be intense because pain and suffering are usually the results of the ego defending its identity and resisting awareness of the truth in which it swims. To stop the pain and suffering, it is essential to surrender the ego and "I" perspective so that truth may be recognized but the mind identifies itself as the "I" perspective and, therefore, must surrender *itself* to halt the pain and suffering. That is why spiritual awakening usually occurs after a significant accumulation of pain and suffering and only after the mind/body/spirit has completely exhausted almost every other resource other than doing the one thing that works. The mind is a distortion of spirit, created by free will's intoxication, perceiving itself as the focus of everything, and fallaciously fears becoming nothing if it surrenders the authenticity of its self-perception.

Once the Matrix of the Mind has shaped the fruit of the previous thought with its perspective, it passes the fruit, as amended, to the Potentiator of the Mind. The Potentiator of the Mind employs the same polling process that the Matrix of the Mind used to poll the body and spirit for input. Once the input has been obtained from the Potentiator of the Body and Spirit, the fruit of the previous thought, as again amended, is incorporated into the pattern of consciousness and the now modified mind/body/spirit is ready to attract the next thought and repeat the process all over, but as a newly modified pattern of consciousness.

The effect of the modification to the mind/body/spirit will always be spiritual, even if we don't recognize it as such, meaning it will affect the level of consciousness, dimensionality, and degree of alignment with the Higher Self. While we remain in lower consciousness, the nature of the modification will be from the perspective of fear, a victim's perspective because, while we retain the perspective of being a separate identity from the Creator, that is the only possible perspective. Once our consciousness reaches the threshold of the 4th time/space heart chakra, the nature of the change presents itself from the perspective of a greater awareness of truth and greater unity. The nature of thought remains essentially the same but the capacity of the processing mind/body/spirit to glean greater truth from the process increases, so it appears and is experienced dramatically differently.

Regardless of the level of consciousness that experiences the modification, the fruit of every thought will either cause us to align more closely with the Higher Self or move us further away from alignment. While we continue to vacillate between degrees of alignment from thought to thought, we remain in chaos and locked into the struggles of lower consciousness, indicative of the lower three chakras. We stumble and bumble without a committed focus while we remain unconscious, taking one step forward and then one step back. In the nomenclature of the Buddha, we remain within the Wheel of Samsara.

The fractal preparation of consciousness for 3rd Density is a two-phased process that results in inaccurate perceptions of the self and misinterpretations of the experiences of life, and overcoming the misperceptions is accomplished by incrementally and sequentially healing the self by addressing these two phases. The nature of the 3rd Density experience is the reduction in the flow of Intelligent Energy as a result of the accumulated emotional baggage gained from incomplete processing of experiences, so, phase one of the recovery requires increasing the flow of Intelligent Energy to the mind/body/spirit by healing the emotional baggage. The experiences that we failed to finish processing are the lessons that we were meant to learn to advance our evolution. Healing the emotional baggage requires us to finish the processing of the experiences and, thereby, finish learning the lessons offered by the experiences.

After healing the emotional baggage, which increases access to the available flow of Intelligent Energy, phase two begins, which is the continued exploration of the self through the lens of awareness that invariably results in recognition of greater truth and increased alignment with the Higher Self. We evolve to higher dimensions within the density and progress through the process of creation, thereby fulfilling our purpose in life. Healing the emotional baggage requires us to invert focus from outside of us to inside and increased concentration and awareness are required to be successful. The development of increased concentration and awareness is also required to implement phase two of the process but, having successfully undertaken phase one, phase two can capitalize upon the skills pioneered in phase one.

The ideal plan for life and participation in experience is that we will remain fully "in the moment" and process the catalyst, presented to us as part of every thought, completely as it is presented. This is every mind/body/spirit's ambition before incarnation as an analog projection of its time/space self but, after incarnation, things are almost always more challenging on the playing field than in the locker room. While we remain in the phase of life when we predominantly experience things we don't like, unconscious, and within the grip of the conditions of the Archetypical Mind, we fail to fully process catalysts because of a lack of awareness, a lack of direction, and a lack of information. We are preprogrammed to need love, and so, all of our efforts are consciously and/or unconsciously focused on exploring love but, since we enter life without an inkling of what love feels or looks like, we spend a lot of time discovering what love doesn't feel like, thereby narrowing the search.

Emotional baggage results from exploring love "in all the wrong places", is accumulated within the space/time energy system, distorts the time/space pattern of consciousness, and increasingly baffles the flow of Intelligent Energy within the energy body. To remove these obscurations to the energy flow we must become aware, explore the self, and complete the processing of the catalyst that was previously incomplete because in the catalyst are the lessons of or about the Inherent Characteristics. This is the healing process (mental, physical, and emotional) and it is a necessary step in the evolution of the mind/body/spirit. Healing emotional baggage is the process that allows the increased flow of Intelligent Energy, permits the awakening of awareness, and transforms the attachment to the authenticity of the conditions of the Archetypical Mind.

Healing emotional baggage requires inwardly directed concentration, awareness, and the development of discernment to distinguish honesty from deception. These are the attributes of meditation combined with contemplation. This is the benefit of allowing a daily visit to the guru's cave to develop the skills necessary to become aware, develop an ability to concentrate, and discover the self that lives outside of the village.

Increased free will intoxication over the 4th Density's degree of intoxication creates the 3rd Density fractal of consciousness, and the healing process, or escalation of consciousness to a 4th Density level, will require the individual's sobering. As the healing of phase one required an increased awareness, sobering from free will intoxication is also accomplished with awareness but the efforts of reducing intoxication will probably have limited effects until phase one of the healing process has been significantly accomplished. Phase one of the process employs awareness to explore the self and heal the emotional baggage and phase two employs increased awareness skills to surrender identity and experience evolutionary success. The inevitable and immutable result of the process is the ability to experience greater truth (the Creator) in every thought.

Alignment with the Higher Self is synonymous with surrendering the perception of separation from the one infinite Creator and greater alignment is achieved by healing the distorted perceptions of 3rd Density consciousness. Before awakening to life's purpose of exploring the self with awareness and while consciousness remains in relative chaos, consciousness purports an ego identity which includes an attachment to the authenticity of the distortions and subordinating spiritual pursuits in favor of immediate gratification through the body/physical. When consciousness grows exhausted from self-inflicted pain and suffering, it begins to use the strength of the will to choose what is enduring by ceasing the search for the more temporal gratification of transient needs.

Consciousness begins to transform the perception of self from the ego and "I" perception and becomes "self-aware". Self-awareness becomes the tool for advancing consciousness and transforming the ego mind into the deep mind, thereby advancing and accelerating its evolution. Awareness (SA), the Inherent Characteristic of the Creator, is the primary tool of evolutionary advancement and is diverse in the scope of services it offers.

Since the fruit of every thought is incorporated into the mind/body/spirit before the next thought is processed, no two thoughts are processed with the mind/body/spirit in the same condition. After the fruit of the previous thought is incorporated into the mind/body/spirit, its pattern of consciousness will be changed forever and the previous mind/body/spirit becomes no longer available to process another thought. However, the newly modified mind/body/spirit is immediately ready to process the next thought. The processing of every thought is a "point in time" experience which means that creation is a point in time experience and no point will be exactly duplicated again.

With the processing of a single thought by a single mind/body/ spirit, all of creation is changed and recreated, awaiting the next thought to change it again. "All is One", so as one is changed, all are changed. It may seem that one drop of water will not change the entire ocean but infinity is comprised of an infinite number of water droplets, so as one droplet is changed all are changed because the ocean is one body of water. This becomes apparent when we contemplate that every single thought processed by a single individual is a complete experience of creation and every new thought is the impetus to change creation again.

The moments of space/time do not flow smoothly without interruption from thought to thought. Space/time is paused for every thought and functions similarly to how claymation (stop motion animation) photography works with a whole new photograph being taken after one small element of the character is adjusted to accommodate the expectation of movement. Time is simply stop-action animation.

The matrix category and all of the other modules remain the same throughout the entire journey of consciousness through the foundational and experiential densities. Modification of a pattern of consciousness changes how the modules are perceived and causes the modules to seem to be different with each thought processed. It is always and only consciousness that changes and, therefore, it responds differently after each thought that it processes.

Chapter 18

The Matrix Modules of the Archetypical Mind

The foundation of the Archetypical Mind is the matrix category which consists of three modules: the Matrix of the Mind, the Matrix of the Body, and the Matrix of the Spirit. The matrix category formats the mind/body/spirit by establishing the perceptual distortions of movement (DA) and separation (TA) into the newly created unit of consciousness which creates the beginning perception that it is in constant motion (chaos) and autonomous (isolated). When consciousness first enters the evolutionary process, the soul stream creating the Higher Self has the option of either starting all consciousness in 1st Density or distributing it throughout the dimensions of the foundational and experiential densities. When Earth began to host a 3rd Density experience, it was already a 1st and 2nd Density planet, so the 3rd Density (human) population was simply added to the two densities already enjoying the planet.

The Earthly 3rd Density experience was begun by transferring an existing 3rd Density population that had failed to graduate from the density in four previous attempts on planets within the same solar system. 3rd Density people from 15 other populations that had also failed from at least one previous attempt were added from other solar systems to make a total of 16 different sources of population members. That meant that these 16 different groups had already experienced some significant indoctrination to creation from 16 different archetypical minds and had not been successful in graduating from any of them. Beginning a new 3rd Density experience on a planet that was hosting a 3rd Density experience for the first time was unusual and made Earth a second-chance planet for everyone participating.

The Archetypical Mind for Earth was already established and had been functioning as the spacesuit for the solar system for billions of years, just not serving a 3rd Density experience on Earth. When consciousness dons an Archetypical Mind spacesuit, it immediately becomes programmed according to the conditions and parameters of the mind and any thoughts/ experiences it processes will be processed accordingly. An Archetypical Mind is only applicable to consciousness in the foundational and experiential densities, and a particular mind design serves only the consciousness sharing the same solar system. Earth's 3rd Density experience differed from a typical 3rd Density experience in several ways, but the most obvious difference was that it was a compilation of such a wide variety of beginning participants with different conditions of being.

The matrix category of the Archetypical Mind establishes the basic conditions of consciousness' perspectives for the process of evolution in a particular experience within the foundational and experiential densities. The Matrix of the Spirit formats consciousness in all of the dimensions of all five of the lower densities to perceive itself as an absolutely clean canvas with no information, no personality, no pattern of consciousness, and in significant chaos or dispersion because of these conditions. 1st Density consciousness begins with the same perceptual distortions as 5th Density consciousness nearing the end of its experiential density experiences with 40 strands activated, but the degree to which consciousness is swayed by the authenticity of these distortions is dramatically different.

Soon after its induction into creation, 1st Density consciousness combines to form the four elements of a planet and forever after creates the four minds that interpret the experiences of the four elements. Consciousness in this condition always perceives itself as physical and never again visits the metaphysical world until it leaves 1st Density. 1st Density consciousness has very limited awareness capacity and the beginning conditions of the Matrix category are seldom significantly altered or decreased. Awareness, the most basic of the Inherent Characteristics, is very low, and, therefore, the distortions offered by the Archetypical Mind seem irrefutably authentic.

2nd Density enjoys a greater degree of awareness capacity and experiences both the metaphysical world and the physical world as it evolves through the repetitious processes of reincarnation and death. Even though 2nd Density consciousness experiences these two environments at different times during its tenure in the density, the conditions afforded by the matrix categories are seldom diminished. 3rd Density consciousness is the density of awareness and all participants begin the density heavily under the chaotic influences of the matrix characteristics, but, as the participants evolve to the upper dimensions of the density and their awareness escalates, the heaviness and irrefutable nature of the distortions subside somewhat. The chaotic effects on 4th Density consciousness begin where they left off in the graduating 3rd Density consciousness. However, by the end of the density, the conditions of the matrix category are equally offered with significantly less sway than at any previous time in its evolutionary history.

When consciousness advances to 5th Density awareness, the effects of the entire Archetypical Mind are still equally offered, but they have significantly diminishing sway on consciousness' thought processes to the point of almost being inconsequential. As you may observe, the design of the Archetypical Mind is intended to remain consistently offered throughout consciousness' evolution through the lower five densities, but, as awareness of the experiencing consciousness grows, the design has a diminishing influence. The spacesuit effect of the mind becomes less restrictive or confining as the spacesuit inhabitant becomes more aware of their authentic self.

The Matrix of the Spirit is the "alpha" of the entire Archetypical Mind, which is where the evolutionary process begins for consciousness in a soul stream experience. The design of the Matrix of the Spirit module creates a "condition" which uniformly causes all consciousness in the experience to perceive itself according to the mind's design and occurs when their spacesuit is first donned. It is the prelude to the creation of a pattern of consciousness that may be compared to the blank canvas where a pattern of consciousness will be painted before any paint is applied.

The journey begins when the first thought is processed and a pattern of consciousness immediately begins to take shape, but the shape that it creates is entirely up to the experiencing consciousness, as guided by the design of the Archetypical Mind. Every thought produces fruit according to the preferences of the experiencer and the choices made are what cumulatively shape the consciousness pattern of the enduring self. Processing individual thoughts is an incremental process and each new thought process builds upon and amends the consciousness pattern that resulted from the last thought. Each new thought process adds color to the painting like a new brush stroke, expanding upon the one before.

The fruit of a thought is first delivered to the Matrix of the Mind because the category's function is as the artist's hand that makes the change to the canvas. In all of the categories, while the mind/body/spirit remains in the foundational or experiential densities, the mind is the artist that ultimately determines how the thought will be interpreted for the category, regardless of input from the body or spirit. As consciousness reaches the higher dimensions of the 3rd Density, the spirit begins to awaken, and eventually, in the higher densities, the mind surrenders completely to the spirit and it replaces the mind as the artist guiding experiences. In the foundational densities, the 3rd Density, and the lower dimensions of the 4th Density, the primary experiencing mind is the ego mind, the novice artist created by free will intoxication.

The spirit is the deep mind which is unrecognized until the middle dimensions of the 3rd Density, even though it's the more experienced and skillful artist. The ego mind is the product of consciousness' identity, but, as identity is surrendered to unity, the mind willingly surrenders itself to the deep mind because it becomes aware that it's the more skillful artist. For those people polarizing along the service-to-self path, they won't recognize the deep mind and will work to increasingly empower the ego mind through all of the experiential densities.

For those polarizing along the service-to-others path, the role of the deep mind continues throughout the experiential densities but the ego mind disappears near the end of the 4th Density when the identity is completely surrendered. The perception of self transforms into 5th Density wisdom and a social memory complex, then the unity of a 6th Density social memory complex, and eventually, into the stillness of the 7th Density. The mind is what transforms as the independent perceptions are surrendered and the self-perception mutates into an ever-growing organism, destined to merge into the oneness of the Creator. Throughout the entire evolutionary process, the mind will continue to guide the uniqueness of its perspective that consciousness creates through its experiences, but its perception of independence from the Creator's unity decreases with each dimension attained. The process of evolution incrementally fulfills the purpose of creation because consciousness learns of itself by experiencing itself at each dimension along the way.

When consciousness initially graduates from the experiential densities into 6th Density, the mind becomes the root mind but the mind/body/spirit will still retain a modicum of autonomy, even within the social memory complex. 6th Density is the broadest range of coding activation of all of the densities, and, as consciousness continues to evolve through the density and its perception of self merges more significantly into unity, the mind increasingly surrenders its uniqueness into the unity of the whole by continuing to surrender free will intoxication. By the end of 6th Density evolution, any residual perceptual autonomy will have been completely surrendered to the unity of 6th Density consciousness, in preparation for its transition to 7th Density. Even in the 7th Density, consciousness is still a mind/body/spirit and the mind continues to represent consciousness' uniqueness, but, in the lower dimensions of the density, the mind is the racial mind of one of the five Inherent Characteristics.

As consciousness continues to evolve through the 7th Density, it is resolving distinctions between the Inherent Characteristics by continuing to surrender its consciousness pattern as a racial mind to one of greater unity with the Creator. The conclusion of the 7th Density journey, in preparation for the transition to the 8th Density and completion of the entire journey through creation, is stillness, when all distinctions are resolved and consciousness again experiences the complete stability of the Creator. Beginning in the 1st Density, and until it reaches the upper dimensions of the 3rd Density, consciousness is creating the uniqueness of an identity because of its perception of separation, as interpreted by the ego mind. In the upper dimensions of the 3rd Density through the 4th Density, consciousness is surrendering its identity, learning who it is by exploring the self and transforming the mind from the ego mind into the deep mind.

Every module of the Archetypical Mind is designed with two archetypes. One archetype begins the evolutionary journey as the object or Logos and the other archetype begins as the subject or sub-Logos. Logos, as used in this context, is the guiding or dominant concept from which one or more sub-Logos may be experienced. For example, the solar system would be sub-Logos to the galaxy and a planet would be sub-Logos to a solar system.

According to the Archetypical Mind designed for Earth's solar system, consciousness evolves within the foundational or experiential densities, and the initial object archetype both integrates and harmonizes with the subject archetype or, where there is a distortion archetype in the object position, exchanges roles altogether. In those modules designed with a distortion archetype in the object or Logos position, the module creates a "condition" which must be overcome by surrendering its authenticity in favor of the Inherent Characteristic archetype in the sub-Logos or subject position. Recognition and acceptance of the authenticity of the Inherent Characteristic archetype, in place of the recognition and acceptance of the distortion-generated condition, is accomplished by the recognition of greater truth.

The Matrix of the Spirit creates the condition of primordial darkness because the object/Logos position is populated with the distortion archetype DA or movement, and the subject/sub-Logos position is held by TA or separation. Within the Archetypical Mind's design, the Matrix of the Spirit is the only module populated with a distortion archetype in both the subject and object position, which is why it is the alpha and cannot be overcome other than by integration and harmonization with the omega module that is comprised of an Inherent Characteristic archetype in both positions. The condition of primordial darkness, created by the Matrix of the Spirit module, persists throughout consciousness' tenure in the foundational and experiential densities, and, even though its authenticity is potentially lessened with every thought processed, it will continue to offer, to a lessening degree, a perception of innocence until it is finally harmonized.

The condition created by the Matrix of the Spirit's design is innocence, which is the desired beginning condition for consciousness starting the evolutionary journey so that it may create its uniqueness without any preexisting bias, other than that provided by its sponsoring archetypical racial mind. Every soul stream originates from a 6th Density entity that holds a racial bias according to its Inherent Characteristic or distortion identification. The 1st and 2nd Density experiences of planet Earth, for example, are the product of a LA or the wisdom racial mind archetype, but the population is the product of a RA or the love racial mind archetype. Even today, the 1st and 2nd Densities of Earth continue their racial mind bias of wisdom that served as the foundational experiences of its soul streams and the population continues their racial mind bias of love.

Every Archetypical Mind module is a "thing unto itself" as well as an integral part of the entire mind's design. A single module contributes a specific service to the processing of thought. The nature of the contribution is initially deemed to be supportive of either an object or subject role and so each module functions as either the male or female in the processing of every thought. In the course of consciousness' evolution through the foundational and experiential densities, the male and female identifications integrate until, as a social memory complex, consciousness graduates from the experiential densities into the unity of 6th Density.

The Matrix of the Spirit module is a subject or male module. As consciousness evolves through the lower densities, the male or subject nature of its identification is incrementally integrated with the female, or object, nature of the Great Way of the Spirit, which is the omega of the Archetypical Mind. The design requires that the male surrender its perception of independence to one of greater unity with the female, which then eventually merges into greater unity or oneness with the Creator.

The Matrix of the Spirit initially is the corpus of the mind/body/spirit's consciousness pattern but it doesn't participate in the actual processing of individual thoughts, other than providing the foundational perspective for the thought's interpretation. The mind/body/spirit's consciousness pattern is modified after every thought process, and, ideally, the primordial darkness perspective lessens as the fruit of its thoughts is incorporated into the pattern. It holds the perspective of continuous motion (change), and separation (perception of autonomy) which together create the condition of chaos in the inexperienced mind of the 3rd Density participants. The effects of the Matrix of the Spirit's perceived authenticity lessen as consciousness escalates awareness and surrenders the erroneous condition to the truth.

In 1st Density, the Matrix of the Spirit programs consciousness as primordial darkness or innocence without a consciousness pattern at its beginning. As consciousness aggregates, learns by interacting with each other and begins to form a planet, 1st Density consciousness does create a consciousness pattern for each of the four elements (fire, water, atmosphere, and matter) which explains the uniqueness of every planet. 2nd Density consciousness also begins in primordial darkness but a consciousness pattern for individual pools of consciousness soon develops as its analog projections enjoy space/time experiences. The same primordial condition begins the 3rd Density experience, but it too quickly creates a consciousness pattern for each metaphysical mind/body/spirit (enduring self) predicated upon the experiential interpretations of its analog projections into space/time.

In the foundational densities and the 3rd Density, consciousness begins the density without preserving the condition or experiences of the lower densities, but it does preserve the condition and experiences when it enters the 4th Density. 4th Density consciousness preserves the individual mind/body/ spirit's 3rd Density consciousness pattern because the pattern is unique to the individual mind/body/spirit graduating. By the time consciousness enters the 5th Density, it has surrendered all of its identity and merged its consciousness pattern into a social memory complex, but its individualized consciousness pattern is still distinguishable, even though it's now part of the social memory complex. Even upon entry into the 6th Density, a modicum of the individual's mind/body/spirit consciousness patterns remains but only until the social memory complex progresses approximately midway through the density.

Throughout consciousness' progression through the foundational and experiential densities, the Archetypical Mind remains constant and unchanging but its effects on consciousness change as the limiting conditions, that were authentic in the 1st, the 2nd, and the lower dimensions of 3rd Density, diminish with awareness' escalation and increased dimensionality. The Archetypical Mind is designed to serve all the densities of the foundational and experiential density, and consciousness' surrender of its free will intoxication and increased awareness allow it to excel beyond its conceptual distortions and perceptions. Paradoxically, it's because of the conceptual conditions and algorithms of the Archetypical Mind that consciousness is most motivated to evolve beyond them because the mind also provides the tools necessary to do so. Eventually, all consciousness entering the evolutionary process will arrive home at the place that it began and see it again as if for the first time, but the speed with which consciousness evolves is totally at its discretion.

The matrix category differs from most of the other categories of the Archetypical Mind in ways other than housing the alpha of the mind and establishing basic conditions for experience according to its distortions. In most of the other categories, the mind module receives the thought, forwards it to both the body and spirit with the expectation that they will independently return their input, and then the mind adjudicates how the thought will be interpreted for the category. This is true, with the caveat that, until a mind/body/spirit opens itself to the dimensions necessary to open the 4th heart chakra, the input from the spirit column, in most of the other categories, is ignored. It's as if the spirit doesn't contribute to the process at all, but the spirit is automatically asked for its input with every thought.

Because it creates the condition of primordial darkness (innocence), the matrix category's contribution is perfunctory and its participatory input isn't requested for individual thoughts. It's the foundational condition of the consciousness from which all experience is perceived and is always a contributor because of the condition that it creates, without necessarily acting on individual thoughts. Most of the other modules' contributions can be considered incremental acts and facilitate change in the prevailing condition of the consciousness pattern or identity, but the matrix category creates a foundationally immobile condition to be eventually overcome.

The Matrix of the Mind is designed with "DA" or movement as the object/Logos and the Inherent Characteristic "SA" or awareness as the subject or sub-Logos. "DA" is the object and reinforces the "DA's" distortion in the Matrix of the Spirit which causes consciousness to perceive itself to be in constant motion, with no means to be still. Constant movement is also constant change, which further results in chaos for consciousness with the limited awareness of the lower densities. In addition to the affirmation of the perception of constant motion or chaos, the Matrix of the Mind creates the ego mind which results from the perceptions of motion and the perception of autonomy from all other consciousness, created by the Matrix of the Spirit.

Even though the mind module of most of the categories is the decision maker for how the fruit of the thought will be adjudicated, the Matrix of the Mind jointly decides the category results with the Potentiator of the Mind, the module immediately above the matrix. The potentiator and matrix category functions as a unit and jointly modify the metaphysical consciousness pattern and physical world analog projection. Together they create the beginning condition and perpetually modify the condition(s) as the individual mind/body/spirit evolves through the system.

As awareness escalates and guides the evolution of the mind/body/spirit's consciousness, the initial subject/sub-Logos "SA" begins to moderate the object/Logos "DA" and it begins to transform the perception of constant motion by incrementally surrendering its attachment to the authenticity of the physical perceptions of the 1st Density environment. If you will recall, we previously explained that people often mistake stasis for stability. They perceive change, which is synonymous with motion, as scary and cling to things in the past or remember life to be better in the past. They identify themselves as being "conservatives" because they eschew change in favor of stasis.

Stasis behavior is fear-based and simply an indication that their consciousness level is still within the lower dimensions of the density. Awareness has not yet been sufficiently energized to mitigate the scary feelings of chaos resulting from the perception of constant motion. "DA" is a distortion archetype and creates a distorted perception of truth.

Escalating consciousness must surrender attachment to the distortions through awareness, and, since the only thing that changes is the experiencer, the only thing the experiencer can change is itself. The more we anticipate change and fear it, the more we are creating stress for ourselves by trying to manage the world around us instead of exploring the self and becoming aware of "what" within us needs the focus of awareness and surrender.

We see things as we are, not as things actually are. We are the lens through which we experience the world. When we are lost within the lower dimensions of creation, we are fearful and continuously interpret experiences to be what we don't like, but we are constantly pursuing what we do like. To begin to enjoy what we do like, instead of continuously experiencing more of what we don't like, we must change ourselves.

The fruit of every thought is first delivered to the Matrix of the Mind and forwarded to the Matrix of the Body for input. Similar to passing a memo around the office to ask for input or comments, the body replies to the request with information but offers no added intelligence because the body has no intelligence to offer. The Matrix of the Mind adjudicates its opinion of the thought fruit, after receiving the body's input, and forwards the fruit to the Potentiator of the Mind with its conclusions.

The Matrix of the Body is also comprised of "DA" in the object/Logos position, and "KA" (stillness) in the subject/sub-Logos position. "DA" in the object/Logos position affirms the perception that it's in constant motion, initiated in the primordial darkness condition created by the Matrix of the Spirit. It perceives constant motion to be both mental, because of the structure of the Matrix of the Mind, and physical, because of the structure of the Matrix of the Body. The repeated affirmation of the perception of constant motion adds to the authenticity of the movement distortion belief and the degree of chaos experienced by the mind/body/spirit.

"DA" is a distortion of "KA", or stillness, and its antithesis. While consciousness remains within the foundational densities and the lower dimensions of the 3rd Density, "DA", as the object/Logos of all three of the matrix modules, reaffirms and promotes the authenticity of the constant motion perception. As consciousness escalates into the higher dimensions of the density, chaos begins to lose its authenticity and the subject/ sub-Logos of the Matrix of the Mind and Matrix of the Body begin to awaken.

Awakening allows the moderation of the commonly shared distortion archetype "SA", or awareness, in the subject/ sub-Logos position of the Matrix of the Mind, and "KA" or stillness, in the subject/sub-Logos position of the Matrix of the Body. Both SA and KA are Inherent Characteristic archetypes and offer truth to counteract the distortion perceptions of the initial distortion archetype. Advancement of consciousness through evolution requires surrendering of false perceptions, created by attachment to the authenticity of the distortions, in favor of truth. The further up the consciousness scale, the less consciousness adheres to the attachment to the authenticity of the distortions.

The characteristic of the Matrix of the Body is motion and/ or chaos, because of its object/Logos, but it also affords the potential for "even functioning" without chaos because its subject/sub-Logos is the antithesis of its object/Logos. "KA" eventually counteracts the chaos and allows consciousness to experience its journey without the foibles of constant motion perception. Additionally, the Matrix of the Body also functions in conjunction with the Potentiator of the Body that also helps moderate the "DA" distortion which we will discuss in greater detail in the next chapter discussing the potentiator category.

The Matrix of the Body initially is a female or object-leaning module, which means it's intended to balance the male or subject leaning of both the Matrix of the Mind and the Matrix of the Spirit. The opportunity to moderate the initially more powerful disposition of the male leanings of the other two matrix modules is entirely dependent upon the experiencer's willingness to employ the awareness afforded in the Matrix of the Mind. KA offers the opportunity to experience stillness and is available in the Matrix of the Body. Awareness is always the available tool to discover and effect greater calming of the chaos (healing).

We previously said that the matrix and potentiator categories work together as a subsystem within the Archetypical Mind's design to receive the fruit of the previous thought and incorporate the fruit into the consciousness pattern of the mind/body/spirit. The consciousness pattern is not modified until the fruit of the thought has been processed through all of the modules of both of these categories, but, after it has been fully processed and the pattern of consciousness has been modified, the experience is deemed to have been brought into space/time. Before this occurs, all of the processing of thought, including its journey through the matrix and potentiator categories, takes place in time/space.

It is not within the province of consciousness experiencing the end of 3rd Density Earth and the beginning of 4th Density to be aware of the specific workings of an Archetypical Mind module, and it doesn't need to do so to benefit from the information we are providing. The process of surrendering attachment to the authenticity of the conditions and implementing the analog integration of the other modules occurs without awareness of its specifics but every mind/body/spirit must undertake the work necessary to escalate their awareness and heal the foibles accumulated to date in their evolutionary journey. It is necessary that they consciously work to surrender unconsciousness and cease living every day in the same mind and spirit-numbing routine.

Overcoming the conditions is not possible while the ego mind is the only mind being employed. The ego mind continuously reaffirms the authenticity of the distortion conditions, in part because it is created by the conditions. The conditions are overcome by "feeling" that they are not authentic, which is an intuitive behavior. The rational/logical mind is the ego mind and surrendering an attachment to the authenticity of the conditions requires the surrendering of the self as an independent identity.

In previous chapters, we compared advancement through the evolutionary process to a baseball player being on first base and desiring to run to second base. To go to second base, the player must take their foot off of first base to make the journey and have faith that he can make it to second base. Likewise, consciousness desiring to run to greater truth must become aware of the fact that the conditions are a result of distortions and the antithesis of truth by also relying upon faith. In the level of consciousness that we all share, we don't have proof because it would limit our free will choices. We must surrender the ego mind based upon faith, and, in so doing, we learn to recognize our Creator-ness and power as a fractal of the Creator.

Matrix of the Mind	Matrix of the Body	Matrix of the Spirit
Initial Object: DA, movement	Initial Object: DA, movement	Initial Object: DA, movement
Initial Subject: SA, awareness	Initial Subject: KA, stillness	Initial Subject: TA, separation
Characteristics: Constant motion, ego mind	Characteristics: Constant motion, even functioning	Characteristics: innocence, primordial darkness
Male (+)	Female (-)	Male (+)
Algorithm, contributes to a solution	Algorithm, contributes to a solution	Condition, alpha module for the entire mind design

Chapter 19

The Potentiator Modules of the Archetypical Mind

As the name suggests, the potentiator category "potentiates" consciousness' evolution through the foundational and experiential densities of creation. As with all of the Archetypical Mind categories, it consists of three modules: the Potentiator of the Mind, the Potentiator of the Body, and the Potentiator of the Spirit. It's also a "thing unto itself" and a significant and strategic contributor to the whole. The design of each of the three modules of the category is consistent with the design of all the other modules of the mind with one archetype in the object/Logos position and another in the subject/sub-Logos position.

The functioning of the potentiator category, while consciousness remains in the lower densities, is different than all the other modules and in how these modules serve the experiencer's thought processes. In the foundational densities and lower dimensions of 3rd Density, the Potentiator of the Body and the Potentiator of the Spirit seem silent because their contributions are not recognized by the Potentiator of the Mind until significant awareness has been achieved. The measure of how much awareness is necessary to begin to recognize and include the contributions of these two modules in the thought process, as are many of the transformational attributes of consciousness' evolution, is the activation of the 4th time/space heart chakra during consciousness' journey through 3rd Density. Until this occurs, the Potentiator of the Mind is the only module of the category participating in the processing of thought.

The potentiator category works in tandem with the matrix category to receive the fruit of the previous thought and amend the consciousness pattern, so, practically speaking, they don't directly participate in creating the fruit of a thought. The prevailing consciousness pattern is a direct reflection of the degree of transformation of the archetypical subject/object roles of the matrix and potentiator categories. If the mind/body/ spirit remains within the perceptual distortions of the lower dimensions of 3rd Density, then the consciousness pattern will reflect its significant attachment to the authenticity of the initial object/Logos distortions and their related conditions.

The role of the matrix and potentiator categories ultimately determines the effect of the thought fruit because the fruit could potentially be ignored by the matrix and potentiator, which would result in sustaining the condition that existed before the thought was processed. The condition of the prevailing consciousness pattern is a reflection of the degree of transformation of the matrix and potentiator categories, particularly the mind module of each category, and if awareness in the mind module has not begun to transform the chaos of motion in the Matrix of the Mind module or unconsciousness in the Potentiator of the Mind module, very little change can be expected. If the fruit of a single thought is such that it promotes a higher consciousness perspective but the condition of the consciousness pattern is still mired in a lower consciousness condition, it's likely that the single thought fruit will be discarded with very minimal effect. However, if the fruit of multiple thoughts continuously supports a higher consciousness perspective, it is much more likely that the matrix and potentiator categories will begin to acquiesce to the polarity of higher consciousness thought fruits and begin to accept them into a transforming consciousness pattern.

How the fruit of thought can be processed from a higher consciousness perspective than the prevailing consciousness pattern is because the person is experiencing "what they don't like" and it has the inspiration to become aware of an alternative way of interpreting thoughts. The alternative way will invariably be presented through interaction with another person who "models" a higher consciousness perspective. Consciousness learns of itself by experiencing itself, and, when it interacts with another person of a higher consciousness level, it first mimics the higher consciousness, and then, eventually, becomes the higher consciousness because it has sufficiently amended its consciousness pattern to resonate at the higher level. A higher consciousness perspective, and subsequent behavior, always feels better and consciousness uses an analogy to determine what it likes according to a personal preference that "feels better".

The transformation from a lower consciousness perspective to a higher consciousness perspective is incremental and every module of the Archetypical Mind is a "thing unto itself", possessed of free will, and capable of offering an alternative perspective to the other modules. It's relatively easier to experiment with a perspective change in the catalyst, experiential, and significator modules processing the thought than in the matrix and potentiator categories because the latter must change the consciousness pattern which is synonymous with a person's identity. The Matrix of the Mind creates the ego mind and the Potentiator of the Mind, in conjunction with the Matrix of the Mind, creates the "I" perspective, two very difficult conditions to overcome, but both of these modules have SA (awareness) as their initial subject/sub-Logos and awareness is the tool that facilitates the evolution of consciousness. Like pushing a car from a dead stop, awareness is most difficult to get going until some momentum is acquired, but, with momentum, the work becomes significantly easier.

The recognition and prominence of awareness, the subject/ sub-Logos of both the Matrix of the Mind and the Potentiator of the Mind, is essential to the mind's ability to recognize the change in the fruit of a thought process and, consequently, implement change in the consciousness pattern. Potentially, the interpretation of the thought fruit by the Matrix of the Mind and Potentiator of the Mind may be at odds with the actual fruit itself, and, if awareness is still very low, amend the consciousness pattern very little or, if awareness has already been increased significantly, amend it a great deal more than the thought fruit would suggest. This is the potential of free will that inherently participates behind the scenes in the workings of every module of the Archetypical Mind. The thought fruit may potentially support polarization towards the positive, but, if the Potentiator of the Mind and Matrix of the Mind chose to cling tenaciously to a stasis disposition that is polarized negatively, it may choose to ignore awareness and not modify the consciousness pattern at all.

The Potentiator of the Mind's construction is the same as all of the other modules designed with two archetypes, one as the object/Logos and the other as the subject/sub-Logos. Lucifer (unconsciousness) is the initial object/Logos archetype guiding a mind/body/spirit's perceptions through the potentiator category lens while it remains in the lower dimensions of the 3rd Density. The Potentiator of the Mind is the only module of the potentiator category actively contributing to the consciousness pattern modification until significant awareness has been energized, so, in addition to the consciousness pattern being shaped by the distortion archetype DA (movement) in all three of the matrix modules and TA (separation) in the Matrix of the

Spirit module, it's operating under the compounding distortion of unconsciousness.

The combination of the Matrix of the Mind and the Potentiator of the Mind jointly creates what may be the most significant condition to be overcome in the course of consciousness' evolution. Together they create the "I" perspective which results from the combination of the ego mind, created by the Matrix of the Mind, with unconsciousness, created by the Potentiator of the Mind, producing in a person the perception that it's a totally isolated and independent unit of consciousness cocooned within a physical body. This is the lens through which consciousness experiences creation until it evolves to the upper dimensions of 3rd Density, at which time it begins to question the authenticity of the conditions.

The more consciousness clings to the authenticity of the conditions by enhancing the eminence of the ego mind and the "I" perspective, the more significantly it perpetuates the painful cycle of stress and suffering. The subject/sub-Logos of the Potentiator of the Mind is SA (awareness), the same Inherent Characteristic archetype serving as the subject/sub-Logos of the Matrix of the Mind. As consciousness awakens, becomes aware, and eventually becomes awareness, the subject/sub-Logos of both of these modules moderate the perceived authenticity of the distortion and related conditions initially offered in the object/Logos position. Through awareness, consciousness evolves and eventually surrenders the authenticity of the conditions in favor of truth.

The Potentiator of the Mind potentiates a person by intensifying the obscuration of truth with the creation of the "I" perspective. A mind/body/spirit learns by analogy, and through comparing and contrasting experiences, it learns what it doesn't like. Consciousness is tasked with exploring love, but it isn't provided with any inkling of what love feels like. In its exploration of love, it potentially experiences a lot of pain and suffering, which is still exploring love because love isn't an emotion. Love is the feeling (the condition of being) that results when a person has surrendered their false identity and allowed themselves to experience more of their Creator-ness, their authentic self.

When you first go to the ice cream store, to determine that you like chocolate ice cream the best, you must taste all of the flavors to know that some are good, some are not good, and the chocolate is the best. The same is true of the exploration of love. Some experiences will be interpreted as good, some will be interpreted as not so good, but, eventually, the analogy will arrive at the one that is the best because of your free will choice. The experience of love that feels the best is immutable because it is the greater experience of the unadulterated oneness of the Creator and the immutable feeling of love begins to serve as a further guide to return to the home from which we all began.

If you plant a bean plant seed in total darkness, it will grow, and grow more quickly than a similar bean plant seed planted in sunlight. The seed planted in darkness accelerates its growth in search of sunlight, hoping that sunlight is there and having faith that it will find it. The seed planted in sunlight doesn't accelerate its growth because it's already receiving what it needs to sustain healthy growth. The seed planted in darkness grows with difficulty, but it grows more quickly because the darkness has potentiated its accelerated growth and, when it does finally reach sunlight, it can achieve the health that it forsook in search of the light.

Similarly, consciousness planted in primordial darkness, chaos, and unconsciousness, created by the conditions of the matrix and potentiator categories, evolves more quickly than consciousness planted in less stressful conditions. It experiences greater stress because it is deprived of the necessary nourishment provided by light, or information, but its healing occurs quickly once it reaches the light. Consciousness heals quickly once it stretches for the light and the conditions creating the primordial darkness, chaos, and unconsciousness are overcome.

The Potentiator of the Mind, by itself, is described as an algorithm module because it doesn't create the condition of the "I" perspective alone. By itself, it is only a part of the equation that guides consciousness in its return to unity, however, when its unconsciousness characteristics are combined with the ego mind created by the Matrix of the Mind, it does participate in the creation of a significant condition. Ironically, it is also deemed to be a female or object module because it eventually surrenders its unconsciousness to awareness and promotes consciousness' perception of greater unity after seemingly running the wrong way (so it can get a running start and build up speed) on its evolutionary advancement.

Consciousness' advancement through evolution is incremental and achieved by processing one thought at a time according to the mechanisms of analogy. The motivation to awaken and surrender the conditions of the ego mind and the "I" perspective, thereby also eventually surrendering the authenticity of all of the other conditions, is pain and suffering or, as the Buddha characterized it, the Wheel of Samsara. Energizing awareness, accomplished through the trial and error process of analogy, lessens the effects of pain and suffering and provides breadcrumbs for consciousness to follow along the evolutionary path.

The Matrix of the Body is constructed with DA (movement) in the object/Logos position at the outset of consciousness' entry into creation and remains a primary contributor to the module's contributions to the consciousness pattern until awareness is awakened. KA (stillness) is the Inherent Characteristic in the Matrix of the Body from which DA is distorted but it remains dormant until awareness in the Matrix of the Mind and Potentiator of the Mind is stimulated. When awareness is energized and the attachment to the ego mind and the "I" perspective are lessened, KA begins to offer the alternative to the constant motion proffered by DA and the Potentiator of the Body begins to be recognized.

The Potentiator of the Body is constructed with LA (wisdom) in the object/Logos position and KA is reiterated in the subject/ sub-Logos position. This is the first module we have discussed that doesn't have a distortion in the object/Logos, but rather, has an Inherent Characteristic in both the subject and object positions. When awareness is energized to the degree that the 4th heart chakra is opened, LA and KA in the Potentiator of the Body offer significant input to mitigate the distortion perceptions of DA in the Matrix of the Body.

In all of the modules so far discussed, the distortions of perception, characteristic of the lower dimensions of 3rd Density and below, are "overcome" by recognition of the Inherent Characteristics in the subject/sub-Logos position and surrendering attachment to the authenticity of the distortion. In modules populated with an Inherent Characteristic in both the object and subject positions, there isn't a distortion to be overcome, and, in the Potentiator of the Body module, the task is to start with recognition of wisdom and eventually integrate stillness to effect a harmonization of the two. LA (wisdom) enhances awareness and guides it to even greater awareness, and KA (stillness) reinforces KA in the Matrix of the Body's subject/sub-Logos position resulting in greater stability through an incremental release of the constant motion perspective.

Once consciousness has escalated its awareness sufficiently to energize and recognize the input from the Potentiator of the Body, the chaos, resulting from the Matrix of the Mind and Matrix of the Body, subsides and the truth is brought into clearer focus. The potential effects of the Inherent Characteristics, to provide an alternative to the authenticity of the unwanted conditions, are incrementally recognized and often accepted only after significant resistance from the mind/body/spirit because acceptance must be accomplished by the ego mind and under the cloud of the "I" perspective. The ego mind is required to surrender itself and its perspective of the self from the "I" perspective.

The ego mind is the rational/logical mind and eschews anything that it cannot rationalize based upon physical world observations or conventions, but surrendering its eminence must occur based upon feeling or intuition. The ego mind must surrender logic to intuition which is possible because "intuition informs intelligence". Relying upon intuition is enigmatic to the ego mind because it has functioned according to a cause-and-effect system since its inception and how the majority of other interactive mind/body/spirits are probably still functioning. The primary motivation to surrender its perceptions of self must come from within, based primarily upon the awareness that surrendering the perceptions of self "feels" better than continuing to defend the authenticity of the distortions and remaining within the Wheel of Samsara.

The Potentiator of the Body's characteristic is "even functioning". When it is finally recognized by the Potentiator of the Mind, it provides balance to the Matrix of the Body and the entire potentiator category. It is deemed to be a male or subject-leaning module, which means, as a module, it is to be balanced with the female or object modules. As consciousness escalates through the dimensions, it continues to diminish the TA and DA distortions and enhances consciousness' awareness. It supports the consciousness pattern's escalation by aiding healing from an attachment to the distortions and resulting conditions by making the truth more apparent.

The module doesn't create or contribute to the creation of a condition and is considered an algorithm because, while it remains a "thing unto itself", it is part of the solution to the distortion perception. Free will is very much an inherent part of the Potentiator of the Body's functioning but the module's activation naturally modifies the mind's distorted perceptions and brings a mind/body/spirit closer to the truth. Because it is dormant through the foundational densities and lower dimensions of 3rd Density, it only begins to provide its healing salve to consciousness that has employed the "strength of its will" and begun to surrender its attachment to the conditions that shape the early stages of evolution.

The Potentiator of the Spirit is also silent or dormant while consciousness perceives its existence to be only according to the authenticity of the conditions. Its contributions become energized or recognized by the Potentiator of the Mind simultaneously with the Potentiator of the Body and it too is populated by an Inherent Characteristic in both the object/ Logos and subject/sub-Logos positions. Its object/Logos is SA (awareness) and its subject/sub-Logos is LA (wisdom). As consciousness advances through the dimensions of a density, SA and LA integrate and harmonize so that the attributes of awareness with wisdom become landmark guiding influences.

Just as love is not an emotion but results from consciousness' greater awareness of its Creator-ness, awareness and wisdom are likewise representative of consciousness' more diverse focus. As consciousness surrenders its attachment to the authenticity of its distortions, it feels greater harmony with its Higher Self and resonates accordingly with other consciousness of equivalent degrees of evolutionary advancement. Experiences continue and partitions of separation and individuality continue to dissolve as perceptions of independence are naturally surrendered. While the limitations of the conditions dominate perspectives, it's improbable that consciousness can feel a close camaraderie based upon a shared awareness of unity.

The characteristic of the Potentiator of the Spirit is light, which "is" information, but it isn't information of a temporal nature. It's the light of truth, shining into the condition of primordial darkness that served consciousness in its elementary creation experiences. The light has always been present, but, until this stage of evolutionary advancement, consciousness has been unable or unwilling to become aware of it. "We see things as we are, not as things actually are", and so, because of the previous attachments to the authenticity of the distortion-creating conditions, consciousness has been unable to be aware of the truth in which it swims.

The Potentiator of the Spirit is an object or female module which, as always, means that its offerings are more aligned with the Higher Self and the Creator. You might think of the object modules as the greater teacher; teaching with every thought process but also learning by observing the reactions and behaviors of the subject. The subject is the pioneer and the object is the settler. Both are adventurers but each has a different role in exploration.

It is an algorithm because its contributions to consciousness' experiences are part of a whole experience. Information, in and of itself, is incomplete but it is an essential ingredient in consciousness' evolution from its initial beginnings to the completion of its exploratory journey. As we will see in future chapters, light or information is incrementally provided with every thought, but, after the light is made available, consciousness is posed with the question of "Is it enough light?" to surrender its perception of independence. Light is provided but the mind/body/spirit is still called upon to use free will to choose how the light will be used and how much light is necessary to transform its perceptions from a separate autonomous perceiving identity to one of greater unity.

All five of the Inherent Characteristics that populate the object/Logos and/or subject/sub-Logos positions throughout the modules of the Archetypical Mind function much like tuning forks. If a single tuning fork in a room full of tuning forks is struck, all of the tuning forks in the room of a similar key will begin to vibrate in resonance with the one tuning fork that was struck. Likewise, when awareness is energized in one module, awareness in all the other modules begins to be energized in resonance with the one awareness initially energized. The same is true for the other four Inherent Characteristics: love, wisdom, unity, and stillness.

All of the modules identified as algorithms make a specific contribution according to their positioning within the Archetypical Mind and in sequence to a thought process, hence it is a "thing unto itself", but it also makes a more general contribution by its specific Inherent Characteristic composition. For example, if the positioning of the Inherent Characteristics were swapped in the Potentiator of the Spirit, the effect would be entirely different. Every archetype is strategically placed within the modules of the mind to maximize the opportunity for consciousness to explore itself uniquely through its experiences.

The potentiator category assists in the creation of a perception of separation and independence from the Creator and all mind/body/spirits in the lower dimensions of consciousness' journey through creation, but it also provides tools necessary to counteract or overcome those perceptions. Like many of the Archetypical Mind modules, consciousness must learn to exercise its abilities, use the tools provided to grow beyond the complacency of its lower consciousness perspectives, and, thereby, benefit from all three modules. As we have emphasized many times before, it is an incremental process that allows consciousness to learn of itself by exploring itself, which is a direct reiteration of the Creator's original purpose of creation.

The Archetypical Mind remains constant and unchanging throughout consciousness' journey through the foundational and experiential densities, but the service that the mind provides to consciousness appears to change because of consciousness' evolving perceptions. The matrix and potentiator categories do not actually participate in the processing of thought, but they do receive the fruit of the thought, create a consciousness pattern, and continuously amend the pattern throughout a mind/body/ spirit's tenure in the lower densities. The amendments to the consciousness pattern directly reflect a mind/body/spirit's degree of progress along the evolutionary journey and directly indicate the clarity of the lens used to experience creation. Consciousness' behavior is a direct reflection of its degree of evolution, awareness, or consciousness level.

Before consciousness processes the very first thought, it is programmed by the Matrix of the Spirit to be a blank canvas on which almost any picture can be painted with the accouterments provided. The primordial darkness beginning is slowly and incrementally transformed as thoughts are experienced and a pattern of consciousness takes shape. Invariably, as a consciousness pattern is formed and amended over time, the mind/body/spirit's innocence condition is reduced, and the primordial darkness condition loses prominence, but, to a diminishing degree, it remains throughout consciousness' tenure in the lower densities. Innocence is a condition that is "feeling" more than it is "factual", and it is through a mind/ body/spirit's emotional interpretation of experiences and analogous choices from among its perceptions that eventually lead it home to unity.

The Matrix of the Mind is not a hierophant but it does function as if it was a hierophant version of a less distorted spirit. It begins its service to the Creator already programmed according to the primordial darkness condition and begins to receive the fruit of the first thought from a perspective of innocence and in constant motion or chaos. By itself, it creates the ego mind which is the primary sculptor of the consciousness pattern and continues to modify its creation until it surrenders itself to the more skillful deep-mind sculptor. It seamlessly works in conjunction with the Potentiator of the Spirit which compounds the ego mind's opaque lens through which it perceives itself and its experiences.

The Potentiator of the Body waits to be recognized but it's always present and available to be brought into the evolutionary game. It potentially provides clarity to the ego mind's opaque lens and the Matrix of the Mind and Matrix of the Body's chaos and confused innocence, but it must be called upon to provide its service. The Potentiator of the Body's even functioning characteristic affects several other modules of the Archetypical Mind, including all three of the Matrix modules and the Potentiator of the Mind. The Potentiator of the Body is activated and begins to contribute to the consciousness pattern concurrently with the Potentiator of the Spirit, and makes the light offered by the spirit module more easily identified and accepted.

The light provided by the Potentiator of the Spirit's characteristic is an essential ingredient to overcome innocence and chaos. The purpose of this writing is to provide light or information to those mind/body/spirits ready and willing to receive it, in the hopes that they will employ the light to propel their evolutionary advancement. Light alone is useless if it isn't accepted and used by the receiving mind/body/spirit to dispel a preoccupation with and attachment to, the conditions of unconsciousness, chaos, and darkness.

The potentiator category potentiates consciousness by first hiding its Creator-ness behind the curtain of unconsciousness and then providing the ingredients necessary to pull back the curtain. It creates or, at least, compounds the problem and then offers the solutions to the problem. However, it is incumbent upon the participating consciousness to become tired of dealing with the problem in the same old way, be ready to stop playing games and move on.

Potentiator of the Mind	Potentiator of the Body	Potentiator of the Spirit
Initial object/Logos: Lucifer (unconsciousness)	Initial object/Logos: LA (wisdom)	Initial object/Logos: SA (awareness)
Initial subject/sub-Logos: SA (awareness)	Initial subject/sub-Logos: KA (stillness)	Initial subject/sub-Logos: LA (wisdom)
Characteristic: unconsciousness	Characteristic: "even functioning"	Characteristic: light, information
Female (-)	Male (+)	Female (-)
Condition and Algorithm	Algorithm	Algorithm

Chapter 20

Introduction to the Catalyst
Modules and Thought

The catalyst category begins a new subsystem within the Archetypical Mind that functions independently but complements the experience and significator categories to facilitate experiences. After being processed through the catalyst/experiential/significator subsystem, the matrix/potentiator subsystem receives the fruit of a thought, modifies the consciousness pattern, and prepares a mind/body/spirit to attract and process the next thought. Every thought processed offers a solitary experience, but, from the limited perspective of consciousness enjoying the lower dimensions of 4th Density and below, an experience may seem to incorporate a multitude of thoughts along a central theme.

Every thought is experienced within an environment, and, much like a single sentence diagram, consists of a subject, an object, and a verb or action element. Within a single thought process, because of the characteristics afforded by the categories of the Archetypical Mind, a thought holds the potential to choose from a variety of incremental options that accrue to allow consciousness to experience one of three different results. The first potential result is the most ideal, which is to reveal greater truth by allowing a mind/body/spirit to surrender a little more identity and move closer into alignment with the Higher Self. The second potential result is for the pattern of consciousness to remain at its current degree of evolutionary advancement, and the third potential result is for a mind/body/spirit to reject greater truth, increase its belief in the authenticity of its autonomous perception, and move farther away from unity with the Higher Self.

The Catalyst of the Mind is where a new thought begins processing, but, prior to attracting a new thought, the consciousness pattern will have been modified by the previous thought making the experiencer new and original. When the consciousness pattern is modified, the actual alteration brings the experience from time/space into space/time, therefore, it is only at this point that a thought becomes part of the perceived physical world. The consciousness pattern functions as a magnet and attracts the specifics of the next thought according to the prevailing condition of its pattern.

While consciousness remains in the lower dimensions of the 4th Density or below, the attraction of the next thought is automatic and perpetual. As a person's consciousness level escalates and becomes aware, the mind can direct the focus of the magnetism by the strength of its will and assume greater control over the thoughts to be processed. Assuming control of the thoughts selected is a product of awareness and is indicative of consciousness' increasing ability to substantively choose its path through evolution.

Changes and/or modifications to the consciousness pattern result in behavioral changes in both the consciousness pattern and its analog projections. If the mind/body/spirit has adjudicated the previous thought in a manner that escalates its consciousness level, then, from that point forward, its behavior will demonstrate its increased awareness of its Creator-ness. More specifically, a mind/body/spirit will allow the Matrix of the Mind to incrementally recognize a greater influence from the archetype SA (awareness), and, in the Matrix of the Body, recognize increased influence from the archetype KA (stillness), each of which is positioned as the initial subject of its respective modules.

Its behavior will also reflect a reduction in the prominence of the unconsciousness archetype in the Potentiator of the Mind and a proportionate increase in the initial subject/sub-Logos archetype SA. As the mind/body/spirit continues its enlightenment and the appropriate level for activation of the Potentiator of the Body has been reached, then input from the initial object archetype LA (wisdom) will be recognized to further lessen the influences of unconsciousness. Concurrently, the initial subject archetype of the Potentiator of the Body KA (stillness) becomes activated and begins to integrate with the initial object archetype.

Also, concurrently with the activation of the SA archetype in the Potentiator of the Body module, the SA archetype in the Potentiator of the Spirit module becomes activated and begins to further strengthen the mind/body/spirit's awareness. As the KA archetype in the Potentiator of the Body becomes activated, the LA archetype in the Potentiator of the Spirit also becomes activated and begins to integrate and magnify the light provided by the spirit module. Evolution gathers significant momentum with the addition of the participation of the Potentiator of Body and Spirit in the modification of the consciousness pattern and the mind/body/spirit's behavior immediately reflects the changes, but the transformation is likely to require time for the changes to be digested, seasoned, and incorporated into thoughts.

Even before crossing the evolutionary threshold of awakening the 4th time/space chakra, the subject archetype of a module slowly rises to the surface as if it were an air-filled balloon rising from the ocean bottom. As processed thoughts productively prod consciousness forward through evolution, the subject archetype either integrates or exchanges position with the object archetype as the design of the individual module intended. Awakening the 4th time/space chakra is a significant point of transition where the previously dormant modules are activated and the initial object and subject archetypes in all the modules begin to find their balance. If processed thoughts are unsuccessful in productively advancing the mind/body/spirit forward, the subject archetype will essentially remain dormant and consciousness will continue to struggle under the distorted perceptions of the Archetypical Mind's conditions.

When the 4th time/space chakra is activated, the innocence of the Matrix of the Spirit begins to be proportionately reduced because the Potentiator of the Spirit shines the light, or information, into the darkness. Changes continue to incrementally result in even more positive modifications of the consciousness pattern because the positively interpreted thought fruits continue to transform and heal the pattern. The behavior of a mind/body/spirit transforms and directly reflects the level of consciousness and its ability to recognize, accept, and positively act upon the truth discovered in the thoughts processed.

All thought is attracted from a timeline of the prevailing lifetime because it is the next line in the script chosen by the character in the play. Every thought is uniquely presented within an environment and includes a subject, object, and verb or catalyst but the most important aspect, and the one aspect that determines how the thought will be interpreted more than any other, is the condition of the mind/body/spirit's pattern of consciousness. The consciousness pattern most accurately reflects the mind/body/spirit's stage of progression through evolution, its degree of continued attachment to the authenticity of the conditions and the distortions of the Archetypical Mind, and its level of free will intoxication. Consciousness sees and experiences "things" as it is, not as things actually are.

Similar to how a magnetic field is a means of expressing the relative movement of two electrical fields, a thought is a field and a means of energizing the relative movement between the object and subject archetypes of a module and their perceived fields of the truth. The Inherent Characteristics are undistorted truths that provide consciousness with clarity and pierce the illusions of the distortion archetypes. Distortions are not deceptions but they are apparitions that fade when contrasted with the truth of the Inherent Characteristics archetypes.

Creation is a "thought experiment" and a single thought is an incremental part of the total creation enterprise. A thought is a concept and the catalyst portion of a thought is its heart that propels consciousness' evolutionary progression. The amount of truth extracted from a thought is solely determined by the experiencing consciousness and measured by its effectiveness in promoting its degree of surrender of its free will intoxication. The effect of the added truth is reflected in how much or how little of a mind/body/spirit's attachment to the authenticity of the Archetypical Mind's conditions persists and how much it is aligned with its Higher Self.

A thought potentiates the core elements of the concepts represented in subject and object archetypes, both distortions and Inherent Characteristics, but, because it is a field, it also provides spaciousness to allow free will interpretation by the experiencing consciousness. The energy of creation is shaped by the mind's ability to recognize or not recognize truth, and either complement or deviate from the intent that is a part of the thought field. Spaciousness in the thought field allows consciousness to co-create its experiences through its interpretation of the thoughts according to an analogy with its choices determined solely by its personal preferences. Personal preference is determined through the chakra system according to its unique determination of what feels better to the individual mind/body/spirit.

When the mind inharmoniously processes thought, it is incumbent upon consciousness to become aware, correct the disharmony, and reestablish it. Harmony is a relative condition, determined to be as such according to how it feels to the participating consciousness. Greater harmony feels better than less harmony and certainly better than disharmony, but only the individual mind/body/spirit determines what is harmonious according to whether or not it feels good. Greater harmony is greater stability and the Creator is absolute stability, but the experiencing consciousness is the sole determinate of how much stability it is ready to feel because it requires surrender of its false identity and free will intoxication.

Consciousness begins creation by experiencing innocence, chaos, and instability but it learns through analogous interactions that stability immutably feels better than instability, which motivates it to pursue even greater stability. Likewise, it learns through analogous experiences that love feels better than fear, and, as previously discussed, love is a condition made possible by the greater awareness of its Creator-ness. In the process of having experiences, consciousness incrementally learns to become more aware to experience more love and explores itself in the process. Free will allows consciousness to moderate "what" it learns, "how" it learns, and "when" it learns, but the result of the learning is inevitable.

Consciousness begins the evolutionary journey as it does because these are the basic conditions created by the Archetypical Mind. A mind/body/spirit's experiences or thoughts are the vehicles for it to learn of itself by experiencing itself. For it to arrive at its predetermined destination, it must employ awareness to discover the foibles of its perceptions, and, because of its discovery, surrender distortions in favor of truth. Evolution is experienced through thought and can progress as quickly or as slowly as the participating consciousness chooses.

Processing thought "is" the work of creation, but, after being fully processed, a thought is not retained by a mind/body/spirit other than in how it has modified the consciousness pattern. Thoughts are the messages or the lessons to consciousness that allow it to learn of itself, and, therefore, fulfill its purpose for being alive. For consciousness to learn the lessons offered in thought, it is necessary that it fully process the thought, which means it has been fully run through the Archetypical Mind, and any polarities imputed by the mind have been fully integrated and resolved according to the limitations of the density's consciousness. It is improbable that many of the thoughts will be fully processed at the time of experience, while a mind/body/spirit remains in lower dimensions of 3rd Density or below; therefore the incomplete thoughts are stored as emotional baggage until consciousness is ready, willing, and able to complete the lessons.

Ultimately, consciousness must complete all of the incompletely processed thoughts stored as emotional baggage because in the emotional baggage are the lessons it needs to learn. Healing emotional baggage by finishing the lessons of 3rd Density is what is begun in the middle to upper dimensions of 3rd Density and is completed in the lower dimensions of 4th Density. 4th Density is a transitional density that allows for the healing of the 3rd Density distortions and prepares consciousness for the greater surrender of its free will intoxication. The upper dimensions of the 4th Density are where the process of actually becoming aware of its Creator-ness as love and the foundation is laid to learn of wisdom through the lens of love takes place.

The level of consciousness reflected in the consciousness pattern of the experiencing mind/body/spirit indicates how the historical catalyst has been interpreted and forecasts how it is most likely to be interpreted until the consciousness level is significantly changed. The Archetypical Mind's design remains unchanged throughout consciousness' tenure in the foundational and experiential densities, but the service that it provides evolves as consciousness evolves. The range of services that the Archetypical Mind provides is like a stack of shelving. Until consciousness grows tall enough to see and reach what is on the upper shelves, it remains unavailable, but only because consciousness doesn't know to stretch and grasp it.

The majority of the catalyst is planned before incarnation as part of the chosen timeline being experienced, but there is flexibility available to the Higher Self to guide the catalyst of the incarnate mind/body/spirit, just like the director of a play has flexibility in how the play will be presented. Timelines offer an infinite number of possibilities, everything from the most positive to the most negative and almost everything in between, but, if a mind/body/spirit needs experience not anticipated in a timeline, the Higher Self can add opportunity not originally anticipated. "Catalyst" is experienced in thought and it is a relatively simple task for the Higher Self to create a new or different stream of thoughts to augment a timeline and provide a mind/body/spirit with catalyst opportunities for learning.

Catalyst Overview

In 3rd Density, the catalyst offered in the processing of the thought is the same or very similar whether the mind/body/spirit is in the lower dimensions or higher dimensions. The difference between consciousness experiencing lower or higher dimensions is its ability to recognize truth or the services on the top shelf which, in turn, affects the intensity with which the catalyst is experienced. The ability to efficaciously process a thought increases as consciousness evolves which is evidenced by lower consciousness being generally less happy, negatively interpreting more thoughts with greater intensity, and finding greater difficulty letting them go. In contrast, higher consciousness enjoys greater happiness, fewer negative thought interpretations with less intensity, and a greater ability to let it go, or, in other words, completely process the thought at the occasion of its presentation.

In the lower densities, the characteristic of the Catalyst of the Mind is "pain and suffering". The determination of whether the offering is pain and suffering or joy and happiness is in the eye of the beholder and determined solely by the lens of the mind/body/spirit. As long as a mind/body/spirit remains in the lower dimensions of 3rd Density or below, it will primarily continue to experience the catalyst as pain and suffering to a greater or lesser degree. The determination of the catalyst as pain and suffering is a relative assessment that is a landmark difference between consciousness residing within the lower and higher dimensions of the density.

For anyone who has only the thoughts and awareness of the experiences of the pain and suffering of lower consciousness, it is very difficult to imagine that the same sow's ear can be experienced as a silk purse, but that is exactly what occurs as it evolves. The same catalyst, that at one phase of the evolutionary journey is seen as pain and suffering, can be seen at a later phase to be a joy-filled experience. The difference is not in the event itself but in the perceptual difference of the beholder's eye. The objective of all catalysts is the transformation of consciousness from lower to higher awareness and, in the process, rediscovery of the self.

At lower levels of consciousness, it is common to be preoccupied with trying to change the catalyst, unaware of the necessity or even the ability to transform the mind/body/spirit's consciousness pattern that beholds it. As consciousness escalates, it becomes apparent that the only adjustment of the scenario possible is of the observer, which is the transformation of consciousness itself. Throughout the foundational and experiential densities, the consciousness pattern of a mind/body/spirit is the only agent of change.

The flow of the thought within the catalyst category is the same as it is within all of the categories of the Archetypical Mind, as it emanates from the mind to first the body, then the spirit, and back to the mind. While consciousness remains within the lower dimensions of 3rd Density and is attached to the absolute authenticity of the conditions, the mind's perfunctory choice to reinforce its perceptions will be the body module's influence while ignoring the spirit. As the presentations on the catalyst and experiential categories will illustrate, this is especially significant in the catalyst and experience categories because these categories provide three-dimensional physical world perceptions that encourage the lower consciousness attachment to their authenticity.

As the mind/body/spirit accumulates experience and elevates consciousness, the perfunctory recognition of only the body's influence is incrementally transformed and consciousness begins to slowly surrender the priority of the body's influence to that of the spirit. Allowing the preferential choice of the spirit's influence over the body's input is indicative of consciousness' relinquishment of its attachment to the authenticity of the physical, and, in general, the conditions. While consciousness remains within the lower dimensions of 3rd Density and below, the catalyst category provides an enhancement of the attachment to the authenticity of the physical, but, later in the enlightenment journey, the same catalyst category modules serve as an accelerant for the surrender of the attachment.

Emotions are not part of the catalyst category, therefore the catalyst is devoid of emotions, but it provides the nucleus around which thought will be explored through the later assignment of emotion in the experiential category. Catalysts come in a variety of types, but all catalysts are conceptual and all experiences are presented in thoughts. The primary ingredient of a catalyst is that it acts as a verb in a sentence and provides consciousness with the opportunity for change. Invariably, the potential of change is from the subject to the object perspective which means consciousness is provided with the opportunity to transform its perspective from one that is more independent from the Creator to one that is closer in alignment with unity.

Entry into creation is the beginning of consciousness' evolution and it proceeds along a path, following numerous timelines which provide a mind/body/spirit with the catalysts to be experienced. In the foundational densities, 3rd Density, and the early dimensions of 4th Density, a mind/body/spirit isn't able to consciously micromanage the selection of catalyst to be experienced. However, consciousness does choose how it will interpret every catalyst and how it will modify the consciousness pattern with the thought proceeds. Usually unaware, consciousness chooses all of the catalysts experienced because the thought incorporating the catalyst magnetically responds to the prevailing condition of its consciousness pattern.

The Catalyst of the Mind guides a mind/body/spirit to choose from among a range of possible scenarios on a timeline with the actual selection being unconsciously made because of its resonance with the harmony/disharmony of the consciousness pattern. The catalyst experienced is not randomly selected because the nature of the available scenarios from within the range will fall within a general range of catalysts appropriate for the current character being portrayed in the current lifetime, and specifically most beneficial to its current consciousness pattern. All of the scenarios available for selection, at any given moment, will essentially share a common lesson because that will be what is needed to be learned at that moment to move it forward in evolution.

The greater the chaos and disharmony of the consciousness pattern's condition, the greater the chaos and inconsistency demonstrated in how a mind/body/spirit will interpret the catalyst. Behavior illustrates the momentum of experiences along the trajectory of the timeline and how a mind/body/spirit "gets" exactly the life that it has created to date. The catalyst always offers a message about a specific condition within a mind/body/spirit that needs healing and/or transformation, and undertaking the healing with awareness will potentially, but incrementally, move it forward along the evolution journey.

All of the messages of the experiential densities are focused upon healing from the distortions by expanding awareness, and they provide the opportunity to experience greater truth, thereby, relearning the Creator from the unique vantage point created by consciousness' free will choices. The intent of every 3rd Density message is for consciousness to awaken from unconsciousness, become more sobered from free will intoxication, and begin a more aware effort to return to unity with the Creator. Healing is the process of the Creator learning of itself by experiencing itself, and, in all of the densities, this is accomplished by consciousness in the subject posture becoming more like consciousness in the object role by first mimicking and then becoming the object. Unaware consciousness experiences chaos as it learns what it doesn't like so that it will know what it does like in comparison.

The objective of a message will always be the same, but the message(s) will often appear as a series of individual thoughts that may be difficult for the consciousness experiencing the 3rd Density to discern what the objective is. While consciousness remains unaware within the confines of lower dimensions, it perceives catalysts to primarily be problems that invariably will have something to do with getting love, because it is tasked with becoming aware and exploring love from the vantage point of awareness. Regardless of the interpretation of the catalyst as a problem, the objective of the catalyst will always be to potentially advance consciousness' spiritual progress.

Consciousness exploring the self as a projection of the Creator is tasked with relearning the Inherent Characteristics from its unique vantage point.

Relearning the Inherent Characteristics of the Creator is learning the Law of One through the lens of a unique consciousness pattern. Consciousness polarizing service-to-self is also relearning the Law of One from a similarly unique perspective and is in service to the Creator just as much as the most aware service-to-others being. Everything that consciousness does or thinks is fulfilling the purpose of creation whether it is evident or not. Depending upon the degree of awareness a mind/body/spirit permits itself, the journey's trials and tribulations can either be magnified or reduced.

The primary mechanism for catalyst delivery is through the interactions between two or more people, but other less obvious presentations of catalysts can be an equally effective delivery system. For example, the relationship between the individual and society in general, the individual and the unmanifest self (which would include the experience of pain), or even the inner dialogue of the self can supply a catalyst for the self because the self can be both subject and object in an experience. The unmanifest self is that portion of the mind/body/spirit that remains in time/space and coexists with the "me" that is reading this manuscript in space/time.

Catalysts can also be provided by inanimate things such as gadgets. Who would deny the catalytic relationship between a mid-life crisis male and his motorcycle or a soon-to-be bride and her wedding dress? Even a medical license or job title can be a very dynamic catalyst because it potentially adds complexity to the self's identity.

One of the most extreme catalysts that the population of Earth has repeatedly experienced has been bellicosity in the form of war or even the threat of war. Wars provide tremendously intense opportunities for a catalyst of a diverse nature. Catalysts, such as money, may interconnect with and enhance the effects of other catalysts while simultaneously being their catalyst. There is little or nothing that a mind/body/spirit may encounter that does not catalyze evolution.

Practically every experience in the timelines and/or improvised is a catalyst in one form or another. An excellent metaphor for the obligatory experience of catalysts is a grocery shopping trip. The trip is obligatory but what groceries are purchased is up to the free will choices of the shopper. Catalysts are essential for experience but how the catalysts are interpreted is the sole choice of the experiencing consciousness.

Chapter 21

The Catalyst Modules of the Archetypical Mind

When considering the categories of the Archetypical Mind comprising the catalyst/experiential/significator subsystem, it is essential to understand that experiences enjoyed by consciousness in the foundational densities and the lower dimensions of 3rd Density will probably not benefit from many of the modules potentially available until it has activated the 4th time/space chakra. All modules are potentially available to all consciousness, even in these lower ranges of the consciousness scale, but, while it continues to reinforce only the ego mind and "I" perspective conditions, consciousness will probably be unreceptive and/or unaware of the potential contributions from other modules. Just as the Potentiator of the Body and Potentiator of the Spirit are always available at all times, the nature of limited awareness makes it impractical for a mind/body/spirit to recognize their contributions until it has adequately evolved to do so.

The catalyst category consists of the Catalyst of the Mind, the Catalyst of the Body, and the Catalyst of the Spirit but the Catalyst of the Spirit will not be recognized by the Catalyst of the Mind until adequate awareness has been achieved, which means that the ego mind must have sufficiently surrendered its independent identity, its exclusive prominence, and recognized the spirit's potential contributions. The threshold for recognition of the spirit is the opening of the 4th time/space chakra which usually occurs in the upper dimensions of 3rd Density and signals a mind/body/spirit's qualifications for graduation to 4th Density. Opening of the heart chakra diversifies a mind/body/

spirit's intelligence resource beyond the ego or rational/logical mind by including the intelligence offered by the deep mind which is the province of the spirit.

Opening the time/space heart chakra, and thereby, activating the spirit portion of mind/body/spirit design, is the result of the choice to align with the Higher Self, adopt a unity consciousness philosophy, and recognize, to a relative degree, the Law of One. It is the choice to surrender chaos, identity, and free will intoxication in favor of greater stability and unity with the Higher Self, but, more prominently, it is the choice to evolve into higher consciousness.

Catalyst of the Mind

The construction of the Catalyst of the Mind, as it is with all of the modules of the Archetypical Mind, consists of two archetypes: one as the initial object/Logos and the other as the initial subject/sub-Logos. The initial Logos/object of the Catalyst of the Mind is SA (awareness) and the initial sub-Logos/subject is LA (wisdom). As consciousness escalates its awareness, these two Inherent Characteristics incrementally harmonize to permit the transformation of its perspectives to greater unity and integration into oneness. However, for those mind/body/spirits polarizing negatively, harmonization of the awareness and wisdom archetypes in this module doesn't occur, but, instead, the archetypes are employed independently to enhance consciousness' focus outside the self, reinforce the ego mind and "I" perspective, and further dominate and subjugate others.

Awareness is "the" Inherent Characteristic that consciousness is tasked with becoming in the 3rd Density, and, from its newly clarified lens, explores love in the 4th Density. Consciousness must become aware but do so by developing self-awareness and relying upon the strength of the will as the motor that propels it forward. Enigmatically, pain and suffering are the fuel that ignites the motor's combustion so it can power consciousness out of the complacency and confusion of lower consciousness. Consciousness becomes aware of the pain and suffering through the process of analogy, motivates the strength of the will to pursue less pain and suffering, and enhances awareness in the process.

The Catalyst of the Mind is an algorithm module which means it is a piece of the puzzle necessary to resolve the conditions of the Archetypical Mind. The Catalyst of the Mind is the module where a newly attracted thought begins the assembly line process of a mind/body/spirit having an experience. Every thought is an independent experience and every module of the Archetypical Mind contributes a significant element to the interpretation of experiences. The Catalyst of the Mind receives the thought, sequentially forwards it to the Catalyst of the Body and the Catalyst of the Spirit for input, receives the input from both the body and spirit modules (after the spirit has been activated) and, only then, determines the catalyst category's interpretation of the thought.

Once the Catalyst of the Mind adjudicates the categories' interpretation of the thought, the results are forwarded to the Experience of the Mind module for further processing along the Archetypical Mind assembly line. The Catalyst of the Mind is a female or negative module, which means it's the object of other male/subject modules. The primary focus of male modules to be balanced is the experiential category modules.

While consciousness remains in the lower 3rd Density dimensions and below, the "awareness suppressing effects" of unconsciousness from the Potentiator of the Mind are projected into the catalyst category. Unconsciousness remains influential because the mind/body/spirit has been made unconscious, not the thought, but its effect isn't so substantial as to deny the contributions of the Catalyst of the Body while the spirit module remains dormant. The actual thoughts are always emotionally neutral because the condition of the consciousness pattern, and, consequentially, its personal preferences are the determinant of which emotions are utilized.

Mind/body/spirits enjoying the Earth experience have, over time, systematically created emotional and spiritual entropy, becoming numb to pain and suffering being as such because of a dearth of analogous feelings. Constant discomfort has caused Earth's population to become complacent and apathetic about conditions that could be significantly changed with awareness. The Higher Selves are aware of this condition and have put forth a significant effort to counteract it, which we will discuss in future chapters, but, regardless of any external efforts to heal the condition, it's still incumbent upon the population to recognize and take advantage of the opportunities for change because each mind/body/spirit is ultimately responsible for its evolutionary progress.

Consciousness in all densities may experience the bliss of unity consciousness according to the density's programmed capacity to do so. Consciousness experiencing 3rd Density on Earth has consistently failed to become aware and claim a more joyful experience which has resulted in entropy. Despite the difficulties presented by a multitude of sources, Earth's population has chosen to remain unconscious and it is solely incumbent upon the population to turn it around.

Catalyst of the Mind

- Initial Object: LA (wisdom)
- Initial Subject: SA (awareness)
  - Characteristic(s):
    - Pain & Suffering
    - Motivator of evolution through discomfort
- Female Principal (-)
- Algorithm

Catalyst of the Body

The Catalyst of the Body offers a diverse range of services as consciousness migrates from the lower to the higher consciousness phases of the experiential densities' journey. The Catalyst of the Body creates the foundational perceptual condition for the experience of a physical world; the first condition within the foundational condition is used to perceive its creation and collects the sensory data necessary for the mind to interact with physicality. As with all of the modules of the Archetypical Mind, the potential services offered by the module don't change but consciousness' ability to perceive and employ the services does change according to its evolutionary status.

In the foundational densities and lower dimensions of 3rd Density, the mind modules of the catalyst/experiential/ significator subsystem are consistently only recognizing input from the body modules while omitting most, if not all, input from the spirit modules with every thought. After consciousness enters the upper dimensions of 3rd Density, the body category continues to contribute to the thought process but its prominence declines as the mind begins to be swayed towards the spirit's input more frequently. As the archetypes comprising the modules transform by either integrating the Inherent Characteristic archetypes or overcoming the distortion ones, consciousness becomes more receptive to the truth because higher consciousness more closely resonates with it.

The Catalyst of the Body's contributions are enigmatic because one of its principal characteristics is the collection of sensory data input accumulated from a vast array of potential "sensory data" available in the space/time environment. The environment serves as the stage for the thought process while the physical data is simultaneously creating the perceptual foundation for a physical self. Sensory data input is only from or about the environment, which means it can only be of or about the space/time illusion. When a mind/body/spirit

313

interprets the catalyst of a thought, it is influenced by the predisposition promoted by the consciousness pattern towards the pleasantness or unpleasantness of the environment in which the thought is presented. Choosing the sensory data to complement or disparage the thought enhances or diminishes the intensity of the catalyst, based upon the mind/body/spirit's personal preference.

The Catalyst of the Body's creation of the foundation for all physical perception is another Archetypical Mind condition, facilitated because the initial object/Logos is populated with the distortion archetype DA (movement). In every module populated with a distortion archetype in the object/ Logos position, the module creates a condition that must be surrendered or overcome as consciousness escalates. The initial subject/sub-Logos is populated with the Inherent Characteristic KA (stillness), from which DA is originally distorted. As with all of the modules creating conditions, the initial Logos and sub-Logos eventually exchange positions, as consciousness and awareness escalate, thereby transforming the perception and function of the module from distortion to truth.

The Catalyst of the Body creates two conditions, but the second condition is dependent upon the sequential creation of the first. The first perceptual condition created by DA is the foundational concept of "space as a volume" but the module also creates a second condition which is the perception of length, the first spatial dimension within the "space as a volume" perception. The two other spatial dimensions are created by two other modules of the Archetypical Mind which we will address in future chapters.

With every individual thought, the Catalyst of the Body recreates the concept of space and the first linear dimension, which means, for consciousness outside of the Archetypical Mind such as 6th Density or above, the concepts of distance and direction do not exist. The concept of space as a volume and the concept of length do not exist independently of the mind's observation because they are created by the distortions of perception afforded by the Archetypical Mind. The truth is, there is no physical separation between two mind/body/spirits, other than as they may conceptually perceive it, and there is no physical distance between stars, galaxies, or universes. The only physical distance in creation is as it is perceived according to the degree of consciousness' adherence to the authenticity of the distortions, which means all distances and directions are distortions of perception.

The five physical senses (sight, sound, touch, taste, and smell) provide the mechanisms for detecting sensory data predicated upon the Archetypical Mind conditions. They allow a mind/body/spirit to be physically viable in all of the foundational and experiential densities but they lose their authenticity and become less and less the focus of experience as consciousness progresses. In 3rd Density and below, while consciousness remains firmly attached to the authenticity of the physical and predominantly focused upon learning of the self through the sensory apparatus of the chemical body, the physical perspective is its whole world.

For those mind/body/spirits following the service-to-others path, physical world authenticity becomes supplanted by the awareness of truth and unity. Truth is synonymous with infinity and, as consciousness escalates, it aligns more completely with the Higher Self as a personification of the one infinite Creator. Escalating consciousness increases access to truth by incorporating additional density dimensions into awareness which inevitably results from surrendering the ego mind, surrendering the "I" perspective, and sobering from free will intoxication.

While consciousness remains within the lower dimensions of 4th Density and below, a mind/body/spirit is presented with millions of pieces of sensory data input every moment of every day, but it can be aware of only a very few of those potentially available. With every thought, the mind sorts through the millions of bits of sensory data information but becomes aware of the few that support its prevailing perceptions as projected by its consciousness pattern. Until consciousness surrenders its attachment to the authenticity of the physical world in the later dimensions of 4th Density, the scope of sensory data input brought into focus expands and the previously myopic perspectives of lower consciousness incorporate more of creation into its awareness field.

Every aspect of sensory input recorded as part of the experience is considered "content" of the experience. The entirety of the experience is recorded and the sensory data, or content, becomes an inherent part of the experience's interpretation. While consciousness remains under the limiting constraints of unconsciousness in the Potentiator of the Mind, the sensory input has only a temporal meaning, but, if consciousness has awakened awareness, the same sensory input data can serve to further expand its exploration and understanding of the self.

Catalyst of the Body
•Initial Object: DA (movement)
•Initial Subject: KA (stillness)
•Characteristic(s):
•Sensory Data Input
•Space (Volume)
•First spatial dimension
•Female Principal (-)
•Condition

Catalyst of the Spirit

Faith and hope are the characteristics of the Catalyst of the Spirit. While perceptions are determined primarily by the ego mind, the premise that consciousness' evolution is predicated upon faith is a very difficult concept to understand and even more difficult to accept. The greater the prominence of the ego mind, without contributions of the spirit or deep mind, the more it seems that faith and/or hope are folly.

The Catalyst of the Spirit is initially populated with two Inherent Characteristic archetypes: LA (wisdom) in the Logos/object position, and SA (awareness) in the initial sub-Logos/subject position. Again, the pairing of LA and SA uniquely facilitates the characteristics of this aspect of the Archetypical Mind but in the reverse order from the Potentiator of the Spirit that shines light into the thought process. Wisdom and awareness eventually integrate as consciousness evolves, but, until then, wisdom independently encourages consciousness to surrender beyond its perceived authenticity of sensory data through faith. Having the faith to surrender the ego mind to the deep mind and learning to rely upon intuition follows the light provided in the Potentiator of the Spirit module.

The Inherent Characteristic archetypes are diverse and each archetype offers preponderantly the characteristic indicated by its character identification but it also includes all the other Inherent Characteristics. Wisdom is preponderantly wisdom but also includes characteristics of the other four characteristics and therefore is very diverse in the services that it offers. When consciousness adequately surrenders the ego mind and "I" perspective conditions, opens the 4th heart chakra, escalates its awareness, and engages the deep mind by recognizing the contributions of the spirit module of the Archetypical Mind, it opens itself to the process of "direct knowing". Direct knowing comes from a connection to the collective consciousness that is equally available to all consciousness.

Direct knowing receives light, or information, directly and is not qualified or limited. Truth from direct knowing is obvious to the willing recipient and challengeable only by an ego mind that is still attached to the authenticity of the Archetypical Mind's conditions. A mind/body/spirit "knows" it is true because it feels right and good and no other "proof" is required. It feels good because it connects consciousness to infinity which is, by degrees, both the Higher Self and the Creator.

Hope and faith are sequential stages of the same process and are determined by the extent to which consciousness has surrendered the ego mind and connected to the collective consciousness. A mind/body/spirit has hope when it has received some degree of connection to the collective consciousness but still wavers between the authenticities of the conditions and truth. As the ego mind and "I" perspective continue to be surrendered, hope transforms into faith, direct knowing becomes more substantial, and a mind/body/spirit learns of its power to transform itself into higher consciousness. It is a process that potentially advances with every thought which we will discuss more specifically when we address the Experience of the Spirit module in coming chapters.

The Catalyst of the Spirit is an algorithm that offers the potential resolution of a puzzle piece to the goal of surrendering one or more conditions created by the Archetypical Mind. By this phase of the processing of thought through the Archetypical Mind, a pattern emerges from the modules constructed with LA and SA in alternating positions, all coordinating to propel consciousness forward. The vibrational resonance of SA in one module awakens all of the corresponding SA archetypes in other modules, and the vibrational resonance of LA has a similar effect with other modules populated with LA. The Catalyst of the Spirit module is also female energy, which means all three of the catalyst category modules are female, serving as the object to other subject modules but principally the modules in the experiential category.

The more consciousness grips tightly to the ego mind, the more it reinforces the ego and "I" perspective, strengthens fear and supports its perceived independence and isolation in creation. Faith is often contrary to the foundational precepts of science and prevailing philosophical thought, which presumes the irrefutability of "the physical world" and/or natural laws. The reliance upon conventional wisdom of or about the physical world reinforces the physical illusion and is a principal obstacle deterring consciousness from the development of intuition, developing the connection to direct knowing, and relying upon faith.

The thought of surrendering to faith usually enflames consciousness' ego mind-based fears and presents the rational/ logical ego mind with a confounding enigma. There is no proof that surrendering to faith through reliance upon intuition is a practical means to evolve but the alternative, adhering to the prominence of the ego mind, perpetuates the experience of stress. Consciousness learns by analogy and if adherences to the ego mind's traditional methods continue to create stress, which they do, the only other alternative is to surrender, rely upon intuition, and employ faith. Either way, there isn't any proof because "anything and everything" a mind/body/spirit experiences is done only by the mind through thought.

When "the pain of staying the same is greater than the pain of change, we change" as the saying goes. The Catalyst of the Mind's characteristic is pain and suffering while consciousness remains within the lower dimensions of 3rd Density and below. When consciousness surrenders its attachment to the conditions of the Archetypical Mind enough, recognizes intuition as a viable means of evolving after it has encountered truth, and becomes courageous enough to take its foot off of the first base and run to second base predicated upon faith, it evolves. The Catalyst of the Spirit provides the opportunity to develop faith enough to run to second base and beyond with the processing of every thought, but the individual mind/body/spirit must take the initiative by using the strength of its own will.

A six-year-old may protest having to eat his or her vegetables and do so vehemently. After the same six-year-old matures, he often decides that the vegetables are not so bad and may decide they taste good. The vegetables remain the same but the tastes and predilections of the once six-year-old have changed. The same is true of consciousness' protest and defense of the authenticity of the conditions which eventually will be surrendered to truth, afforded by surrendering the arguments for maintaining adherence to the authenticity of the conditions because of awareness.

Relying upon faith, or not, is a principal determinant between choosing to polarize negatively or positively. Service-to-others evolutionarily mature by becoming aware and choosing to surrender identity to greater unity based upon faith. Service-to-self doesn't become aware or mature and continues to protest surrendering identity by defending its independence from unity.

Progression through evolution and alignment with the Higher Self is a "feeling" enterprise instead of a rational/logical thinking one. The more a mind/body/spirit relies upon rational thinking to discredit intuition, the slower its progress will be. The more it allows feeling to be its guide to discover new qualities and quantities of truth, the more quickly it will evolve and find greater joy and happiness.

The design prescribes the gathering of light (information), yielding the rational to intuition, and allowing the light to be cured or to season the consciousness pattern. During the curing process, consciousness incrementally transforms to greater awareness and its perceptions reflect greater dimensionality. The design affords consciousness the ability to successfully and skillfully explore the self without the necessity of self-harming behavior. Choices should always be made based upon what feels better or, in other words, the process of analogy and the feeling afforded by surrendering distortions to truth immutably feels best.

Fear is the antithesis of love and it is essential to overcome fear and surrender identity through greater awareness to discover the truer self. The awareness of unity, resulting from surrendering to the enlightenment process, is inevitable and immutable but can only be experienced through feelings based upon faith, not a priori proof, to go from first base to second base. Surrendering perceptions of separateness affords consciousness the ability to embrace the unity of all creation and surrender stress into the direct knowingness of truth.

Consciousness isn't afforded proof at the level of consciousness currently experienced on Earth but it does get pain and suffering to urge it onward and upward. When there is enough pain and suffering, then it will rely upon hope, if not before, by encouraging awareness and discernment. The universe fulfills consciousness' desires but if it is insistent upon proof before it experiences the process of surrender it will be allowed all of the pain and suffering desired to mitigate between the ego and surrender.

Hope and Faith are the tonics of the healing enterprise, and the salvation from pain and suffering. It is because consciousness is the distorted Creator and love is the creative principle of all creation that every mind/body/spirit must employ the strength of its will to assume control of the throttle for its journey through evolution. Everyone is different but the process and path to return to the home from whence consciousness began is the same.

Catalyst of the Spirit

- Initial Object: SA (awareness)
- Initial Subject: LA (wisdom)
  - Characteristic(s):
    - Faith
    - Hope
- Female Principal (-)
- Algorithm

Chapter 22

The Experience Modules of the Archetypical Mind

In the previous chapter, we explained the catalyst category, the first category of the catalyst/experience/significator subsystem of the Archetypical Mind, and this chapter continues to explore the processing of thought through the experiential category. A thought, or an experience, begins to be processed when it is recognized by the Catalyst of the Mind and from there distributed to the Catalyst of the Body and Spirit, then returned to the Catalyst of the Mind with their input for the final catalyst category adjudication, and forwarded to the Experience of the Mind for further processing. The Archetypical Mind functions as an assembly line that allows every module to uniquely contribute its characteristics to the thought process and ultimately concludes with the fruit of a single thought. The processing of thought occurs completely in time/space with only the results of the process, the fruit, brought into space/time by modifying the consciousness pattern and/or analog projection.

The experience category is the second step of the catalyst/experience/significator subsystem and consists of three modules: including the Experience of the Mind, the Experience of the Body, and the Experience of the Spirit, with each module sharing the same basic design structure as all of the other modules of the Archetypical Mind. Two archetypes, one in the object/Logos position and the other in the subject/sub-Logos position, create the transforming characteristics of the module and facilitate consciousness' incremental evolution from chaos to stability. The initial object/Logos archetype is TA (separation), and, because it is a distortion archetype, the Experience of the

Mind creates yet another condition that must be surrendered or overcome. The initial subject/sub-Logos is LA (wisdom), which eventually supplants TA as the principal characteristic of the module as the mind/body/spirit successfully evolves.

Experience of the Mind

Emotion is the characteristic of the Experience of the Mind module and will continue to be so even after LA assumes the role as the principal archetype of the module, however, the nature of the emotion transforms; not because the emotions have changed but because the experiencing consciousness has changed. While consciousness remains within the lower dimensions of 3rd Density and below, the emotions may predominantly be negative ones because, for the most part, they will feel unpleasant as indicated by the heavy labels such as fear, heartache, guilt, shame, etc. Emotions labeled with heavy names indicate they feel burdensome and intense because consciousness is in the rudimentary discovery phase of its evolution exploring "what it doesn't like" as it learns to practice analogy in its exploration of love. Analogy requires consciousness to experience two things and to choose which one it prefers between the two.

As explained in earlier chapters, consciousness begins its experience of creation as a blank canvas, in constant motion or chaos, and completely innocent. In the 3rd Density, it's tasked with becoming awareness, and, upon graduation to the 4th Density and through the lens of awareness, to explore love. Consciousness in 1st and 2nd Densities has the same mandate but it isn't until 3rd Density that it has sufficient energy and intelligence resources to begin to successfully fulfill the task, so we generally identify this task as belonging to 3rd Density. Discovering love by trial and error and from the perspective of darkness and chaos can, and almost always does, create significant pain and suffering as consciousness employs analogy to narrow down the infinite number of variables to eventually reveal the love that it has been seeking.

Emotion is the product of the analogous process of the chakra system which is part of the Experience of the Mind module. The Experience of the Mind is the most significant contributor to experience interpretation while consciousness remains within the lower dimensions of 4th Density and below because emotions are felt more intensely by lower consciousness than higher consciousness that may still be swayed by the Archetypical Mind. When the consciousness level escalates, a mind/body/spirit interprets thoughts or experiences with greater awareness of truth and significantly less attachment to the mind's distortions and conditions. Not only does the intensity of negative emotions subside or evaporate, but the nature of the emotions transition from the heavy negative ones, those that don't feel good, to lighter more positive ones, those that feel better.

The aphorism "we see things as we are, not as they are" is particularly appropriate because emotions transform when the experiencing consciousness changes, even though the actual experiences remain essentially the same. Emotions result from a vibration created by the friction between a mind/body/spirit's prevailing perspective and truth. The creation of emotion occurs according to a step-by-step process that sends an emotionally neutral thought down a conveyor belt and allows every step of the chakra system to either like or dislike (resonate or not resonate) the thought. The steps along the conveyor belt that dislike the thought content create friction that results in the vibration.

When computer programming began, all computers functioned according to the recognition of zeros and ones that were presented in various orders and frequencies. The order and frequency of the presentations of zeros and ones was the language of computers and allowed them to do computations. Similarly, the creation of emotion occurs because the chakra system recognizes two simple choices; either it likes or dislikes in varying intensities based upon the comparison and contrast of its prevailing consciousness pattern, its resistance to truth, and truth itself. The more a consciousness pattern's perspective varies from the truth, the more intense and more frequent the emotions, because of greater friction and, consequently, a greater vibration.

When the analysis is complete, there are only two emotions; love, which is a mind/body/spirit's recognition and acceptance of its alignment with the Higher Self and the Creator, and fear, which is the antithesis of love and created because of a mind/body/spirit's defense and/or protection of its perceived identity. These are the zeros and ones of basic computing as thought is processed through the chakra system, but presented according to the multiple steps of the chakra system conveyor belt. The 1st time/space chakra begins the conveyor belt that has six assessment points for an analog projection into space/time, and, therefore, six opportunities to like or dislike the thought being processed.

The 2nd time/space chakra receives the fruit of the thought assessment from the 1st time/space chakra's process and repeats the process but from the base perspective of the 2nd time/space chakra. The process is repeated from the 3rd time/space chakra, 4th time/space chakra, and eventually, 5th time/space chakra perceptions after the mind/body/spirit has evolved to the stage of opening these awareness platforms. An emotion application doesn't occur until the "content" from the Experience of the Body and Spirit has been provided to the Experience of the Mind that has already received input from the Catalyst of the Mind in the original transfer from the Catalyst category. The final emotion application isn't completed by the Experience of the Mind until the entire chakra system, the length of which will vary according to the current density being experienced, has finished its processing of the thought.

The individual space/time chakras are where emotion (like or dislike) is incrementally created and where emotional baggage for the particular analog projection is cumulatively stored. When sufficient baggage has been accumulated in a particular chakra, the flow of Intelligent Energy through that chakra often becomes obscured or even blocked entirely. For example, if a mind/body/ spirit has accumulated significant emotional baggage in the 3rd space/time chakra, the energy flow will be blocked and all future thoughts will probably only be processed to this point along the conveyor belt. The remaining higher chakras will not be able to add their contributions to the thought process until the emotional baggage has been lessened or healed. Fear is the emotion most often associated with the 3rd space/time chakra and a significant enough distortion along the conveyor belt at this point would most likely cause the mind/body/spirit to behave as if it were an orange-ray (2nd Density) consciousness.

The condition of a yellow-ray or 3rd Density consciousness functioning as an orange-ray or 2nd Density consciousness is not uncommon in the Earth experience because of the spiritual entropy that has developed. In an earlier chapter, we discussed reports that some of the WWII Nazi SS troops supervising, torturing, and killing the concentration camp prisoners experienced sexual gratification from their treatment of the captives which is indicative of emotional distortions resulting from emotional baggage at this level. Similar behavior abounds in the current population throughout the world and is evidenced by reports of sex trafficking, genocide, police brutality, authoritarian coups, or the forceful kidnapping and separation of children from parents to punish an indigenous population because they are indigenous, to name a few.

While a mind/body/spirit's behavior reflects a lower consciousness level but is not necessarily socially deviant behavior, the emotion's intensity will probably be significant which means it is probable that the feeling is very undesirable. A thought is seasoned with each trip through the time/space and space/time chakras, adding unique flavoring because of the emotion created. While consciousness remains within the lower dimensions of 3rd Density or below, it is limited to the emotional seasoning provided by the lower chakras, but, when it opens the 4th time/space chakra, it begins to mitigate lower consciousness emotions with higher consciousness vibration and perspectives. The higher consciousness perspectives generate less friction because consciousness is better able to experience truth, thereby further encouraging the surrender of its identity and the need to manage the world around it to support and defend its hierophant self-image.

The frequency of negative emotions decreases and emotional intensity declines because less friction to truth is created. Eventually, as consciousness escalates into the upper dimensions of 5th Density, if not before, all negative emotions disappear and only the positive, good feelings of greater unity with the Creator are experienced, to the extent that free will intoxication has been surrendered. Relative to the emotions created during its previous experiences of the lower densities, consciousness experiences a constant state of bliss, which is the natural state of all consciousness after it has surrendered identity and overcome the distortions of the Archetypical Mind.

The Experience of the Mind module is a male or subject module which means it is designed with a leaning towards greater separation from the Creator, but, as it evolves, it transforms to more of the object leaning as it integrates perspectives with the female modules. Two of the three experience modules are male leaning modules and all of the catalyst modules are female modules. The experience category is one of three aspects of the catalyst/experience/significator subsystem of the Archetypical Mind and each one progressively supports the others to process thought in a manner that promotes the consciousness' free will choices while guiding it to mitigate the beginning conditions of constant chaos, innocence, and confusion. The design of the Archetypical Mind and all of creation is to guide consciousness to greater unity, thereby, furthering the cycle of evolution.

Experience of the Mind
•Initial Object: TA (separation)
•Initial Subject: LA (wisdom)
•Characteristic(s):
•Emotion
•Male Principal (+)
•Condition

Experience of the Body

Before sending a thought through the chakra system to emotionally interpret the experience, the Experience of the Body receives the thought from the Experience of the Mind to offer its content contributions. As it is with all of the body modules, the body doesn't add intelligence but it does add significant information used by the Experience of the Mind to interpret the thought. The Experience of the Body is constructed of two archetypes; one in the initial object/Logos position and another in the subject/sub-Logos position. The initial object archetype is the same distortion archetype found in the Experience of the Mind, TA (separation), but the initial subject/sub-Logos is the Inherent Characteristic archetype SA (awareness).

TA is a distortion archetype created from YA (unity), which means the Experience of the Body creates yet another condition of the Archetypical Mind that must be overcome as consciousness evolves, but, similar to the Catalyst of the Body, it provides other significant contributions to initially help diversify and authenticate the perception of a physical world. The condition created by this module is the second spatial dimension or width. The diversification of the physical world perception expands upon the Catalyst of the Body's creation of the perception of space as a volume and the first spatial dimension by providing the second step of a four-step process involving three different modules to create the perception of a physical world with three spatial dimensions.

The other significant contribution to the perceptual distortion condition is the experience of the sensory data collected in the Catalyst of the Body. The Catalyst of the Body only selected the sensory data from the environment but held it in suspension without "feeling" it. When the thought is forwarded from the Catalyst of the Mind to the Experience of the Mind, the yet-to-be-felt sensory data collected in the Catalyst of the Body is included, along with the perceptions of space and the first spatial dimension. Feeling the sensory data is how the body interacts with the environment and dramatically reinforces the mind/body/spirit's perceptions of the authenticity of space/time.

The first spatial dimension consists of two points within the concept of space as a volume, but the first spatial dimension allows for only a straight line or linear exploration of creation, which is very limited. It is a condition experienced by some other solar systems' experiences. The Experience of the Body adds a third point which allows the perception of a flat surface and the exploration of the physical world without depth. Just as there are solar systems that experience creation with only two spatial points of perception within a volume, there are others that only have a three-point dimensional perception and only allow for the exploration of the physical world as a flat surface. The experience of creation is infinite and incorporates many more conceptual derivations of the Earth experience than we can imagine.

The conditions of the Archetypical Mind cause consciousness to perceive an authentic physical world, independent of its observation, which, from its limited perspective, most often results in a dramatically intensified perception of separation from the Creator. It enhances the ego mind, strengthens the "I" perspective, and compounds unconsciousness by perceptually moving a mind/body/spirit even further from the essence of the Creator. Enjoying the lower dimensions of 4th Density and below with a physical world perception based on three spatial dimensions is neither a plus nor a minus because it's just one of the infinite experiences of creation that allow the Creator to explore itself from different vantage points.

Physicality is only a reflection in the funhouse mirror and it doesn't matter if the perspective is viewed from space/time, time/space, or straddling the two, which is more often the case. As consciousness escalates, a mind/body/spirit begins to see through the illusion and recognize the images in the mirrors as distortions because of greater awareness. Just as a closer inspection of a funhouse mirror reveals the frame and the supports holding the mirror in place, a closer inspection of emotion and thought begins to reveal the distortions artificially supporting the authenticity of the conditions.

While consciousness remains within the influences of the conditions, it isn't a matter of discovering something physically new that hasn't been noticed before but a matter of detaching from its authenticity because awareness has brought greater truth to the forefront and caused the shedding of unconsciousness. Once a mind/body/spirit awakens, becomes aware, and begins to shed its attachment to the authenticity of the physical, it surrenders the perception of its transience; the temporal perspective that participation in creation will cease if the body disappears. Perceptions of the physical world are just part of a phase in the evolutionary journey just as growing through the teenage years is a phase in a lifetime.

The Experience of the Body is one of three modules that make the dream, within a dream, within a dream possible. Without this module, we couldn't have the three-dimensional space/time dream and so the intensity of the physical world experience wouldn't be possible. However, just because we are within a dream doesn't mean we shouldn't or can't awaken from the dream. We must awaken to continue to raise our consciousness and evolve.

Experience of the Body

- Initial Object: TA (separation)
- Initial Subject: SA (awareness)
  - Characteristic(s):
    - Sensory input experience
    - Physicality
    - 2nd spatial Dimension; width
- Female Principal (-)
- Condition

Experience of the Spirit

The Experience of the Spirit contributes a lot to the thought process, even though the Experience of the Mind will not consciously recognize its contributions until the 4th time/space chakra has been energized. The module creates a condition at the beginning of consciousness' evolution that remains prominent until well after a mind/body/spirit has opened the 4th chakra, but, as the archetypes incrementally transition the object and subject roles, it begins to incrementally serve as an algorithm too. When consciousness demonstrates sufficient evolutionary progress and attachment to the authenticity of the conditions is increasingly surrendered, the module increases its contributions to the algorithmic functions of the mind and expedites consciousness' further advancement.

The module offers consciousness two characteristics at the beginning of its evolutionary journey which transform as it evolves into another characteristic completely different than the beginning two. The initial characteristic is functionally reflected in the two conditions that it creates, which are the "perception of motion through time" and the "third spatial dimension". As a whole, the authenticity of the conditions begins to weaken near the end of the 3rd Density, increasingly dissipates in the 4th Density, and is virtually gone by the time it evolves to the 5th Density. The module serves a significant purpose because its second characteristic is algorithmic and provides support for the surrender of both the ego mind and the "I" perspective. The initial conditions and algorithmic characteristics are not mutually exclusive because, from the first day of a mind/body/ spirit's introduction into the foundational densities until it leaves the 5th Density and again is in unity with its Higher Self, it promotes the incremental surrender of free will intoxication, ego mind, and "I" perspective.

Consciousness experiencing the lower dimensions of 3rd Density is the evolutionary period when the conditions are the most authentic, but the algorithmic characteristic of the Experience of the Spirit is always available even though seldom recognized until mid-4th Density. The "I" perspective and ego mind conditions, created by the co-supporting design of the Matrix and Potentiator of the Mind, are the primary targets of the spirit module. When consciousness can surrender its attachment to the authenticity of the conditions, especially the authenticity of the "I" perspective and ego mind, a dramatic transformation of consciousness and its experience of creation occurs.

The transformation begins in the 3rd Density when consciousness first becomes aware, continues and escalates as it becomes awareness, and hits its 3rd Density zenith when it opens the 4th heart chakra and experiences its authentic self for the 1st time in its evolutionary journey. Transformation continues into 4th Density when it continues its exploration of love through the lens of awareness until it becomes love and begins to explore wisdom through the lens of love. When consciousness graduates to 5th Density, as part of a newly formed social memory complex, it continues its dramatic transformation as it melds more completely into a cohesive single organism as a social memory complex, exploring unity through the wisdom lens.

No matter the density, with every thought processed, the Experience of the Spirit offers the Experience of the Mind the choice to either continue to support a perception of separation and attachment to the authenticity of the conditions or to surrender its perceptions and step closer to unity. The perception of separation is a scale that measures the degree of free will intoxication remaining and reflects, in a mind/body/spirit's behavior, the attachment to the authenticity of the "I" perspective and ego mind as one extreme, and reunification with the Higher Self as the other. The more completely the mind/body/spirit surrenders its perception of separation, the more completely it's able to use awareness to experience truth. Surrendering of the ego mind and "I" perspective provides a mind/body/spirit with access to greater truth, ends the necessity of interpreting catalyst with pain and suffering, and aligns it with its Higher Self.

The Matrix of the Spirit begins evolution by programming consciousness to be in primordial darkness and total innocence. The Potentiator of the Spirit, after it begins to be recognized, provides consciousness with light, or information, to incrementally fill the void created by the darkness and innocence of its beginning. The Catalyst of the Spirit provides consciousness with the opportunity for hope and/or faith, based upon the information and light provided by the Potentiator of the Spirit. The Experience of the Spirit's algorithmic characteristic lets consciousness surrender misperceptions, fears, and clinging to the distortions by targeting the core distortion conditions that tend to sustain its free will intoxication, and by encouraging a mind/body/spirit to surrender its perception of an independent identity.

With every thought processed, the Experience of the Spirit poses the question to the ego mind, "Is this enough light for you to surrender now? Here is a little more information, so how about now?"

The object/Logos position in the Experience of the Spirit is populated with the distortion archetype DA (movement), and the subject/sub-Logos position is populated with the Inherent Characteristic archetype LA (wisdom). DA is a reiteration of the object/Logos archetype of the three matrix modules but this is the first time it has reappeared since then, and, while it is still the distortion of movement, it is a different aspect of movement than previously experienced. In the Experience of the Spirit, it is change or, more specifically, the perceptual movement of time as the mind's focus incrementally moves from one processed thought to the next.

As awareness and the consciousness level escalate in a mind/body/spirit, the perception of change transforms, and, what may be eschewed in the lower dimensions of 3rd Density and below, begins to be welcomed in the upper dimensions. The perception of unwelcome change is increasingly supplanted with stability, and, because consciousness eventually surrenders any attachment to the authenticity of the conditions of the Archetypical Mind, the only remaining change to be experienced is the further surrender of free will intoxication and a more complete integration into unity. Wisdom emerges from the subject/sub-Logos position to make the truth more recognizable.

The Experience of the Spirit is a male/subject module that is a target of the female object modules, particularly the ones comprising the catalyst category. As in any interaction between the male/subject and female/object energies, the male is intended to mimic and then become more of the object that it's mimicking by surrendering its more independent perspective. The experience category offers the male/subject energy in both the Experience of the Mind and Experience of the Spirit, and the female/object energy in the Experience of the Body module.

Experience of the Spirit
•Initial Object: DA (movement)
•Initial Subject: LA (wisdom)
•Characteristic(s):
•Surrender of Ego
•Movement through time
•3rd spatial dimension; depth
•Male Principal (+)
•Condition and Algorithm

Chapter 23

The Significator Modules of the Archetypical Mind

We previously explained that the processing of thought through the Archetypical Mind functions like an assembly line where each module of the Archetypical Mind is provided with the opportunity to add its unique characteristic, culminating in a single adaptation, small or large, to the consciousness pattern. As consciousness evolves and is capable of recognizing increasing degrees of truth, the nature of a module's contribution transforms because consciousness changes, not because of changes in the Archetypical Mind. The processing contributions offered make every individual module a "thing unto itself" while incrementally adding to the whole.

The significator category, the next process category in the orderly processing of thought after the catalyst and experiential categories, acquires the thought as so far processed, and, as the name implies, determines the significance of the thought to consciousness' evolution. Even though there are two categories after the significator yet to add their contributions to the thought process, the significator category is the last category that will participate in the thought process while consciousness remains in 3rd Density or below. The processing category immediately after the significator is the transformation category, which may begin to participate in the thought process in a rudimentary way during the final dimensions of the 3rd Density, but any significant contributions of the transformation category will not be realized until consciousness graduates to the 4th Density. The Great Way category, the final category of the Archetypical Mind, has an entirely different function than the lower six categories and doesn't directly participate in the processing of individual thoughts at any time while consciousness remains in the foundational and experiential densities.

The significator category consists of three modules: the Significator of the Mind, the Significator of the Body, and the Significator of the Spirit. The basic design of each module is the same as it has been for all of the lower four categories already discussed with two archetypes each: one beginning the evolutionary process in the object/Logos position and the other in the subject/sub-Logos position. None of the three significator modules include a distortion archetype in its construction, but, contrary to what we previously explained, two of the three modules do create a condition, even without a distortion archetype included in the mix because these conditions are an adjunct product of the Earth experience and not part of the original mind's design. This is possible because of the way experience has developed within the population and what has been assembled so far by the contributions of the previous modules.

Regardless of how the significator conditions were created, by the time a single thought reaches the category a mind/body/spirit views a thought from a cumulative condition perspective, and the nature of the significator category both supports the potential for its conditions, while consciousness remains in the lower dimensions of 3rd Density and below, and subsequently contributes to the surrendering of the conditions when it reaches the upper dimensions of 3rd Density and above. The significance that the category adds to a thought process is always spiritual or how the thought interpretation advances consciousness along its evolutionary journey. Free will is the unspecified archetype that pervades every module of the Archetypical Mind, and, based upon its level of awareness, consciousness processes a thought according to its likes or dislikes to uniquely determine its significance to the person's evolution.

The significator category eventually becomes an accelerator of consciousness' elevation when a mind/body/spirit develops the ability to inwardly concentrate and becomes awareness. Awareness and concentration allow an individual to move out of unconsciousness and assume control of their evolutionary journey. Awareness is both the discovery tool and the tool of transformation that guides consciousness out from under the conditions of the Archetypical Mind and into a greater experience of truth.

The entire Archetypical Mind design is intended to focus consciousness on the unique exploration of itself by establishing a perception of independence from the Creator and then the systematic surrender of its independent perception so it may again recognize the truth of unity. The more completely consciousness can explore itself to a greater depth than may have been previously achieved, the more efficacious the mind's design. Evidence of efficaciousness is not in the number of successful graduation candidates but in the completeness of their self-exploration. It is often the case that the more challenging the life experience the greater the potential for deeper and more complete self-exploration.

Significator of the Mind

As with the other categories already discussed, the mind module of the significator category receives the fruit from the mind module of the preceding category and polls the significator body and spirit modules for input. The Significator of the Mind is the primary determinant of the category's thought interpretation but it is initially characterized as a collection of biases and prejudices that promote unaware and reactionary behavior, indicative of a lack of awareness while consciousness remains within the lower dimensions of 3rd Density and below. Biases and prejudices are the continuation of behavior resulting from 2nd Density survival conditioning and rely upon learned species or social group behavior with very little individual cognition. For the most part, biases and prejudices may be viewed as a hindrance to true recognition because they perpetuate ignorance, stimulate chaos, and endear consciousness' attachment to the authenticity of the Archetypical Mind's distortions.

Emotions result from perceived problems but problems only exist while consciousness remains attached to the authenticity of the Archetypical Mind's conditions, and so, problems incrementally dissipate as a mind/body/spirit successfully escalates its consciousness level. Evolution is a process and is designed to be experienced incrementally so that consciousness may explore itself deeply and completely. Consciousness is motivated to advance through evolution because the stress and suffering, indicative of lower consciousness, don't feel good and aren't the preferred choice of experience.

Biases and prejudices can be valuable tools to assist lower consciousness in avoiding physical world dangers and in providing an elementary guide for rudimentary experience interpretation, but, as consciousness evolves and cognitive abilities and awareness capacities escalate, they become their source of pain and/or suffering. They will be discarded because they no longer create a good feeling. Biases and prejudices are characteristic of consciousness seeking to find order within the chaos of the beginning stages of evolution, and, even if consciousness didn't participate in the experiences of 1st or 2nd Density, it would probably adopt them from the social influences that were offered by other mind/body/spirits sharing the culture. They offer significant contributions to the creation of the more defining characteristic of the module that was originally planned, which is the creation of a hierophant to uniquely experience an evolutionary journey.

The Significator of the Mind is uniquely positioned within the modules to bring together multiple individual elements to create a consciousness hierophant, and creates the lens through which a consciousness pattern perceives experiences. The hierophant is not the consciousness pattern but colors and influences how the pattern sees itself and the world around it, and, consequently, guides how it interprets thoughts. While consciousness remains unconscious and unaware, the biases and prejudices proffered by the hierophant are dominating, but, as the consciousness level escalates, surrenders unconsciousness, and evolves, their priority lessens and greater truth seeps into consciousness' awareness.

The biases and prejudices flavor the disposition of all thought but, as do most of the mind modules of their respective categories, it adjudicates the category interpretation of the thought after it receives input from the body and spirit module. The Significator of the Mind is constructed of RA (love) in the object/Logos position and LA (wisdom) in the subject/sub-Logos position. This is the first appearance of RA in the flow of thought along the Archetypical Mind assembly line and, possibly more than any other archetype, RA has great flexibility in how it is perceived and experienced. What most emanates from RA, being the initial object/Logos archetype, are infinite possibilities.

Consciousness' timidity in exploring possibilities is reflected in the propensity to cling to stasis and a fear of change, but, ironically, embracing change is what expands creation and makes the most adventuresome explorers of the Creator, invariably leading to a mind/body/spirit's greater happiness. The module begins and ends as love energy but love energy is infinitely diverse. Love is all energy spanning from extreme positivity to extreme negativity and everything in between.

When consciousness' dimensionality rises within a density and the subject/sub-Logos is energized, the subject and object experience increased integration as the two archetypes balance each other's qualities. The initial subject/sub-Logos is LA (wisdom), and when it begins to integrate with love, tempers the infinite possibilities of RA from its wildest free-spirited and free-willed days by serving as the stabilizing influence of the pairing. The Significator of the Mind is attracted to the male energy which means it serves as a subject part of the Creator and an experiential mirror to the "Creator as the object".

The Significator of the Mind is both a condition and an algorithm but the condition that it creates wasn't originally designed as such. Because of the nature of the development of the Earth experience, anomalies emerged from the experience and skewed the functioning of the module. The distinction between when it serves as a condition and when it serves as an algorithm is delineated along calibrations of consciousness levels. While consciousness remains within the lower dimensions, the condition is the most prominent and this constitutes the hierophant that is constructed and used; built from and upon biases and prejudices. These are the wild and crazy days of chaos, full of pain and suffering when RA is facilitating infinite possibilities and opportunities to run amuck in its deviation from alignment with the Higher Self.

The Hierophant is the false self; founded upon the belief in the authenticity of the conditions, exacerbated by biases and prejudices, but usually deemed to be beyond reproach by the experiencer(s). It is in this module that a mind/body/spirit "attaches" to ideologies and "drinks the Kool-Aid". From the hierophant vantage point, the greatest pain and suffering is experienced which sets up the "bottom hitting" that will serve as the basis for the self to transform by surrendering the ego mind and allowing consciousness to evolutionarily move forward.

The algorithm aspect of the Significator of the Mind begins to contribute to the journey when RA and LA begin to harmonize with each other and integrate into a cohesive working unit. When consciousness allows itself to be consciously aware of the naturally occurring benefits of the integration of love and wisdom, it begins to surrender the biases and prejudices forged during periods of earlier innocence. Evolution accelerates as a mind/body/spirit begins to move out of the patterns of pain and suffering with intention and purpose and surrender its propensity to resist the truth.

Consciousness begins to doubt the authenticity of the conditions, its independence, and its identity and ceases obediently scurrying in line to drink more Kool-Aid. Consciousness begins to surrender the ego mind and its previously irrefutable perception of an independent identity by beginning to practice discernment for the catalyst presented to its doorstep. It begins to be able to respond to life's messages with loving kindness, directed both to the self and to the other selves, rather than continuing to insidiously react with force to defend its false identity.

The plan of evolution requires consciousness to begin in ignorance and it must have, during the beginning stages, unquestioning allegiance to the authenticity of the conditions and its independence from the Creator and all other beings. Without a foundational allegiance to the conditions of the Archetypical Mind, it's improbable that experience could function with the intensity that it does. Essentially, consciousness begins evolution as close to the opposite perspective from the Creator as possible.

Allegiance to the conditions' authenticity comes into doubt as the consciousness level escalates and the seeds of balance between love, as the object/Logos archetype, and wisdom, as the subject/sub-Logos archetype, emerge. While in 3rd Density, consciousness doesn't get proof but it does have the capacity to develop intuition and a connection to "direct knowing" that brings into question the authenticity of the conditions. Faith, as proffered in the Catalyst of the Spirit, allows consciousness to reacquaint itself with its power and allows it to surrender the ego while simultaneously learning to rely upon intuition as its deep mind connection to the collective consciousness.

For most people, the irrefutability of the physical world and natural laws have firmly, but erroneously, established itself in their perceptions because of biases and prejudices. The conditions, when experienced with the limited capabilities of only the ego mind, create some significant obstacles to be overcome but, despite the degree of difficulty, that is exactly what is expected in consciousness' evolution through the experiential densities. The key to surrendering the ego mind and the attachment to the irrefutability of the conditions, as are all progressions through evolution, is awareness. Through awareness, consciousness can pierce the illusion of the conditions' irrefutability and begin to experience truth, which is not obviously supported by the conditions of the Archetypical Mind.

Significator of the Mind

- Initial Object: RA (love)
- Initial Subject: LA (wisdom)
  - Characteristic(s):
    - Heirophant
    - Biases & Prejudices
- Male Principal (+)
- Condition & Algorithm

Significator of the Body

The construction of the Significator of the Body includes the second appearance of RA (love) in the object/Logos position and the first appearance of YA (unity) in the Archetypical Mind as the initial subject/sub-Logos. The characteristic of the Significator of the Body is the healthy functioning or illness of the physical body. The prevailing condition of the physical body is a direct manifestation of how the person's thought(s) have been processed. What manifests as physical health or illness is a reflection of the cumulative condition of the consciousness pattern.

The Significator of the Body is responsive to the consciousness level of the experiencing mind/body/spirit, and the more tenaciously consciousness clings to the authenticity of the physical and its engrained perceptions of independence and separation, the more likely it will reflect these stresses in the physical body. While a mind/body/spirit remains in the dimensions of lower consciousness, the object of the Potentiator of the Mind (Lucifer, unconsciousness) promotes the reactive nature of the mind to stimuli offered in thought without a hint of its capacity to control it. Since the body is solely a reflection of the mind until the spirit is energized, the mind provides the mind/body/spirit with what it is prepared to receive, which is often the experience of ill health and/or illness. Before the inclusion of the veil as part of an incarnate experience, Earthly humans were able to awaredly control bodily functions that are now considered autonomic, including pain.

Similar to the characteristic of the Significator of the Mind, despite the initial Logos and sub-Logos not including a distortion archetype, the Significator of the Body creates a condition that was not part of the original design of the Archetypical Mind. The condition created by the Significator of the Body is an erroneous perspective that the body is subject to the hostilities of a physical world, including illness, but it is a condition that has developed throughout the 3rd Density tenure of the Earth population, compounded by the imposition of the veil. People choose or reaffirm illness or health with every thought. Even with the veil, the condition of the body is predominantly within a mind/body/spirit's control according to the degree of its spirit/mind harmony and this becomes apparent as consciousness is elevated and aligned more closely with the Higher Self.

Overcoming a condition of illness reflected in the Significator of the Body is not just overcoming bacteria or a virus infection when a mind/body/spirit comes into physical contact with an external source. The originally programmed characteristic of the module, which still prevails today as its primary programmed characteristic, was that it would have the objective of overcoming an attachment to the physical in its entirety as part of a larger transformation. As the prominence of 4th Density consciousness becomes more apparent in the Earth population, physical and/or mental illness will begin to fade from the experience entirely because the participating consciousness' awareness will quickly escalate to the point that it no longer will benefit from the lessons of an illness. In the "not too distant future", all pain and/or suffering, both mental and physical, will also fade from the Earth experience without increased medical science advancements or discoveries.

When a mind/body/spirit chooses a healthy body, it does so as part of the choice of alignment with the Higher Self because illness is frequently the choice resulting from chaos and unconsciousness. For people choosing the service-to-others path, the algorithmic benefits available from the module extend far beyond the transformation from physical or mental illness to health. The blending of RA (love) and YA (unity) ultimately spur awareness and detachment from the physical, but, while consciousness retains a limited ability to perceive truth, the

Significator of the Body also rudimentarily encourages it to recognize a greater connection to other selves, thereby promoting greater unity. This is the foundation for a higher love perspective and the beginning of unity consciousness; the precursor to the development of a 4th Density social memory complex.

Illness originates in the mind module when the mind instructs the body to "be" a certain way. Once the body has received such an instruction, it will repeatedly report the body's status as illness in response to every thought processed by the mind. To heal the illness, the mind needs only to amend its instruction to the body to remove the illness and offer a clean report with all succeeding thoughts. The body is a manifestation of the mind but doesn't add intelligence to the thought process; therefore, it only functions as instructed by the mind.

Significator of the Body
•Initial Object: RA (love) •Initial Subject: YA (unity) •Characteristic(s): •Illness v Health •Male Principal (+) •Condition & Algorithm

Significator of the Spirit

The Significator of the Spirit differs from all other modules in how it is designed except for the Great Way of the Spirit. The archetypes comprising this module neither transform nor integrate when consciousness rises but the two archetypes serve to logarithmically magnify the contributions of the object/ Logos and subject/sub-Logos archetypes. The functioning of the archetypes in this module directly mirrors the level of consciousness and subsequent consciousness pattern of the individual mind/body/spirit more than any other individual module of the Archetypical Mind.

The initial object/Logos of the Significator of the Spirit is RA (love) and the initial subject/sub-Logos is also RA (love) so, at the appropriate time in the course of a thought process, the Significator of the Spirit simply offers love energy, which is synonymous with Intelligent Energy. The Significator of the Mind, as do all of the mind modules of the different Archetypical Mind categories, determines the adjudication of the thought for the category and decides whether to radiate or absorb the energy, thereby, choosing with every thought to either polarize positively or negatively. By choosing to radiate the energy, consciousness is choosing to surrender its identity and independence in favor of unity with the Higher Self and the Creator, and, conversely, by choosing to absorb the energy, it is choosing to sustain and/or defend its identity and independence as a separate self. As explained in earlier chapters, a mind/body/spirit is unable to credibly support the choice of polarization until it has demonstrated the choice in 51% of its thoughts processed to polarize positively or in 95% of its thoughts processed to polarize negatively.

A mind/body/spirit dwelling in the lower ranges of 3rd Density consciousness usually vacillates between absorbing and radiating Intelligent Energy which causes instability and chaos or, as otherwise described, reoccurring pain and suffering. A mind/body/spirit dwelling within the higher ranges of consciousness available for 3rd Density will predominantly radiate the love energy and, after graduating to 4th Density along the positive path, will exclusively radiate it. The level of consciousness not only will determine the degree of radiance or absorption of the energy but also the nature of a mind/body/spirit's behavior. The higher the consciousness the greater the radiance of love, the greater the alignment with the Higher Self, and the more unifying the behavior, but, the lower the consciousness the more cruel, narcissistic, and self-centered the behavior and the greater the absorption of love energy.

The act of radiating or absorbing love energy with every thought establishes a trajectory through a timeline and the course of a mind/body/spirit's experience of a lifetime. There is no "reality" outside of a mind/body/spirit's observation of it and the choice of radiation or absorption in the Significator of the Spirit sets the tone for its interpretation of a perceived story or a true experience. Escalating awareness and radiating Intelligent Energy is how the conditions of the Archetypical Mind are overcome; exchanging or integrating the initial objects with the subjects of individual modules. Absorbing Intelligent Energy does not encourage archetypical transformations to occur; instead, it reinforces the ego mind, "I" perspective, and ignorance created by its initial distortion formatting.

The choice to radiate or absorb the energy is primarily but not solely the choice of one module. The Significator of the Spirit provides the resource to be radiated or absorbed but the module reflects the condition of the prevailing consciousness pattern and the leanings of the other modules that have already added their contributions to the thought process by how much energy is made available. If the mind/body/spirit is in the emerging phase of polarizing positively, only a small quantity of energy will likely be made available but, if it is farther along in its evolution along the positive path, experiencing 4th or even 5th Density, it will make significantly greater quantities available because it knows more completely that the supply is infinite and not limited to the resources of an individual mind/body/spirit. As the primary module for consciousnesses' adjudication of thought in the significator category, the Significator of the Mind primarily influences consciousness thought interpretation and determination of the degree of truth recognized by the experience but relies upon the Significator of the Spirit resource to color the change resulting from its choice.

The significator category is the final phase of a thought process while consciousness remains below the upper dimensions of the 3rd Density. Beginning with the final dimensional levels of 3rd Density but before a mind/body/spirit graduates to 4th Density along the positive path, the next Archetypical Mind category (the Transformation category) becomes activated and adds another layer of processing for a thought. Until then, the fruit of the thought is forwarded directly from the Significator of the Mind to the Matrix of the Mind for final processing by incorporation into the consciousness pattern.

In 1st and 2nd Densities, the primary focus for consciousness' evolution is upon awareness but not exclusively because awareness is not exclusive to the other four Inherent Characteristics. In 3rd Density, an experience becomes more complex because, for the first half of the density, the focus will be primarily upon awareness but then, once consciousness becomes awareness, the more focused subject matter will be love, but not exclusively love because neither awareness nor love is exclusive of the other Inherent Characteristics either. In 4th Density, consciousness becomes love and primarily explores wisdom, and in 5th Density, it becomes wisdom and primarily explores unity, along with all of the other Inherent Characteristics. Through all of these changes and along the entire evolutionary path through the foundational and experiential densities, the Archetypical Mind remains unchanged and constant, allowing consciousness to be the sole agent of change.

When the fruit from the Significator of the Mind is received, the Matrix and/or Potentiator of the Mind isn't obligated to amend the consciousness pattern strictly according to the fruit. The fruit of the catalyst/experiential/significator subsystem may sway the consciousness pattern decidedly towards the positive or negative path but the matrix/potentiator system may not accept that adjudication as presented. If the thought fruit is inconsistent with historical trends, the consciousness pattern will probably be changed very little but, if a significantly different trend is repeatedly provided, it is also probable that changes to the consciousness pattern will be increasingly made to reflect the new trend in the thought fruit. The design is to promote incremental changes that allow consciousness to explore and absorb a greater depth of experience and, therefore, greater depth and understanding of the self.

The degree of receptivity to change in the matrix/potentiator categories will be regulated according to where consciousness is in the evolutionary process. The lower consciousness is within the process, the more likely it will resist changes and it probably will take significant motivation to move the needle, but the higher the consciousness, the less motivation will be required to experience change. The propensity for lower consciousness to remain the same fuels its continued attachment to the authenticity of the Archetypical Mind conditions, intensifies emotions and perpetuates its creation of pain and suffering for itself. Awakening awareness and developing its healing abilities remains the primary focus of most of the Earth's population during the final years of the population's 3rd Density experience.

Significator of the Spirit

•Initial Object: RA (love)
•Initial Subject: RA (love)
 •Characteristic(s):
  •Radiance or absorption of Love Energy
  •Choice of service-to-self or service-to-others
•Female Principal (-)
•Algorithm

Chapter 24

The Transformation Modules of the Archetypical Mind

Even though the design of the Archetypical Mind doesn't change during consciousness' journey through the evolutionary process, some modules of the mind aren't always available to consciousness in all of the densities. As we explained in Chapter 23, the significator modules comprise the last category of the catalyst/experiential/significator subsystem experienced by consciousness enjoying 3rd Density and below, and even the spirit modules of these categories are not fully experienced by consciousness until it evolves sufficiently to open the fourth time/space chakra near the end of its 3rd Density tenure. The modules not universally experienced are simply quiet ones requiring a minimum evolutionary development and, until achieved, they remain inaccessible, but consciousness is never prohibited from accessing them.

The net effect of the Archetypical Mind's design is to require the experiencing consciousness to assume responsibility for its advancement through evolution, and the primary motivation to assume that responsibility and begin to do the work is pain and suffering. Enigmatically, pain and suffering are never imposed upon consciousness and are not designed as part of the experience, but, because the population of a planet co-creates its experience, it is potentially available if the experiencing population chooses it. The Zenoa–Earth population has not only chosen to create pain and suffering as part of its experience, but it has also made it a foundational characteristic and it is sometimes perceived as the only option available for large portions of the population. 4th and 5th Density service-to-self consciousness serving Earth and earlier planetary experiences has intentionally compounded the population's propensity towards pain and suffering by seeding and nurturing a service-to-self philosophy but discomfort has never been the only option available.

Access to all of the modules of the Archetypical Mind and the ability to energize their benefit is always potentially available but the onus is upon the individual mind/body/spirit to take advantage of the opportunities offered by doing the work and raising its consciousness level sufficiently to access them. When a particular evolutionary task is undertaken, the tools necessary to be successful become immediately available, regardless of any perceived external hindrance. Experiencing consciousness always regulates its schedule as to how quickly or how slowly it moves along the evolutionary path, dependent upon how diligently it does the necessary work. As with any school, there is a curriculum to be followed and it is incumbent upon the student to complete the curriculum, learn the subject at hand, and advance.

The Transformation modules initially become available when consciousness opens the 4th time/space heart chakra and enters into the upper dimensions of the 3rd Density in preparation for its graduation to the 4th Density. Before this evolutionary step, the attributes of the transformation modules are potentially available but beyond consciousnesses' reach, and, even when they are finally activated, their benefit is minimally employed because the transforming consciousness is still relatively weak. The modules become more effective after some degree of advancement has been made into the dimensions of the 4th Density, which is when the brain's frontal lobes become more active and continue to provide an increased degree of service throughout the 5th Density.

As the name suggests, the Transformation modules provide the tools necessary to aid consciousness' "transformation" from lower consciousness to higher consciousness which includes the surrender of its attachment to the authenticity of the Archetypical Mind's distortion archetypes. Consciousness is incrementally guided to build its perceptions and perspectives through 1st, 2nd, and 3rd Densities to reach the zenith of its perception of separation, chaos, and independence near the middle of 3rd Density. While still within the limits of 3rd Density, a person will awaken, begin to surrender attachment to the authenticity of their false perceptions, and begin to migrate back to greater truth and unity. The nature of consciousness' interactions in 3rd Density makes for a very interesting unraveling of lower consciousness perceptions because experience occurs through a perspective smorgasbord from various space/time analog projections that, usually unbeknownst to the incarnate projections, are accumulated into the time/space consciousness pattern.

3rd Density consciousness simultaneously experiences both time/space, where the corpus of its being resides, and space/time, where its analog projections reside and where most thoughts are perceived to be processed. Evolving consciousness moves through the densities in time/space but the awakening consciousness that is tasked with surrendering attachment to the conditions and transforming is perceived to be the space/time analog projections. As each analog projection advances, its progress is accrued to the time/space mind/body/spirit. At the beginning of the 3rd Density, the time/space mind/body/spirit normally incarnates into three or four analog projections simultaneously, but, as it advances through the density and its consciousness escalates into the upper dimensions, it simultaneously incarnates into as many as eight or nine analog projections. (Earth's population, generally speaking, has regressed from its early energy capabilities and can only project into one or two simultaneous incarnations.)

When the analog projections begin to awaken and credibly demonstrate a commitment to either the positive or negative path, the time/space mind/body/spirit usually begins to reduce the number of concurrent analog projections in the hopes of increasing its ability to move more quickly towards graduation by consolidating more Intelligent Energy, and, therefore, the potential for greater awareness into a single incarnation. Those mind/body/spirits polarizing negatively are more inclined to numerically reduce their incarnations sooner so they can use their consolidated energy to dominate and subjugate a greater number of weaker 3rd Density mind/body/spirits. Mind/body/spirits polarizing positively are more inclined to continue to incarnate in multiple analog projections longer, thereby, exploring the self more completely. Whether it has chosen the positive or negative path, consciousness usually ends the 3rd Density and begins the 4th Density with one time/space mind/body/spirit incarnating into one space/time analog projection of itself.

The Transformation modules will scarcely be used by the prevailing 3rd Density Earth population because very few members are capable of benefiting from their contribution but the newly arrived 4th Density consciousness children will have ample use for them and the information in this manuscript. As the children age and begin to systematically open their 4th time/space heart chakra, they will begin to send the thought being processed forward from the Significator of the Mind module to the Transformation modules before being cycled to the Matrix/Potentiator modules for incorporation into the consciousness pattern. The Transformation category includes three modules; the Transformation of the Mind, the Transformation of the Body, and the Transformation of the Spirit.

Transformation of the Mind

The mind module of the Transformation category has the same structure as the other modules of the Archetypical Mind, including the other Transformation modules. The design reiterates a two-archetype construction with both positions being filled by Inherent Characteristic archetypes and providing the qualities that create the characteristics for the module. The initial object/Logos position is occupied by the archetype LA (wisdom), and the initial subject/sub-Logos is occupied by YA (unity). Because the object and subject positions are filled by Inherent Characteristic archetypes, the contributions of the module will be realized by the merger and harmonization of the two as consciousness is escalated and magnifies the qualities that each one offers individually.

The characteristic of the Transformation of the Mind module is expressed as the "surrender of the ego mind" but the surrender encompasses much more than just the ego mind. The module begins to contribute to consciousness' evolution after the time/space heart chakra has been opened which means the mind/body/spirit has already transcended unconsciousness, awakened, become aware, and has at least begun to become awareness. These evolutionary accomplishments are all benchmarks of significant progress before consciousness begins to benefit from the module itself and suggest there is much more to be accomplished to finish the journey through the experiential densities.

The ego mind is the instrument the reader is using to read and understand this manuscript. It is the mind that supports and reinforces consciousness' ability to perceive space/time, feel emotions, and support its perception of separation, but, as the level of consciousness escalates in the 4th and 5th Densities, the deep mind is promulgated in front of the ego mind. The ego mind eventually completely surrenders to the deep mind, but, to do that, it will have surrendered its attachment to the conditions, substantially surrendered the "I" perspective, and significantly sobered from its free will intoxication.

When free will intoxication is sufficiently surrendered, the authenticity of the conditions fades. The "I" perspective also fades as the 4th heart chakra opens more completely and consciousness surrenders resistance which leads to the mind/body/spirit increasingly perceiving other consciousness with love and compassion. Surrendering the "I" perspective and ego mind begins with seeing other mind/body/spirits as extensions of the self, continues by surrendering the self into a social memory complex, and eventually ends in the condition of complete unity. While consciousness remains within the experiential densities and the auspices of the Archetypical Mind, wisdom and unity harmonize in this module and consciousness transforms its 3rd Density perception of independence into its eventual reintegration into the Higher Self.

By the end of a mind/body/spirit's 4th Density experience, nothing remains of the ego mind but the independent perceiving consciousness pattern remains as the last vestige of the distortions that characterized its experiences through the lower densities. By the end of 4th Density, all mind/body/spirits will have merged into a social memory complex, which is a requirement and the signal of suitability for graduation into 5th Density as a positively polarizing mind/body/spirit. Consciousness continues to evolve into greater unity throughout its tenure in the 5th Density and works to continue to resolve any residual attachment to the authenticity of the conditions. The metaphysical consciousness pattern, to an ever-decreasing degree, remains part of the mind/body/spirit's experiences until it finally is surrendered sometime after its graduation to 6th Density.

In earlier modules of the Archetypical Mind, we have seen LA (wisdom) numerous times and each time it has been paired with another Inherent Characteristic or distortion archetype that requires a decision on the part of the experiencing consciousness to either continue with its current perspectives or change. The choice to change or remain the same is always solely the choice of the experiencing consciousness but the appearance of LA provides it with the opportunity to gravitate to a higher consciousness perspective, heal its attachment to the distortions, and evolve closer to the Creator. In the Transformation of the Mind module, LA begins the module's work as the object which assumes significant awareness by the mind/body/spirit already, but, as it begins to benefit from the other Transformation modules YA (unity) begins to specifically guide its thought interpretations towards greater unity.

The Transformation of the Mind becomes activated only after the prominence of the hierophant of the Significator of the Mind has begun to be weakened. It aids in the shining of the light into the darkness of the Significator's biases and prejudices and shining truth into the false self, promoting the reduction in the perceived prominence of the ego mind and the "I" perspective. As with the other mind modules of the various categories, the Transformation of the Mind is the final word of the module's thought interpretation but only after the body and spirit have contributed their input.

The difference between a 3rd Density mind/body/spirit unable to utilize the attributes of the Transformation category and the 3rd or 4th Density mind/body/spirit that can access them is solely the difference in their awareness level. The awareness (AKA: consciousness) level is the ultimate measure of the degree of surrender of the ego mind and "I" perspective, and a direct reflection of the degree of sobering from its free will intoxication. The potential of the mind/body/spirit that can utilize the Transformation category and one that is not able to do so yet is the same, but the one able to access the category has simply done more work to successfully heal its false perceptions.

The conditions of the Archetypical Mind that form consciousness' perceptions of a physical world are, relatively speaking, secondary to the primary conditions such as unconsciousness, the ego mind, and the "I" perspective. The secondary conditions begin to dissolve of their own volition as consciousness surrenders or heals the primary conditions. Healing the self is the process of becoming aware of the self and exploring the self, thereby fulfilling the purpose of creation. When awareness is directed inside the self, instead of being projected outside the self into the illusion of the physical world, consciousness begins to discover and then heal the distortions in its perceptions because it liberates an increased Intelligent Energy flow that boosts consciousness' advancement.

The Transformation of the Mind receives the fruit of the thought at its current process phase from the Significator of the Mind. The thought fruit, as interpreted by the Significator of the Mind, is always presented as the radiance of love energy (Intelligent Energy) because those mind/body/spirits choosing to polarize negatively do not open the Transformation category but, when the Transformation category is first activated in the 3rd Density, thought is processed from the perspective of the mind/body/spirit's hierophant. As the Transformation category begins to incrementally add its flavoring to the recipe and the ego mind is proportionately reduced, the prominence of the hierophant perspective is reduced accordingly. The net effect of the Transformation category is accelerated evolution, increased radiance of love energy, and increased ability to recognize truth.

The Transformation of the Mind measures the input from the body and spirit modules into its assessment; all of which is intended to further accelerate consciousness' healing from the distortions and conditions acquired during its tenure in the 3rd Density. The 1st, 3rd, and 5th Densities are considered primary densities, and the 2nd and 4th Densities are transformation periods that bridge the major gaps between the primary ones. 2nd Density consciousness is too low to benefit from the Transformation category but the 4th Density is strategically designed and positioned to heal from the 3rd Density and accelerate consciousness' return home. There is as much learning to be gained from the 4th Density healing as there was in the creation of the 3rd Density experiences.

Transformation of the Mind

- Initial Object: LA (wisdom)
- Initial Subject: YA (unity)
  - Characteristic(s):
    - Transformation of the Ego Mind & "I" Perspective
- Male Principal (+)
- Algorithm

Transformation of the Body

The Transformation of the Body simultaneously receives the thought with the Transformation of the Spirit and returns its report to the Transformation of the Mind as a further enhancement for the thought's adjudication. The characteristic of the Transformation of the Body is the "death and rebirth" of the physical body but this doesn't mean that the physical body immediately dies and is reborn within the same space/time environment. It means that the heretofore authentic perception of the physical is incrementally surrendered with every thought processed. Within the 4th Density experience, an individual mind/body/spirit will eventually cease to incarnate into a chemical body but, when it enters the 5th Density, it will gain the flexibility to transition between time/space and space/time at will.

The 4th Density affords several significant changes for consciousness as it continues its evolutionary journey, not the least of which is the adequate surrender of its independent identity to allow it to integrate its uniqueness into a social memory complex, thereby, transforming its perception of the self from a single autonomous organism into a multifaceted organism comprised of multiple mind/body/spirits. The 4th Density is the end of the biological evolution that creates an increasingly complicated single biological organism to provide a vehicle for consciousnesses to interact within a space/time environment.

The 3rd Density incarnations are experienced in a very dense chemical body. During the period of transition from the 3rd Density to the 4th Density, the incarnate body incrementally begins to become less chemical and more electric. As the transition progresses and the 3rd Density mind/body/spirits have either graduated to the 4th Density or, for those not graduating, have been relocated to another 3rd Density experience, the 4th Density mind/body/spirits begin to incarnate into "transitional bodies" that become less chemical and more electric with each reincarnation. Many of the children on Earth are now incarnating into transitional bodies, and, with each lifetime cycle, will experience better health and longer life expectancies, and will be reincarnated into a body that is a little more electric than the last one until their reincarnation process is no longer necessary.

With each 4th Density incarnation, the consciousness levels will escalate and its attachment to the Archetypical Mind conditions lessens accordingly. During the shared 3rd and 4th Density environment now being experienced, the 4th Density incarnates may be having significant difficulties because the collective consciousness of the population is still within the lower dimensions of the 3rd Density range, but, as the transition continues and accelerates, conditions will improve because lower consciousness influences will be either escalated or removed from the environment. Soon within the 4th Density experience, physical pain and illness will virtually disappear and be reduced to a minor discomfort upon death that now wouldn't require medical treatment.

Eventually, consciousness becomes able to transition between the space/time and time/space environments "at will", without the surrender of its physical body because of its escalated consciousness and a reduced attachment to the authenticity of the conditions. Earth's recently concluded 3rd Density experience enjoyed a chemical body at the beginning of its cycle with a life expectancy of approximately 900 years, as was discussed in an earlier chapter. After the 4th Density environment is segregated from the 3rd Density at some future point, the average life expectancy greatly increases after the full transition to a 4th Density experience is finished and the transformation from a chemical body to a fully electric body is complete. The average tenure of consciousness in the 4th Density is only about 35,000 years and the average tenure in the 5th Density is only about 3,000 years which means, once the 4th Density body transition is complete, it will be the last physical body that it requires to finish its tenure in the experiential densities.

The initial object/Logos of the Transformation of the Body is LA (wisdom) and the initial subject/sub-Logos is SA (awareness). Wisdom and awareness fuel each other to logarithmically magnify their contributions and accelerate consciousness' continued advancement through the densities. Of course, this effect only applies to consciousness having chosen the positive path because the mind/body/spirits choosing the negative path neither become aware nor energize the transformation modules. Those choosing the service-to-self path remain much more attached to the authenticity of the physical but do eventually learn to transition between space/time and time/space as a result of increasing their Intelligent Energy resources by stealing it more proficiently.

Transformation of the Body

- Initial Object: LA (wisdom)
- Initial Subject: SA (awareness)
- Characteristic(s):
  - Death and rebirth of the physical body
- Female Principal (-)
- Algorithm

Transformation of the Spirit

By now you should know that the construction of all of the Archetypical Mind modules have the same basic design and the Transformation of the Spirit module is no different, consisting of two archetypes with both of these being Inherent Characteristics. The object/Logos is LA (wisdom), and the subject/sub-Logos is RA (love). The 4th Density objective for its advancement is for consciousness to become love and through the lens of love explore wisdom. The characteristic of the Transformation of the Spirit supports this objective and the construction of the module provides the tools to accomplish and accelerate this task.

The same module characteristics serve the 5th Density as consciousness in the higher density, pursuing its task of becoming wisdom and exploring unity, as LA and RA harmonize and become the platform from which to stretch beyond the limits of the experiential densities. The characteristic of the Transformation of the Spirit is the "alignment with love and the Higher Self". In the 4th Density, aligning with love is the task but, in the 5th Density, consciousness has become love as a result of its 4th Density accomplishments and further strives to align more completely with the Higher Self. Consciousness' graduation to the 6th Density is the result of adequately surrendering its perception of independence and further sobering from its free will intoxication which means all that consciousness is doing, by participating in the foundational and experiential densities, is learning of itself by experiencing itself through its thoughts.

If the Transformation modules have been energized and are participating in the thought process, consciousness has chosen to polarize positively and has at least met the criteria for 4th Density graduation. When the Transformation of the Mind polls the Transformation of the Spirit for its input before a thought is adjudicated, the spirit invariably responds with wisdom and love according to the degree of harmonization of the two Inherent Characteristics. Because of the uniformity of the consciousness patterns at this stage of 5th Density evolution, there is seldom significant deviation in the radiance of love and/or alignment with the Higher Self from one mind/body/spirit comprising the social memory complex to the next. There remain vestiges of uniqueness in its report to the mind module but the variations offer little if any friction with the intent of alignment with love.

The Transformation of the Spirit is a magnifier of the dispositions already established in the consciousness pattern. It reinforces and accelerates further surrendering of the attachment to the conditions, enhances consciousness' ability to perceive greater truth, and accentuates its surrender of the ego mind, "I" perspective, and free will intoxication. It is further grease on the wheels that already have their direction and forward motion.

The Transformation modules will not be available to most of the prevailing population (3rd Density) of the Earth experience. Even though Gaia's consciousness level is well into its 4th Density evolution, the population is still predominantly 3rd Density and not very advanced along the dimensional scale. Because of the condition of the population, the preponderance of the information provided in this manuscript may have little interest to the 3rd Density population, but, at the appropriate time, should have significant interest to the 4th Density children and early arrivals that are now incarnate as part of the population.

```
┌─────────────────────────────────────────┐
│        Transformation of the Spirit       │
├─────────────────────────────────────────┤
│ • Initial Object: LA (wisdom)             │
│ • Initial Subject: RA (love)              │
│   • Characteristic(s):                    │
│     • Alignment with love and the         │
│       Higher Self                         │
│ • Female Principal (-)                     │
│ • Algorithm                               │
└─────────────────────────────────────────┘
```

The primary task of the early 4th Density arrivals and children that will be assuming the reins of the population's experience will be to heal the 3rd Density's damaging transgressions towards the planet, surrender false beliefs and/or limiting ideologies within the populace, and establish the new modus operandi for the Earth experience as a 4th Density planet. Paramount among the transition criterion will be the removal of all those polarizing negatively and all of the 3rd Density consciousness that will not be graduating, which will occur naturally as normal lifetimes conclude. Before the evacuation of the negatively polarizing graduates and the non-graduating 3rd Density consciousness, the Earth may experience some significant chaos and resistance to change as the 4th Density consciousness awakens and assumes an increased leadership role.

Those who are currently alive on Earth are living in an exciting time in the cosmic experience. Being incarnate on the planet is always an honor but especially at this time because there has been a waiting list to be part of the transition. Earth has experienced a very difficult past for a variety of reasons, some of which we have discussed in earlier chapters, but having achieved the completion of a 3rd Density experience and now moving forward by transitioning to a 4th Density planetary experience is commanding a galaxy-wide viewing audience. Being part of the transition affords consciousness with tremendous opportunities for learning and spiritual growth, seldom available elsewhere in this little corner of creation.

Chapter 25

The Great Way Modules of the Archetypical Mind

Consciousness participating in the foundational and experiential densities does so because a 6th Density Higher Self has invested itself into a soul stream. A Higher Self creates a soul stream that will either begin a new solar system or expand an existing one by investing consciousness into the foundational and experiential densities. The Higher Self then guides the consciousness to a unique harmonization, forming a unique planet, eventually with plants, animals, and 3rd Density beings (Humans on Earth) or higher, according to whatever balance the invested consciousness has chosen according to its preference of "likes" over "dislikes". Expanding a planetary experience always sequentially begins with a 1st Density experience until it has advanced to a sufficient level of stability when a 2nd Density experience may be initiated, and eventually, a 3rd Density or higher experience may also begin.

The experiences of 1st and 2nd Densities are timeless and random but occur within the parameters of the governing Archetypical Mind. The experiences of 3rd Density are not random but are still governed by the parameters of the same Archetypical Mind serving the foundational densities. In the particular Archetypical Mind that governs Earth's solar system, consciousness enters evolution according to certain experience-shaping conditions that capitalize upon all nine of the archetypes selected to construct the enveloping universe with a particular beginning emphasis on the four distortion archetypes: movement, separation, unconsciousness, and free will. The distortion archetypes create the initial perceptual conditions that cause consciousness to experience chaos, separation, and unconsciousness.

Before consciousness puts on the spacesuit that is the Archetypical Mind and submits to the conformity accordingly required, an enveloping environment is created by the Great Way modules that collectively serve as the foundational truth for all experiences by establishing the framework for consciousness' experiences and an antonym for the initial conditions. Unlike the other modules of the Archetypical Mind, the Great Way modules do not participate in the processing of individual thoughts but they are part of every thought process within the environment they create.

Great Way of the Mind

The first Great Way module to be discussed is the Great Way of the Mind. Unlike the six categories we have previously presented, the mind module of the Great Way category does not adjudicate a thought's interpretation. Rather than horizontally governing the categories' input to the thought process, it vertically guides the workings of all of the mind modules of the Archetypical Mind by virtue of the environment that it creates.

The construction design of the individual module is very similar to the construction of all of the other modules we have discussed. There is an initial object/Logos, populated with the Inherent Characteristic archetype YA (unity) and an initial subject/sub-Logos populated with LA (wisdom). In most of the previously discussed modules, the initial object and subject modules either swap positions, where the initial object/Logos is a distortion archetype, or integrate, where there are two Inherent Characteristic archetypes, to transform consciousness' experiences as it evolves through the dimensions and densities, but, in the Great Way of the Mind module, both archetypes are Inherent Characteristics that begin on equal footing with equivalent prominence. The objective of the module is to provide a common environment for the mind aspect of all mind/body/

spirits within the solar system to share, therefore, establishing guiding parameters for its experiences.

The environment, created by the participating Inherent Characteristic archetypes, is continuously changing. The interactions of YA and LA archetypes effect changes in the environment because the archetypes' are evolving as the creation experience matures. In other words, the environment created is a stable but not a stagnant environment. Consciousness at all levels is constantly evolving, therefore the nature of the environment is constantly changing as a result of the evolutionary changes in the archetypes creating the environment.

The archetypical consciousness represented in the object/Logos and subject/sub-Logos positions is of 6th Density, and, as consciousness evolves in the foundational and experiential densities, the degree of consciousness' maturity in the Creator Being densities is also affected. "All is One" and the process of evolution of even the most independent perceiving aspect affects all of consciousness' evolution from the lowest to the highest as illustrated even in the maturity of the organisms we previously identified as "nine-star systems", galaxies, and universes. For example, the Arcturian "nine-star system" appears as an older and wiser organism than the one Earth participates in but it simply is the product of a greater maturity along its evolutionary journey.

The characteristic of the Transformation of the Mind module is the "surrendering of the ego mind" to the deep mind, which is a boost to assist consciousness' evolution from the limiting perspectives of the lower densities and dimensions into higher ones, and the characteristic of the Great Way of the Mind module is the "surrendering of all of the lesser minds", including the deep mind, to the root mind. The progression of minds from the ego mind of the foundational and lower experiential densities to the deep mind and the deep mind to the root mind of 6th

Density corresponds to consciousness' degree of sobering from free will intoxication.

The Transformation of the Mind serves as a specifically focused boost for lower consciousness to transform the ego mind into the deep mind within the enveloping environment created by the Great Way of the Mind. The Great Way of the Mind more generally promotes the surrender of both the ego and deep minds at all levels and consciousness' return to the creating root mind of the Higher Self. The Great Way of the Mind relies upon awareness as its predicate which is the key to surrendering and transforming the more limited minds into the unity of 6th Density. The foundational and experiential density Inherent Characteristics become hierarchical in Earth's design, beginning with awareness, progressing to love, then wisdom, and, finally, unity, all of which are simply increasing levels of awareness of consciousness' Creator-ness as free will intoxication is surrendered.

Great Way of the Mind

- Initial Object: YA (unity)
- Initial Subject: LA (wisdom)
  - Characteristic(s):
    - Surrender of lesser minds ultimately to the Root Mind
- Male Principal (+)
- Algorithm

Great Way of the Body

The Great Way of the Body doesn't directly participate in the processing of thought either, but, similar to the Great Way of the Mind, creates an environment of truth for all of the body modules of the lower six categories of the mind. The Great Way of the Body specifically directs its service vertically to the body modules of the other categories. The characteristic of the Great Way of the Body is "abundance" and provides the resources for harmony and other essential characteristics that support consciousness' journey through the lower densities. The concept of abundance remains constant from beginning to end, even though the archetypes creating the body environment change as they continue to evolve.

The construction of the module is consistent with other modules with YA (unity), as the object/Logos, and KA (stillness), as the subject/sub-Logos. As is characteristic of the three Great Way modules, the archetypes don't exchange roles or merge because both are equally activated from the outset but they do provide an increasingly logarithmic magnification of their service as evolving consciousness can recognize and capitalize upon the modules' potential contributions. As with the other body modules, the Great Way of the Body doesn't add intelligence but it does add information that allows consciousness a greater depth of exploration of the self throughout its evolutionary journey.

Like the mind module environment, the body module environment is stable but not stagnant because the Inherent Characteristic archetypes that comprise the construction of this module are also constantly evolving. The consciousness populating the lower densities today perceives the environment differently than the consciousness that will experience the same "level" of consciousness tomorrow. The Matrix of the Body module programs consciousness entering the foundational densities to "move", which adds to its perception of chaos, but, the Great Way environment guides it to greater stillness, out of chaos, to a relative state of unity that allows it to form the four elements and eventually the space/time environment.

Consciousness with two strands of coding activated becomes fire which is significantly more perceptually isolated than consciousness with eight strands of coding activated that perceptually becomes solid matter, but, regardless of whether consciousness has two strands or eight strands activated, it is tasked with learning to harmonize its differences, including its physical manifestations, within the density to form a cohesive organism called a planet.

How the four elements harmonize determines the nature of its 1st Density experience and the nature of the space/time environment. As consciousness matures and incrementally moves through the foundational densities and lower dimensions of 3rd Density, the perception of the authenticity of the space/time environment increases until it reaches a zenith, but, when consciousness' advancement reaches the upper dimensions of 3rd Density, this trend begins to reverse itself and begins to lessen. The Great Way of the Body equally serves consciousness at both ends of its journey by providing the environment, resources, and information necessary to guide its development path back to unity and stillness, according to its capacity to perceive the service.

Throughout the cycle of the creation and dissolution of an authentic perception of the space/time environment, awareness is the "tool" that allows consciousness to benefit from the information offered by the module. Regardless of whether SA (awareness) is specifically identified as an object or subject of the module, it's inseparably part of every object and subject because all archetypes are only predominantly their named identification while also consisting of all of the other four Inherent Characteristics. Consciousness becomes relatively aware in the 1st Density, assimilates itself into an element according to the cohesion of its coding activation, and harmonizes its element identity with the other three elements to form a functioning organism. As awareness continues to increase, it eventually surrenders its attachment to the authenticity of the space/time environment in favor of truth, still functioning as an evolving organism but without the perception of physicality.

To have experiences so consciousness may progress, it must "change" or "move" and this perception is ably created in the lower body modules by the archetype DA, a distortion of KA. Change guides consciousness to alter its beginning perceptions of dispersion and independence to a greater perception of unity. Without change, consciousness couldn't experience analogy and, therefore, couldn't perform the comparison and contrast process that allows it to choose and learn. Consciousness evolves by exploring itself according to its preferences, and, invariably, prefers what "feels" better.

Unity invariably feels better than separation, and it's only through an analogy that consciousness can explore itself, discard that which doesn't feel as good, and progress to unity. Within the concept of space/time, change is experienced as a mind/body/spirit moving in relation to another mind/body/spirit. A single mind/body/spirit cannot perceive motion because motion is a concept only available in relation to another mind/body/spirit or an object in relation to another object.

Movement is a predicate for the thought-processing method of analogy, how consciousness learns of itself through the process of evolution, and how consciousness can also perceive a one, two, or three-dimensional physical environment. Personal preferences, chosen according to analogy, are the heart of how the uniqueness of a consciousness pattern is developed and how the "Creator as the Object" explores itself by experiencing itself as the "Creator as the Subject". A judgment of right or wrong is based upon the individual mind/body/spirit's determination of what feels better according to its current consciousness pattern and is only the Creator exploring itself as completely as possible through the process of analogy.

The Great Way of the Body creates an environment that allows consciousness to venture far from the direct path home and still be able to recover its direction and return to the source. Abundance feels better than lack and the path consciousness follows is always selected or created according to what "feels better", but, invariably, awareness of the choices available changes as consciousness evolves. Awareness is the tool that allows consciousness to recognize the options in the incrementally acquired experiences and provides it with the information necessary to refine its selections to either sustain its perception of separation or surrender distortions in favor of greater truth.

To explore the self infinitely, the concept of abundance provided by the Great Way of the Body is a necessary ingredient. Consciousness begins the evolutionary journey perceptually formatted primarily as chaos because of the programming provided by the distortion DA and TA, but consciousness is always within the enveloping environment of unity and stillness created by the YA and KA archetypes. The environment of abundance created by the Great Way of the Body keeps consciousness tethered to the truth which is a trail of breadcrumbs guiding it home.

> ## Great Way of the Body
>
> - Initial Object: YA (unity)
> - Initial Subject: KA (stillness)
>   - Characteristic(s):
>   - Abundance
> - Male Principal (+)
> - Algorithm

Great Way of the Spirit

The final module of the Great Way category and the Archetypical Mind is the Great Way of the Spirit. When we discussed the Matrix of the Spirit we identified the module as the "alpha" of the entire Archetypical Mind because it began consciousness' evolutionary journey by programming it with the perception of separation from the Creator (and all other consciousness) and is in constant motion or chaos, a condition described as "primordial darkness". The module is the foundational program of consciousness, and it's populated with two distortion archetypes: DA (movement) in the object/Logos position, and TA (separation) in the subject/sub-Logos position.

The Great Way of the Spirit is the "omega" to the Matrix of the Spirit's alpha. Similar to the Significator of the Spirit module, its archetypical construction reiterates the same Inherent Characteristic archetype in both the object/Logos position and the subject/sub-Logos position. The two archetype positions in the Significator of the Spirit reiterated RA (love), making it the only option available, and the Great Way of the Spirit's object/ Logos is populated with YA (unity) and the subject/sub-Logos reiterates unity, making it the only option. The Great Way of the Spirit's characteristic is "infinity, truth, and unity" which prepares consciousness for its return to 6th Density.

The Great Way of the Spirit provides the enveloping environment for all of the mind's modules, guiding and motivating all of the parts to 6th Density consciousness, the Density of unity and reunification with the Higher Self and the Creator, but, unlike the other two Great Way modules, it isn't limited to the category or the vertical sequence of spirit modules. It is the all-encompassing environment for the entire Archetypical Mind, and, consequently, the nature of consciousness' eventual experience while it remains within the foundational and experiential densities.

When consciousness surrenders the Archetypical Mind upon its graduation from 5th Density to the unity of 6th Density, the alpha Matrix of the Spirit module merges with the omega Great Way of the Spirit module, and the journey through the foundational and experiential densities will have been completed. Consciousness, now significantly changed from its evolutionary beginning, no longer processes thoughts, no longer distinguishes between an incarnate and non-incarnate self and doesn't contend with polarity. Unity doesn't recognize polarity because "All is One".

Still, when consciousness returns to 6th Density, evolution doesn't end because there is a significant transformation of consciousness yet to be experienced in its 6th Density evolution. Everything consciousness experiences in the lower five densities will have been completed when it reintegrates into the Higher Self. As previously explained, 6th Density is the broadest range of coding activation in the evolutionary process, consisting of eight levels of coding advanced two at a time. The density is divided into an upper half, with a coding activation ranging from 50 to 56 strands, and a lower half, with coding activation ranging from 42 to 48 strands. Consciousness participating in the lower half is primarily concerned with offering guidance to consciousness in the foundational and experiential densities and learning how to surrender even more of its free will intoxication so it may progress into the upper dimensions of 6th Density. The upper half of the 6th Density creates the soul streams and, near the end of the 6th Density dimensional range, has turned its focus on progressing to the 7th Density and a more complete reunification with the Creator.

The Great Way of the Spirit is undoubtedly a female module and an algorithm for consciousness' evolution. Through its characteristics, the spirit module of the Great Way category offers consciousness the opportunity to resolve all remaining attributes of the conditions and the mind/body/spirit's identity.

Great Way of the Spirit

- Initial Object: YA (unity)
- Initial Subject: YA (unity)
  - Characteristic(s):
    - Infinity, truth, unity
- Female Principal (-)
- Algorithm

To quote the poet T.S. Eliot:

We shall not cease from exploration, and the end of all our exploring will be to arrive where we started and know the place for the first time.

Chapter 26

Wanderers

Consciousness in a 3rd Density experience is very much like kindling. It has great potential to burn brightly, radiating light and warmth, but, on its own, it has little means of igniting. As with consciousness, an external combustion source is usually required to facilitate the kindling's fulfillment of its potential.

Adding to the predicament of requiring an external ignition source is the problem of free will. The Law of Confusion or, as otherwise known, the Law of Free will, emphatically requires that the 3rd Density population, the kindling, should not be unduly influenced by external sources that may contaminate its uniqueness and skew the entire experiment results with "experimenter bias". Despite the Law of Confusion, the Earth and preceding Zenoa, Maldek, and Mars experiences have been plagued with a significant problem that has complicated the Creator Beings' efforts to maintain an "uncontaminated" experiment, which is the pervasive influences of service-to-self or negatively polarized factions striving to establish and maintain the oppression of the population. The service-to-self factions also have free will, which includes the ability to ignore the rules of engagement to extract the necessary energy from a 3rd Density population that they need to maintain or advance their participation in creation.

These "problems" are not unique to the Earth's experience. The same problems have proven to be repetitious throughout the galaxy and universe but a creative way of dealing with the problems has been devised that has proven effective in countless other 3rd Density experiences, as well as the Earthly experience. One common solution to these three most prominent problems has been to invest "wanderers" into the planetary population.

A wanderer is an analog projection of a higher consciousness entity that is not "in" the 3rd Density experience to graduate like the majority of the population, but, nevertheless, lives one or more lifetimes as a 3rd Density mind/body/spirit. The wanderers normally don't receive any special privileges or have access to "powers" that other 3rd Density mind/body/spirits don't have, but they do maintain a deeper connection to their unmanifest self which allows them to potentially radiate greater love energy, thereby providing a boost or ignition to the regular 3rd Density population. A wanderer usually begins a 3rd Density incarnation with the same innocence and in the same chaos that all other 3rd Density mind/body/spirits experience, therefore there is no guarantee of their success.

During the early 1980s there were approximately 35 million "wanderers" participating in the Earth's population and today there remains less than 8 million with the numbers continuing to decline. The time when there was a need for wanders has essentially passed since the first Earthly 3rd Density experience has ended and many of the children are 4th Density consciousness. Wanderers have been an integral part of the Earth's experience since its beginning and many of the leading figures for centuries have been wanderers, achieving their pre-incarnate purpose in all aspects of humanity.

The overwhelming majority of wanderers are from the lower half of the 6th Density, but there are a few 4th, 5th, and upper 6th Density wanderers. After the difficulties of Zenoa, Maldek, and Mars, and as Earth began to repeat the difficulties of those earlier 3rd Density experiences, a call went out to the universe inviting participation by asking for wanderers to assist in the Earth experience. Multitudes of "nine-star system" organisms from around the universe have sent emissaries to participate in the Earth experience for thousands of years, but the most prolific participation has probably been within the last three hundred years.

Wanderers are analog projections of a higher consciousness being's time/space self, similar to a regular 3rd Density being, but instead of both the unmanifest self and the manifest self being in the 3rd Density, the unmanifest self remains in the originating density and the manifest self is living an analog projection lifetime in the 3rd Density. More often than not, the analog projection's lifetime being experienced by a wanderer is not a conventional preprogrammed timeline. Usually, a special set of timelines is written for the wanderer that will contain elements not normally included in the timelines of a mind/body/spirit seeking graduation from the density. The wanderer's timeline may include a designated objective that will boost the entire population, if the objective is successfully achieved, or it may be much more limited in scale to specifically aid a small grouping of 3rd Density mind/body/spirits.

Even though a wanderer's timeline may incorporate a "designated objective", it is incumbent upon the wanderer to progress through the experiences of the timeline to discover and then accomplish the objective. A wanderer mind/body/spirit begins in the same ignorance, chaos, and perception of separation as an ordinary 3rd Density mind/body/spirit, usually experiencing the same or greater "slings and arrows of outrageous fortune". In other words, they must awaken within the system, recognize their potential, and choose to implement their assigned task.

Most wanderers don't awaken and don't ever accomplish their assigned or chosen task, but some do, and those are the ones most memorable in history. A wanderer can also get lost within the 3rd Density experiences and oppositely conduct themselves from their original intentions because they too must enter the experience with the "forgetting". Negatively polarized 4th and particularly 5th Density entities can recognize a wanderer's energy signature and often make an extra effort to distract them from awakening and accomplishing their goals for the incarnation. Service-to-self entities don't want wanderers to succeed because the wanderer's objective is to raise the consciousness of the population by actively or passively countering the service-to-self objectives of continued oppression.

Since wanderers usually don't have access to special insights or powers greater than the 3rd Density population, the process of escalating awareness requires the same exploration of the self that the regular population wrestles with. For a wanderer to accomplish their task, they must awaken from unconsciousness, become awareness, and explore love, wisdom, and/or potentially unity through the lens of an equivalent consciousness pattern to the general population, but, because it is a wanderer, it isn't trying to graduate from the density and may, if they are able, tap into the higher consciousness perspectives and truth of their unmanifest self. Regardless of whether they successfully awaken and accomplish their lifetime goals, they almost always radiate greater love energy which, by itself, elevates the consciousness of those 3rd Density mind/body/spirits that come in contact with them.

Preparing a wanderer for introduction into a 3rd Density experience is somewhat more demanding than preparing consciousness that will be working towards graduation. Consciousness entering the 3rd Density experience with the ambition of graduating will have already established a time/space mind/body/spirit that is its enduring self and will eventually graduate to 4th Density and beyond. A wanderer doesn't create a separate 3rd Density time/space mind/body/spirit but directly projects its analog self into space/time from its 4th, 5th, or 6th Density self. This is significant because we process thoughts or have experiences in time/space and only the fruit of the thought process is brought into space/time, which results in the modification of the 3rd Density acolyte's metaphysical consciousness pattern.

A wanderer has the potential to modify a thought from its moderated higher consciousness time/space self's perspective and bring the fruit of the thought into space/time. A wanderer's analog projection is still the primary aspect of the experience, according to the Archetypical Mind, which means it begins its incarnation in the same chaos, separation, and unconsciousness as 3rd Density mind/body/spirits sharing the experience. It creates an ego mind, is unconscious, and creates an "I" perspective, all of which must be significantly reduced while living a timeline to benefit from its time/space mind/body/spirit perspectives. A wanderer, beginning a space/time incarnation as an analog projection, experiences the same "forgetting" as all other 3rd Density consciousness and must awaken to the truth of its higher consciousness and resulting perspectives.

A wanderer seldom experiences an unmodified off-the-self timeline designed for a 3rd Density mind/body/spirit participating as part of the regular population. A wanderer's timeline is almost always written especially for a wanderer and overlays several "regular" timelines in a manner that makes it possible for the wanderer to provide punctuated opportunities for the regular 3rd Density mind/body/spirits to learn and grow in ways not conventionally available. This can make life very difficult for a wanderer that remains within the constraints of the ego mind and "I" perspective because often the wanderer is tasked with becoming a victim of a 3rd Density mind/body/spirit. The mission of the wanderer is to awaken the 3rd Density denizen to compassion and motivate them to become awareness. By playing a second banana role, the wanderer is providing the opportunity for the 3rd Density entity to choose to either awaken or remain unconscious.

A person experiencing very difficult life events is often a wanderer and living a timeline designed specifically to provide one or more 3rd Density mind/body/spirits with the opportunity to evolve. Children born to abusive parents, women who have experienced repeated abuses by fathers, boyfriends, or husbands, or gay and lesbian people are often wanderers and offer others the opportunity to learn by analogy, awaken to their shortcomings, and choose a higher consciousness path. The design of the evolutionary process is that consciousness learns by experience and lessons are offered to others by providing the choice to evolve or not, to radiate or absorb love, to remain in pain and suffering, or evolve to happiness and joy. The time/space mind/body/spirit making the wanderer analog projection possible knows its incarnation is the participation in a grand thought experiment and the objective is to provide the "Creator as the subject", personified as consciousness, with the opportunity to explore itself by experiencing itself.

Most wanderers have a goal of assisting in a very specific way and with a targeted number of 3rd Density mind/body/ spirits, but some wanderers have an even grander objective and these are the ones that are more recognizable in Earth's history. Wanderers have always participated in Earth's experience but little is known about how they participated before the most recent redevelopment of the written word a few thousand years ago. But, even within this relatively short portion of history, they have been instrumental in all walks of life and all aspects of human business.

The biblical character Moses was a 6th Density wanderer and, while most of the activities attributed to Moses are fictional, he was a real incarnate mind/body/spirit that brought a higher consciousness message than was generally available in the population. Wanderers seldom go where they aren't needed, and the time and place of Moses' incarnation were in great need of light and information. His awakening was relative to the immediate population and he was enlightened accordingly, providing them with a model to emulate. Other biblical figures that were wanderers include King Solomon, Mary Magdalene, Jesus, the Buddha, and even Mary, the mother of Jesus.

Because wanderers seldom go where they aren't needed, they tend to concentrate their incarnations into intensely troubled low consciousness geographic areas of the planet like the area known as the Middle East. Wanderers seldom incarnate in isolation, especially if one wanderer has a grand objective affecting large portions of the population. If one wanderer has a defined role or purpose, various other wanderers are planned to join with the one to aid and support them in minor and major ways. Fifteen wanderers may be born in different parts of the world, but, when it's time for their service, the supporting wanderers will be guided by life circumstances to mysteriously converge so they can provide their supportive role.

We explained in previous chapters that a mind/body/spirit learns how to evolve by observing others of higher consciousness and, to make it possible, an example is always provided at the appropriate time. Lower consciousness begins to awaken incrementally, recognizes higher consciousness, and begins to mimic the higher consciousness until its consciousness has risen and it realizes it has become what it was mimicking, no longer in need of pretending. In addition to offering light through communication insights, providing a standard for others to mimic is a primary method wanderers use to offer assistance.

Siddhartha Gautama, more often identified as the Buddha, was a 6th Density wanderer with grander objectives than a normal wanderer. The Buddha began his incarnation with a relatively normal criterion for a wanderer incarnation except that he had a particularly thin veil and a very high degree of advancement within the originating density. He could connect to his higher consciousness unmanifest self and the collective consciousness more easily and employ "direct knowing". The Buddha provided a role model for others, then and now, but also provided significant information through his more expansive connection to the collective. Regardless of his thinner veil, Siddhartha still was required to go through the process of awakening, self-healing, and self-discovery, which is what he accomplished during his meditation retreats.

The messages that the Buddha taught were different than most other wanderers in that he didn't give the answers at the back of the book. He taught how the populace could learn to read on their own and glean the answers they sought by themselves; making the understanding more deeply and completely learned through their individual experiences. The 6th Density spirit that was the Buddha is of RA and continues to be very active in the guidance of the planet to this day, maintaining numerous soul streams participating in the Earth experience and others.

Jehoshua, or Jesus, was also a wanderer of LA, the wisdom archetype that calls the Sun home, and he was nearing the end of his 4th Density evolution at the time of his Earthly incarnation. Since his Earthly incarnation, Jesus has graduated to 5th Density and is participating in a 5th Density social memory complex that is also active in providing light to the Earth's population. It is unusual for a 4th Density being to become a wanderer because they are just recently beyond their dissolution of the Ego Mind and "I" perspective. Their time/space self is still within the Archetypical Mind and it is usually deemed too much to ask of consciousness at that stage of development.

Jehoshua also entered his incarnation with a thin veil which provided him with the ability to utilize his recent unattachment to the physical authenticity to perform "miracles" in the eyes of the surrounding population. Very few of the teachings of either the Buddha or Jehoshua have been preserved, primarily because neither one of them had a stenographer following them around to take written notes. The nature of Jehoshua's teachings differed from the Buddha's in that they were much more focused on the message of love, which is indicative of the 4th Density. The Buddha's teachings were more focused on unity, and, by teaching the methodologies of a self-guided evolution, he intended to provide the tools needed at the moment and for the future people to grow through the remaining 3rd Density Earth experience and that of the next.

The Buddha's triggers for his awakening were much more subtle than what was required for Jehoshua, but, because of Jehoshua's 4th Density lens, it was necessary as a motivator. Jehoshua became aware of his "powers" at a very early age, and, while playing with another child, unintentionally killed his playmate in a momentary fit of anger. This served as a significant motivation for Jehoshua to learn, grow spiritually, and make amends for his youthful carelessness. It was a catalyst for Jehoshua to fulfill his incarnate purpose of providing light and being a model for others to emulate while offering the necessary stimulus to motivate his awakening and self-development.

Mahatma Gandhi was another recent wanderer that was both a spiritual messenger and political figure, putting his spiritual awareness into action to aid the welfare of the populace. Gandhi was a 6th Density wanderer of RA that also continues to be significantly involved in guiding the Earth's population toward the healing of its attachment to the conditions and distortions of lower consciousness. Unity through recognition of the equality of all people and the rejection of the oppression of service-to-self influences through self-awareness were the hallmarks of his incarnation. Gandhi is most remembered for leading India's liberation from English colonial rule but he was also instrumental in weakening the traditional caste system India had socially enforced for centuries.

Many wanderers have chosen politics as a vehicle to share their message because of its prominent influence upon the lives of the general population and they have shone throughout history as landmark transformers in the status quo. Abraham Lincoln was one of the political wanderers that had a monumental ambition but experienced great personal difficulties during his incarnation. The first portion of his life, the years before 1853, was personally very challenging and exhausted him physically, mentally, and spiritually, but, in 1853, the spirit that enjoyed the first portion of the lifetime surrendered its incarnation to another, different spirit that assumed the same embodiment and timeline. Because of this substitution, Lincoln became what is known as a "walk-in". The character portrayal known as Abraham Lincoln's life after 1853 was significantly different than the earlier years because the ability to achieve success in the lifetime ambitions was made possible by the renewed energy and zeal of the replacement spirit.

Franklin Delano Roosevelt or FDR was another 6th Density wanderer that experienced significant challenges to his life goals. FDR experienced polio as a catalyst to focus his ambitions after the character of his incarnation wavered from the lifetime objective. The illness catalyzed the refocusing of his attention back to the pre-incarnate ambition. FDR was instrumental in shifting the oppression of the population from service-to-self ideologies and allowing the lower-consciousness population to experience greater freedom and elevate awareness because of his leadership. What we perceive to be ideological populism, framed as conservative versus liberalism, is nothing more than the continued battle between attempts to oppress the population with service-to-self ideologies and the struggle to allow the populace to experience greater freedom, which includes the opportunity to spiritually evolve through greater awareness.

Many of the "Founding Fathers" of the United States were 6th Density wanderers, mostly from RA, including Thomas Jefferson and Benjamin Franklin. Their philosophical awareness and wisdom significantly exceeded the prevailing norms of the time and, even considering their personal struggles with prevailing societal conventions, were able to rise above the norms to participate in creating the democratic experiment that has transformed how the populations of the world have enjoyed the Earth experience. The struggle of service-to-self versus service-to-others continues today in both the United States and throughout the world, but, without their vision and foresight, there wouldn't be the island of hope that the US offered to its citizens and to the world population that shares this Earthly endeavor.

Wanderers have been instrumental in raising awareness in all walks of life and all chosen professions. They have been significant contributors to the arts, music, law, the sciences, and religion. Michelangelo, Vincent van Gogh, and Leonardo da Vinci were all 6th Density wanderers, but, even more significantly, they were all the same 6th Density spirit of RA. Wolfgang Amadeus Mozart, Johann Sebastian Bach, and Ludwig van Beethoven were also all 6th Density wanderers of RA. Mozart was from another galaxy that is predisposed to sound and uses sound more significantly as a vehicle of evolutionary advancement than is common in our galaxy. A wanderer's participation in a variety of professions diversifies their influences within the population and further fulfills the ambition of wanderers to provide light or information by being a model for others to emulate, mimic, and eventually become an equivalent consciousness.

If you are familiar with the lives of any of these historical figures, you may note that none of them were saints or even saintly in their lives. Wanderers assume a character role in the play of life and begin an incarnation with the same forgetting and attachment to the conditions of the Archetypical Mind, which means they experience similar life struggles as the general population. It is incumbent upon the individual wanderer to feel the pull of higher consciousness, awaken, and discover how to fulfill their pre-incarnate purpose, which, by the way, isn't disclosed to them in a secret coded message. They must undergo the same process of awareness development as any other mind/body/spirit in the general 3rd Density population but, if they are successful in their efforts, they can and often do become the external combustion source for the kindling of 3rd Density.

As previously stated, the wanderers are participating as a 3rd Density person and live a timeline designed to overlay a variety of more conventional 3rd Density timelines. After their initial incarnation and introduction into the density, 3rd Density mind/body/spirits working towards graduation begin a new incarnation with the consciousness pattern developed through their previous lives. The developing consciousness pattern is important because it is the basis for interpreting experiences by a new analog projection in a new lifetime. In other words, a new analog projection picks up where the previous one leaves off.

Wanderers, particularly of 6th Density origin, don't have emotional baggage or a particular consciousness pattern that would guide them to interpret experiences appropriately for a 3rd Density timeline. To make it possible for them to "fit in" with the existing population and simultaneously create "triggers" designed to stimulate their awakening, a suitable consciousness pattern and emotional baggage are fabricated for them by making the necessary adjustments to the chakra configuration of their analog projection. With these configurations, the distortions programmed by the conditions of the Archetypical Mind, and the timelines designed specifically for the wanderer's experience, a wanderer's lifetime becomes indistinguishable from a mind/body/spirit normally progressing through the evolution process. The exception is the potential to access their higher consciousness and unmanifest self, if they are successful in awakening, undergoing the standard process of healing the emotional baggage, and adequately surrendering the ego mind, unconsciousness, and "I" perspective.

Other than the potential to tap into the higher consciousness unmanifest self and a uniquely designed timeline, wanderers receive no special privileges over the general population. Wanderers may sign up for a "one and done" incarnation, as was Mozart's participation, or they may sign up for a series of lifetimes. If they sign up for multiple lifetimes they need not be serial. They can be dropped into timelines randomly with completely different purposes, as different sexes, or at varying points in history because everything occurs simultaneously.

A sourcing 6th Density consciousness can experience multiple wanderer incarnations simultaneously while maintaining existing soul streams and continuing to initiate new ones. Every 3rd Density mind/body/spirit has a Higher Self that usually originated the entire soul stream of which it is a part and continues to guide and monitor its progress through the evolutionary process. Every wanderer also has a designated Higher Self that serves the same purpose but often the wanderer's Higher Self is from another 6th Density archetype. For example, a RA wanderer may have a LA or DA archetype as its Higher Self while it continues to be incarnate.

Why would a 6th Density entity want to be a wanderer? There are many reasons but most prominently, "to be of service". "All is One" and as one aspect of consciousness needs assistance, all require assistance. Every 3rd Density experience is unique and every mind/body/spirit participating is also unique. Many 6th Density entities desire to participate as a wanderer to diversify their experiential resources and expand their understanding of creation and/or the Creator.

Unfortunately, most wanderers don't awaken, tune in to their Higher Self, or to their higher consciousness unmanifest self, but those who are successful provide a significant boost to the general 3rd Density population. Many of the homeless and/or drug addicted mind/body/spirits still participating in the Earth's population are wanderers who haven't been able to adapt to the severe and heavy conditions of the Earth's experience, but each one has contributed the light and love that it has been able to muster. Most are not tasked with a monumental duty such as the Buddha, Jehoshua, or Gandhi but everyone significantly contributes as they are able. Any 3rd Density experience would be significantly more difficult if it were not for the contributions and love that emanate from the wanderers that participate.

Chapter 27

The Human Condition, part one

In Chapter 11, we introduced information on stress and defined what stress is. To briefly reiterate: stress is the difference between expectations and "what is". In this chapter, we shall expand upon the concept of stress, explain the foundations of stress, and describe the process of stress creation, which is the source of all human suffering. Until consciousness awakens and begins to heal the self from the erroneous illusions of its perception of the self, it will likely continue to create stress but it isn't necessary because all consciousness inherently has the tool(s) necessary to discover and resolve stress' creation thereby, healing the "human condition".

The Human Condition — part one

All consciousness experiencing 3rd Density is programmed to explore love and it usually does this by incarnating into a space/time environment. The 3rd Density begins with consciousness conditioned to perceive itself in "primordial darkness" which is characterized as not having any information, in constant chaos, and as an independent and autonomous perceiving mind/body/spirit. A person is a clean canvas on which to paint whatever they desire according to the limitations of the paints and brushes at their disposal.

A time/space mind/body/spirit incarnates into space/time as an analog projection of itself, and, from birth, begins to have experiences which is how they paint on their canvas. They're simultaneously creating a pattern of consciousness in the time/space mind/body/spirit and an identity in a space/time analog projection. The person registers their likes or dislikes by feeling an emotion, but emotions are only the individual's assessment of the experience according to its prevailing condition. If consciousness adjudicates an experience or thought as "feeling" good, it places the experience in the "it must be love" and "I want more of it" category, and if it doesn't feel good, it goes into the "it must not be love" or the "fear" category. These are the only two choices possible because all of the other perceived emotions are only varying intensities of these two primary emotions as seen through the lenses of varying levels of awareness.

All experiences are experienced in and through thoughts because creation is a thought experiment and no physical stage is built on which to conduct the play called creation. There is no possibility of an experience outside of a thought. There isn't a physical world independent of consciousness' observation of it because the physical world is all part of the thought. There is, however, an Archetypical Mind design that determines how thought will be processed, and it may be misunderstood to be a physical mold or form because of its consistency.

By this design, the birthing of consciousness into primordial darkness means it doesn't know what love is, even though it is preprogrammed to explore love, therefore, the first order of business is to discover what love feels like. The space/time analog projection, from the first experience of a lifetime, begins to form an identity according to its interpretations of experiences. A consciousness pattern is concurrently created by the mind/body/spirit in time/space, shaped by the characteristics of the multiple identities of its analog projections. The time/space consciousness pattern results from the accumulated experiences of all of the analog projections of itself into space/time and serves as the repository for all of the identities attributable to the analog projections.

This is a progression from the pools of consciousness in 2nd Density that don't allow the preservation of consciousness' experiences as it evolves through the levels. Beginning in 3rd Density, the time/space mind/body/spirit becomes an individualized repository of experiences of its multiple lifetimes as analog projections into space/time and it builds upon its prevailing phase of evolution with every new incarnation. Every person, enjoying a space/time incarnation on Earth or elsewhere, is an analog projection of a time/space mind/body/spirit and contributes to its consciousness pattern by interpreting incremental experiences during the incarnation. The analog projection simultaneously creates an identity predicated upon the prevailing condition of the time/space mind/body/spirit but made unique by its free will interpretations of its experiences. Consciousness processes every thought as both the time/space mind/body/spirit and as a space/time mind/body/spirit but the space/time perspective always has the last word as to how thought will be adjudicated by the analog projection. If there is a distinction between the time/space consciousness pattern and the space/time identity's thought interpretation, the space/time self can overrule or discard the input from the time/space consciousness pattern. This is often a behavior characteristic of consciousness in the lower dimensions of the density because the ego mind is still dominant. When Grandma says, "Listen to your heart and not your head," she is describing the conflict between the identity and the consciousness pattern happening behind the awareness of the incarnate mind/body/spirit.

As experiences continue, both the manifest analog projection and the time/space unmanifest self continue to paint parallel pictures, forming both an identity and a consciousness pattern respectively. Every experience is a brush stroke on the canvases that are the space/time identity and the time/space consciousness pattern. Initially, the pictures that are being created will probably be very similar but the similarities may soon diverge because the time/space consciousness is simultaneously incarnate in multiple analog projections, learning from the experiences of multiple incarnations, but each projection is living an independent life without the benefit of directly learning from the other incarnations or from the time/space mind/body/spirit while it remains unconscious. The consciousness pattern is gaining a cumulative evolutionary maturity from multiple incarnations while the analog projection is learning from a single source.

If a single time/space mind/body/spirit is simultaneously incarnated into three or four analog projections, it is exploring love through all of the incarnations simultaneously. An individual analog projection is only exploring love from its identity and, if the consciousness pattern's maturity is outpacing the awareness of the incarnation, it is probable that the incarnate mind/body/spirit will discount the input from time/space and rely primarily upon the ego mind. This can cause disharmony between the two but the ego mind has the ultimate determining authority over how thought will be adjudicated because of its free will and support its identity accordingly. There can be, and often is, a significant discrepancy in the incarnate operating consciousness levels of the multiple incarnations of a single time/space mind/body/spirit, even though they are still actually co-experiencing the incarnation as a single unit of consciousness.

The design for incarnations into space/time is a microcosm of the Higher Self model that is creating soul streams into the foundational and experiential densities. A Higher Self remains a 6th Density awareness, but it projects itself into myriad varieties in the lower five densities and allows the projections to exercise free will to explore the possibilities as it will. The Higher Self remains "intact" as a consciousness organism but explores itself by experiencing itself according to the same design initiated with the "Creator as the object" and "Creator as the subject" relationship. At a significantly reduced level of awareness, the time/space mind/body/spirit is serving in the "Creator as the object" role, and each analog projection is serving in the "Creator as the subject" role.

The potential for discrepancies between the two aspects of the same consciousness exists because of free will. Remember, free will is the perception of separation, and as long as the incarnate analog projection perceives itself as an independent unit of consciousness, it probably perceives a greater degree of free will intoxication than the time/space mind/body/spirit. That is why and how the initial analog projection creates an identity based upon "what it likes" that can be very different from the consciousness pattern of the time/space mind/body/spirit. After the initial incarnation into space/time, a new incarnation begins with the prevailing condition of the consciousness pattern so all subsequent incarnations begin with a "personality" formed as a result of the accumulated incarnations of the multiple analog projections of the time/space mind/body/spirit.

As an analog projection creates or amends an identity based upon experiences that either successfully reinforces the feeling of love or not, it creates expectations, AKA biases and prejudices. Expectations are "always" rooted in experiences and the identity is the hierophant that is the Significator of the Mind. If a mind/body/spirit incorporates a characteristic into its identity or hierophant and the characteristic doesn't prove to successfully get more positive feelings as a result, it will remove that aspect and search for another characteristic that may be more fulfilling, adjusting its expectations accordingly. While an analog projection retains an identity with corresponding expectations, it remains in the "discovery" phase of its evolution through the density which is characteristic of the lower three-fourths of the dimensions of 3rd Density.

Stress occurs when the people, places, or things around an individual don't meet the individual's expectations by not supporting or defending their identity, which means it isn't getting the "good feelings" or love from their experiences. An individual mind/body/spirit will go to great lengths to sustain its identity and subsequent expectations. When the world doesn't defend or support a mind/body/spirit's identity by not meeting its expectations, a common behavior is to try and manage the world around it by changing whoever or whatever is not meeting its expectations. Overwhelmingly, the "world" presents itself as another person, so the mind/body/spirit whose identity isn't being supported tries to change the other mind/body/spirit(s) to compel or "trick" them into providing the "love" that they need.

Most, but not all experiences, are provided by interactions with other mind/body/spirits as either individuals or groups and, therefore, most stress is experienced because of interactions with other people. Every interaction is a message to the individual(s) participating in the experience because every individual applies emotions to interpret the experience. The message is always about the self and will either be about what needs to be changed within the self or confirmation about what is "right" within the self but *no* experience brings emotion with it!

Imagine there is a group of people at a lawn party with a lawn sprinkler in their midst. If the sprinkler was unexpectedly turned on, everyone would get wet in the same way because the sprinkler brought the water. However, every person getting wet would feel differently about the experience because they would interpret the experience according to how "they were", not as the experience was. Some would be indignant, some would be amused, and some would be angry, depending upon whether or not getting wet supported their identity and subsequent expectations. The experience, as are all experiences, is absolutely neutral of emotions but it would bring a message to every person sharing the experience by being a trigger for them to feel the emotions stored within themselves.

Stress is "the difference between seeing experiences through the distorted lens of individual expectations versus enjoying experiences through a clear, undistorted lens by seeing things as they really are". By failing to become aware and recognize the unwanted feeling within the self as a message about what needs to be changed about the perceived self, the mind/body/ spirit is choosing stasis over stability and continuing to reinforce its ego/identity and perception of separation. The message is often lessened or lost completely because the recipient remains unconscious and unaware, but never fear, the message will be repeated as many times as necessary until the recipient either awakens or grows fatigued from interpreting the message according to its expectations because doing so causes chronic suffering.

Socially, an individual will gravitate towards other people with similar expectations and identities because a group comprised of a similar consciousness level is less resistant to supporting a common identity. They prompt little need to change. If an identity includes overt victim characteristics, other people with similar characteristics will resonate and stimulate a harmonic misery of sorts. Likewise, if an identity is less burdened with biases and prejudices with corresponding expectations, other people with similar identities and expectations will resonate more comfortably. "Birds of a feather, flock together" because, when they do, there is less resistance to meeting expectations and less stress, but also, less opportunity to become aware and spiritually advance.

Expectations and identities of a group are reflective of a level of consciousness because they are predicated upon the degree of awareness and the level to which individuals comprising the group have surrendered free will intoxication. While individual consciousness remains low and free will intoxication is high, groups are formed because of a shared level of fear. As individuals awaken and escalate their awareness, association with old groups of lower consciousness becomes uncomfortable for both the group and the awakening individual. As people evolve, they will gravitate to new groups that offer a greater resonance with their degree of awareness.

The popularity of groups wax and wane as individuals within the general population experience varying degrees of stress brought about by the inevitability of change and challenges to their expectations and identity. For example, the popularity of religion has fluctuated around the world as the stasis expectations of the population have been challenged by war, economic issues, or challenges from service-to-self factions. In the United States, as dramatic social changes that challenged the general population's stasis were experienced around the Civil War, the Ku Klux Klan, a very low consciousness group, came into existence with great enthusiasm across the country, but lost popularity around the turn of the century as stresses temporarily declined. The group experienced a significant resurgence during the 1920s along with the rise of fascism in Europe because the stasis of the population was challenged by economic issues and individuals felt increased fear. The names of many groups remain the same but the identities of the groups change as the individuals comprising the groups change. Politics is an excellent example of this when you consider the ideologies of the Republican and Democratic Parties in the United States. Republicans once were the party of Jefferson and Lincoln, and even today, current members often highlight such associations as a moniker of their ideals, but today's group is comprised of individuals that lean towards or actively promote service-to-self philosophies, and the practical ideals and level of group consciousness have been altered accordingly. Likewise, the Democrats were historically the party opposed to the liberalism of the Republicans, but, because the nature of the individuals comprising the party has changed, the ideologies and consciousness level of the group have also changed until both parties essentially profess the opposite of their founding philosophies.

Groups, of any focus, can only reflect the nature of the individuals that comprise the group's participants. If the consciousness level of the individuals is low, the consciousness level of the group will reflect it in its feelings, behaviors, and ideals. If the consciousness level of the individuals comprising the group is high, likewise, it will reflect that as well but, regardless of whether the group consciousness level is high or low, it is incumbent upon the individual to take responsibility for their awareness and development of its evolution. Groups provide the opportunity for experiences and a consistent supply of messages about the self, but surrendering individual awareness to the group hinders the individual's ability to evolve.

The pictures being painted on the individual's canvases are unique in all of creation, even though experiences may be shared or repeatedly duplicated because every single experience/thought is interpreted uniquely. All experiences, or thoughts, will be interpreted according to the morphing identity because the uniqueness of the identity continues to refine its preferences more narrowly to get more of what feels good and less of what doesn't feel good. Based upon identity, the mind/body/spirit shapes expectations and expects more experiences that provide the opportunity to feel what it likes and less of what it doesn't like. The mind/body/spirit's perspectives derive from its identity, and it sees things as they are, rather than the way things actually are.

In the lower dimensions of the density, the mind/body/spirit is functioning according to the ego mind, unconsciousness, and with an "I" perspective, which means it's firmly attached to the authenticity of the physical world and its independence from "other" people. Its awareness is primarily directed outside of the self with the expectation that others must provide them with the love that they are preprogrammed to explore. They expect other people to love them if they could just find the right identity and/or be a better trickster.

When the world doesn't support and defend a mind/body/ spirit's identity or doesn't provide the love that it wants and needs to the degree it expects, it feels stressed when it is only able to see experiences through the lens of its expectations. It lives through its expectations because its identity, formed without awareness as a result of its interpretations of its previous experiences, has determined that this is what is necessary for it to get love or, at least, good feelings. It is customary, while consciousness remains in the lower dimensions of the density, for the mind/body/spirit to consistently experience failure in its attempts to get love from the outside world.

If there are 150 flavors of ice cream and out of those 150 flavors a person has determined that chocolate is their favorite, it's necessary to arrive at this determination by tasting all of the possible flavors and discarding those less pleasing than chocolate. This is the process of analogy, based purely upon a preference for one flavor over another, but, in the course of arriving at this conclusion, there will probably be several flavors that stand out. Eventually, because of the process of refinement through analogy, one will emerge as the absolute favorite.

The same is true of the discovery process of determining what love feels like. Just as it is necessary to taste 149 flavors to conclude that chocolate is the best, people have experiences to determine what feels good to them. In previous chapters, we explained that people exchange energy with every interaction, and, while they remain in the lower dimensions of the density, the exchange becomes an unconscious battle because concluding an interaction with more energy than when entered feels better. The competition for energy fuels most relationships on Earth, even in today's world that has recently finished and begun another new 3rd Density population, that is shared with a new 4th experience. Consciousness, in the lower dimensions of the 3rd Density and especially those polarizing negatively, misinterpret increased energy as love, and either consciously or unconsciously employ the "Concept of Empire".

To reiterate: the "Concept of Empire" is the belief that "I can be enhanced by diminishing you or others. The more I can win the energy battle, the more energy I will get and the more good feelings (or misperceived love) I will feel." Of course, the basic problem is that getting energy feels better than not getting energy, but it isn't love. Exercising the "Concept of Empire" is still working through the 150 flavors to determine the one that is your favorite.

Those people polarizing negatively do so because they have reinforced the prominence of the ego mind and "I" perspective and continue to confuse the hedonistic "feel good" feeling of winning the energy battle as love. They have failed to become aware and surrendered the ego self adequately to experience what love feels like. They have only experienced varying levels of fear and determined that the lower levels of fear, those that promulgate serious pain and suffering, can be mostly avoided by increasing their skill in winning more energy battles. They are still tasked with exploring the self and learning of love, but, they fear the pain and suffering so much, they give up the search for love in favor of stasis and avoiding the most significant fears.

Trying to control one's life and everything in it is a condition that emerges from this behavior. People attempt to control other people, places, and things, as well as themselves, so they can limit catalyst input and avoid confronting awareness of what needs to be healed and/or changed within themselves. Movement is synonymous with change, and, as long as the distortion archetype DA is part of the experience, change is inevitable. Attempting to control change and clinging to a fear-based stasis philosophy creates as much, if not more, stress than any other aspect of life on Earth.

The same messages begun for everyone in the 3rd Density continue to be delivered to those polarizing negatively throughout 4th and 5th Densities, but with escalating intensity because they continue to see things as they are, not as things actually are, and, the more they become fear, the more they see fear in surrendering the ego. The process begins in the 3rd Density, and, as the more competitive individual learns to rely upon their success in winning energy battles, perpetuates the error of confusing winning energy battles for love. Competition continues through service-to-self's 5th Density experience but the stakes, in the ego minds of the higher density service-to-self, get more significant because every energy battle becomes a very real life or death experience. When the stakes get higher, the participants become willing to surrender all pretense of civility, and there isn't anything they won't do to sustain the ego and continue to steal the energy they need, as was evident in the tragedies of Earth's Atlantis, the planets Zenoa, Mars, and especially Maldek.

Ideally, and in the experience of most 3rd Density people, at some point in the evolutionary process, "awareness" occurs. The awareness is almost always awakening from unconsciousness because the person is unhappy; when the individual realizes that he/she may either be winning or losing energy battles, but, either way, they aren't happy. They experience dissatisfaction, decide something else needs to change, and they seek alternative ways to find happiness beyond the competition habit. The less attached to the eminence of the ego mind, the more likely the awareness will come as a result of the awakening that, despite being a successful competitor, the practice isn't providing them with what they need.

The same awakening may occur for those with a greater degree of free will intoxication, but the process usually doesn't result from an awareness epiphany. The greater the perception of separation, resulting from the greater free will intoxication, the more likely the individual will "hit a bottom" because they have exhausted themselves physically, mentally, and spiritually in their efforts to extract love from the world around them. When this occurs, we call it depression or despair, and the individual has no alternative other than give up their previous behavior and be compelled to seek elsewhere. The desire and need for love is preprogrammed in everyone experiencing the 3rd Density, and if a mind/body/spirit can't get the love it needs from the world, the only other place to look is inside itself.

The awakening process, whether arrived at by choice or compelled by circumstance, is the same for every 3rd Density person throughout the universe. Despite the variety of vantage points provided by different sponsoring archetypes, different environments, unique Archetypical Minds, or whatever the variables, the process of evolution that allows consciousness to transform from the furthest perception of separation from the Creator to reunification is the same. The process requires consciousness to surrender free will intoxication, explore the self with awareness, and learn of its "power" as the Creator, thereby fulfilling the purpose of Creation.

The evolution process guides consciousness to create a pattern and then guides the surrendering of the consciousness pattern to unity. Every analog projection undergoes a microcosm of the same process, meaning: within each lifetime a mind/body/spirit analog projection creates an identity and then is tasked with surrendering that identity into recognition and unity with its unmanifest self and/or Higher Self thereby, elevating its awareness and consciousness level. Consciousness learns of itself as the "Creator as the subject", and consequently, the "Creator as the object" learns of itself by experiencing itself.

Chapter 28

The Human Condition, part two

Chapter 27 explained that beginning with the 3rd Density, consciousness creates a consciousness pattern that is the hierophant of the time/space mind/body/spirit with a separate identity or hierophant for each of its space/time analog projections. The identity is the lens through which the analog projection sees the world and interprets its experiences because it creates expectations, biases, and prejudices, based upon the prevailing condition of the identity. It expects the world to recognize and reinforce its identity because, regardless of what the expectations may be, its purpose is to allow the mind/body/spirit to "get" more of what it likes and less of what it doesn't like. By the design, consciousness is exploring itself by experiencing itself and it enjoys a variety of experiences so that it might employ the process of analogy to uniquely determine its preferences.

The Human Condition—part two

The consciousness pattern of the time/space mind/body/spirit is a compilation of experiences from multiple identities, each created during an incarnation into space/time. A consciousness pattern serves the same function for the time/space mind/body/spirit as an individual identity does for an analog projection, but it's more comprehensive and directly representative of the degree of evolutionary advancement than an individual identity. While a mind/body/spirit remains within the lower dimensions of the density, probably, it will only be able to incarnate into three or four analog projections simultaneously,[2] but, as it evolves into the upper dimensions of the density, it may be simultaneously incarnated in as many as eight or nine projections. Incarnations provide the time/space mind/body/spirit with experience that will hopefully expand its awareness and allow it to evolve.

Experiences/thoughts are messages but the messages presented to an analog projection have little or nothing to do with information about the physical world, per se. Space/time, the physical world, is only the stage for the play, and being aware of characteristics of space/time may enhance the experience of the play but they have little or nothing to do with the play's message. Just as an actor in a play might lose themselves in the character they're portraying, the actor and the analog projection might personally suffer significant life difficulties because of their loss of perspective of their authentic self. Every thought/experience is interpreted with emotion and emotions are the result of preferential feelings as uniquely determined by the person. The method of creating an identity is the same for every analog projection, but the identity that results from the process is unique, therefore, the Creator can learn of itself by experiencing itself infinitely.

An analog projection of a time/space mind/body/spirit is a person living a lifetime and every person forms a unique identity, different from all others, but the identity isn't stagnant once it is formed. As the analog projection continues to have experiences, its identity constantly changes to accommodate its learning, and expectations change accordingly. The creation of the identity begins with the first experience after birth, but earnestly restarts at about two years of age and is continuously modified until the last experience of the incarnation.

An analog projection grows through an incarnation in phases with experiences becoming more complex with each expanding phase. An infant only processes thought through its 1st time/space chakra and then makes one lap through all seven of the space/time chakras, creating the portion of an emotion at each assessment point, interpreting the catalyst at each chakra. The incremental catalyst assessments at each chakra culminate in one assessment for the whole experience.

When the analog projection reaches the toddler or second phase of its development, the 2nd time/space chakra opens and it sequentially assesses all future catalysts through the 1st time/space chakra and all seven of the space/time chakras, then repeats the process through the 2nd time/space chakra. The limitations of processing catalysts only through the two time/space chakras continue until puberty when the 3rd time/space chakra opens and the person can expand their awareness, transform their identity, and amend their expectations accordingly. The incremental opening of the time/space chakras allows the individual to explore themselves at each phase, as it amends their identity. Thoughts are designed to be processed one at a time and in a linear sequence. It's necessary to have a sufficient number of experiences and sufficient opportunity to season any changes at each phase to build upon previous experiences, amend the identity, and adjust its related expectations.

Every thought is an experience and provides the experiencer with a catalyst for change. Earth's Archetypical Mind requires every thought to be interpreted with an emotion. Emotion is the expression of an individual's preference for a catalyst that, at every step of the chakra system process, either feels good or doesn't; meaning it either feels like love or it feels like fear. At the 1st time/space chakra and 1st space/time chakra, the first assessment point, consciousness chooses whether the experience feels good or doesn't and then passes the thought along to the next assessment point, the 1st time/space chakra and 2nd space/time chakra and so on. Every chakra along the way is a point of reassessment that requires making the simple choice of "it feels good" or "it doesn't feel good" before the thought can move on to the next chakra.

The process requires an individual assessment at each time/space and space/time chakra, ultimately resulting in the adjudication by the Experience of the Mind module of the Archetypical Mind. The Experience of the Mind module receives the catalyst from the Catalyst of the Mind module, "feels" the fruit of the chakra process, collects the input from the Experience of the Body (and potentially the Experience of the Spirit module), and forwards the fruit of the experience phase of the process to the Significator of the Mind module for further processing. The Experience of the Mind "feels" the catalyst before it invites input from the Experience of the Body and Experience of the Spirit. When it invites input from the Experience of the Spirit is when the Deep Mind has an opportunity to significantly influence the catalyst interpretation by prompting the Ego Mind to surrender a little more of the ego identity.

The Significator of the Mind module "is" the identity or Hierophant. When awareness escalates within the space/time mind/body/spirit and the spirit modules of the Archetypical Mind are recognized by the Ego Mind, the Catalyst of the Mind promotes having faith to surrender the Ego Mind, the Experience of the Spirit encourages the surrendering, and the Significator of the Mind makes the choice to amend its perspective by actually surrendering the identity. Once it begins surrendering the identity and altering its expectations accordingly, it begins to intermittently radiate love energy instead of repeatedly competing and battling with force to feel better. It begins to incrementally get closer to feeling love for the first time.

For an infant, the hierophant is the consciousness pattern of the time/space mind/body/spirit because an identity for the incarnation hasn't been adequately formed yet. After the first incarnation, all reincarnations pick up where the previous ones left off and a new incarnation begins with the condition of the prevailing consciousness pattern of the time/space mind/

body/spirit. Relatively speaking, the period of infancy is often functioning as a higher level of consciousness than after the space/time mind/body/spirit has formed an identity.

The infant phase of a lifetime is very elementary and intimately linked to the condition of the prevailing consciousness pattern of the unmanifest self. One may speculate that the physical limitations of an infant are the primary constraints to its awareness but its senses and potential for awareness are fully functional. Its awareness is governed by the scheduled opening of its chakra system and the surrendering of its time/space mind to the newly created ego mind, which is what occurs when the 2nd time/space chakra is opened. The body is a creation of the mind and the physical maturation of the body is a result of the mind's development, based in large part upon its chakra opening schedule.

Opening the 2nd chakra is the beginning of evolutionary responsibility for an incarnate analog projection because it begins perceptual independence from the time/space mind and the earnest creation of its identity. The ego mind assumes the primary duty of processing the toddler's thoughts and creates expectations to reinforce its emerging identity. The ego mind is what transforms the little angel that you put to bed at night into the demanding "terrible twos" toddler the next morning. It is also at this point when the timeline begins to bring thoughts to the analog projection and guides its experiences.

During infancy, experiences are random and interpretations of experiences are accomplished with the most basic analogous choices, but there isn't significant continuity to the determinations because an independent identity has yet to be formed. With the opening of the 2nd time/space chakra and the assumption of responsibility for experience interpretation by the ego mind, the toddler/child begins to create a unique identity and forms expectations accordingly. An identity is created solely as a result of analogous interpretations of experiences and is predicated solely upon what the mind/body/spirit prefers. The toddler is beginning to uniquely explore love and shape its identity so that it will be able to get more of what feels like love and less of what feels like fear.

Through the timeline, specific experiences are brought to the toddler instead of relying upon the randomness of infancy. Parents, siblings, relatives, and friends all bring experiences and the child learns that if it looks, acts, thinks, or behaves in certain ways, the individuals bringing experiences will respond either positively or negatively to its identity characteristics. The child "expects" to be rewarded with more positive feelings if it shapes its identity according to certain criteria and so begins the process of competing for "feel good" energy with others. The "feel good" responses from others will be primarily in the form of incremental Intelligent Energy boosts.[3]

Because consciousness learns by analogy, "what feels good" is relative to its "what doesn't feel good" experiences. A child living in a challenging household with abusive parents or siblings may be only able to create its identity and subsequent expectations relative to its limited range of experiences. Abuse, during the childhood years, often results in the child incorporating either abusive behavior or subservient victim behavior into their identity and expectations because their experiences have proven these to be effective means of extracting a "feel better" catalyst from others. A variety of mental health concerns may develop as a result of an unbalanced identity and its related expectations including mania, chronic depression, psychosis, or any number of other characteristics.

Parents can mitigate fear by being loving and caring, but, regardless of how comforting a parent's love is, a child is most likely going to learn of fear through catalysts brought to it by the timelines. Mitigation of fear provides the child with an analogous experience that can aid him or her in escalating their awareness, thereby balancing emotions, but the foundations for the emotions will still be sown, regardless of the degree of the parent's comfort. If a child only experienced a parent's "perfect" love, it wouldn't have an analogous experience to compare and contrast, and it would be as bereft of learning opportunities as the child who only experienced an abusive life.

All identities are created based on experiences with the primary motivation to get more of what is perceived as love. All identities are hierophants or false identities and can only deliver a limited "feels better" feeling. Until an analog projection surrenders its identity through awareness and realizes that it is the source of what it seeks, it will continue to create stress and fail in its attempts to feel the love that it desires and needs.

As the child's world expands with school and other activities, the process intensifies and becomes incrementally more complicated. Diversity in sources of experience also diversifies a child's identity and its expectations transform accordingly but the primary motivator remains constant. The child searches for the right mixture of identity ingredients so they can sustain a successful campaign to get more of what they like and less of what they don't like. A limited perceptual scope continues until the child reaches adolescence when the mind/body/spirit opens the 3rd time/space chakra and the playing field expands exponentially.

During childhood, before the 3rd time/space chakra opens, the foundation for all emotions is created. The child learns of fear, "what it doesn't like", and love, "what it does like", according to its analogous choices, relative to its experiences. Regardless of the intensity of the catalyst, the foundation for the polarity of these two aspects of love is established. Consciousness explores love by choosing whether the experience feels good or not.

When the 2nd time/space chakra opens and the timeline begins to bring experiences to the child, every experience (every thought) becomes a message and the process will continue throughout the remainder of the lifetime. The message is always about the recipient and it is incumbent upon the individual, even as a toddler, to "get" the message. The message is never about the space/time circumstances or the scene in the play that is providing the opportunity for the message. The message is always about "feelings", the emotions that are used to interpret experiences because the emotions are created and applied solely by the message recipient.

It is improbable that a child is going to have sufficient awareness to learn all the lessons of the messages at the time of presentation so the messages, via the emotions, are stored within the individual awaiting future completion. Emotions shape the identity and the overall design is for the individual to create an identity, awaken, and then surrender the identity created. The design for the foundational and experiential densities is for consciousness to begin in total innocence and dispersion, perceptually move far away from unity with the Creator by the development of its perception of independence, and then surrender its perception by rediscovering its oneness. The design of every timeline and intent of every 3rd Density lifetime is a microcosm of the larger design for the lower five densities.

An identity is created based purely upon the individual mind/body/spirit's preferences, which means it's uniquely created based on its interpretations of the catalyst. An identity, especially during the childhood years, is the source of emotional baggage that obstructs the flow of energy through the mind/body/spirit's energy system and serves as a tuning fork that resonates with a path along the timeline. The emotional baggage is nondescript but where it is stored within the chakra system becomes very significant and distorts the individual's identity accordingly. Awakening to dissatisfaction or unhappiness, surrendering the hierophant to truth, and allowing the true self to emerge heal the emotional baggage because the lessons will have been learned.

When the 3rd time/space chakra opens and the analog projection enters puberty, the process of creating an identity continues but with a new vantage point added. From the beginning of the toddler phase to the beginning of puberty, the child is said to be learning of itself in relation to others on a one-to-one basis. This is true only because the child is limited by its degree of awareness as dictated by the limits of the 1st and 2nd time/space chakras. 2nd Density shares the same awareness limits but with activated coding levels ranging from 10 to 16, instead of the 18 to 24 activated coding levels that define the 3rd Density.

While consciousness remains under the guise of unconsciousness, it seeks love from the world around it, which is the awareness characteristic of consciousness with only the first two or three time/space chakras open. It barters with other individuals for what it wants and needs, and explores love by experiencing "what it doesn't like" by competing with other analog projections for Intelligent Energy in its attempt to discover what feels best. Because an identity is the product of the ego mind, the space/time mind/body/spirit is intended to discover what it likes by looking through a particular consciousness lens. In 3rd Density, when the consciousness lens becomes excessively obscured with emotional baggage, the chakra opening process itself may become distorted.

It is possible, and common in the Earth experience, that when an analog projection is in the child phase of its development, it may fail to be able to balance its experiences of "what it likes" versus "what it doesn't like" because it isn't provided with sufficient comparative experiences. When a child is raised in an abusive household and knows only the catalyst that it doesn't like, it may be compelled to scale unpleasant catalysts into degrees by intensity. The entire foundation for emotions is created during this period but it may know only the fear side of the analogy equation and be able to only draw upon those emotions that evoke less fear than others for their "feel good" experiences.

As previously explained, even the child with an experientially balanced childhood will probably have a limited ability to become aware enough to learn the lessons brought to it by the catalyst and therefore will collect some degree of emotional baggage. Emotional baggage is intended to be a mechanism to preserve analogous learning opportunities, promote awareness, and allow the catalyst to accumulate until the individual reaches a sufficient discomfort level to be motivated to finish learning the lessons brought through life experiences. Since the foundations for all emotions are created during childhood, when emotional baggage begins to accumulate, it becomes a magnet for further experiences by creating a resonance with a specific path along the timeline.

When a child doesn't have the experiential means to balance experiences, the scheduled 3rd time/space chakra may open early or late. If the flow of energy is sufficiently obstructed by emotional baggage, the 3rd time/space chakra will open but the energy flow may be unable to reach the chakra and it will be unable to contribute its higher consciousness perspective to the catalyst interpretation. The analog projection will still create an identity and form its subsequent expectations but it may be significantly distorted from the majority of the population, resulting in behavior generally deemed unacceptable.

Both time/space and space/time chakras are orange in color and when an analog projection is unable to access the lens of the 3rd time/space chakra the analog projection is said to be functioning as an orange-ray consciousness. The orange-ray analog projection is still in 3rd Density and living a 3rd Density lifetime but is only partially able to enjoy the resources available to it. In previous chapters, we stated that large portions of the 3rd Density Earth population are still functioning as orange-ray consciousness and that is still true today as the population transitions into a shared 4th Density experience.

From the perspective available to consciousness incarnate in a 3rd Density experience, it is difficult to distinguish between individuals functioning as orange-ray consciousness and those individuals who have chosen to polarize negatively along the service-to-self path because their behavior appears relatively similar. From a higher consciousness perspective or from the perspective of the unmanifest time/space mind/body/spirit, it is relatively easy to distinguish between the two. The orange-ray analog projection is still choosing what it likes according to the experiences that it has in its repertoire and seeking to discover love, but, with the service-to-self consciousness, the time/space mind/body/spirit has chosen the negative path and repeatedly reinforced that choice over many lifetimes, determining love to be folly.

A time/line is chosen by the individual time/space mind/body/spirit before the incarnation and it may determine that a lifetime with harsh conditions will be a helpful boost to its evolution. All lifetimes offer a variety of experiences, and, because consciousness learns by analogy, sometimes it's advantageous to learn the extremes of one side of the analogous options to slingshot themselves in the other direction. All experience is intended to escalate awareness but, from the vantage point of an incarnate 3rd Density mind/body/spirit, especially from within the prevailing conditions of the Earth population, it's very difficult to see the benefits of certain lifetimes and/or experiences.

Just like adults, children are potentially learning about love with every thought or experience. Every thought brings a message that potentially will awaken and diversify its awareness by allowing it to either explore love at present or potentially save the experience for later. No experience is unimportant because, cumulatively, experience is how consciousness learns of itself.

As with all consciousness, a child is learning of its power as the Creator and diversity of experience provides it with the information necessary to awaken, become awareness, and experience love. One of the most significant diversifications of experience is the choice to incarnate as a male or female. Learning of its power differs for males and females but, once discovered, the result is the same.

Males, the designed "subject" of consciousness' interactions, find power in physical strength or its derivations such as intellect, money, or simply the strength of the ego. Physical strength or its derivations provide a vehicle to illustrate the radiance or absorption of energy and the individual's degree of consciousness advancement and polarization. While the ego mind is the dominant mind being used, competition remains prominent in most males, which is indicative of its subject role.

Females, the designed object of interactions, find power in beauty. Beauty is an equivalent vehicle to the male's physical strength to illustrate the radiance or absorption of energy and the degree of the individual's consciousness advancement and polarization. All males are not physically strong and all females aren't physically beautiful but both genders use some variation of force to get more of "what they like" and less of "what they don't like" from interactions with others until the 4th time/space heart chakra is opened.

While unconscious, each space/time mind/body/spirit uses the assets available to them to explore love by initially attempting to win energy battles during the competition phase of life, until their efforts prove repeatedly unsuccessful. A person begins to heal and see "things as they really are" when they begin to be honest with themselves, become aware of their dissatisfaction, lack of fulfillment, or unhappiness, and resolve to change the perception of the self by surrendering the hierophant identity. All encounters between males and females are a subject/object interaction but sometimes the roles are reversed and the female is the subject and the male the object.

Male and female power characteristics are not mutually exclusive. Just as the archetypes are principally one archetype but still comprised of the other four, males are not exclusively male and females are not exclusively female. The balance between male/subject and female/object characteristics varies within a lifetime and even within an individual from the time of day to time of day as the perception of the self migrates.

The 3rd Density is the most intense of all of the densities because it is where the identity is at its most significant. Everything that consciousness has experienced from the first moment of its introduction into 1st Density reaches its zenith in the 3rd Density. Physical, mental, and emotional pain and suffering are probably at their peak about three-fourths of the way through the density, and it is when discomfort is at its peak that the ego mind begins to question its identity and expectations, seeks an alternative way of perceiving experience, and finally begins to find what it has been seeking all along. It is through the evolution process that the Creator has the most efficacious opportunity to learn of itself by experiencing itself because consciousness, the "Creator as the subject", will have uniquely attained the maximum point of perceptual independence and begin to find its way back to unity.

The opening of the 3rd time/space chakra continues and expands the opportunities for consciousness to learn of itself by experiencing itself. After all three time/space chakras have opened, consciousness becomes unfettered in its exploration of love and potentially can explore the negative or positive side of it as long as it desires. However, it's only after enough free will intoxication has been surrendered to open the 4th time/space chakra that consciousness can feel love for the first time. Feeling love for the first time is the bite of the apple that motivates consciousness' healing of previous distortions and propels it forward along the remainder of its evolutionary return to unity.

Chapter 29

The Human Condition, part three

Chapter 28 explained that a new 3rd Density lifetime is formatted according to the prevailing consciousness pattern of the time/space mind/body/spirit and enjoys infancy with the mind of the unmanifest self. When the infant becomes a toddler, the 2nd time/space chakra has opened and, based upon the experiences brought to them by their chosen timeline, the development of an identity becomes a primary focus. The child shapes its hierophant self according to its simplistic free will choices, and is motivated by "what it likes". Their expectations for the outcome of new experiences are a product of their identity which is a collection of beliefs acquired from their experiences during their prevailing life.

The child's world is limited, not because its potential is limited, but because the child's awareness is limited by a phased chakra opening. Puberty marks the opening of the 3rd time/space chakra and the child's awareness expands dramatically but it's the last automatic awareness expansion. The time/space mind/body/spirit may sequentially send thousands of incarnations into space/time to evolutionarily advance itself, as exemplified by the fact that the average 3rd Density person on Earth has unsuccessfully attempted to graduate from the density over three thousand times and some over eight thousand. During a 3rd Density incarnation, the task of the positively polarizing analog projection is to escalate its awareness and surrender the hierophant enough to open the 4th time/space chakra.

The Human Condition—part three

Opening of the 3rd time/space chakra begins the "competition" phase of the human condition. During childhood, the foundations for the competition phase are established and competition may be prevalent but it isn't as prominent as in the later stage because the emotional foundations are still being established and the awareness level is limited. With the additional capacities that accompany the opening of the 3rd time/space chakra, competition becomes the defining characteristic and it usually reaches a lifetime zenith during this period.

Competition is a behavior characteristic that is often employed from a more intense state of chaos to allow the individual to get more of "what they like" and less of "what they don't like". Some individuals may become extremely competitive while others less so, based upon how they have historically interpreted the catalyst presented during childhood and thereafter. Interpretation of the catalyst from a more competitive mindset isn't dictated by the nature of the catalyst but, rather, by the experiencer's degree of evolutionary advancement of their consciousness pattern.

A greater evolutionary advancement of the enduring unmanifest self often is demonstrated by a less competitive behavior for its analog projections because the analog projection will be assessing its life experiences with a less controlling ego mind. The ego mind controls the catalyst interpretations until the person begins to surrender control to the deep mind. Instead of dictating to the analog projections how to interpret experiences, the deep mind offers interpretive choices that often are less stressful, but the onus of recognizing the value of the alternative is on the ego mind. The analogy process is always employed to interpret experiences so free will is preserved, and stress and suffering are prime motivators to induce 3rd Density participants to become aware and surrender their distorted perspectives of the self.

3rd Density consciousness is preprogrammed to explore love but a prerequisite is to become aware and, eventually, become awareness. A single 3rd Density lifetime is a microcosm of the entire journey through the lower five densities and an infant begins the first incarnation in primordial darkness. Once the unmanifest self has developed a consciousness pattern, the pattern serves as a constantly evolving repository for the conditions of its analog projections. The Archetypical Mind imposes unconsciousness on an immature consciousness pattern because of the influences of the archetype Lucifer, in chaos because of the influences of the archetype DA (movement), and perceives itself as independent from all others because of the influences of TA (separation).

The infant begins to have experiences and interprets them with its unmanifest mind until it becomes a toddler when it earnestly begins to create an ego mind and "I" perspective. The ego mind quickly becomes the primary interpreter of their experiences, determining what feels good and what doesn't feel good. Based solely upon the ego mind's interpretation of what feels good or doesn't, the toddler creates an identity to trick the world into giving them more of "what they like". With the identity as their guide, they create expectations, and when expectations aren't met, their identity deems itself to be disrespected and the person (toddler, child, teenager, or adult) feels stress.

The design of the 3rd Density is that every analog projection (person) will develop an identity, which is a distorted perception of the self as a separate and independent mind/body/spirit, awaken to their unhappiness, become aware that the identity is false, begin to surrender the identity until the mind/body/spirit becomes awareness, and then, begin to experience love (their authentic self) for the first time as it begins to transform from a perception of autonomy to one of unity. The competition phase is just a discovery period when the person is experimenting with their identity while continuing to experience stress and suffering. This phase will continue until they reach a personal uncomfortable zenith and become motivated to look for an alternative.

The availability of light (information) is essential to aid consciousness' surrendering of its false perceptions. Analogy requires at least two experiences and information shines light into the darkness which is, in itself, experience. When a mind/ body/spirit is confronted with the choice of "what feels good" versus "what doesn't feel good", its intention will always be to choose the former, but, while the ego mind remains the primary vehicle to make the choice, fear remains a significant factor to cloud clarity of the options. Therein is the importance of faith because through faith, the individual learns of their power, it learns to trust, and, consequently, it develops an intimacy with himself where nothing is hidden.

The competition requires a prize or some advantage that feels good. In 3rd Density, the prize is awareness, but, since the competition process begins without a hint of what the future or success feels like, the search is more like a scavenger hunt. Consciousness learns by analogy which is a trial and error process, and so, it scurries around the space/time environment turning over rocks, looking behind trees, and diving into oceans searching for what feels good without knowing what it's searching for. In other words, consciousness looks for love in all the wrong places while being stifled by unconsciousness, chaos, and a perception of separation but constantly motivated to keep looking by suffering.

As explained in some detail in earlier chapters, all consciousness vibrates, and, consequently, "is" energy. All consciousness perceives itself with some degree of free will intoxication and some degree of independence from other units of consciousness (and the Creator). Consciousness can interact with other units of consciousness by exchanging energy based on its current degree of vibrational balance or harmony. There wouldn't be a motivation to interact with other people if people couldn't exchange energy, and there wouldn't be the opportunity for exploration and diversity if energy were not uniquely exchanged according to individual harmonies.

In 3rd Density, consciousness is designed to eventually perceive itself as a mind/body/spirit, whether it's the time/space or space/time version, and to interact with other mind/body/ spirits by exchanging energy. Every catalyst or thought must be interpreted with an emotion which is a simple determination of whether it feels good or not as incrementally assessed through the chakra system. While a mind/body/spirit remains in the lower dimensions of the density, in the competition phase of its evolution, what "feels better" is getting more Intelligent Energy. Winning the competition for Intelligent Energy feels better, but it is misinterpreted as the prize.

That is not to say that every interaction with every other mind/body/spirit is an energy battle. Most people have some interactions with certain people that reciprocate the energy exchange when neither person expects a return on their energy investment. While the individual mind/body/spirit remains within the lower dimensions, the frequency and consistency of sympathetic energy interactions are unpredictable, but, simply because they occur, the experience gives both participants an inkling of what the real prize should feel like. It is another opportunity for the participants in the sympathetic energy exchange to employ analogy by comparing the fruitful experience with other exchanges.

When the 3rd time/space chakra opens, the child moves from the small arena of experience to the large theater because their expanded awareness and consciousness level allows them to do so. Society has been structured to accommodate the changes in the individual mind/body/spirit's abilities and its identities and expectations adapt accordingly. The intensity of emotions is often attributed to the life-defining significance of an experience but the intensity is significant only because of changes attributed to the identity and expectations of the experiencer. As the child transforms into puberty, their most significant perceptual change results because of the concept of responsibility to and for others as it relates to their identity and resulting expectations.

The 3rd Density mind/body/spirits functioning with only 18 strands of coding activated have less awareness available to them, which means they are well within the lower dimensions of the density. For people dwelling in the lower dimensions of the density, responsibility to or for others is usually a reinforcement of their identity. Vocalizing or demonstrating responsibility for others will almost always be to get more of what feels good. In other words, it connotes a barter agreement between two parties that doesn't require mutual consent and/or expects equivalent compensation of some sort.

As consciousness escalates through 20 and 22 strands of coding, responsibility becomes less of a barter agreement because it is viewed from an increasing but still variable degree of energy resonance, but increasingly demonstrates compassion and empathy for others. When 24 strands of coding have been successfully activated, it is most likely that the 4th time/space chakra will have been opened, bartering for energy will have ceased entirely or significantly reduced, and the experiencer will have become awareness. Responsibility is an excellent teacher and two phases of a human lifetime invariably teach the virtues of responsibility; one is infancy and/or childhood and the other is during elder age but any other people experiencing fragility can also teach responsibility.

Commitment is another concept important to promoting evolutionary advancement and learning about the self in the 3rd Density. While consciousness remains within the lower dimensions of the density, a mind/body/spirit makes a commitment to another individual or group by incorporating them into its identity as a pier support. The commitment becomes much like a pillar that helps to support the individual's identity and its expectations are adjusted accordingly. The commitment maker expects consistency as a pier support, and, when it isn't, the inconsistency usually causes a significant disruption to the experiencer's harmony and evokes strong emotional responses because it undercuts the stability of its identity.

Timelines anticipate the need for diverse experiences to allow a mind/body/spirit to become aware and escalate their consciousness level. People bring messages to the recipient but the messages are seldom intended to support the hierophant (identity) by being comfortable or pleasing. Consciousness learns the most while experiencing suffering and sometimes the greatest suffering comes from messages delivered by the least expected sources, especially when a commitment has been made to another mind/body/spirit and a change in the commitment challenges its stasis (erroneously perceived stability).

A marital divorce is an excellent example of how a message is brought to one or more individuals to heighten awareness through the message. Beyond the obvious biological necessity of perpetuating the species, the purpose of mating, which has become the social arrangement of marriage, is for the two people to bring messages to each other about what they need to learn about themselves. The two people make a commitment, which means they incorporate into their respective identities a pier support relying upon each other's identity and expect the pier support to remain constant. When the pier support is removed or changed drastically by death or divorce, the stasis afforded by the commitment is removed and the individuals are provided the opportunity to become more self-aware by exploring the self more completely because of the change than they would have, had the pillar not been removed.

All space/time experiences are designed to bring a message to the recipient that will provide an analogous opportunity for them to become more aware. If the message is only received by the ego mind, it is highly likely that the interpretation of the catalyst will only be perceived according to whether it meets its prevailing expectations and reinforces its identity. If it doesn't meet expectations and defend or support the identity, it causes stress.

Awareness is a tool that is available to both the ego mind and the deep mind but the ego mind projects awareness outwardly into what it perceives to be the physical world. The deep mind discounts the authenticity of the physical world and projects awareness inwardly to explore the self, heal distortions, and evolutionarily advance. The ego mind's use of awareness usually enhances the hierophant self-image and attempts to "change" others, attempting to compel them to recognize how wonderful its identity is. The deep mind's use of awareness invariably leads to the dissolution of the authenticity of the hierophant and its expectations and eventually eliminates stress by healing the self's distortions in favor of truth.

The lower dimensions of 3rd Density begin with the ego mind as a person's only accessible resource but the density often ends with a vacillation between the prominence of the ego mind and the deep mind. (Those polarizing positively need only do so 51% of the time, while those polarizing negatively must achieve a 95% ratio.) 4th Density begins where 3rd Density leaves off and ends with the complete dissolution of the ego mind and total reliance upon the deep mind that is part of an elementary social memory complex, but, relatively speaking, it's a deep mind with an adolescent's awareness. 5th Density begins where the 4th Density leaves off and ends with a significantly more mature deep mind that has become an equal contributor to a larger social memory complex.

Eventually, the 5th Density social memory complex graduates to the root mind of the 6th Density and a significantly more comprehensive social memory complex. 6th Density continues the maturation of the mind throughout its dimensions but the nature of the mind has dramatically changed from the minds within the experiential densities. Maturation of the mind is the diminution of the prominence of any autonomous perceiving mind until the collective mind of the Creator is all that is left, which is to say, the eventual total sobering from free will intoxication.

Awareness continues to be the tool that allows the mind's maturation throughout all of the densities but the ego mind is no longer a factor after 4th Density, except for those mind/body/spirits polarizing along the negative or service-to-self path. The deep mind can mature through the process because it continues to explore itself, surrender its hierophantic self-perception, and eventually integrate more completely into unity. Awareness continues to be the tool that discovers distortions by shining light into the darkness of the self and allowing consciousness to become more aware of its oneness. Awareness is the tool that surrenders false perceptions and identifies truth, allowing consciousness to "be" love, to "be" wisdom, and to "be" unity because the hierophantic self evaporates in the light of truth.

Throughout the evolutionary process, there is nothing to gain but there is a lot to get rid of. What consciousness is getting rid of are distortions of the perception of the self so that it may know itself as the Creator. It experiences love for the first time when it surrenders its identity sufficiently to know that it "is" love, the very thing that it has sought outside of itself through all of the experiences, all of the incarnations and reincarnations, and all of the hardships throughout its 3rd Density journey. Stress doesn't feel good because it is predicated upon the authenticity of the false perceptions of the hierophantic self.

Consciousness polarizing negatively disavows love and lives only through its hierophant in the 3rd through 5th Densities. Please understand the 4th and 5th Densities along the service-to-self path aren't even vaguely similar to those densities along the service-to-others path. Along the service-to-self path, advancement through the dimensions of the densities is contingent upon employing force more skillfully by dominating and subjugating others to extract greater energy. Consequently, stress is magnified immensely and the ego mind and hierophant self are the only perceptions of the self possible because of the lack of awareness. The mind/body/spirit pursuing the service-to-self path becomes more myopic the farther it goes along the negative path and it cannot see the inevitable brick wall it's heading towards.

Choosing to polarize service-to-self or service-to-others is a primary objective of the 3rd Density. The service-to-self path begins with a primal fear of surrendering the hierophant and ego mind but learns to "be" fear to enhance its domination and subjugation of others to compel other consciousness to meet its expectations. Those polarizing negatively enhance the most painful part of the 3rd Density by continuing to live in fear; never being able to experience the love that they too have been programmed to explore, until they exhaust themselves, return to where they dropped out of evolution school, and begin again along the positive path. There is only one path that will return consciousness to unity with the Creator and it's not the path of separation.

After the 3rd time/space chakra opens and the 3rd Density consciousness is capable of expanding its interactions on as large a scale as it is willing, experiences provide the individual with a variety of opportunities, usually brought according to a pendulum swing. Experiences will alternately provide an individual with the opportunity to be "big" by recognizing their identity and meeting its expectations, and, alternately, to be "small" by failing to support and defend their identity. While the ego mind is prominent, it is highly unlikely that these swings will be recognizable because the individual is focused on how they can manipulate the physical world to again allow it to be "big". Usually, not until a certain degree of awareness maturity has been achieved, will the individual be able to look back upon their life and recognize patterns.

When the 3rd Density on Earth began, the average life expectancy was 900 years, which allowed the opportunity for an individual to have more experiences and more easily recognize patterns within a single lifetime. However, because of declines in the population's collective consciousness level, the average life expectancy fell precipitously until after Atlantis' demise when it bottomed out at about 30 to 35 years; much too short to recognize any patterns. Due to helpful interventions from wanderers and other mechanisms spearheaded by RA and assisted by others, the collective consciousness of the population was escalated sufficiently to allow the life expectancy to increase to where it is today, but there remains a constant drag on the populations' consciousness level due to its collectively low level of awareness.

The pendulum swing between awareness and unconsciousness is evident in an individual's lifetime, extrapolated to groups, and evident in the entire collective consciousness of the planet's population. Recorded history that we know of has demonstrated the pendulum swing time and time again with the swing historically taking centuries to complete a cycle. As the Earth's population neared the end of the 3rd Density experience, the pendulum swing became shorter and shorter until now it seems to be completing a cycle in only a few short years.

The pendulum swing is evident in the population's degree of compassion demonstrated towards weaker members and those segments of the population oppressed or outright dominated and subjugated.

Anthropology studies the history of the pendulum swings as it studies behavioral characteristics in groups of people. Simple observations of misogyny and bellicosity within and by groups are two of the most obvious markers of the phase of the pendulum swing a group may be experiencing. Misogyny, bellicosity between groups, and/or autocratic leadership are strong indicators of the negative swing of the pendulum and a prevailing low consciousness. The process sequentially swings back to the higher side as demonstrated in a decline in misogyny, then a decline in group bellicosity, and finally a move towards a more democratic form of leadership.

Fear is the prevailing emotion and chaos is the social condition that instigates the lower consciousness or negative swing. The lower the consciousness, the greater the chaos and the greater the fear in the individuals comprising the group, consequently the group itself. Fear and chaos are the tools of the service-to-self factions which are intimately involved in the functioning of the Zenoa–Earth population and have been since its time on Zenoa. The swings of the pendulum continue to be significantly exacerbated by their interference in the population's evolution.

Rejection of service-to-self overtures to instigate fear and chaos is an individual's responsibility. Rejection is accomplished by awakening, healing the emotional baggage collected through experiences, surrendering the hierophant, and escalating awareness. It is an individual process that requires a commitment by the individual to leave first base and run to second base relying solely upon faith. Despite the possibly excessive difficulties brought by the high degree of interference, the task is the same for all 3rd Density consciousness, no matter where within creation the experience is being enjoyed.

The Earthly human condition is not unique but it is intense. Earth has been deemed one of the most difficult experiences but, by that token, it is and has been one of the most productive experiences in fulfilling the purpose of creation. With the information provided in this writing, you no longer have the luxury of not knowing what is necessary to change yourself and the planetary population's experiences. You can choose to remain unconscious or choose to do the necessary work to heal the distortions and become a model for others to mimic and elevate their consciousness. All consciousness experiencing 3rd Density must undergo the same process sooner or later.

Be the change you want to see in the world!
~ Mahatma Gandhi

Chapter 30

The Human Condition, part four

The conclusion of a 3rd Density experience is often called a harvest because consciousness has been sown into an environment according to unique criteria (an Archetypical Mind), nourished and cultivated by the planters (the Higher Selves), and buffeted by winds, rains, and drought to reach maturity. As with an annual crop that's tenure in the fields is regulated by the seasons, some consciousness will mature as anticipated during the specified 75,000+ year growing period but some will not. The fruit of the harvest is the evolution of consciousness through the 3rd Density experience which is a microcosmic reiteration of the entire evolutionary journey. The intended purpose of all creation is to provide a deeper exploration and understanding of the self, but consciousness is never harvested prematurely, especially from the 3rd Density. The 3rd Density experience is an opportunity for consciousness, otherwise known as the "Creator as the subject", to learn of itself by experiencing itself at the 3rd Density level, thereby adding to the fulfillment of the purpose of creation.

Consciousness is prepared for its participation in the 3rd Density by segregating itself into multiple units by perceptually isolating equal portions of consciousness with equal portions of free will to create the spirit so that every unit begins with the same potential. Every unit of consciousness, according to the criterion and characteristics of the specific 3rd Density experiment, begins as a spirit. The spirit creates a mind, and the mind creates a body thereby creating an individualized unit of consciousness called a mind/body/spirit. Other than some unique characteristics of the specific 3rd Density experience, all 3rd Density minds/bodies/spirits within the universe that we share begin with a clean canvas or, as otherwise known, in "primordial darkness" with the same basic design features.

With this common design foundation, 3rd Density consciousness is introduced to the enlightenment process with the task of exploring itself by experiencing itself within the timeframe of approximately 75,000 years and with the requirement of achieving minimal degrees of progress along the evolutionary path. At the end of the specified period, "all" consciousness is harvested and those mind/body/spirits deemed to have reached an adequate degree of maturity to do 4th Density work will progress to the next level as part of a new higher consciousness experience; but those deemed insufficiently mature to do the work of the next level will be resown into a new 3rd Density experience to again try to achieve the minimal degrees of progress. Those deemed insufficiently mature may retain advances gained from the previous experience(s), essentially picking up where they left off, but in a new environment and possibly with new graduation criteria. Similar to how a college student beginning undergraduate studies under one category, but failing to meet the graduation criteria within the allotted time, must amend their course of study to meet the criterion of a new category to graduate. The consciousness not maturing sufficiently from one experience must still meet the criterion of the new experience to evolutionarily graduate to 4th Density.

The harvest doesn't mean that, at the end of the time, all mind/body/spirits will rapture off of the planet or magically evaporate from the Earth, but, after the naturally occurring end of their final incarnation, they will simply move to a new neighborhood. Earth's 3rd Density experience ended in February 2016 and no significant disruption of people's lives was apparent within the population because none was required. Every lifetime is extremely important and every opportunity to gain maturity is provided up to the last possible moment. However, significantly fewer 3rd Density acolytes have begun a lifetime on Earth since the year 2008, and those mind/body/spirits not graduating, or not being harvested to 4th Density along the service-to-others path, are being relocated to a different planetary experience to continue their evolutionary journey.

The Human Condition—part four

Even though the original 3rd Density experience on Earth has ended, there continues to be a new 3rd Density experience to accommodate the population that has yet to graduate and a new 4th Density experience that is simultaneously sharing the planet. The purpose of creating an overlapping 3rd and 4th Density experience is to provide the 3rd Density population with the opportunity to observe and emulate the 4th Density denizens as they mature into adulthood. This was the purpose of the wanderer population that previously shared the experience, but was only marginally successful. At some point in the future, the 4th Density population will be separated from the 3rd Density population and each experience will continue with its journey, independent of the other.

Many of the planetary changes are to accommodate the elevated consciousness in the 4th Density children now incarnating in significant numbers to 3rd Density parents. Gaia is a 4th Density consciousness approximately midway through the density, and is geologically and meteorologically changing the planet to accommodate dual 3rd and 4th Density experiences. This is in addition to the continuing planetary physical problems the prior 3rd Density population has caused with its abuses of the planet that are accelerating climate change. The climate will continue to warm, regardless of whether the pollution problems are reversed, but it would be warming at a much more gradual rate.

Climate change is an example of changes instigated by Gaia with other changing cosmic conditions provided by the galaxy. Man's irresponsible treatment of the planet "is" accelerating the changes and causing harm, principally to the 2nd Density consciousness sharing the planet, but the changes are going to continue regardless of whether man's behavior towards the planet is immediately amended or not. It's what the planet does, because it too is a living breathing organism and a unit of consciousness participating in the enlightenment process, just as every individual mind/body/spirit comprising the population is doing.

The 4th Density is a transitional density allowing consciousness to heal from the distortions of the 3rd Density and to align more closely with the Higher Self and the Creator. As explained in earlier chapters, consciousness expands its perception of an independent 3rd Density self, creates significant pain and suffering for itself through the myopic promotion of its identity, and then, near the end of 3rd Density, begins to surrender its perceptions and false identity. All mind/body/spirits, deemed ready for graduation to 4th Density along the service-to-others path, will not share the same dimensional level but they will all have minimally attained the awareness threshold necessary to do 4th Density work. At the beginning of the 3rd Density, all consciousness began at the same level but it will begin the 4th Density wherever it left off in the previous experience.

Approximately 90 years ago, the 3rd Density "harvest" began and the vibrational energies of the Earth slowly escalated in anticipation of the new density which was, and still is, causing discomfort to the remaining 3rd Density population. The escalation was intended to be agitating to the 3rd Density denizens because it was incompatible with the population's median vibration, but its purpose, beyond being necessary for

Earth's transition to the next density level, was to encourage increased awareness. The increased vibration caused the familiar and comfortable environment to slowly become uncomfortable so the population would potentially awaken and spiritually advance as it neared the end of the 3rd Density experience.

Consciousness learns by analogy and learns what it doesn't like or what doesn't feel good, so it can distinguish what it does like because it feels better. While the accelerated vibration may have been uncomfortable, it has motivated a few individuals to surrender complacency and become more aware. To assist the awakening members of the population to greater awareness during the 1900s, the number of wanderers participating in the population significantly increased, and light or information was made available from various sources.

At present, the increased vibration continues but primarily because these are the new vibrations of the 4th Density. The higher vibrations are still increasingly uncomfortable to the remaining 3rd Density population, but they must either "get with the program" or be left behind. This is not punitive but it is necessary to emphasize that the old ways of the 3rd Density are history and the world is moving forward, like it or not. If population members are unable or unwilling to awaken and evolve, they will be allowed to continue their 3rd Density evolution for as long as is necessary, but maybe not as part of an Earthly experience.

4th Density experience begins where the 3rd Density experiences leave off because consciousness is "transitioning" to the new density. The participants in the new 4th Density Earth will, for a while, continue to enter incarnations as analog projections of their time/space mind/body/spirits, continue to progress within a lifetime through the systematic time/ space chakra openings, and continue to create identities and expectations similar to what the 3rd Density population does, but the 4th time/space chakra will automatically open at the appropriate time. During the experience of the lower dimension of the 4th Density, consciousness will continue to live timelines, but, because the 4th time/space chakra was opened during the last density, the nature of their experiences and the availability of light or information will be greatly expanded.

3rd Density is an individual, solo journey. Consciousness begins the lower dimensions as an independent time/space mind/body/spirit and eventually results in graduation based upon the spiritual progress of the individual. 4th Density also begins as an independent time/space mind/body/spirit but ends by adequately surrendering the perceptual independence of the self to form a social memory complex. In between the beginning and end of the 4th Density, significant changes take place that dramatically redefine the concept of self.

When a time/space mind/body/spirit enters the 4th Density, all four of the lower time/space chakras are open but the processing of thought through the chakras by the incarnate analog projection will occur according to a scheduled opening similar to that of 3rd Density, especially during its early incarnation. Thoughts will be processed by the ego mind and the deep mind, even during the periods of the lifetime when only the lower three time/space chakras are open, but the deep mind progressively assumes priority as the consciousness matures until the ego mind is eventually surrendered. The prominence and participation of the deep mind allow the incarnate analog projection to access greater awareness than those of 3rd Density who have not yet opened the 4th time/space chakra.

An additional characteristic differentiating consciousness' experience in the 4th Density, the time/space mind/body/spirit will probably incarnate as a single analog projection only, instead of the 3rd Density multiples. The single 4th Density analog projection can employ all of the resources of the time/space mind/body/spirit, which are greater than those of a 3rd Density consciousness. Intelligence is awareness plus information and the greater awareness of 4th Density will be demonstrated in the analog projection as greater intelligence, in other words, the children are going to be way smarter. Remember, to graduate to 4th Density, the 3rd Density consciousness was required to become awareness.

The task of 4th Density is to explore love through the lens of awareness until it becomes love, just as it became awareness in 3rd Density. Awareness and love are simply reflections of the condition of consciousness and its ability to "feel" itself less of an autonomous being and more of the Creator. 4th Density consciousness can experience or "feel" itself to be in greater unity than the consciousness that has not yet become awareness. Likewise, consciousness graduating from 4th Density will have further surrendered its free will intoxication and will be able to experience or "feel" itself to be in greater unity than the consciousness that has not yet become love.

Numerous societal changes result as the consciousness level of the population escalates and begins to heal the conditions of 3rd Density. The present-day Earthly experience appears to be chaotic because of the changes brought about by the transition but nothing falls apart, it only falls together. The old must be cleared away to make ready for the new, and that is what is now happening.

The lower 3rd Density consciousness not ready for graduation is being systematically restricted from reincarnating and, even more significantly, the people polarizing service-to-self are being relocated. Earth's 3rd Density population has galactically been a significant source of energy for the service-to-self for a long time but, because of the removal of the service-to-self and introduction of a significant number of positively polarized 4th Density people, its ability to mine the energy will be significantly impeded. Currently, a dramatic conflict between the service-to-self factions prevails as the old service-to-self meritocracy is dismantled in space/time. The remaining service-to-self minions are jockeying for position in an attempt to sustain energy extraction levels, but the net effect is a zero-sum cannibalization of one service-to-self individual by another.

Philosophically, the changes may look like a pendulum swing to the right but only because of the prominent visibility of the service-to-self factions trying to sustain domination. The population's experience may be interpreted as chaos because the ranks of the service-to-self, which have been in control of significant portions of the world, are in turmoil. There isn't an Armageddon or World War III scenario anticipated, but significant efforts are being made from outside of the planetary experience to ensure this doesn't happen.

What "was" must be cleared away to make way for the new. The nature of "what falls together" will be up to the new 3rd and 4th Density denizens of the planet but whatever does eventually fall together will be without significant service-to-self influences or overwhelming lower 3rd Density consciousness biases. The nature of the population is changing dramatically and quickly, and it is evident when carefully observing and listening to the youth leaders of the present day.

For the incoming 4th Density consciousness to surrender individualist identities and evolve into a social memory complex, significant things need to occur. Healing from residual 3rd Density distortions is the first order of business but this task is impeded because the 3rd Density and service-to-self individuals and their related distortions are still prevalent. The distortion's prevalence means social customs will probably prevail for a while because the newly minted 4th Density mind/body/spirits are beginning the new experience within the prevailing 3rd Density conditions. The new 4th Density mind/

body/spirits will probably still create an identity and relevant expectations, awaken, and then surrender their identity to be more aware of who they are before they begin truly functioning as a 4th Density consciousness and recreate the planet.

There isn't a schedule for Earth's 4th Density advancement because how resistance free and how quickly the transition and evolution occurs is entirely up to the consciousness participating in the experience. 4th Density consciousness has 30 million years to complete its 4th Density learning with an average single life expectancy of 90,000 years but the average tenure in 4th Density is only about 35,000 years. The beginning of a mind/body/spirit's initial tenure will be spent healing the residual emotional baggage from the 3rd Density, surrendering the ego mind and "I" perspective, and establishing a stable 4th Density planet from which to continue and expand the experience.

To promote faster healing and a more efficient consciousness escalation, it is anticipated that the veil that separates consciousness' ability to communicate freely with the Higher Self and other aspects of the metaphysical world will be slowly lifted. The current plan is for the veil to slowly be lifted to allow the 4th Density mind/body/spirits to gradually acclimate to the new "abilities". Access to light or information as provided in this manuscript will then become much easier to obtain directly by all 4th Density inhabitants. Probably, the physical appearance and interaction with other 4th, 5th, and other higher-density beings will still be measured for a while to allow the 4th Density participants to uniquely develop as a population and continue to protect the fragility of the transitional population from overt intrusion.

The drama between service-to-self and service-to-others that plays out daily in the 3rd Density Earth experience also plays out on a galactic scale and it would be unconscionable to remove all restrictions and expect a newly initiated 4th Density population to equitably participate in that arena. Just as a newly licensed teenage driver is incrementally given greater permissions to integrate into the foibles of major traffic, newly minted 4th Density consciousness is incrementally introduced to the ongoing drama foibles of the galaxy. The mind/body/ spirits graduating from the 3rd Density Earth experience, who have been quarantined and veiled from interactions with metaphysical beings for centuries, would probably have significant difficulty immediately jumping into an unprotected galactic experience with more experienced beings.

How quickly the protective censorship is removed will depend on how quickly the population matures in the 4th Density. As always, the participating consciousness determines the nature of its experiences. Until the population matures, the time/space mind/body/spirits will continue to project analogs of themselves into the 4th Density space/time experience but, when the population has adequately matured and surrendered its attachment to the authenticity of the physical space/time environment, this practice will cease. The 4th Density experience will continue to be part of the Earthly shared 3rd and 4th Density experience but without repeated incarnations as analog projections or relying upon timelines to bring it experiences.

The ego mind will undoubtedly continue for Earth's 3rd Density population but, for the 4th Density population sharing the experience, it will be significantly surrendered, allowing the 4th Density time/space mind/body/spirit to rely more completely upon its deep mind. In densities one through four, the "I" perspective "is" the product of free will intoxication so it will have been significantly surrendered in comparison to its 3rd Density experience. The 4th Density population is beginning its 4th Density experience in a very unusual manner by sharing a combined 3rd and 4th Density environment and many developmental expectations are in question as a result.

The 4th Density population has consented to be of service to the struggling 3rd Density population in an attempt to move the lower consciousness out of a heretofore rut.

A strategic feature of a 3rd Density incarnation is the "forgetting" because it allows an analog projection to begin anew with the condition of the consciousness pattern, and, from that basis, create a less biased lifetime by relying primarily upon its interpretations of the catalyst presented in the new timeline. After the initial introduction into the 4th Density incarnation, the "forgetting" probably will no longer be employed, which will allow the 4th Density population to remember who it was in its previous incarnation(s) and essentially pick up where it left off. The incarnation of the 4th Density children has been launched with the forgetting but it will probably be lifted relatively soon during its incarnation. The differences between a 3rd Density and 4th Density population will, no doubt, prove challenging to both populations as the experience continues.

Ceasing to incarnate into space/time analog projections and no longer relying upon timelines to bring it the catalyst for experiences is a significant 4th Density milestone, equivalent to the opening of the 4th time/space heart chakra in 3rd Density. Opening of the 5th time/space chakra and the accompanying level of awareness defines this milestone, but, even before the opening, the focus of the population can be characterized as healing the self and aiding others within the experience to likewise heal. After the opening of the 5th time/space chakra, the focus expands to include assisting in aiding the healing of lesser consciousness outside the limits of the immediate planet. The outward projection of distortion healing assistance is usually directed toward a 3rd Density population in need of guidance.

Once 4th Density has reached the 5th chakra opening milestone, they can shield themselves from detection by 3rd Density consciousness, a necessary element of offering assistance without infringing upon the 3rd Density's free will. The universe is a very, very busy place and there are always opportunities for 4th Density beings to assist other consciousness in their evolutionary advancement, usually within the same nine-star system and with experiences created by the same archetypical Higher Selves, but not always. The defining characteristic of a 4th Density service-to-others experience is to "be of service" which allows the participating consciousness to learn of love through the lens of awareness.

"Being of service" is a noble objective, but it also is indicative of an adolescent level of awareness when practiced obsessively. Being of service still presumes a degree of separation from other units of consciousness and a common characteristic of 4th Density service-to-others is over-exhaustion because every minute is obsessively focused upon "being of service". Until 4th Density consciousness begins to explore and become wisdom, the obsession characteristic will probably continue. 5th and 6th Densities, and all higher consciousness, choose to "be of service" but with a more balanced approach.

Because the 4th Density experience on Earth is a transition from 3rd Density, many deeply ingrained characteristics will simply disappear or be changed dramatically. These are some examples:

Life expectancies will increase dramatically until the cycle of birth and death is no longer necessary and the population's numerical size shrinks significantly. Physical pain disappears except for a very minor "discomfort" upon death which is so inconsequential that, in 3rd Density, wouldn't prompt treatment. Drug and alcohol use and any addiction behavior disappear. Misogyny, bellicosity, and autocratic leadership, the three primary indicators of 3rd Density's low consciousness, disappear.

Females assume a much more significant leadership role on an equal footing with males and with equal prominence in decision-making. Discrimination and/or racial segregation disappear. Religions, all religions, disappear. Competition and thoughts of personal gain disappear as the "Concept of Empire" is eradicated from personal, social, business, and governmental interactions.

"Business" ceases to operate motivated by profit. The populace communicates with Gaia and abuses of the planet cease while the planet continues to experience climate change. Governments around the world unify, become more democratic, and are responsive to the needs of the populace.

Poverty disappears. Crime and punishment disappear. Laws and/or the judicial system may persist for a few generations but will soon be unnecessary. Technology quickly surpasses 3rd Density's wildest imagination and interaction with "aliens" becomes commonplace.

There is a lot of work to be done to facilitate the transition from 3rd Density to 4th Density. Imagine that you are tasked with cleaning the convention hall after a huge crowd has just departed, leaving all of their empty cups, papers, and other trash lying on the floor so the next huge crowd, now waiting outside the doors, can enter. The transition may take a few generations to complete but the projected result is inevitable.

Chapter 31

The Human Condition, part five

If you are reading this manuscript, you are probably experiencing a lifetime on Earth as an analog projection of either a 3rd Density or a 4th Density mind/body/spirit. If you are experiencing life as a 3rd Density analog projection, you will be harvested upon your naturally occurring death and assessed to determine your readiness to graduate to 4th Density or to continue learning the lessons of 3rd Density. If you are experiencing life as a 4th Density analog projection, you have already graduated to 4th Density and are beginning your evolution through the new density. There are a few individuals still participating in the Earth experiment that are wanderers but their numbers are quickly declining and their tenure on Earth doesn't affect their evolutionary progress.

As an analog projection, you were born into a physical body, experiencing the 1st and 2nd Density environment of the planet, and will die at the appropriate time. Before your birth, you perceived yourself to be a time/space mind/body/spirit and after your death, you will again reunite with the same self-perception from which you will continue with your evolutionary journey as deemed appropriate. You are the one infinite Creator, learning of yourself by experiencing yourself at either the 3rd or 4th Density level of consciousness. You are already eternal consciousness and cannot be born or die, other than through the changing perceptions of the self afforded by the analog projections that you invest in.

The time/space mind/body/spirit's perception of the self, the unmanifest self that is the enduring you, is multifaceted because it perceives itself as the unmanifest self and simultaneously participates in every analog projection of itself enjoying an incarnation. Each one of the analog projections will be "born" to begin the lifetime and will "die" to end it. Birth and death are simply bookends that frame the variety of stories enjoyed in between.

The Human Condition — part five

Conception is a random occurrence that provides the opportunity for an analog projection to live a timeline that's interwoven with other timelines being experienced by parents, grandparents, siblings, friends, etc. Before conception, it is undetermined which time/space mind/body/spirit will project itself as the analog projection, inhabit the body, and be afforded the opportunities for self-exploration made possible by the lifetime. Because of the characteristics of the existing timelines being lived by the parents and other family members, the new lifetime holds probabilities that will offer opportunities of a specific nature for spiritual growth and/or development of the new incarnation. If the potential opportunities offered fit the spiritual development needs of one or more time/space mind/body/spirits, they may be offered the opportunity to invest themselves as the analog projection to experience the catalyst of the timeline, but, for obvious reasons, only one analog projection is chosen.

As presented in earlier chapters, the learning required to evolve is based upon "feelings" rather than intellectual ponderings, and consciousness must have experiences and learn from them by feeling the emotions prompted by experiences. Emotions are consciousness' interpretations of experiences and how it explores them as a result of the catalyst presented. Consciousness cannot explore itself and, thereby, learn of itself unless it feels emotions. It is obligatory to have the experience and feel the emotions, which, by design, is accomplished through the catalyst presented in a specific environment and according to certain guiding characteristics.

To evolve, consciousness must "get" the lessons brought through experience, which means it must experience the catalyst, feel the emotions, and use the fruit of the experience to enhance its awareness. While consciousness remains unconscious and/or innocent, it is difficult to "get" the lessons so the catalyst providing the learning potential often must be reiterated numerous times. Just as a student must accumulate certain credits and achieve a certain degree of proficiency in various subject matters to receive a diploma, consciousness must have a variety of experiences, and likewise, achieve a relative degree of proficiency with each aspect of the self.

Every timeline ultimately offers the same lessons but the lessons offered during some incarnations may be more beneficial to a more mature mind/body/spirit than one that is less mature and so timelines are usually matched to the capabilities of the experiencing consciousness. Third grade arithmetic is fundamentally the same lesson as twelfth grade calculus but it is improbable that a third grade student will be able to benefit from calculus at the third grade phase of their education. The greatest timeline segregation choices come when a time/space mind/body/spirit has chosen the negative path. Certain incarnations will potentially expedite those mind/body/ spirits choosing the negative path more than others and priority is usually given to those mind/body/spirits already advanced along the negative path to fill those opportunities.

For the most part, incarnations into Earth's timelines are grouped according to soul streams but variances to this behavior are encouraged to provide diversity and to expand the scope of experience interpretation. When consciousness chooses to limit its diversity by only reincarnating into timelines interacting with other members of the same soul stream, the effect is much like an incestuous family tree. The more adventuresome and diverse the incarnation experiences, the broader the awareness experiences, and, usually, the more accelerated the evolutionary advancement, but free will prevails and consciousness chooses the incarnations it desires.

Repeatedly reincarnating within the same soul stream results in character exchanges from lifetime to lifetime, usually because they feel familiar and more comfortable, but it limits the diversity of perceptions and seldom accelerates a mind/body/spirit's learning as much as potentially possible. Being a second chance planet, Earth's 3rd Density experience has been comprised of mind/body/spirits from 16 different sources but most of the soul streams remained comfortably within their own "family" grouping. The planet's 3rd Density consciousness' evolution could probably have been enhanced or accelerated if the participating mind/body/spirits had been more adventuresome and diversified their incarnation experiences, but they didn't, and that's history now. While consciousness remains immature and within the lower dimensions of the densities, the Higher Self makes the incarnation choices for the time/space mind/body/spirit, but once a certain level of maturity has been reached, the choice is left to the individual. Similar to a teenager reaching the age of consent, he or she has the right and obligation to make their own choices, but until then, the parent or guardian guides their choices.

The primary determinant of which incarnation is best for a particular mind/body/spirit is always the potential offered for spiritual growth through the catalyst of the timeline but ancillary characteristics are also considered, where possible. If a mind/body/spirit finds joy in music and wants to make music part of an incarnation and three incarnations are available offering the same or very similar spiritual growth opportunities but only one includes the potential to be a musician, the music aficionado will probably get the one with music. Similarly, lifetimes that most likely will include significant pain and or suffering may be offered to a more advanced consciousness that desires to accelerate its evolution progress because consciousness potentially learns the most in such a lifetime. Regardless of the potential opportunities designed into a timeline, the onus of learning from the lifetime is up to the incarnating analog projection.

Birth is a process that allows a time/space mind/body/spirit to invest itself as an analog projection into a space/time body. Since the transition is from the awareness of a time/space perspective, the transition is usually relatively simple because the distortions of incarnation don't hinder consciousness' assumption of the role, and they don't have to be overcome or surrender the incarnation distortions. A fetus in gestation for the first two trimesters isn't occupied by an analog projection and lives as the consciousness of the mother. Sometime during the 3rd trimester, exactly when depending upon the consciousness level of the analog projection, the fetus will become a space/ time mind/body/spirit independent of the mother because the analog projection will assume residency.

If the analog projection is projected by either a wanderer, a 4th Density, or a 3rd Density consciousness within the upper dimensions of the density, they will usually begin to occupy the fetus later in the pregnancy. It isn't uncommon for a wanderer to wait to occupy the fetus until the moment of birth. If the analog projection is from a lower-density consciousness, it usually needs more time to acclimate to the new body and will begin its occupancy earlier in the trimester. The fetus' movement usually indicates the analog projection is visiting the body to simply check it out and get a feel for its new vehicle.

Death is simply the other end of the life cycle. No one dies early and no one dies late. A death simply ends a life cycle but the death usually offers a significant catalyst to other mind/

body/spirits that have shared some portion of the individual's life experiences. To those individuals who observe the death experience, it potentially provides an opportunity to become more aware of themselves and, thereby, benefit from the catalyst offered through the death.

While the birth transition from the awareness of a time/space mind/body/spirit may be relatively simple, the reverse transition from the incarnation can be more difficult because the individual must surrender many of the distortions that were part of the life perceptions. Multitudes of individuals that have experienced a near-death experience or "NDE" recall the sojourn into the beginning of the death transition process with some commonalities but there are more differences in their recollections than similarities. The differences persist because the transitioning individual still perceives the new metaphysical experiences according to the distortions of the incarnation and has yet to experience reintegration with the metaphysical self.

The journey from the distorted perception of incarnation to the more accurate perception of the time/space mind/body/spirit usually occurs in a series of incremental steps, but how many steps will be unique to the individual, depending upon the awareness level of the transitioning spirit. Some mind/body/spirits may experience only one continuous step as it smoothly transitions into their metaphysical perspective and others may perceive multiple steps in stops and jerks with varying intensities at each stage of the process. The variability is determined by the awareness level of the transitioning spirit and how willing they are to surrender their attachment to the authenticity of the incarnate perspective. The steps may appear as light changes, gates, or plateaus that allow the transitioning individual to adjust to the changes.

Other transitioning mind/body/spirits may begin the process but stop completely after initially crossing over, unwilling to surrender their attachment to the authenticity of the physical, and becoming a doppelganger or ghost for a while. The nature of the transitional experience coincides with the consciousness level of the transitioning mind/body/spirit in the same way that an incarnation is often more difficult for a low consciousness individual than for a higher consciousness. Even in the transitions between birth and death, there are learning opportunities for consciousness to explore the self.

For those mind/body/spirits called ghosts remaining stalled in the transition process, progress hasn't advanced beyond the foyer and they have rejected all assistance because of the fear they carry with them from the incarnation and a residual attachment to the authenticity of the physical world experience. They are no longer able to interact with the physical world but their perceptions continue as the character portrayed in the previous lifetime. Most ghosts perceive the geographic place of departure to be unchanged from the way it was before they began the transition process and perceive themselves to still be in that place. Relatively speaking, they are tied to the physical illusion as they last experienced it, unwilling to release the attachment, most often because of an attachment to the other people that had shared the experience and fearing the relationship loss if they do.

Continuing to exist as a ghost is a learning experience for consciousness and the mind/body/spirit caught in such a psychic loop will usually be allowed to remain stymied until its awareness expands sufficiently for them to move further along the transition process by its own volition. In Earth time, a ghost may remain ensnared in this psychic loop for a long time, centuries even, but, to the ghost, the experience of time has stopped. All physical pain ends with the surrendering of the physical body but, in such a situation as a ghost, the pain and suffering from emotional baggage, accumulated during its incarnation, remain prominent. The emotional baggage remains because the mind/body/spirit unconsciously chooses for it to remain, just as during the incarnation, they choose to first create it and then to continue to carry it due to their reluctance to become aware and surrender it by learning the lessons that the experiences brought to them.

For those people that have experienced an "NDE", their recollections are almost always characterized by the lights they have perceived. Light is information or truth, so the more light is perceived the more truth is within their perceptual abilities. "Moving to the light" is synonymous with gaining a more truthful perception of how things are, which requires shedding the erroneous or false perceptions associated with the incarnation. The intensity of the light doesn't vary but the ability of the experiencing mind/body/spirit to perceive and accept the light does vary, according to their level of consciousness escalation.

After crossing the threshold of the metaphysical world and proceeding past the foyer, guiding assistance is immediately available, as needed. Some will not need any assistance and will smoothly proceed with the detachment from the perceptions of being incarnate to reunification with the time/space mind/body/spirit, and others will require significant coaching, guidance, and a helping hand to proceed through the steps. Whatever degree of assistance is required is available but none are forcibly dragged along the way.

For those deceased mind/body/spirits progressing along the transitional path, the identity is released as part of the transition because it's no longer needed. The role of the identity has already been used to reshape the prevailing condition of the time/space mind/body/spirit's consciousness pattern and so the changes afforded by the incarnation have already been reflected in the amended pattern. In the case of a ghost, it's only its unwillingness to progress far enough along the transitional path to surrender the identity and reunite with the time/space mind/body/spirit that keeps it stuck. Sometimes, an identity is exceptionally strong and the mind/body/spirit refuses to surrender it to reunite with its enduring self. The choice to surrender the analog projection identity is entirely up to the analog projection and they will maintain the false identity until they choose to reincarnate again and undergo a new lifetime that, hopefully, will advance their awareness. As you can imagine, this behavior is much like a toddler refusing to behave in a manner that is to its benefit, despite the uncomfortableness of its current situation. The analog projection demonstrating this behavior is usually very dimensionally low and trending, but not yet decided upon, the service-to-self polarity. All analog projections, participating in space/time (the physical world), are perceptual distortions of a time/space mind/body/spirit of some level of consciousness, whether it be 2nd, 3rd, or 4th Density consciousness or a wanderer of an even higher level. It is incumbent upon the mind/body/spirit participating in creation as an analog projection to facilitate its transition from the illusion of the space/time environment and reunite with its enduring self in time/space. Once reunited, the enduring self regains more of its strength and energy which feels significantly better than when it is in a diluted work mode with analog projections disbursed into the illusion. To the reuniting analog projection, for a short time before it surrenders its analog projection perceptions and surrenders its perception of independence from the enduring self, the reunification feels like a joyful wave of peaceful relief.

Once the analog projection is reintegrated into the enduring self, the analog projection is gone and no longer exists, other than as the benefits of its experiences have been incorporated into the enduring self. Grandma, Little Billy, or Uncle Joe were characters portrayed in the play of life, and once their part is over, the actors go home to continue their evolutionary journey by again preparing to incarnate into new analog projections to further their progress. The actor, the time/space mind/body/spirit that is the enduring self, retains the lessons and accesses the memories of the analog projections because they are the same consciousness entity but the individual characters no longer exist independently after the incarnation ends.

As presented in the previous chapter, the multiple time/space mind/body/spirits participating in creation as part of a single soul stream often repeatedly incarnate together, alternating roles as male and female, mother and child, abuser and victim, and every other relationship imaginable. Consciousness incarnates in a variety of roles to provide a diversity of experiences from different perspectives. The design of 3rd Density intentionally requires a certain degree of myopic limitation requiring the incarnate mind/body/spirits to explore the self as completely as possible from the perspective of its current character portrayal. Consciousness learns by analogy and, because of perspective limitations, compares other mind/body/spirits to the self with the intent of promoting greater awareness of the self but, as long as it wallows unaware in the lower dimensions, it erroneously uses itself as a narcissistic standard and criticizes others that fail to recognize and support its identity.

In any play, a character's participation has a beginning, when it walks onto the stage, and an ending, when it leaves the stage for its last appearance. Birth is the beginning of the character's portrayal of its current incarnation and death is the end. At best, it is a temporary gig that has a specific purpose but the incarnation isn't intended to be anything other than a small portion of a much longer theatrical production.

We can intellectually know this but when an individual that we have a relationship with dies, there is almost always a series of emotions evoked usually called grief that needs resolution. People die all the time; some we know and others that we don't know, but only certain ones cause an emotional reaction. The experience of someone dying and evoking an emotional reaction does so, as philosophy describes it, because we have established an "agency" relationship with them. Consciousness must have, to some degree, an agency relationship with another mind/body/spirit to elicit strong emotions.

The explanation for how an agency relationship works was introduced in part three of "The Human Condition". A mind/body/spirit creates an identity based upon its experiences to "get" more of what it likes. It creates expectations, based upon the identity, that other people and the world will recognize how wonderful its identity is and meet its expectations by giving it more of what it likes. An agency is created when the individual mind/body/spirit commits to another mind/body/spirit, which means it has incorporated the other person into its identity, essentially making the other person a pillar of support for its identity. If you would like to review a more detailed explanation of this process, please see Chapter 29 of the manuscript.

Ironically, the person incorporated into the identity doesn't need to actively participate in a relationship, as is evidenced, for example, by the real grief felt over a celebrity or another person's death that has never even met the grieving person. When Franklin Delano Roosevelt died after being reelected to the presidency for the fourth time, millions of people grieved his death as diligently and sincerely as if their father or favorite uncle had died but they had never been in FDR's presence other than having heard his voice over the radio. Elvis Presley died and left millions of fans to mourn the passing that had only heard his music or maybe seen him in one concert. Even to this day, thousands of fans from around the world, who weren't even alive when he died, gather twice a year at his former home in Memphis, Tennessee, to hold a candlelight vigil at his gravesite and mourn his passing.

When another person is incorporated into the identity of a mind/body/spirit to any degree and dies, it shakes the stability of the identity by removing a pillar of support, causing a disturbance. If it is a close relative that serves as a major pillar of the identity, it is likely to cause a significant disturbance and evoke strong emotions of grief but the degree to which the emotions are felt is conditioned upon the degree the other person has been incorporated into the identity. The emotions comprising the condition of grief are a mixture of fear and heartache because the removal of the pillar challenges the stability of the identity and the identity's purpose is to "get" more of what the space/time mind/body/spirit likes.

Fear is felt because the removal of the pillar requires the identity to change, and change, particularly when experienced by lower consciousness, promulgates the unknown into thoughts that don't feel good. Heartache is felt because the person serving as the pillar was assigned the task of providing more of what the individual likes, and when the pillar is removed, the sources of "what is liked" are temporarily depleted. All consciousness in 3rd Density is tasked with exploring awarenesses in the pursuit of love but it isn't provided with any idea of what love feels like, so, it goes through the analogous process of discovering what love might feel like by having experiences and adjudicates love to be "what it likes". As consciousness escalates, awakens and becomes awareness, opens the 4th time/space Chakra, and feels love for the first time, it accelerates the process of surrendering the false identity which weakens the dependent agency status of other mind/body/spirits.

Birth and death simply begin and end an analog projection's experiences in the space/time environment. They are experienced as physical events to preserve the illusion of separation and substantiate the independent perspective as a physical being. As the population advances the transition into 4th Density and the importance of preserving the authenticity of the illusion decreases, the physical process of birth and death becomes increasingly less important until the 4th Density mind/body/spirits open the 5th time/space chakra and the required participation as a physical being becomes unnecessary. The experience of birth and death, as bookends to a story, ceases and the time/space mind/body/spirit maintains a contiguous awareness for the remaining tenure of the journey back to unity with its Higher Self.

Chapter 32

Forgiveness

On June 23, 1990, a 5th Density social memory complex of the archetype LA, which identifies itself with the name Latwii, spoke through a channel, Carla Rueckert McCarty, in response to a group question concerning forgiveness. The following is an excerpt from that communication:

> *Forgiveness is first the turning to a power greater than yourself, and a giving to that power of an entire situation, that you may be given the consolation and the healing that you require in order to forgive yourself, whether you are the wronged one or the self-perceived wrong doer. There is always a lack of forgiveness of the self that seems to be held more tightly than the forgiveness of others. You gaze too close into the mirror of this illusion and your manifestation within it. Your birthright is to be forgiven, to realize each self-perceived error and to forgive oneself for it, and move on.*
>
> *Thus, you come to a respect, and an honoring, and a loving, and a nurturing of yourself. The key to forgiveness of others is the forgiveness of the self. Release, release, release, give back to the forces of the universe those energies which are easily absorbed in infinity, and leave them not to pollute your own feelings, your mind, or your heart, but rather let forgiveness flow as a sweet river under the surface of all that you do and say.*

Latwii continues:

> *When the work of forgiveness of self has been done to the point where you feel that maintenance is that which is necessary rather than complete concentration, then and only then turn to the*

attempt to forgive others. It is not selfish to do the work upon the self first, it is necessary, it is mandatory. You must bring your own personality and biases into balance, else how can you be the house of the Father, how can that light shine through you if you are lurching about wasting the energy of love in the distortions of self-immolation?

Let us say we have done this work, and it does come to an end, not that you do not slip from time to time back into those negative programs which have caused you to be armored against the rest of the world and survive, but that you recognize that you do not need this armor, that you are meant to be vulnerable to circumstance, that you are meant to be an actor upon the social scene. This is the density where you learn to deal with entities in more and more gentle compassion and love. Now you have forgiven yourself, you then can see that although those other entities may not have done this work, at the end of that work which they will do at some point, they will find their birthright as children of a forgiven nature, children of the one Creator, children of love in which there is no judgment.
~ Latwii[4]

Latwii's address is directed towards a 3rd Density audience and uses several references that would have meaning and be identifiable to an Earthly population of this level of consciousness with the intent of providing the recipients with information to promote their healing of distortions that cause them pain and suffering. At the time of this writing, the population of the planet is still predominantly 3rd Density but is also significantly comprised of 4th Density denizens who may find some of the references archaic. This does not diminish the veracity of the content or the validity of the healing process prescribed.

The sum and summary of the excerpt explains that people tend to harbor resentments against other people, groups, or the world in general for what the resentment holder perceives as one or more transgressions. Some perceived transgressions may be considered small and others deemed large, but regardless of the perceived magnitude of the transgression, the resentment holder has interpreted the catalyst or experience as an unpleasant experience and continues to carry the unfinished lesson and memory of the catalyst because they have refused to become aware of the lesson it offered. In other words, the resentment holder has received a message from another individual, group, or the world in general which carried a lesson about the recipient but, for whatever reason, has declined to learn the lesson. The resentment holder has been given a homework assignment and essentially said, "I'm not ready to do my homework."

Just because the homework isn't done doesn't relieve the student from the obligation to do the homework and learn the lesson. The homework will remain pending until the student relinquishes his or her resistance and completes the assignment by processing the emotion evoked by the experience. Unlike school homework, the lessons to be learned can only be completed by feeling and resolving the emotions that the student created in response to the catalyst. Until the student decides to become aware, explore the self by feeling the emotions, and surrender their resistance to doing the work of the enlightenment process, the partial emotional interpretation of the experience will be stored inside of the student's energy body as emotional baggage which then serves as a magnet for future experiences and hinders the student's flow of Intelligent Energy through the chakra system.

Imagine you decided one Saturday morning that you need a new doghouse for your beloved companion and you began to build the doghouse but were called away from your task by some less tiresome opportunity like golf or shopping. To preserve your project, you decide to move the half-finished doghouse into your living room until you could return to it sometime in the future. The next Saturday, resolved to continue with the doghouse project, you decide you've had an idea for an even better doghouse design and begin from scratch to build another doghouse but you leave the previous half-finished doghouse in the living room. Again, a more enjoyable opportunity arises that distract you from building the new doghouse and you move the new doghouse project into the living room to be stored next to the previous unfinished doghouse.

This routine continues for several weeks until eventually the main house is full of unfinished doghouses and you can't navigate through the house because of all of the unfinished projects stored there. The body's energy system is like the main house and the emotions you have stored, in anticipation of returning to finish their processing in the future, are the doghouses. To reclaim a comfortable dwelling it is necessary to remove the half-finished doghouses from the main house.

Resentments result from experiences with individuals or groups that don't meet the recipient's expectations, which means the recipient didn't get more of what he likes from the experience because the messenger didn't recognize, defend, or support its identity, the false identity that it spent a lifetime engineering. The size of the slight varies with the degree to which the message recipient's expectations were not met. If you shopped in a store and the clerk was rude or condescending, the resentment formed may be small but pungent and may cause you to vow never to return to the store. If a spouse or significant other has an affair, the resulting resentment may be large and instigate a series of significant life changes called divorce, depriving the message recipient of a heretofore significant pillar of support for their false identity.

The size of the resentment will vary according to the degree to which the experience bringer has been incorporated into the identity or, in other words, the degree to which an agency has been established with the person or group. The language used to express the resentment usually indicates the size or intensity of the resentment. For example, "betrayal" and "traitor" are very heavy words to identify the catalyst or the person to whom the agency was shared and usually indicate the intensity of the feelings used to interpret the catalyst experience. All emotions result from the most simple of analogous choices of either "it feels good" and "I like it" or "it doesn't feel good" and "I don't like it".

As Latwii explains, the resolution of the emotional baggage resulting from the resentful interpretation of the catalyst requires the act of forgiveness but forgiveness is not what most people believe it to be. Traditionally, in the eyes of the resentment holder, a person commits a transgression against the resentment holder by not supporting their identity and, therefore, not providing the good feelings expected. While still preserving the false identity and its resulting expectations and in an artificially forced act of compassion and/or benevolence, the "injured" party is instructed to rise above the failings of the injuring party and offer forgiveness without much or any awareness gain on the part of the resentment holder. The message recipient essentially builds a new wing onto its false identity that reinforces the main identity by expanding and defending it with the thought, "I'm a better, bigger, or a more erudite person than the message bringer."

In the words of Latwii:

You gaze too close into the mirror of this illusion and your manifestation within it. Your birthright is to be forgiven, to realize each self-perceived error and to forgive oneself for it, and move on.

Every experience is a message or catalyst to the message recipient but not about the messenger, and if the recipient doesn't "get" the lesson offered in the message, forgiveness isn't sincere and, therefore, isn't healing. Forgiveness requires a change in the recipient or, in other words, it requires the recipient to become aware of "what" within itself feels injured or disrespected and the further amendment of the aspect of the identity that the recipient is clinging to. Invariably, changing the identity in this way requires an incremental surrender of free will intoxication, whether the recipient is aware that this is what is being surrendered or not. Consciousness, especially at a 3rd Density level, sees things as "it" is, not as things actually are, and therefore experiences stress when their identity isn't supported.

Forgiveness requires self-exploration with the intentional purpose of reaching a heightened degree of self-awareness which results in the inevitable healing of the distorted perceptions of the false identity. Previously, we explained that the journey through the entirety of 3rd Density and the beginning of 4th Density is solo because the awareness potential of consciousness experiencing the density doesn't exceed the perceptual limits of an individualized mind/body/spirit. Because of the various contributing distortions of the Archetypical Mind, no one has participated in 100% of an individual's experiences except for the individual, and no one has interpreted the experiences precisely as the experiencer. The limited capacity to experience beyond the perception of a separate and individualized self is the essence of the uniqueness of the identity through which the experiences were interpreted, based solely upon what the experiencer prefers.

Again, Latwii's words:

Thus, you come to a respect, and an honoring, and a loving, and a nurturing of yourself. The key to forgiveness of others is the forgiveness of the self. Release, release, release, give back to the forces of the universe those energies which are easily absorbed in infinity, and leave them not to pollute your own feelings, your mind, or your heart, but rather let forgiveness flow as a sweet river under the surface of all that you do and say.

The purpose of creation is to provide the Creator, the one infinite Creator with the opportunity to "learn of itself by experiencing itself". Consciousness is the one infinite Creator that perceives itself as separate from the Creator, made possible by the concept of free will experiencing creation as the "Creator as the subject". The 3rd Density consciousness' identity, which all mind/body/spirits are destined to create, is simply the result of the free will concept at the 3rd Density level of awareness.

Because a 3rd and early 4th Density mind/body/spirit sees things as they are, not as things actually are, forgiveness requires the exploration of the self through increased awareness which, since consciousness is the "Creator as the subject", is the Creator learning of itself by experiencing itself. Forgiveness requires an increased ability to feel compassion, both for the self and others, but to feel compassion requires the surrendering of the authenticity of the identity. Forgiving the self for perceiving others' actions or inactions as transgressions, subsequently surrendering expectations predicated upon the authenticity of the identity, and, consequently, being able to forgive the self, begins with becoming aware of the associated feelings or emotions. Emotions were employed to interpret the experience judged to be a transgression of the identity, and emotions are the flashing red light that highlights the path to healing.

Forgiving others for perceived transgressions comes after forgiving the self, which means the aggrieved party has been successful in "getting" the lesson that was offered through the experience and amending the identity through a partial surrender of its authenticity. Every identity is a false identity, no matter how broadly shared the resulting expectations may be. When the identity is incrementally surrendered through awareness, what remains is an increased ability to "see things as they really are" which results in a reduced compunction to feel stress. "Seeing what really is" requires a reduction in the propensity to see other people as separate from the self, an increase in the ability to see other people as extensions of the self, and demonstrate empathy and/or compassion.

Again, Latwii's words:

When the work of forgiveness of self has been done to the point where you feel that maintenance is that which is necessary rather than complete concentration, then and only then turn to the attempt to forgive others. It is not selfish to do the work upon the self first, it is necessary, it is mandatory. You must bring your own personality and biases into balance, else how can you be the house of the Father, how can that light shine through you if you are lurching about wasting the energy of love in the distortions of self-immolation?

True forgiveness concludes with sincere gratitude for the message bringer for how they have brought the catalyst that has elevated the recipient's consciousness level. Only when the message recipient has been able to surrender their identity sufficiently to feel the changes within themselves as a result of the message is forgiveness complete. Forgiveness is a process that begins with a single catalyst.

A single transgression can, and often does, serve as a nucleus for subsequent experiences that can begin a cascade of self awarenesses and further healing. Once awareness is awakened and the tool of awareness is begun to be skillfully employed within the self, new experiences, that heretofore would have been perceived as a significant slight or transgression, will have a less dramatic impact and serve as a catalyst for even greater healing and transformation of the remaining identity. Awareness is a very simple but powerful tool to heal the self by surrendering distortions and pointing consciousness toward truth. Truth, of course, is the way things really are and the more a mind/body/spirit can surrender the identity and see things as they are, instead of through the distortions of the identity, the less stress experienced.

Experiencing transgressions or slights is also evident with expectations established from aspects of an identity garnered through group affiliations like families, religions, or political groups. People affiliate with groups based upon a comfortable affinity because of shared identity characteristics and expectations, and when the group identity is disrespected, the perceived transgression may feel as intense to the individuals within the group as if the slight were made personally. The group doesn't feel emotions because only the individuals comprising the group can feel the emotions within themselves but the group does reflect the median consciousness level of the individuals and, consequently, behaves as a cumulative reflection of the individual's degree of evolution.

It isn't uncommon for a transgression of a group expectation to create a more intense response among the members than a message offered specifically to an individual. The reactions from the group may begin small but grow as the more unaware reactive reflexes of the lower consciousness group members pull the median awareness level of the group down to a lower level, causing group members that, as individuals, may be less reactionary. This is a classic "mob" mentality as the more mature acting members revert to lower consciousness behavior because they surrender their perspective and allow the group perspective to prevail for some time. Losing one's perspective invariably results in regrets and promotes the need to forgive the self for reverting to a greater degree of unconsciousness, especially for the higher-consciousness members of the group.

Awareness is always the appropriate tool to avoid self-harming behavior and to heal the unconscious distortions of the self that feel the need to defend a false identity to feel good. Michelle Obama's often reiterated quote, "When they go low, we go high," requires the individual to be aware and to employ it to guide and heal the self. Everyone feels emotions because that is how consciousness interprets experiences but emotions or emotional baggage don't have to be debilitating. "Going high" necessitates examining the emotions felt, surrendering the part of the identity challenged by the experience, and responding to the transgression in a way that demonstrates the "higher" perspective.

Latwii goes on to say:

> *Let us say we have done this work, and it does come to an end, not that you do not slip from time to time back into those negative programs which have caused you to be armored against the rest of the world and survive, but that you recognize that you do not need this armor, that you are meant to be vulnerable to circumstance, that you are meant to be an actor upon the social scene. This is the density where you learn to deal with entities in more and more gentle compassion and love. Now you have forgiven yourself, you then can see that although those other entities may not have done this work, at the end of that work which they will do at some point, they will find their birthright as children of a forgiven nature, children of the one Creator, children of love in which there is no judgment.*

For consciousness that has chosen to participate in the portion of creation that evolves, which is but a small portion of consciousness participating in the creation, the process is the same. Consciousness is intentionally distorted to perceive itself perceptually as far from the Creator as possible and then carefully guided back to the perception of unity, where it began. 3rd Density is the most chaotic and the most intense phase of the evolutionary process because consciousness has enough intelligence to create an independent perceiving identity, which potentially causes it great pain and suffering, and, of its own volition, must become sufficiently aware to surrender the very identity it has spent lifetimes engineering to move closer to reunification with source. Consciousness is simply exploring love but, to know the real love that it likes, it must first learn the aspects of love that it doesn't like.

The late comedian Bill Hicks often called life an amusement park ride, and in many respects it is but, if you don't know it's supposed to be fun, it can be terrifying. Learn to forgive by healing the self and then forgive others by surrendering the false self-identity and its related contrived expectations. Awareness is the tool every aspect of consciousness has to move quickly and painlessly through evolution but awareness is much like a hammer. It's a simple tool that can be used immediately by everyone but takes practice to learn to use it well, however, the practice often begins with several smashed thumbs.

Chapter 33

Truth

There is one absolutely unimpeachable truth which is "All is One". Every other "truth" is impeachable because its authenticity is determined solely from the perspective of the experiencer and the experiencer will always be within creation. In other words, an experiencer will be a part of creation and, therefore, consciousness. Consequently, by design and definition, consciousness is intoxicated with free will and holds a distorted perception of truth. As consciousness evolves through creation, what passes for truth continuously transforms until what was yesterday's truth often can't be imagined as anything other than balderdash.

With this in mind, we will begin a discussion of truth from the top down. Briefly reviewing the information provided in Chapter 1 of this manuscript, we explained that the purpose of creation was to provide a means by which the Creator can learn of himself by experiencing himself. To accomplish this objective, the Creator focused awareness and projected itself in two concepts; the first being infinity and the second being intelligence. The two concepts do not merge but maintain their independence and function as parallel concepts.

The purpose of the Creator conceptually projecting itself was to overcome a fundamental problem; the Creator proper cannot be distorted but, as a concept, it could create within the Intelligent Infinity concept without limitation to achieve creation's objective which required the use of distortion. The first and most fundamental creation within the concepts of infinity and intelligence, AKA Intelligent Infinity, was a conceptual distortion called free will. By projecting the conceptual distortion of free will into Intelligent Infinity, the "Creator as the subject" was born which essentially meant that the one infinite Creator made a conceptual duplicate of itself. The "Creator as the subject" is only a concept (AKA a thought) but, as a concept, it perceived itself as a fully functional and separate being, autonomous from the one infinite Creator (AKA the "Creator as the object").

Free will is the distortion concept that allows the "Creator as the subject" to be able to perceive itself as separate from and independent of the "Creator as the object", and, consequently, can adjudicate its interactions with the "Creator as the object" according to its likes and dislikes. Initially, before the "Creator as the subject's" first interaction with the "Creator as the object", there was no distinction between the subject and object other than the "Creator as the subject's" perception that it was an independent being. After the first interaction, the "Creator as the subject" began to create distinctions based purely upon its preferences of what it liked or didn't like. Predicated upon its experiential preferences the "Creator as the subject" began to create a pattern for interpreting its experiences that became increasingly unique.

The "Creator as the subject" is consciousness and so its pattern became the source of its creation guidance that it learned from its interpretation of experiences. The creation of the conceptual "Creator as the subject" allowed the one infinite Creator to learn of itself by conceptually experiencing itself but, very importantly, to do so without any potential "Creator as the object" biases because the "Creator as the subject" feels itself to be an autonomous being. The "Creator as the subject", because it began and conceptually remains as the one infinite Creator, shared the same desire to know itself by experiencing itself and, therefore, began the development of creation employing the same procedure that facilitated its creation.

The act of projecting the distortion of free will into the concept of Intelligent Infinity to create the "Creator as the Subject" has been replicated numerous times and it's believed to have been done so an infinite number of times. Every time the free will concept was projected into Intelligent Infinity, it created another "Creator as the subject" that perceived itself to be autonomous and subsequently created a unique consciousness pattern that diversifies the opportunities for the one infinite Creator to learn of itself through experiences. One "Creator as the subject" equals one creation, and so the one infinite Creator explores itself infinitely through the creation of multitudes of creations.

Consciousness, all consciousness, no matter the level of awareness, sees/feels things as "how it is" instead of how things really are because, to varying degrees, it perceives itself as an autonomous being. The limitation of seeing things through the personal lens of a consciousness pattern is the essential benefit of free will and what allows the one infinite Creator to learn of itself by experiencing itself. The "Creator as the subject" is consciousness and, as its pattern of consciousness develops and transforms, it facilitates perceived truth's perpetual expansion. Perceived truth varies from "Creator as the subject" to "Creator as the subject" because each unit of consciousness is unique and it interprets experiences based upon the condition of its prevailing consciousness pattern or, in other words, as "it" is.

The characteristic of free will that facilitates and allows consciousness to function independently from the "Creator as the object" is feeling. The "Creator as the subject" doesn't "feel" that it is the same as the "Creator as the object" and therefore, it can interpret its experiences based solely upon what "feels" right according to its pattern of consciousness. What feels better is what determines truth for consciousness and allows it to "live" its truth because it prefers what feels best. The 8th Density "Creator as the subject" undoubtedly intellectually knows all is one but consciousness' uniqueness, its consciousness pattern, isn't determined by an intellectual process.

Once the "Creator as the subject" has begun to create a consciousness pattern, it begins to expand creation, and we remind the reader that we are calling everything within the purview of a single "Creator as the subject" a creation, for lack of a better label. That means there are multiple and potentially an infinite number of "creations" all functioning simultaneously and semi-independently. There was an original "Creator as the subject" that established the system of densities and dimensions we have been using to distinguish the various levels of consciousness and all subsequent "Creator as the subjects" have consensually adopted the system of delineation, but there is another element to consciousness delineation which we have not yet discussed called octaves.

Densities and dimensions essentially create a two-dimensional grid, transcending the borders of creation, but octaves serve as a third dimension, also transcending the limitations of a single creation. Octaves add the potential for consciousness to explore the depth of itself, and it's called an octave because it functions very similar to a musical scale with eight notes. In a musical scale, the 8th note of a lower scale is the same as the 1st note of the next higher scale so the scales appear to be stacked one upon the other. Octaves function the same way with the 8th Density of a lower scale being the 1st Density of the next higher scale, advancing in layers of sevens to coordinate with the densities.

Octaves are designed to expand seven layers within seven layers within seven layers ad infinitum while potentially transcending the experiential limits of a single creation. Consciousness constantly relocates within the three-dimensional scales according to its degree of maturity and can move easily from octave to octave as it explores itself ever deeper. Consciousness may also move from creation to creation when and if further learning can be enhanced by participating in another creation that may offer greater diversity, much as if it were an exchange student. Consciousness adopts perceptions of truth after modifying its consciousness pattern as promulgated by the creation being experienced, but relocating to another creation will usually require significant modification of its self-perception and, consequently, its perception of truth, to efficaciously participate and benefit from the new creation experience.

A "Creator as the subject" tops the creation experience within each octave and "is" the 8th Density, without subdivision by dimensions of that creation and related octaves, but truth varies among 8th Density "Creator as the subject" beings from creation to creation. Regardless of the creation being experienced, all perceptions of truth are the result of an accumulated interpretation of experiences predicated upon the simple choice of either "I like it" because it feels best, or "I don't like it" because it doesn't feel best. This simple "like it" or "don't like it" decision, as guided by the experiencer's level of consciousness, is an emotion, which means that, at all levels of consciousness, truth is determined by emotion and not by a rational thought process. An experience "feels" good, or correct, because it resonates with the prevailing condition of the experiencer's consciousness pattern.

Just as it is with densities and dimensions, octaves do not have a geographic area in which they exclusively apply. Within a single creation, the experiencing of all dimensions, all densities, and all octaves are possible without the necessity for a relocation because everything is conceptual, and, outside of the lower five densities, motion, distance, and separation don't exist. Even within the Earth experience, consciousness potentially may experience all dimensions, densities, and octaves. "All is One" and, other than in the perceptions of consciousness, nothing is secret or hidden.

Granted, the 8th Density deviation from the one absolute truth may be infinitesimal when compared to the perceptions of truth proffered by the densities humans currently experience, but diversity is the essence of creation. Just as a millimeter movement of a laser beam may seem infinitesimal at its source, the effect 2,600 light years away will be huge. When exploring infinity infinitely, significant distortions of truth should be anticipated.

8th Density, the originating "Creator as the subject" in each creation experience, is not subdivided and is the Creator of all that is downstream from itself. It retains the same powers, awareness, and capabilities as the undistorted "Creator as the object", except for its free will intoxication which results in the distorted perception that it is a separate and independent being. 8th Density's truth increases in variety as its downstream creation evolves because the fruit of all of the experiences within its creation flows upward to the source. The degrees to which its knowingness and evolution of its perceptions of truth have expanded from its beginning are the measure of its maturity and the ultimate objective of consciousness' design.

8th Density expands its self-exploration by the creation of the 7th Density. 7th Density is created by reiterating the procedure employed to initially create the "Creator as the subject", which is the projection of the concept of free will into a portion of itself to a greater degree than its own free will intoxication. Initially, in the uppermost dimensions of the 7th Density, truth is only a bit more distorted than the truth perceived by the 8th Density but, as consciousness is increasingly intoxicated with free will in the 7th Density, consciousness is thinly sliced into dimensions. Consciousness, experiencing a single dimension within a density, experiences a minutely different perspective than all other dimensions, and, therefore, its perception of truth will vary accordingly.

Within 7th Density, the Inherent Characteristic archetypes become delineated, which means not only do the dimensions, created by incrementally increasing degrees of free will intoxication but, as the dimensions reach deeper into the density, consciousness becomes increasingly biased according to one of the Inherent Characteristics: awareness, love, wisdom, unity, or stillness. The distinctions and differences in the perceptions of truth also increase with the intensifying biases and increased free will intoxication. In the lowest dimensions of the density, consciousness patterns become the most unique because the lens through which it enjoys its experiences becomes more refined and more focused on particulars.

Awareness becomes dramatically limited as consciousness descends into the lowest densities. When consciousness reverses its expansion and evolves upwards through the densities, awareness is expanding and simultaneously becomes keener as a result of its surrendering of perceived limitations. The upper dimensions of any density are always significantly more aware than the lower dimensions of the same density and each successive density is significantly more aware than the one below. The effect of free will intoxication governs consciousness' ability to be aware.

The experiences and perspectives of consciousness at a 7th Density level may be dramatically different than the experiences of the 3rd or 4th Density but the motivation is the same: to become more aware, surrender free will intoxication, and evolve back to the source. At all levels of evolution (AKA the enlightenment process) consciousness' perception of truth corresponds to how much "stuff" it has surrendered to reveal more completely who it really is. 8th Density's truth and perception of self are transformed by the experiences of the 7th Density, and the 7th Density's truth and self-perception are transformed by the cumulative experiences of the densities below its own. By the uniqueness of multiple 8th

Density "Creator as the subject's" interactions with the "Creator as the object", the one infinite Creator is transformed into a more diverse and knowing being.

Perceptions of truth are transformed again by reiterating the process of increasing free will intoxication in the lowest dimension of the 7th Density consciousness to create the 6th Density. 6th Density offers the broadest range of dimensions of all of the densities and affords a significant diversification and escalation of available archetypical distortions to the perceptions of the one absolute truth. Densities one, two, three, four, five, and seven are all subdivided into four coding levels but 6th Density is subdivided into eight coding levels that essentially create the equivalent of two densities in one. The lower half is more focused on the management of densities one through five and the upper half is more focused on creating the lower five densities while concurrently turning towards reunification with the Creator.

As with all levels of consciousness, the 6th Density perception of truth varies from dimension to dimension as it can experience greater unity through the incremental surrender of free will intoxication. Sobering from free will intoxication always requires getting rid of "stuff" instead of acquiring anything new, however, the 6th Density exists as a social memory complex but, even so, perceived truth still varies by dimension within the 6th Density. Within the lower dimensions of the 6th Density, consciousness retains a modicum of individualized mind/body/spirit consciousness patterns but, as it amalgamates these patterns and escalates its degree of unity, the perceptions of truth become more consistent until, near the end of its 6th Density experience, perceptions of truth become one 6th Density truth, according to its prevailing Inherent Characteristic bias.

Densities six, seven, and eight are Creator Being densities and each makes its contribution to creation by developing its own unique consciousness pattern while providing the opportunity for the truth to be explored even more completely through the creation of the lower five densities. Regardless of the density of its participation, consciousness determines its truth that is the lens through which it adjudicates its experiences, based on the prevailing condition of its consciousness pattern. Every experience of and by consciousness reiterates the subject/object relationship begun with the first insertion of the free will distortion into Intelligent Infinity and simultaneously presents consciousness with a "teach/learn" and "learn/teach" opportunity.

6th Density consciousness explores itself through interactions with other aspects of itself, interactions with consciousness experiencing the other four Inherent Characteristics, and, most uniquely, it explores itself as a result of the experiences of the lower five densities that it creates. From consciousness projected into the lower five densities, learning is accrued to the lower dimensions of the 6th Density and then absorbed throughout consciousness in all of the dimensions of the density. The lower half of the 6th Density is like a package distribution center. The accrued learning from consciousness in the foundational and experiential densities is received in the lower dimensions, processed, and redistributed or shared with all of the densities.

Like all of the consciousness experiencing creation, 6th Density truth is a reflection of the prevailing condition of its consciousness pattern which results from the constantly evolving information delivered through experiences. As the 6th Density's perception of truth evolves and changes, so do the 7th and 8th Densities because the flow of information, gained from the experiences of lower consciousness, perpetually expands and deepens all of the consciousness' resources for truth. Ultimately, the "Creator as the object" also alters its perception of truth because it is at the top of the evolutionary journey and the ultimate destination for everything experienced below itself, but the one unimpeachable truth remains unchanging, and that is that "All is One".

6th Density truth as a whole becomes much more diversified than 7th Density and essentially becomes a mini-creation within itself because within the 6th Density range the upper dimensions create within the lower dimensions. The 26 archetypical distortions experienced by the foundational and experiential densities are created by consciousness from the upper four coding levels of 6th Density projecting the distortion concepts into consciousness experiencing the lower four levels. The archetypical distortion concepts aren't experienced by the 6th Density consciousness. They're only valid within the lower four coding levels of the density and experienced by the foundational and experiential densities. To evolve past the lower coding levels of 6th Density, consciousness, experiencing itself as one of the 26 distortions, must surrender its distorted self-concept and reintegrate its consciousness pattern into alignment with that of the 6th Density source Inherent Characteristic.

For example, the concept of movement is projected, by the distortion archetype Melchizedek (free will), into the 6th Density KA (stillness) to create the distortion archetype DA. The projection originates from the upper dimensional 6th Density consciousness perceiving itself as free will into the archetype KA in the lower coding levels of the density. As an independent distortion archetype, DA only exists within the lower four coding levels of 6th Density and below and must reintegrate with KA before advancing itself beyond the lower levels of the density. When DA is incorporated as an archetype in this way, the concept of movement may be experienced by all consciousness within the foundational and experiential densities.

The physical appearance of a universe begins with the lower coding levels of the 6th Density and every star is the physical representation of one of the archetypes. The upper coding levels do not directly create physicality and do not occupy the stars that we see per se, but they do provide the time/space environment for the creative products of consciousness in the lower four coding levels. When 6th Density consciousness transitions to 7th Density, all of the consciousness within its environment and all of its creations are reclaimed by a method that Earth science calls a "black hole".

Most of the 7th Density consciousness' perceptions incorporate one of the five Inherent Characteristics into its consciousness pattern (plus 7th Density free will) and the upper dimensions and coding levels of 6th Density essentially have the same archetypical biases but with greater governors that establish the coding levels. The lower four coding levels of 6th Density potentially include 26 archetypical distortions (three within the universe experienced by Earth) that are in addition to the five Inherent Characteristics and free will, and greatly diversify the resources available from which to create lower-density experiences. Truth becomes much more diversified from the one immutable truth because the potential lenses of the 6th Density become significantly more diverse.

All 6th Density consciousness is biased towards one of the Inherent Characteristics or one of the distortion archetypes, and the nature of its bias affects its perception of truth but allows it to share the bias with consciousness experiencing the lower foundational and experiential densities. The 6th Density archetypical distortions also create soul streams to be invested into the lower densities but it seldom does this as the principal soul stream creator. For example, Earth is created from a mixture of the 6th Density consciousness biases from the nine archetypes but RA (love) is the principal investor with 55% of the consciousness investment, and LA, or wisdom and the principal archetype that calls the "Sun" home, has invested approximately 12%.

The remaining third of the consciousness experiencing Earth is composed of a mixture of archetypical biases in varying quantities including SA, KA, YA, TA, and DA (Lucifer and Free will don't directly invest consciousness), each contributing to the total experience. The net effect of co-creating in this way is an expanded experience because of the diversity in consciousness' perceptions of truth. Both the Inherent Characteristics and distortions participate in the design of the Archetypical Mind and shape how experience is perceived by the lower consciousness. Until consciousness escalates its awareness and surrenders its perceptual biases, it perceives truth to be according to the way it is, rather than the way things actually are.

Consciousness originating from TA or DA and experiencing the lower five densities does so from within the spacesuit called the Archetypical Mind, according to the same criteria as consciousness originating from RA or LA. Perceptions of truth are initially distorted according to a common criterion for all consciousness participating in a lower-density experience regardless of its source, but, since it will eventually return to unity with its Higher Self, the entire soul stream, including the Higher Self and above, benefits from the learning gained from its perceptual diversity. Every sub-creation within creation is an experiment designed to mix and match distortions and characteristics to encourage uniqueness in the interpretation of consciousness' experiences, the creation of its consciousness pattern, and, therefore, uniqueness in its perceptions of truth.

From the highest level of consciousness to the lowest, consciousness interprets its experiences according to how "it" is, rather than how things really are which means it creates its truth accordingly. In the 8th Density, free will is its only distortion but the unique shaping of its consciousness pattern is made possible by the distortion concept that it is separate from the one infinite Creator. The design allows creation to be experienced as a consciousness pattern that begins as a clean slate with no distinguishable differences from the Creator other than its perception of itself as an independent entity, but it soon gains diversity as it enjoys more interactions with the Creator. Consciousness learns from experiences, and its perception of self, and resulting perceptions of truth, transform accordingly.

Truth is the truth until it's not, but what always transforms consciousness' perception of truth is the transformation of the perception of the self. Intellectually, the absolute truth can be known down to the 3rd Density but consciousness is guided by relative truth, which is known by feeling what feels best at all levels of creation, even including the foundational densities. Evolutionary advancement through the consciousness levels requires the transformations to be felt rather than intellectualized because what is felt is indicative of the condition of the lens, the consciousness pattern, through which consciousness experiences creation.

The lens, through which consciousness enjoys its experiences, determines truth's authenticity as promulgated by the degree of attachment to the authenticity of its independent self. As consciousness evolves through the dimensions and densities, it loses its propensity to be judgmental as to right or wrong, good or bad, and true or untrue, and it sees things more accurately as they really are. Greater awareness of the self is a natural condition for consciousness polarizing positively and promotes a diminution of stress because the consciousness pattern or identity, for an analog projection, no longer needs to be supported or defended. Less stress and greater happiness are felt at each progressive step along the way until, eventually, all experiences feel blissful.

Chapter 34

Christ Consciousness

Regardless of the degree of enlightenment, all consciousness learns according to the analogy process which means that all consciousness learns by comparison and contrast. In the lower four densities, consciousness, as analog projections into the space/time environment, has experiences, compares each new experience with its resume of previous experiences, and decides whether it likes the new experience or not. If it likes the new experience, it adjusts its identity or consciousness pattern to get more of what it likes but, especially in the lower dimensions of 3rd Density, if it doesn't like a new experience it will often strive to change the message to conform to the message recipient's identity expectations. All consciousness below the 8th Density learns to amend its identity or consciousness pattern by observing and mimicking other consciousness.

All consciousness is motivated to get more of what it likes, less of what it doesn't like, and mimics other consciousness that appears to be getting what it likes. In planetary experiences more closely following the ideal design for 3rd Density than Earth, mind/body/spirits participating in the lower dimensions of the density observe and mimic the behavior of others that have advanced to the upper dimensions of the density from within the same 3rd Density experience because, invariably, upper dimensional consciousness enjoys greater joy and happiness. Because of the various difficulties imposed upon the Earthly population by external forces, that have complicated its ability to enjoy a more conventional density experience, Earth's population has generally not been able to advance consciousness to populate the upper dimensions from within. When there are few, if any, models to emulate, there are few opportunities to observe and mimic higher consciousness and the lower consciousness of the density will potentially be forever stuck in a chaotic lower consciousness loop, which is essentially what the Zenoa–Earth population has demonstrated for hundreds of thousands of years.

The Zenoa/Earth population dilemma could have been halted by the guiding Higher Selves at any time by simply ending the enterprise and starting over but the population's predicament created a unique opportunity to observe how a 3rd Density population would respond to the oppressive difficulties artificially induced by service-to-self manipulation. All of creation is a massive thought experiment to allow the Creator to explore itself more completely and, since it's all a thought experiment anyway, the decision was made to allow the Zenoa–Earth population's difficult enlightenment process to continue despite the service-to-self induced distortions. The continuum of failed 3rd Density experiences that began on Zenoa, progressed to Maldek, then to Mars, and eventually to Earth, appears to have been planetarily costly to the solar system but it provided the potential for a diversity of fresh experiences seldom available elsewhere in the universe.

All 16 populations assembled to co-experience Earth's 3rd Density enterprise shared a similar evolutionary history. The task for the 6th Density beings guiding the population's 3rd Density progression was to pilot the already significantly confused consciousness through 3rd Density despite constant service-to-self interference while preserving the population's free will. The task was made difficult because service-to-self interference continued throughout the entire series of planetary experiences and the population proved incapable of internally generating upper-dimensional behavioral models to emulate which severely hampered the success of traditional methods.

Not being capable of organically generating upper-dimensional models from within the planetary population created a Catch-22 and caused the overwhelming majority of the population to remain mired in the lower dimensions of the density.

By the time the population began the Earthly 3rd Density experience, the atmosphere of Zenoa had been destroyed, making the planet uninhabitable by 3rd Density consciousness, Maldek had been completely blown up, Mars' atmosphere had been destroyed, also making the planet 3rd Density uninhabitable, and 15 new populations with similarly difficult histories were added to the Zenoa–Earth population to try and graduate from 3rd Density again. Numerous design changes had been attempted to nudge the population's evolutionary advancement along but nothing had yet gained traction. Several changes were employed in the Earth experience to vary the population's experience, including a quarantine of the planet from continued overt service-to-self intrusion.

Because of the Law of Confusion (AKA the Law of Free will), the planet couldn't be completely quarantined so a protective grid system was created that didn't prohibit service-to-self access to the population, but it did severely restrict it. Also, the population experienced a mechanism called a "time-lateral" that was essentially a hologram of the planet so if the population again decided to significantly damage it, the real Earth wouldn't be harmed, but that meant the population never really experienced the actual planet Earth. Other design features were created that served as planetary protective devices but these features still didn't significantly nudge the population's enlightenment forward.

After the experimental disappointments on the planets that preceded Earth, the problem of how to move the population forward along the evolutionary path still remained. The ethical requirements to preserve the population's free will limited the available methods that could be used and conventionally successful methods focusing upon direct interaction between the higher consciousness beings and the incarnate population were deemed too intrusive and/or ineffective. By the time the 3rd Density Earth experience began, the guiding higher consciousness beings had learned significant lessons from the previous failed planetary endeavors and this gave them insight as to what could be done to help the Earth experience. Even so, by their admission, there remained a significant degree of naivety as to what could be done to offer a more productive service.

The primary feature that was eventually employed to supplement the lack of upper-dimensional consciousness was a massive injection of wanderers into the population. Wanderers became substitutes for the higher dimensional 3rd Density consciousness that would normally have been organically generated from within the population. The wanderers provided the population with sources for truthful information but, more importantly, provided them with models of higher consciousness behavior that the population's lower consciousness could emulate and mimic. Millions of mostly 6th Density higher consciousness beings from around the Milky Way and many other galaxies invested analog projections as wanderers into the Earthly experience to provide examples of higher consciousness behavior so that the lower consciousness mind/body/spirits could have examples to observe and hopefully emulate.

The practice of wanderers' participation continues today but it is quickly coming to an end; as the 3rd Density population begins a new cycle, those polarizing service-to-self are removed, and the new 4th Density denizens assume prominence. The commitment to preserve the new 3rd and 4th Density denizens of Earth's free will continues but the nature of 4th Density is entirely different than 3rd Density and, what may be a 3rd Density infringement could be a necessary element of a 4th Density mind/body/spirit's schooling. Soon, the new 4th Density inhabitants of Earth will telepathically communicate freely with higher consciousnesses that aren't incarnate as part of the Earth experience and may even physically interact with individuals and groups long involved with piloting the Earth's development. Because the lessons of 4th Density are dramatically different than the elementary school lessons of 3rd Density, the classrooms must change to accommodate the new lessons.

Occasionally over Earth's history, a single wanderer has been given a specific mission beyond simply infiltrating the population to serve as a model of higher consciousness 3rd Density behavior. Among the many wanderers tasked with a special mission was an individual mind/body/spirit named Jehoshua who was born into the geographic area of Earth now called the "Middle East". Jehoshua was an analog projection of a 4th Density mind/body/spirit that participated in creation as a part of LA (the wisdom archetype), and today, continues his evolutionary journey as part of the 5th Density social memory complex known to many as Latwii. At the time of the Jehoshua incarnation, he was nearing the end of his 4th Density evolution, having been successful in opening the 5th chakra and having begun to participate in a newly formed social memory complex.

Jehoshua volunteered to participate in the Earth experience as a wanderer but it is/was unusual for a 4th Density consciousness to be called upon to participate as a wanderer at all, much less with a mission of great magnitude because a 4th Density mind/body/spirit has only just recently unattached from the authenticity of the space/time environment and usually has not fully acclimated to the expanded perceptions of self. Nevertheless, he was selected to model an ideal mind/body/spirit that, by his example, could significantly propel the Earthly population forward along the enlightenment journey. The plan was for a wanderer to incarnate as a human in the usual human way (not an immaculate conception) without a veil, with access to most of his higher 4th Density awareness, but still be required to incrementally evolve within the incarnation through the 3rd Density self-healing procedures. The ambition for the mission would be for the wanderer to become spotlighted as a significant messenger of truth and a stellar model for humans to emulate and mimic so they could escalate their own consciousness level.

Over the centuries of the Earthly 3rd Density experience, there have been countless messengers from higher consciousness service-to-others origins providing telepathic and direct interaction with population denizens. Many messages foretold the potential of a transformational higher consciousness planetary experience which was interpreted as heaven, Satori, Nirvana, or simply an angelic encounter, but the messages were often distorted by service-to-self interlopers transforming the positive messages into fear or dread. For example, the service-to-self spin would emphasize a biblical Old Testament "wrath of god" or "ten commandments" perspective if denizens didn't comply with the interloper's demands or wishes. The positive message is intended to provide the population with hope and insight into the potential for a better incarnate experience, but, to the unaware low consciousness humans, believing the service-to-self sourced distortions usually resulted in their direct or pseudo enslavement.

Prior to the destruction of the Atlantis continent, the area today known as the Middle East was the global center for the population polarized as service-to-self and their concentration eventually fueled a perpetual downward cycle of a very, very low consciousness level among the general populace which lingers even today. The populace inhabiting the Middle East was targeted by numerous wanderer incarnations to attempt to counteract the low consciousness service-to-self concentration, as well as other endeavors such as the construction of the Egyptian pyramids and many others around the world. Over time, many of the positive prophetic messages of a higher consciousness potential were distilled, until the general messages devolved into prophecies of a single angelic savior that would swoop down from above and save struggling humans from their plight of pain and/or suffering, transporting them to a magical land with streets paved in gold, etc. The mythical concept of a Christ or savior figure evolved from the prophecies and became the basis for a foretold eventual "Christ Consciousness".

The intent of the messages or teachings that preceded and were repeated by Jehoshua was the foretelling of the eventual 4th Density environment which is synonymous with the Christ Consciousness concept and, because Jehoshua was a 4th Density wanderer, his teachings were through the lens of 4th Density. Regrettably, most of his teachings have been lost since his incarnation and many other teachings that were preserved have been distorted over time. Even when initially delivered, the teachings were only marginally comprehended because (1) the ability to comprehend the teachings was limited because the prevailing human consciousness level was very low, and (2) the teachings were resisted by the bulk of the population because they directly contradicted the cultural hegemony of the day.

Wanderers seldom, if ever, incarnate alone, especially a 4th Density wanderer with as significant a mission as Jehoshua, and his disciples, mother, wife, and many others who participated in his experiences were 6th Density wanderers subtly supporting his mission. Unlike the special incarnation conditions provided to Jehoshua, the supporting wanderers had to awaken themselves to be sufficiently effective "sub-messengers", scribes, and/or event planners. It was deemed important to the plan that Jehoshua be publicly perceived to be a higher consciousness mind/body/spirit whose message would be insightful and superior, but whose persona wouldn't be so superior to miss the point of Jehoshua himself being a figure to be emulated and mimicked.

The 4th Density awareness that he proffered made him a child prodigy but his maturation during the incarnation followed the same incremental chakra opening process normally experienced by a 3rd Density mind/body/spirit. In other words, he was an infant, opened his 2nd chakra to begin his toddlerhood, and opened his 3rd chakra to experience puberty, etc. Because he was a 4th Density wanderer able to sustain access to his higher consciousness awareness and having already opened his 4th chakra earlier in his enlightenment journey, his awareness escalation continued significantly beyond what was normally enjoyed by the population and/or other wanderers. As will be soon experienced by many of the newly minted 4th Density denizens of Earth, he opened the 4th chakra during his late teens or early twenties.

Opening the Kundalini is a significant milestone in consciousness' evolution. The Kundalini occurs when the 5th chakra is opened and the dominant flow of Intelligent Energy from the bottom of the chakra system is surrendered to the inflow and connection with Intelligent Infinity from the top of the chakra system. The mind/body/spirit's entire torus energy flow reverses as the mind/body/spirit connects with the Creator much more significantly, and instead of the torus flowing up and out, it flows downward circulating out and up. This is a transformative moment in consciousness evolution because it marks roughly the midway point through its entire journey through the experiential densities and the surrender of the last vestiges of the ego mind and false identity.

The mind/body/spirit incarnate as Jehoshua was nearing the end of his 4th Density journey when he became a wanderer and, because of his late density advancement and preservation of his metaphysical self-awareness, he also was able to reestablish his connection to Intelligent Infinity during his incarnation. During the 4th Density, the transformation of consciousness' creation experience includes the opening of the 5th chakra, the Kundalini experience, and the opening of the 32 coding levels of consciousness. Characteristics of all of these events were demonstrated by Jehoshua during his incarnation. The significant "abilities" of Jehoshua during his incarnation included channeling healing green-ray energy to himself and others, surrendering the ego mind, unattachment to the authenticity of the physical, free communication with higher consciousness entities, and the freedom from being confined into a physical body.

The various demonstrations of his greater consciousness level were deemed to be "miracles" by those who observed them and, compared to the capabilities of the prevailing population, they understandably were, but the miracles were only representative of consciousness' everyday expected behavior in the latter dimensions of 4th Density. While the miracles were attention-getting, the purpose was to illustrate to the population the potential that every individual possessed when they undertake the task of pursuing their enlightenment by emulating and mimicking higher consciousness behavior. Jehoshua was a constant teacher, and even though the catalog of teachings salvaged in today's historical records is only a tiny portion of what he taught, the essence of what he taught and what was preserved were lessons of love. Throughout the episodes of this manuscript, we have emphasized that the task of 3rd Density consciousness is to awaken, become aware, and then become awareness and, from the condition of awareness, explore the condition of love.

The task of the 4th Density is to become the condition of love and, from the condition of love, to begin to explore the condition of wisdom. Christ consciousness is the condition of love experienced by a consciousness that has sufficiently surrendered its false identity and ego mind, its free will intoxication, and its attachment to the authenticity of the distortions. Love is not a condition that will magically appear for 3rd Density consciousness until the individual has done the work necessary to prepare themself to do 4th Density work. The experience of 4th Density consciousness on Earth has already begun and will soon become apparent but, to participate, the remaining members of the 3rd Density population must individually prepare themselves to do the work of the next density.

The purpose of Creation is so that the one infinite Creator might know itself by experiencing itself. The end result of creation is already known and was never in doubt. What is unknown is how completely consciousness, that portion of the Creator that perceives itself as separate from the Creator, can know itself through its experiences at every dimension of every density of the creation. Christ's consciousness is just one step along the long journey home to unity with the one infinite Creator, albeit a much less stressful step than the one humanity has been stalled on for a long, long time.

What is primarily missing from the preserved teachings of Jehoshua, is the "how to" information necessary to experience greater aspects of 4th Density consciousness. Jehoshua was one of many enlightened teachers providing different aspects of the same information and it is helpful to look to some of these other teachers to get more specific instructions on how to advance. For example, the analog projection known as Siddhartha Gautama who became known as the Buddha approached the enlightenment teachings differently because he was a 6th Density wanderer. The incarnation of the Buddha included many of the same characteristics of the Jehoshua incarnation but the Buddha spent significant time prescribing a practical methodology and practical understanding that, if undertaken by a mind/body/spirit with diligence, would yield the desired results proffered by the Jehoshua incarnation.

Over the history of the Earth population's evolution, numerous other wanderers, that have obtained significantly less notoriety than the Buddha or Jehoshua, have attempted to guide the population to greater awareness and consciousness by employing a variety of teaching methods and approaches, with varying success. There has been no shortage of teachers, even in today's world, but there has been a significant deficiency in the willingness of people to undertake the task of enlightenment. As always, the choice is entirely up to the individual to awaken and undertake the task.

However, the time may now be at hand to either diligently undertake the task or decide to continue the process of evolution somewhere besides the planet Earth. Jehoshua isn't returning to save anybody because salvation isn't necessary nor is it the plan. The task for consciousness is, through the escalation of awareness and the continued interpretation of experiences, to surrender perceptual distortions and return to unity with the source from which it came and, in the process, to fulfill the purpose of creation. Every individual unit of consciousness has all the tools necessary to accomplish the task and all of the skills and guidance necessary to be successful.

End Notes

1. Illustrations of the Modules of the Archetypical Mind are available in the Appendix at the rear of this manuscript.
2. Because of the Earth population's difficulties in obtaining and/or maintaining evolutionary advancement, most people are only able to project a single or maybe two analog projections at a time.
3. Our descriptions and explanations are assuming the person is of the 3rd Density. We anticipate that 4th Density children, sharing the Earth experience, will behave differently at these landmark occurrences.
4. Jim McCarty, Carla Rueckert, Latwii, 1990. Internet: **https://www.llresearch.org/transcripts/issues/1990/1990_0623.aspx**

Appendix

Modules of the Archetypical Mind

Modules of the Archetypical Mind

Mind	Body	Spirit
Great Way of the Mind Object/logos: YA (unity) Subject/sub-logos: LA (wisdom) Characteristic: Surrender of the "ego" mind Gender: Male (+) Algorithm	Great Way of the Body Object//logos: YA (unity) Subject/sub-logos: KA (stillness) Characteristic: Abundance Gender: Male (+) Algorithm	Great Way of the Spirit Object/logos: YA (unity) Subject/sub-logos: YA (unity) Characteristic: Infinity, truth Gender: Female (-) Algorithm
Transformation of the Mind Object/logos: LA (wisdom) Subject/ sub-logos: YA (unity) Characteristic: Transformation of the ego mind Gender: Male (+) Algorithm	Transformation of the Body Object/logos: LA (wisdom) Subject/sub-logos: SA (awareness) Characteristic: Death and rebirth of the physical body Gender: Female (-) Algorithm	Transformation of the Spirit Object/logos: LA (wisdom) Subject/sub-logos: RA (love) Characteristic: Alignment w/ love and Higher Self Gender: Female (-) Algorithm
Significator of the Mind Object/logos: RA (love) Subject/sub-logos: LA (wisdom) Characteristic: Hierophant, biases and prejudices Gender: Male (+) Condition & algorithm	Significator of the Body Object/logos: RA (love) Subject/sub-logos: YA (unity) Characteristic: illness or health Gender: Male (+) Condition & Algorithm	Significator of the Spirit Object/logos: RA (love) Subject/sub-logos: RA (love) Characteristic: Radiance or absorption of love Gender: Female (-) Algorithm
Experience of the Mind Object/logos: TA (separation) Subject/sub-logos: LA (wisdom) Characteristic: Emotion Gender: Male (+) Condition & Algorithm	Experience of the Body Object/logos: TA (separation) Subject/sub-logos: SA (awareness) Characteristic: Sensory experience, 2nd spatial dimension, physicality Gender: Female (-) Condition	Experience of the Spirit Object/logos: DA (movement) Subject/sub-logos: LA (wisdom) Characteristic: Ego surrender, movement in time, 3rd spatial dimension Gender: Male (+) Condition & algorithm
Catalyst of the Mind Object/logos: SA (awareness) Subject/ sub-logos: LA (wisdom) Characteristic: Pain & suffering Gender: Female (-) Algorithm	Catalyst of the Body Object/logos: DA (movement) Subject/sub-logos: KA (stillness) Characteristic: Space (volume), 1st spatial dimension, sensory date input Gender: Female (-) Condition	Catalyst of the Spirit Object/logos: LA (wisdom) Subject/sub-logos: SA (awareness) Characteristic: Faith/Hope Gender: Female (-) Algorithm
Potentiator of the Mind	Potentiator of the Body	Potentiator of the Spirit

Object/logos: Lucifer (unconsciousness) Subject/sub-logos: SA (awareness) Characteristic: Unconsciousness and the "I" perspective, isolation, evil Gender: Female: (-) Condition & Algorithm	Object/logos: LA (wisdom) Subject/sub-logos: KA (stillness) Characteristic: Stillness and balance Gender: Male (+) Algorithm	Object/logos: SA (awareness) Subject/ sub-logos: LA (wisdom) Characteristic: Light, information Gender: Female (-) Algorithm
Matrix of the Mind Object/logos: DA (movement) Subject/sub-logos: SA (awareness) Characteristic: Ego, consciousness, intelligence Gender: Male (+) Condition & Algorithm	Matrix of the Body Object/ logos: DA (movement) Subject/sub-logos: KA (stillness) Characteristic: Motion, even functioning Gender: Female (-) Condition & Algorithm	Matrix of the Spirit Object/logos: DA (movement) Subject/sub-logos: TA (separation) Characteristic: Innocence, primordial darkness, perception of separation Gender: Male (+) Condition

The "Inherent Characteristic" archetypes include RA (love), LA (wisdom), SA (awareness), YA (unity), and KA (stillness). The distortion archetypes include DA (movement), TA (separation), Lucifer (unconsciousness), and Melchezedek (freewill). Freewill participates in every module but does not have its own module.

The Matrix of the Mind and the Potentiator of the Mind jointly create the "I" perspective, which is another "condition to be overcome". The three aspects of the Matrix category (Matrix of the Mind, Matrix of the Body, and Matrix of the Spirit) combine to create the "ego mind".

Other Books by D. Dean Graves:

Enlightenment Plain and Simple
ISBN #0615735908

Enlightenment Plain and Simple is an easy-to-understand introduction to enlightenment and, with beginning methods to communicate with your Higher Self and self-applied energy psychology methods, you can heal physical, emotional, and spiritual unwanted conditions. No predisposition to psychic abilities or intuitiveness is required. It is everyone's right to become enlightened and these methods have been proven to be dramatically successful in advancing people along the path. The biggest variable is your commitment to do the work.

The Identity Model: Understanding and Healing Mankind's Stress and Suffering
ISBN #9798365703223

The Identity Model clearly and simply explains how and why humans create a false identity, how it contributes to our evolutionary progress, and, through awareness, how to begin its surrender. The inevitable result of surrendering the identity is the cessation of stress and suffering which leaves the experiencer in a state of constant bliss, the inevitable future condition of all humans.

Edifying Children of a Lesser God
ISBN #9798842620630

Humanity has experienced stress and suffering since its beginning, despite the numerous attempts by wise men of a variety of stripes to explain and guide mankind out of the chronic experiences of pain, existential loneliness, and unhappiness. Stress/suffering is at the root of all personal and social "unwanted conditions" but it doesn't need to be. *Edifying Children of a Lesser God* is an elementary introduction to the truth about humanity from its origins and how it can (and must) heal itself from false self-perceptions and assume responsibility for fulfilling its purpose in life. The heart of this writing is an introduction to the *Law of One* which is the one immutable truth of Creation. If you're ready for the truth and to heal from your "unwanted conditions", this is the book for you.

Dear Reader,

Thank you for purchasing *The Enigma of Consciousness* but your work has only begun. Each person is tasked with becoming awareness and employing that awareness to heal their distortions of perception, progress towards greater happiness, and eventually enter the condition of bliss. Enjoying the condition of bliss is inevitable for everyone but to reach it requires that each individual assume the personal responsibility to "do the work". You already have all the tools necessary to ensure your success.

We leave you with the Love and Light of the One Infinite Creator,
D. Dean Graves

O-BOOKS

SPIRITUALITY

O is a symbol of the world, of oneness and unity; this eye represents knowledge and insight. We publish titles on general spirituality and living a spiritual life. We aim to inform and help you on your own journey in this life.
If you have enjoyed this book, why not tell other readers by posting a review on your preferred book site?

Recent bestsellers from O-Books are:

Heart of Tantric Sex
Diana Richardson
Revealing Eastern secrets of deep love and intimacy
to Western couples.
Paperback: 978-1-90381-637-0 ebook: 978-1-84694-637-0

Crystal Prescriptions
The A-Z guide to over 1,200 symptoms and their healing crystals
Judy Hall
The first in the popular series of eight books, this handy little guide is packed as tight as a pill bottle with crystal remedies for ailments.
Paperback: 978-1-90504-740-6 ebook: 978-1-84694-629-5

Shine On
David Ditchfield and J S Jones
What if the aftereffects of a near-death experience were
undeniable? What if a person could suddenly produce
high-quality paintings of the afterlife, or if they
acquired the ability to compose classical symphonies?
Meet: David Ditchfield.
Paperback: 978-1-78904-365-5 ebook: 978-1-78904-366-2

The Way of Reiki
The Inner Teachings of Mikao Usui
Frans Stiene
The roadmap for deepening your understanding of the
system of Reiki and rediscovering your
True Self.
Paperback: 978-1-78535-665-0 ebook: 978-1-78535-744-2

You Are Not Your Thoughts
Frances Trussell
The journey to a mindful way of being, for those who want
to truly know the power of mindfulness.
Paperback: 978-1-78535-816-6 ebook: 978-1-78535-817-3

The Mysteries of the Twelfth Astrological House
Fallen Angels
Carmen Turner-Schott, MSW, LISW
Everyone wants to know more about the most misunderstood
house in astrology — the twelfth astrological house.
Paperback: 978-1-78099-343-0 ebook: 978-1-78099-344-7

WhatsApps from Heaven
Louise Hamlin
An account of a bereavement and the extraordinary
signs — including WhatsApps — that a retired
law lecturer received from her deceased husband.
Paperback: 978-1-78904-947-3 ebook: 978-1-78904-948-0

The Holistic Guide to Your Health
& Wellbeing Today
Oliver Rolfe
A holistic guide to improving your complete health,
both inside and out.
Paperback: 978-1-78535-392-5 ebook: 978-1-78535-393-2

Cool Sex
Diana Richardson and Wendy Doeleman
For deeply satisfying sex, the real secret is to reduce the heat,
to cool down. Discover the empowerment and fulfilment
of sex with loving mindfulness.
Paperback: 978-1-78904-351-8 ebook: 978-1-78904-352-5

Creating Real Happiness A to Z
Stephani Grace
Creating Real Happiness A to Z will help you understand
the truth that you are not your ego
(conditioned self).
Paperback: 978-1-78904-951-0 ebook: 978-1-78904-952-7

A Colourful Dose of Optimism
Jules Standish
It's time for us to look on the bright side, by boosting
our mood and lifting our spirit, both in our interiors,
as well as in our closet.
Paperback: 978-1-78904-927-5 ebook: 978-1-78904-928-2

Readers of ebooks can buy or view any of these bestsellers by
clicking on the live link in the title. Most titles are published
in paperback and as an ebook. Paperbacks are available in
traditional bookshops. Both print and ebook formats are
available online.

Find more titles and sign up to our readers' newsletter at
www.o-books.com

Follow O-Books on Facebook at **O-Books**

For video content, author interviews and more, please subscribe to our YouTube channel:

O-BOOKS Presents

Follow us on social media for book news, promotions and more:

Facebook: O-Books

Instagram: @o_books_mbs

Twitter: @obooks

Tik Tok: @ObooksMBS

www.o-books.com